VISIONS OF AN UNSEEN WORLD:
GHOST BELIEFS AND GHOST STORIES IN EIGHTEENTH-CENTURY ENGLAND

RELIGIOUS CULTURES
IN THE EARLY MODERN WORLD

Series Editors: Fernando Cervantes
                    Peter Marshall
                    Philip Soergel

TITLES IN THIS SERIES

Possession, Puritanism and Print: Darrell, Harsnett, Shakespeare and the
Elizabethan Exorcism Controversy
Marion Gibson

FORTHCOMING TITLES

Diabolism in Colonial Peru
Andrew Redden

The Religious Culture of Marian England
David Loades

www.pickeringchatto.com/religious

VISIONS OF AN UNSEEN WORLD:
GHOST BELIEFS AND GHOST STORIES IN
EIGHTEENTH-CENTURY ENGLAND

BY

Sasha Handley

LONDON
PICKERING & CHATTO
2007

Published by Pickering & Chatto (Publishers) Limited
21 Bloomsbury Way, London WC1A 2TH

2252 Ridge Road, Brookfield, Vermont 05036-9704, USA

www.pickeringchatto.com

BRITISH LIBRARY CATALOGUING IN PUBLICATION DATA

Handley, Sasha
  Visions of an unseen world: ghost beliefs and ghost stories in eighteenth-
century England. – (Religious cultures in the early modern world)
  1. Ghost stories, English – History and criticism 2. English fiction – 18th
century – History and criticism 3. Ghosts in literature
  I. Title
  823'.087330906

ISBN-13: 9781851968886

This publication is printed on acid-free paper that conforms to the American
National Standard for the Permanence of Paper for Printed Library Materials.

Typeset by Pickering & Chatto (Publishers) Limited
Printed in the United Kingdom at Athenaeum Press, Ltd.

CONTENTS

ACKNOWLEDGEMENTS

One of the main arguments presented in this book is that texts are collective productions, and not simply reflections of the author's imagination. I am happy to report that this is as much the case now as it was in early modern England. In the course of writing this book I have incurred numerous debts, both personal and professional. For funding the initial research, I would like to offer warm thanks to the Arts and Humanities Research Board, and to the University of Warwick. My gratitude also extends to the Humanities Research Centre at Warwick for awarding me a Doctoral Fellowship. Sue Dibben provided a level of support and encouragement above and beyond the call of duty. The participants of a one-day conference, 'Perceptions of the Supernatural in the Long Eighteenth Century', made me think and rethink exactly what it was I was trying to achieve. Collections at Birmingham University Library, the British Library, Manchester University Library, Melbourne University Library, Nottingham University Library, the Royal Greenwich Observatory, the Wellcome Trust Library, Dr Williams's Library, Senate House Library and the Friends Library have provided essential resources and endless food for thought over the past few years. Special mention goes to Gareth Lloyd and Peter Nockles at the Methodist Church Archives, Josef Keith at Friends House, the Special Collections staff at Melbourne University, and especially to Sarah Jackson at the University of London for invaluable advice and encouragement.

I could not have undertaken or completed this research without the constant support, guidance and friendship of Peter Marshall and Carolyn Steedman. The enthusiasm, expertise and all-round conviviality that they have shown me represents a debt too hefty to repay. Alexandra Walsham and Colin Jones have shown great skilfulness and generosity in sharing their thoughts about this project. For that and for their insightful comments about the structure and direction of this research, I am truly grateful. Many staff members at the University of Warwick have offered invaluable advice and references, but particular mention must go to Maxine Berg, Bernard Capp, Juliet Chester, Chris Clark, Angela McShane-Jones, Tim Reinke-Williams and Sarah Richardson for taking the time to read parts of this manuscript, or for having the patience to listen to my early musings. The efficiency and know-how of Ros Lucas and Molly Rogers made my time at Warwick much smoother than it might otherwise have been. More recently, the School of History at the University of Manchester has proved a productive environment in which to bring this project to fruition. Special thanks go to Zoe Burkett for her diligence and hard work. I would also like to acknowledge the professionalism and patience of staff at Pickering & Chatto, and particularly of Michael Middeke and Julie Wilson. Any mistakes that remain are mine alone.

As always, my friends have provided me with constant support, laughter and chocolate. To name them all here would take too long but mention must go to Dan O'Connor and James Campbell for reading sections of this work, and to Matt Milner for his technical and culinary expertise. To Brooke, Dave, Matt, Cathy, Nik, Kerryn, Kate, Robert, Gemma, Kelli, Oliver, Helen and Paul – thank you for listening and for giving me hours and hours of entertainment. Azmina, Caroline, Catherine, Elinor, Sarah and Steph have proven to be true friends through an arduous but enlightening journey. My family continues to be my greatest source of support and comfort. This book is dedicated to you for always being there when I need you.

LIST OF ILLUSTRATIONS

INTRODUCTION: THE GHOSTS OF EARLY MODERN ENGLAND

Speaking in 1778, the famous man of letters and social commentator Samuel Johnson usefully summed up the uncertainty surrounding visions of ghosts in eighteenth-century England: 'It is wonderful that five thousand years have now elapsed since the creation of the world, and still it is undecided whether or not there has ever been an instance of the spirit of any person appearing after death. All argument is against it, but all belief is for it.'[1] Johnson was unwilling to credit every reported appearance of ghosts, yet he remained firmly convinced that the souls of the dead could and did revisit their former habitations. Johnson's faithful friend James Boswell endorsed his opinion, and members of Johnson's learned acquaintance also claimed personal experience of such otherworldly encounters.[2] Far from being idle tittle-tattle, Johnson considered the subject of ghosts to be 'one of the most important that can come before the human understanding.'[3] This book seeks to place Johnson's thoughts on this subject in a wider historical context. It will explore the ways in which ghost beliefs both fitted and clashed with the changing cultural landscapes of English society in the long eighteenth century, and with the daily lives of the men and women who lived in it. Through an analysis of ghost stories, which are understood here as complex expressions of ghost beliefs, this is a study in the imaginative force and flexibility of an idea, or rather a set of ideas, surrounding the nature, status and location of the dead, and the changing meanings attached to their appearances.

Particular ideas and beliefs have particular histories; they enjoy cycles of influence and are also subject to revision, transformation and rejection. In the case of ghosts, the religious, social and political transformations of early modern England presented a series of challenges to well-established explanations of what ghosts were and where they came from. Spirits of the dead were believed to visit the living on a regular basis in medieval England, and these episodes were closely associated with the theology and devotional practices of the Catholic Church. It was widely accepted that ghosts were the souls of the dead who returned to confess their sins to the living to speed their passage through the fires of purgatory. Clergymen readily accepted reported visions of ghosts, and they were routinely overlaid with didactic messages to encourage the lay community to prepare their souls for the afterlife through repentance and holy living.[4] The mortuary culture and liturgical practices of late medieval England similarly encouraged the widespread conviction that the communities of the living and the dead were inseparable.[5] However, in the aftermath of England's Protestant Reformation from the mid-sixteenth century, the theology of ghosts was radically transformed. The doctrine of purgatory was abolished by Protestant reformers who deemed it both unscriptural and unscrupulous, since it had allowed the Catholic Church to exploit widespread fears of purgatorial pain for pecuniary gain.[6] The elimination of this middle place between heaven and hell meant that the theological rationale that explained *how* dead souls were able to return to earth was swept away. A number of Protestant apologists also advocated the complete eradication of ghosts from the eschatology of the English Church, because their Catholic opponents continued to perform miracles and exorcisms to articulate claims that theirs was the true faith. Nevertheless, this topic was hotly contested and many Protestant clergy and lay folk were not ready to abandon the possibility that some orders of spirit might yet appear in the material world. Within the theological strictures favoured by English Calvinists, it seemed increasingly illogical to argue that spirits were the souls of the dear departed. The doctrine of predestination taught that the fate of human souls in the afterlife was preordained, and since purgatory no longer existed the dead were stripped of independent agency. Instead, it seemed much more likely that humans were visited by ministering angels carrying out divine orders, or by the devil's minions who sought to tempt the faithful from the path of righteousness. In 1585 such speculations led Archbishop Sandys to confidently declare that 'the gospel hath chased away walking spirits'.[7]

The history of the *theology* of ghosts must, however, be distinguished from the history of ghost *beliefs*. Peter Marshall has recently produced an impressive survey of changing attitudes towards ghostly visions in Elizabethan and Jacobean society, which powerfully demonstrates how these episodes stubbornly refused to go away. Protestant opinion about the nature and existence of ghosts was clearly divided, and a flexible discourse of providentialism allowed large sections of the population to incorporate preternatural wonders within their religious worldviews. Ordinary people also displayed too deep an emotional attachment to the dead to fully discount the possibility that departed loved ones might communicate with them once more.[8] Changes in the theological landscape thus had a profound, though by no means predictable, effect upon public and private conceptions of ghosts in post-Reformation England.

The long-term effects of these religious shifts will be examined in the pages that follow. Yet the meanings of ghostly appearances, and the existence of ghosts per se, were also challenged by the tenets of the so-called scientific revolution. The term 'revolution' is a somewhat imprecise way to describe the piecemeal incursions that natural philosophers (or scientists) were making into Aristotelian and Ptolemaic teaching about the make-up of the material and immaterial worlds. Nevertheless, what *was* revolutionary was the emergence of a new epistemology – that is, a new way of thinking about the world. Typified by the work of Francis Bacon, natural philosophers insisted that received wisdom about natural, preter-natural and supernatural phenomena had to be tested and proven by hard fact. The years 1660–1800 therefore represent a particularly significant phase in the history of ghost beliefs, since this period saw them put under the microscope as never before. The scientific laboratories of the Royal Society destabilized the traditional epistemological structures of early modern England by insisting that all new and known facts were authenticated by direct observation and empiri-cal data. The principles of this new metaphysics also pervaded cultural life and literature thanks to the blossoming of a vibrant public sphere via a network of coffee-houses and the periodical press. Reports of ghostly visits and supernatural occurrences were consequently dissected and anatomized by enlightened phi-losophers, medical practitioners, ladies and gentlemen of fashion, and some of the leading lights of natural philosophy. Countless ghost stories were exposed as frauds, impostures or as mental delusions of the weak and credulous as a result of an obsessive drive to distinguish fact from fiction. The rapid commercial suc-cess of the middling and upper sorts also led to an attendant desire for social distinction, in which ghost beliefs were increasingly marginalized as the fantasies of the vulgar who had not been blessed by the light of reason. Couched in the rhetoric of Enlightenment, religious life seemed scarcely less corrosive of such notions, with many clergy arguing that miraculous signs and wonders were com-pletely out of step with the age of reason, especially since the Protestant Church now appeared secure in its triumph over Catholicism. In light of these develop-ments, it is hardly surprising that many historical narratives of eighteenth-century England and Europe have assumed the rapid demise of belief in the supernatural and occult worlds.

In practice of course, the apparent decline of ghost belief was far from clear cut. The story that remains untold, and the one that forms the core of this book, describes how ghost beliefs negotiated these obstacles, retaining both vitality and relevance in a period of large-scale social, economic, religious and political change. If ghost stories and other occult phenomena were subjected to closer scrutiny as a result of the new empirical philosophy, the networks of gentlemanly science were not uniformly hostile to such reports, especially when they were attended with creditable circumstances and substantial witnesses.[9] Enlightenment obsession with unseen and invisible powers in fact ensured that ghost stories could sometimes command widespread fascination, since they had the potential to reveal hidden secrets about the orders of God and nature. Even if individuals were unwilling to admit belief in the physical reality of ghosts, the *idea* of ghosts, of an existence beyond the human and domestic, played a significant role in the construction of personal identities. The ghosts of gothic fiction and sublime poetry complemented explorations of the interior self, satisfied longings for individual immortality, and provided fuel for the creative imagination. Contemplation of ghost stories helped to frame particular questions that lay at the heart of polite society, and which in turn cultivated the human mind, which was the cornerstone of Enlightenment endeavour. In many ways then, ghost stories expressed the priorities and preoccupations of eighteenth-century life and thought.

On a day-to-day basis, ghost stories also have important things to say about the character of religious life and spirituality, and about the lifestyles, social mores and emotions of ordinary men and women. They similarly provide important insights into the psychological side effects of enlightenment, consumerism and imperialism. The wider historical import of these tales lies in the access they can provide to the thoughts and concerns of people who might otherwise remain hidden from the restricted gaze of the historian. The central aim of this book is to reinsert ghost beliefs and ghost stories into the imaginative and material histories of the long eighteenth century and to suggest that they played a significant role in forging the distinctive character of English society in these years. Ghost beliefs must then be rescued from the realm of *superstition*, since this term implies a stasis and discordance with the prevailing historical forces that characterized eighteenth-century English society – something that is simply not borne out by surviving evidence. This study reconstructs the diverse public and private contexts in which ghost stories performed as legitimate and effective social narratives by focusing on the places, spaces and circumstances in which they featured. Ghost beliefs and the ghost stories through which they were expressed were then a vital part of the eighteenth-century cultural experience.

Post-1770s England has been identified as the golden age of gothic fictions, and the literary significance of English ghost stories in eighteenth-century culture has been explored in some depth.[10] By contrast, the historical import of these narratives remains underexplored. This historiographical gap is no mere oversight and must be attributed in large part to the commanding influence of Sir Keith Thomas's canonical text, *Religion and the Decline of Magic*. Thomas offered a brilliant and comprehensive survey of why men and women of the sixteenth and seventeenth centuries believed in ghosts. So convincing was his thesis that people stopped seeing ghosts in the eighteenth century because they 'were losing their social relevance' and were rendered 'intellectually impossible' by the progress of Enlightenment thought and practice that few have dared to challenge his conclusions.[11] Although the quality of Thomas's work has since the 1970s given legitimacy and impetus to historical studies of a wide variety of popular belief, paradoxically, it may have proved a deterrent to more in-depth historical investigations of ghost beliefs in eighteenth-century England. Alongside Thomas, Ronald Finucane has briefly examined eighteenth-century ghost beliefs as part of a broader chronological span, but neither account has done much to dethrone the prevailing characterization of this period as a time of dwindling belief in the preternatural world, dominated instead by discourses of empiricism, desacralization and rationalism.[12] This historiographical neglect provides a central motivation for this study, since the decline of ghost beliefs has been both overstated and mistimed. Historians have neglected the variety and fragmentation of learned opinion surrounding the reality of ghosts, as well as the complex attitudes towards ghosts that surfaced among different religious, social, gender and age groupings in this period.

Historians of eighteenth-century England frequently assume a disjuncture between the idea of ghosts and the civilizing missions of Enlightenment thought, the commercial and colonial emphasis of Georgian society, and the growing desire for social distinction implicit in new developments in art, philosophy and literature. The few historians who have addressed the status of otherworldly phenomena in this chronology have largely rejected its significance. Lorraine Daston and Katherine Park described an emerging cultural opposition between the enlightened and the marvellous, with the former triumphant and the latter characteristic of vulgarity and ignorance.[13] According to such narratives, belief in the interventions of the divine and of ghostly messengers was deemed to be in conflict with the central Enlightenment focus on man as a perfectible being and as the essential motor of social development and progress.[14] At one level, historians are of course correct to identify some clash between ghost stories and the new intellectual currents that circulated in these years. Ghostly interventions undermined the self-regulating mechanisms of the natural world and questioned overly optimistic views of man and nature, reminding contemporaries of the omnipotence of God and of the fragility of the human condition. By highlighting inconsistencies in historical discourses of enlightenment and desacralization, ghost beliefs deserve a more sophisticated interpretation as sites of cultural contestation. Indeed, the sheer volume of ghost stories that was produced and purchased between 1660 and 1800 suggests that a reassessment of these narratives is long overdue. Furthermore, the familiar expectation that ghosts intervened amongst the living to regulate social mores and to publicize and punish moral abuse locates these preternatural phenomena as essential accompaniments to the historical developments of eighteenth-century life, restraining the worst extremes of empiricist and materialist thought, and combating the immoral excesses of an increasingly consumer-orientated society. As the fundamental expression of ghost beliefs, ghost stories must be recast both as essential complements to processes of so-called modernization, and as notable evidence of counter-currents in eighteenth-century thought. It will become clear in the chapters that follow that ghost beliefs were geographically and socially diffuse, incorporated multiple meanings, surfaced in diverse contexts, and were subject to ongoing revision, rationalization and transformation between 1660 and 1800. Ghost stories were important barometers of cultural change that add balance and complexity to characterizations of eighteenth-century society as a secularizing, rational and anti-miraculous monolith.

Borrowing from the sociological terminology of Max Weber, it was Bob Scribner who associated the late seventeenth and eighteenth centuries with accelerating the process of disenchantment begun by the Protestant Reformation. Scribner and Keith Thomas both noted the exceptions and ambiguities in this thesis, and recent revisionist work by Jonathan Barry, Stuart Clark, Marion Gibson, Peter Lake, Michael Questier, Jane Shaw and Alexandra Walsham has further enhanced our understanding of how Protestantism fostered its own lively brand of signs, miracles and wonders.[15] Nonetheless, with the exception of Owen Davies and Ronald Hutton, who have examined the vitality of witchcraft beliefs in the nineteenth and twentieth centuries, such a comprehensive reassessment has yet to be attempted for the eighteenth century in general and for ghost beliefs in particular.[16] This is partly due to the traditional and somewhat artificial division of labour between historians of early modern England, who tend to study the period up to 1640 or 1700, and historians of the eighteenth century, who have tended to shape their narratives in anticipation of nineteenth-century economic, social, political and religious change. As a result, important continuities between these two chronologies have been obscured and the eighteenth century has all too often been regarded as a very different world from that which went before, and to which the heyday of ghost beliefs, and supernatural beliefs more generally, supposedly belonged.

Histories of the Supernatural

Thanks to the work of Peter Marshall, Jean-Claude Schmitt and Nancy Caciola, a more respectable historiography of ghost beliefs is now emerging for medieval and early modern Europe, but this has not extended to include the long eighteenth century in England.[17] This neglect provides another justification for the present work and a further reason for the current marginalization of ghost beliefs in historical studies of this period, which have been subsumed thus far under the well-heeled historiography of witchcraft. Keith Thomas classified belief in ghosts as an allied belief of witchcraft and too few historians have distinguished between the two categories, even though contemporaries frequently did so. To explain both the persistence and cessation of belief in supernatural wonders historians have employed regional and national comparisons. Yet the category of the supernatural must itself be broken down to appreciate the important differences between the phenomena generally included under this heading.

Whilst concepts of gender will feature in this study and played a part in fashioning responses towards ghost stories, discussions of female physiology and psychology are less relevant in explaining the intensity and longevity of ghost beliefs than they are in delineating attitudes towards witchcraft.[18] Moreover, the need to separate the historical trajectory of ghost beliefs from that of witches is further demonstrated by the work of Ian Bostridge, which has reinforced the association between the early eighteenth century and the flagging influence of witchcraft beliefs on the public stage. Bostridge also described how the Witchcraft Act was removed from the statute books in 1736 amidst heated religious and political squabbles between opposing Tory and Whig politicians.[19] Debate over the existence and nature of ghosts did take on significant political overtones at various intervals over the course of the eighteenth century and became tainted with popish associations in contemporary polemic. But these beliefs were not exclusively linked to a dwindling Tory or High-Church faction and were variously adopted and appropriated by men and women from a variety of political and confessional backgrounds. Moreover, the repeal of the Witchcraft Act was intimately linked to the legal and criminal context of witchcraft accusations that again marks a key distinction from the status of ghost beliefs. It was never a crime to believe in ghosts, or to claim to have seen and conversed with one, and ghost beliefs provided no direct justification for torture, trials or executions, or for outbreaks of informal persecution.

Owen Davies's work has highlighted the persistence of popular belief in witchcraft beyond the 1736 repeal: the criminal associations of witchcraft remained intact, with individuals and communities attempting both to prosecute and persecute suspected witches for material crimes into the nineteenth century and beyond.[20] Moreover, as the examples of John Webster and Francis Hutchinson demonstrate, distaste for the idea of witchcraft, for the material consequences of its punishment and for its polemical associations created greater hostility towards the idea of witchcraft among educated men and women in the years 1660–1800 than did the idea of ghosts. Both Webster and Hutchinson publicly dismissed the legitimacy of witchcraft whilst affirming that ghost stories retained important spiritual meanings. If diabolical witchcraft was conceived of as an inversion of right religion, then ghost stories by way of contrast were more flexible and could be fashioned more easily as orthodox supports of Restoration and eighteenth-century Anglicanism and Methodism. These key differences help to explain why ghost beliefs deserve an independent historiography from that of witchcraft, since they were less offensive to the educated and to the clerical ministry and thus enjoyed a longer shelf life, in various forms of public discourse.

In the field of witchcraft studies, the new social history of the 1960s has led to a flood of micro-histories, extending and complicating understandings of the chronological, geographical and social spread of witchcraft beliefs, presenting the ideas of ordinary people and introducing feminist discourses to transform historical understandings of this phenomenon. Historical conceptions of ghost beliefs have not developed along such lines and have only been studied for the eighteenth century in outmoded intellectual terms that neglect the variety and fragmentation of scholarly opinion and that lay a heavy emphasis on the impact of natural philosophy in exploding the legitimacy of ghost stories. Michael Hunter and Stuart Clark, among others, have outlined the limitations of this functionalist approach, and the complementarity of natural philosophy with deeply-held convictions about the intervention of otherworldly forces is now commonplace. The response of natural philosophers and medics to the realm of ghost beliefs supports the contention that the scientific and preternatural arenas could be mutually reinforcing. Nonetheless, exclusive focus on intellectual responses to ghost beliefs relies too heavily on the presumed chasm between learned and unlearned conceptions of the spirit world. Thus, whilst Peter Burke's suggestion that the eighteenth century witnessed the divergence of high and low cultures remains credible, the presumed conflict between the 'great' and 'little' traditions requires qualification since it oversimplifies fluid social categories, downplays important cultural interactions and neglects the agency of the more marginalized social groupings.[21] This study will highlight a two-way process of cultural exchange by refusing to correlate the labels of 'sceptic' and 'believer' with hierarchies of wealth and social status. Such a standpoint is essential in explaining how and why real-life experiences of ghosts were repeatedly translated from speech communities into manuscript and into diverse printed forms. The production and consumption of ghost stories highlights important exchanges between different social groups, and between local and national cultures.

Finally, historical interpretations of ghost beliefs have been heavily influenced by literary scholars, who identify the late eighteenth century as a crucial moment in the evolution of the ghost story. The explosion of gothic fictions and dramatic representations of ghosts has been interpreted as part of a wider reassessment of attitudes towards the preternatural world, in which the decline of serious belief in ghosts was replaced by an appreciation of ghost stories as aesthetic spectacles. This thesis will be contested by analysing the ambiguous relationship between fact and fiction in these tales. Fictional ghost stories must also be positioned within a wider historical framework to appreciate the multiple contexts in which the figure of the ghost was configured. The simple reduction of ghost stories to the category of frivolous entertainment seriously neglects the complex cultural meanings attached to them.

Ghosts and the Preternatural

Before proceeding any further, the type of ghosts that haunt this text must be defined more carefully. In order to distinguish the particular meanings attached to ghosts, I am not concerned here with anonymous angelic or evil spirits such as are generally involved in cases of witchcraft and demonic possession. Instead I have followed contemporary terminology in defining the eighteenth-century ghost, and my object of study, as 'A spirit appearing after death'.[22] Most often, these ghosts were well known or related to those who saw them. The term 'ghost' was most often used in this period to refer to the familiar spirit of a dead person, but there was also significant crossover with the words 'apparition' and 'spectre'. According to Samuel Johnson's *Dictionary* of 1755, 'spectre' referred to 'a walking spirit' or an 'appearance of persons dead'.[23] Where these terms were used to refer to the spirit of a dead person, they are included in this study. The shifting vocabulary of ghosts will form an important part of the chapters that follow.

Just as the concept of ghosts must be separated from that of witches, so the term *supernatural* must be carefully distinguished from *preternatural*. *Supernatural* refers to something above the power of nature, whereas *preternatural* denotes something irregular, or out of step with the natural way of things. This distinction is especially important for understanding the fluctuating legitimacy of ghost stories in intellectual discourse throughout the long eighteenth century, which took place amidst wrangles over the correct identification and classification of natural and spiritual phenomena. Preternatural wonders should be located somewhere in between the natural and supernatural worlds, as something out of the ordinary, yet potentially explicable by a combination of natural law and divine agency. The ghosts of this book hovered on the boundaries of these categories, but the most frequent descriptions and pictorial representations of ghosts suggest that, by and large, they should be classified as preternatural phenomena, as they were by Samuel Johnson.[24] Ghosts usually appeared in familiar human form, sometimes in the clothes they wore when alive or more often in the winding sheets in which they had been buried. Contemporary advances in optical instrumentation and chemical knowledge destabilized the iconography of ghosts and slowly rendered some of them incorporeal and shadowy substances. Yet, in spite of this, ghosts were rarely described or depicted as transparent. Instead they were regularly invested with human qualities, and were thought capable of moving material objects and of inflicting physical harm upon the living. Similarly, those who were confronted by ghosts believed that they could inflict material damage by shooting or stabbing the spirit with conventional weapons.[25] Ghosts were thus thought to possess a curious hybrid of divine qualities and human characteristics, which must be partly explained by their intimate association with the physical processes of death and decomposition. The prominent position of ghosts within contemporary mortuary culture ensured that they retained important affinities with the natural world; indeed they provided an important bridge between the natural and preternatural worlds. These associations help to explain why ghostly phenomena were important objects of study for natural philosophers, and why reports of their appearance inspired morbid contemplations about death and immortality.

Ghost Beliefs and Ghost Stories

How do historians access the question of belief? This perennial historical problem is one to which scholars have offered a variety of solutions, all insightful but
none comprehensive. By their very nature, personal beliefs are ephemeral, elusive
and almost impossible to reconstruct on a large scale from the sources available to
the historian. The material that does survive in the form of diaries, for example,
is usually weighted to reflect the views of literate, middle- and upper-class men
and neglects the histories of more marginalized social groups whose literacy skills
were less developed or who found little leisure time or need to record their own
thoughts and feelings in writing. In order to combat this bias and to gauge the
depth and social diffusion of ghost beliefs, I am not going to focus solely on the
rich canonical literature of the period in which a few eminent individuals debated
the reality of ghosts, but on a whole gamut of genres and texts in which ghost
stories cropped up and that were accessed by men, women and children of all
kinds. Guided by the pioneering work of Bernard Capp, Margaret Spufford and
Tessa Watt, who have done so much to underline the importance of the cheap
print market for delineating the attitudes and beliefs of even the poorest sections
of early modern society, my analysis begins at the least expensive end of the print
market, with the ghosts of ballad and chapbook fame.[26] From the most widely
disseminated texts, my study extends through to the most expensive and socially
exclusive works.

Eighteenth-century England saw a great proliferation in the publication and
purchasing of ghost stories in a wide diversity of forms and genres, but my decision
to examine this inclusive spread of texts also has methodological implications. By
juxtaposing different kinds of texts and audiences, I want to emphasize the place
of eighteenth-century ghost stories as sites of cross-over and interaction between
oral and literate communities, and between different confessional, gender and
age groupings. The physical production, dissemination and consumption of ghost
stories will also be used to highlight the mixed marketplace that existed for these
publications. This study therefore approaches the question of belief through narrative, and it combines close textual analysis with a broad conception of historical
change. Concepts drawn from socio-linguistic theory and from the sociology of
literature are therefore crucial to this discussion. Focus falls on why ghost stories were told, the ways in which they were manufactured and disseminated, how
they performed as texts and how they tried to shape the imaginations of consumers. Readers must be granted a degree of autonomy in constructing independent
meaning from the written word, but these meanings were inevitably influenced
by the text itself, which was the product of dynamic interaction between market-
conscious writers, commercially-minded publishers and reader expectations.

By focusing on the production, circulation and consumption of ghost stories, I
also hope to avoid a reductive analysis of *elite* and *popular* ghost beliefs. The same

texts could appeal to mixed audiences, and many ghost stories were collective productions that highlight mutual exchange between different social, religious and gender groupings in a chronology that has often been associated with the distancing of high and low cultures, the fragmentation of Protestant denominations and the separation of male and female activities into public and private contexts.[27] These publicly-instituted narratives therefore had important affinities with the beliefs, experiences and attitudes of the society that they represented. Relevant here is Pierre Bourdieu's concept of the field of cultural production, in which the value of a cultural product is determined by the way it fits with the interests and preoccupations of the society in which it is produced.

> Given that works of art exist as symbolic objects only if they are known and recognized, that is, socially instituted as works of art and received by spectators capable of knowing and recognizing them as such, the sociology of art and literature has to take as its object not only the material production but also the symbolic production of the work.[28]

In the words of Kevin Sharpe and Steven Zwicker, 'we are what we read'.[29] The ghost stories of eighteenth-century England were constructed from the raw imaginative materials available to their authors. In so far as these texts were intended for commercial success, they had to connect with the expectations and tastes of readers rather than simply reflecting the views of an isolated and culturally dissonant individual. As Terry Eagleton has argued, a text is not valuable in and of itself. Readers determine its value in relation to their own ideals and preferences.[30] The relationship between text and society, between ghost stories and ghost beliefs, was characterized by symbiosis and mutual exchange. Ghost stories are therefore understood in this book as *things*, as desirable material products, but also as imaginative resources that linked up to the mental processes and narrative habits of daily life. These texts reflected the complex and often contested nature of ghost beliefs, but they also shaped them afresh in line with the priorities of public and private discourse. The imaginative and physical production of ghost stories, the techniques used to entice and persuade readers, and the reception, recycling and raw statistics of publication success are thus of central importance. The changing status of ghost beliefs will be studied through the material culture of individual texts and also by assessing the importance of the diverse literary genres in which ghost stories appeared. I want then to support Lennard Davis's contention that there are important, if complex, connections between literary genres and historical change.[31] The migration of ghost stories between different categories of literature therefore reflects shifts in the way that they were conceived in wider society.

People read ghost stories for a number of different reasons, which was reflected in the myriad ways that authors, printers and publishers catered for divergent consumer interests by varying the format, content, linguistic structure, typeface, illustration, length and price of these publications. The role of the printing industry is foundational to this study since it configured ghost stories in a wider range of printed forms than ever before, including cheap ballads and chapbooks, sermons, extended religious tracts, medical treatises, scientific journals, educational treatises, newspapers, periodicals, national histories, folkloric collections, local histories, novels, poems, drama and working-class autobiography. Such diversity highlights the fluidity of the idea of ghosts as well as the persistent social relevance and flexibility of ghost stories that migrated between traditional texts and new literary genres.

Refinements of the formal techniques of printing also enabled texts to be produced more cheaply and distributed more widely than ever before, and the physical circulation of ghost stories in eighteenth-century England certainly benefited from these advances. However, the impact of the volume and variety of printed ghost stories for delineating perceptions of ghosts is nonetheless ambiguous and the proliferation of these narratives was not a straightforward reflection of serious belief in the existence of ghosts. As Walter Ong has argued, the technology of print could also be a 'time-obviating and otherwise radically decontextualising mechanism'.[32] In this sense, the positive benefits of the commercialization process to which ghost stories were subjected in these years must be regarded with a degree of caution. By translating these essentially oral narratives into printed forms and thus distancing them from the original contexts that often secured their legitimacy, the enshrining of ghost stories in print may have helped in the long term to undermine the authenticity of these narratives as their key formulas became more familiar, less extraordinary and increasingly vulnerable to manipulation.

This tension between the physical production of ghost stories and the ways in which they influenced belief will be addressed by examining how authors and publishers intended readers to believe the essential truth of ghost stories. Advocates of reader-response theory have demonstrated the plurality of ways in which individual readers appropriated the same texts, and yet the assumed relationship between narrative and belief has persisted as one of the key modes of historical enquiry in recent years. As Eamon Duffy, Ian Green, Peter Lake, Alexandra Walsham and Tessa Watt have demonstrated, it was the presumed connection between the printed word and the shape of lay piety that led Protestant churchmen of the sixteenth and seventeenth centuries to engage with a whole variety of cheap printed wares.[33] As the main body of this book will illustrate, this technique was still current in the eighteenth century, although the messages with which these texts were inscribed were updated to suit contemporary need and the popularity of printed sermons provided an alternative outlet for this process of instruction and modification.

Since this study relies heavily on textual analysis of ghost stories, it is imperative to emphasize that contemporaries perceived the relationship between text and belief to be a dynamic and affective one. Indeed, the ghost stories examined here display important techniques that were intended to fascinate, persuade and instruct potential readers. As Chapter 2 describes in more detail, the ghost stories of cheap print were especially notable for incorporating dialogue, a high density of circumstantial detail and character analysis – techniques usually associated with oral forms of communication. This methodology may well have been favoured to keep printed ghost stories as close as possible to their original oral contexts and to allow them to flow back into speech by facilitating the public performance of these narratives in the local alehouse or in domestic settings. The frequent and dramatic use of visual imagery in printed ghost stories is also suggestive of the way in which readers were expected to interpret these texts. As if fresh from the grave, striking images of ghosts in winding sheets regularly accompanied many of the narratives studied here and they helped to underline the serious, contemplative meaning of the text. Indeed, as Roger Chartier insists, such images were intended to engage 'the unfailing adherence of the beholder and, even more than or better than the text that it accompanied, to induce persuasion or belief'.[34] Walter Ong's proposition that print radically distanced the reader from the original context of the narrative and allowed the authenticity of the text to be questioned must then be qualified. The ghost stories that feature in this study are especially illustrative of the interdependence of the spoken and the written in eighteenth-century print culture and this mixture was intended to inculcate rather than to suspend belief. Adam Fox's description of the ways in which print overlaid and reinforced the authority of speech and oral culture firmly underpins this study.[35]

Of course, the extent to which ghost stories had the potential to encourage or discourage belief depended on access to these narratives and, in the case of printed ghost stories, on levels of literacy and reading practices. Adam Fox and Roger Chartier have most recently demonstrated that access to print culture cannot be quantified by counting the number of people with the ability to read and write. The sources available to the historian inevitably render this a flawed task, but such a strict definition of literacy also neglects the myriad ways in which early modern men and women were able to engage and interact with printed texts. Thanks to the work of Bernard Capp, Margaret Spufford and Tessa Watt we now know more about the widespread practice of communal reading in early modern England than ever before.[36] The ghosts of ballads and chapbooks lent themselves to public readings whilst taverns, alehouses, fairs and markets provided the spaces in which these readings were carried out. In the eighteenth century, access to print was facilitated by the proliferation of booksellers in the capital and in provincial centres, by the establishment of circulating libraries and subscription libraries across Britain, by a sophisticated second-hand book trade and by the informal but regular habit of borrowing and lending books, pamphlets and textual ephemera to friends, family and neighbours.[37] New technologies of print and new modes of dissemination fostered new kinds of reading practices, with fictional novels and poetry encouraging habits of private reading. Moreover, as John Brewer has illustrated, circulating libraries provided a reliable source of entertainment and instruction for large numbers of men and women who were captivated by such texts.[38]

The early modern period in general and the eighteenth century in particular thus witnessed a series of mini-revolutions in reading practices. However, following the recommendation of Margaret Spufford and on the understanding that ghost stories were desirable commodities, this study will also take account of reading tastes as well as reading habits and abilities. The specialization of the print market enabled ghost stories to appeal to diverse tastes and audiences. The ghosts of novels and verse were designed to shape private sensibilities, and in the second half of the eighteenth century publishers increasingly catered for a youth market, encouraging the habit of childhood reading and of polite parents interacting with their children as readers. The prominence of ghost stories among this literature will be an important focus of the final chapter. Although this study emphasizes diverse constructions of ghost stories in printed texts, I recognize that the vast majority of ghost stories that were published in this period originated in oral communities and, as Walter Ong has argued, 'Writing can never dispense with orality'.[39] Where possible I have traced the ways in which these narratives spread through oral channels, emphasizing the performative aspects of this mode of transmission and the heightened persuasive force of face-to-face storytelling.

I want to suggest then that, although the two were not coextensive, important connections existed between eighteenth-century ghost stories and ghost beliefs. Further proof of the affective impact of ghost stories on the eighteenth-century imagination surfaces in contemporary complaint literature. John Locke in his *Essay Concerning Humane Understanding* most forcefully articulated the particular success of these narratives for instilling ghost beliefs in the minds of young children. Locke's rejection of the concept of innate ideas underlined the perception that eighteenth-century ghost beliefs were manufactured rather than inherited. Locke's disapproving commentary also identified one of the major sources of narrative reproduction and dissemination in the storytelling of servants.[40] Familiar echoes of Locke's concerns persisted throughout the eighteenth century and intensified in its closing decades when good parenting manuals advised conscientious mothers and fathers to ban ghost stories from the vocabulary of servants and thereby save their children from a lifetime of fear and credulity. According to Locke and a whole host of educational reformers who were influenced by his work, youthful introduction to frightening and dramatic tales of ghosts stirred human emotions, clouded reason and judgement and made an indelible mark on the fancy. A stream of working-class autobiographies at the close of the eighteenth century similarly attested to the formative influence of ghost stories recounted in childhood, emphasizing the importance of spoken and printed ghost stories in cementing belief in the real existence of ghosts and the scenarios in which they could be expected to materialize. Indeed, the history of ideas, and the history of ghost beliefs in particular, can be understood as a history of what people remember and it seems that ghost stories exerted an especially potent force upon the memory.

Thinking with Ghosts

Given that ghost stories wielded an important influence on the individual and collective imagination, it is important to outline the kinds of messages that were inscribed in them. Underpinning this study is the assumption that ghost beliefs were intimately connected with the mortuary culture of eighteenth-century England. They expressed important emotional and spiritual meanings for individuals and communities that were confronted with their own mortality or with that of loved ones. As dramatic representations of immortality, ghost stories diluted the finality of death by extending the ritual process of mourning and by bridging the physical and conceptual gap between this world and the next. By haunting familiar places and people they reinforced structures of social memory and provided an important source of cultural continuity. Almost inevitably, eighteenth-century ghost stories say something interesting about attitudes towards death and towards the dead, and yet historians who have focused on these themes have treated these narratives as curious remnants of popish and pagan superstition or have disregarded them entirely. Ralph Houlbrooke's *Death, Religion, and the Family in England, 1480–1750* offers a cohesive and insightful survey of the evolutions of early modern death culture, and yet he makes only brief reference to ghost beliefs.[41] Clare Gittings linked the mortuary culture of eighteenth-century England to discourses of individuality and yet, instead of tracing the connections between ghost beliefs, interiority and the persistence of the personality after death, she dismissed them as 'superstitious practices' with no contemporary relevance.[42] Throughout this book I will outline the ways in which ghost stories linked up to diverse anxieties and expectations surrounding death and the imagined fate of the dead beyond the grave. As material products, the ghost stories of cheap print and the vivid woodcuts of ghosts in winding sheets that accompanied them must be understood as a form of *memento mori*, as visual and textual reminders of the fragility of human life and the social levelling that it entailed.

By way of contrast, the poems of the Graveyard School in the mid-eighteenth century present a sense of revulsion and morbid fascination with the dead that was focused through the lens of ghost stories. Philippe Ariès's sweeping generalization that the eighteenth century saw a physical and imaginative distancing of death must also be revised in light of the dramatic physical representations of death furnished by ghost stories.[43] Ariès's assertion that death was tamed in the Enlightenment age focused too heavily upon intellectual discourses of death.

The evidence of ghost stories suggests that terrifying ideas of death were at best displaced, but not subdued. Ruth Richardson's insightful work has highlighted the liminality of death in the eighteenth century and the centrality of the human corpse to the mortuary culture of this period. According to Richardson, people 'believed and feared that the dead could return' and she also identified consistent desires to preserve and identify the dead.[44] In so doing, Richardson's work suggests that the complex patchwork of beliefs that surrounded death in this period has not been sufficiently elucidated. The relation of ghost stories to this social history of death is thus an important contribution.

By locating ghost beliefs and ghost stories within the social history of death, this study owes a debt to the pioneering work of Peter Marshall who has explored the role of ghost beliefs in fashioning cultural responses towards the dead in Elizabethan and Jacobean England. Marshall's work is also foundational to the present study thanks to his analysis of how ghost beliefs integrated with the complex formation and fragmentation of religious identities in Reformation England. This study is both a continuation of and a departure from Marshall's work in its examination of the relevance of ghost beliefs to theological debates and processes of confessional formation between 1660 and 1800. Particular attention will be paid to the ways in which traumatic memories of civil war radicalism helped to refashion ghost stories as more orthodox supports of the Church of England. These narratives also fitted more easily with the changing theological emphases of post-Restoration Anglicanism, figuring strongly in polemical attacks upon supposed atheists and Sadducees, and complementing efforts at parochial renewal from the 1690s.

The spiritual meaning of ghost stories was the most consistently expressed context in which they were recommended to readers in the years 1660 to 1800. Ghost stories were used to encourage but also to offset anxieties about the ambiguous process of salvation, and to promote good devotional habits. These stories also responded to the particular challenges of religious life in these years. Reported visions of ghosts lent succour to formal doctrines of the soul's immortality, bodily resurrection and the authority of the Trinity. They also furnished fresh evidence of the workings of the Holy Spirit, which was particularly important against a growing chorus of attacks from rational dissenters who were seeking to exorcize revelation from spiritual life. The rejection of miraculous signs and wonders and all things supernatural by rational dissenters has led historians to overlook the theological significance of ghost stories, or to suggest that they represented an essential perversion of eighteenth-century spirituality. Of course, elements of contemporary rhetoric support these findings. Yet evidence from grass-roots level, from published sermons and tracts, also suggests that ghost stories were tacitly accepted or openly encouraged by Anglican and dissenting ministers who used connections between ghost beliefs and the religious faith of the laity to promote good devotional practice. This study therefore represents an important contribution to historical assessments of eighteenth-century religion. The consistent association of ghost stories with orthodox defences of the Trinity also suggests that these narratives might sit closer to the mainstream of Protestant theology and worship than has so far been allowed. Indeed, Samuel Johnson's definition of a 'ghost' in his 1755 dictionary included reference to 'The third person in the adorable Trinity', whilst 'Ghostliness' was described as something with 'spiritual tendency' that was decidedly 'not secular'.[45]

The adoption of ghost stories by leaders of the early Methodist movement accentuated points of dissension between fragmented Protestant groupings. But the recasting of these narratives as attacks on atheists and immorality and as vehicles for anti-Catholic and patriotic propaganda also highlights important points of confessional unity. Anti-Catholic emphases of eighteenth-century ghost stories are especially significant since they suggest that ghost beliefs were no longer perceived as popish survivals but were now thoroughly suffused with the priorities of Restoration and eighteenth-century Protestantism. Changing theories of providential intervention will also be explored, since the idea of a transcendent divine power that rarely intervened in the natural world had a significant influence on the way that ghost stories were perceived. The place of special or particular providences has been somewhat underestimated within this schema and within historical assessments of eighteenth-century spirituality. These findings add a new dimension to the revisionist work of Anthony Armstrong, William Gibson, Jeremy Gregory, Donald Spaeth and John Spurr, who have rightly debunked the idea that the Church of England was disengaged from the spiritual priorities of the laity, as well as emphasizing the common interests of orthodox and dissenting Protestants.[46]

Peter Marshall, Jean-Claude Schmitt and Malcolm Gaskill have shown how assumptions about the providential intervention of ghosts were manipulated to encourage lay piety, but also to achieve specific practical objectives.[47] Understood as expressions of divine displeasure, ghost stories publicized instances of social injustice, exposing secret murderers, deceitful executors and adulterous spouses. Ghosts continued to protest against these crimes in the long eighteenth century, but they were also vehemently opposed to usury and to expressions of atheism or irreligion, instances of which were thought to be particularly rife in these years. Indeed, ghost stories were increasingly fashioned to articulate anxieties about the evils of eighteenth-century economic life. Functioning as important expressions of anti-consumerist rhetoric, ghost stories can be linked to a neglected aspect of the economic history of this period that is usually dominated by descriptions of a burgeoning imperial economy and the luxury goods that were increasingly imported onto the British market.[48] As I emphasize throughout this study, the primarily oral roots of ghost stories allowed them to be utilized by men and women of differing social backgrounds. Disgruntled servants and abused, neglected or abandoned wives and fiancé(e)s regularly manipulated belief in preternatural phenomena to gain revenge on masters, husbands and lovers. The persistence of these practices and the attention that they received show how the revelations of a ghost could do considerable damage to personal reputations, sometimes leading to arrests or even executions. Pervasive belief in the providential agency of ghosts allowed the female and servant voice to be authorized outside of purely domestic contexts, thus highlighting the interrelationship of public and private discourses. Ghost stories were not simply harmless or entertaining tales and could be both affective and effective. The narrative act itself must then be understood to have important imaginative and material consequences. In this context, this study reinforces and extends the work of Bernard Capp and Laura Gowing by figuring ghost stories as weapons of the weak and dispossessed.[49]

If the perceived imminence of the holy sustained the legitimacy of ghost stories for some, new philosophical arguments also emerged to justify the telling and retelling of ghost stories in more secular frames of reference. The newly-established periodical press forged an innovative association between ghost beliefs and codes of gentlemanly behaviour, emphasizing how contemplation of these narratives was an important exercise for the creative imagination, helping to instil values of moral fortitude and civic virtue. These philosophical discourses had a transforming influence on the status of ghost stories as instruments of instruction and sources of entertainment. The truth or falsity of ghost stories gradually became less significant than the moral lessons that they taught, helping to explain how ghost stories gradually shaded into the genres of poetry, drama and novels. Imaginary ghosts had appeared in print for centuries but the configuration of ghosts in new literary genres intensified this process of fictionalization in the eighteenth century. By eroding the true-to-life status of these narratives, ghost stories were subtly displaced from the particular settings and contexts that lent them meaning and the idea of ghosts was reformulated and internalized as an imaginative tool with which to frame thoughts about personal immortality and morality.

This process was however both gradual and inconsistent. Real and imagined ghost stories coexisted for much of the period studied here and, as Terry Eagleton points out, insistence on a sharp distinction between fact and fiction had more relevance for twentieth-century audiences than for eighteenth-century readers.[50] The relationship between truth and fiction must then be understood as one of instability and ambiguity and this was especially true in the eighteenth century, where influential discourses of domesticity brought the idea of fiction closer to the human life-world and where the novel was distinguished 'by being more often related to real life'.[51] As Raymond Williams points out, poems, plays, novels and other literary texts were first and foremost social products, growing out of and responding to the ideas, anxieties and preoccupations of a particular society at a particular moment in time.[52] The process of fictionalization and invention bore close relation to the narrative practices in which people took part during everyday life and thus Lennard Davis's assertion that 'certain social forces manifest themselves fairly directly on literary works' has particular relevance.[53] Samuel Taylor Coleridge recognized the importance of this fit between fiction and reality in preserving the element of belief in fiction, enabling the reader to sanction 'a willing suspension of disbelief'.[54] If ghost stories did not always offer particular truths, they could confidently claim to articulate more general truths that were intimately related to the experiences of social life. Indeed, inscribed in these narratives were important cultural reactions against the narrow rationalism of empirical philosophy, against the geographical and social dislocations of imperial expansion. The ghosts of verse, prose and drama did not fatally undermine the *possibility* of ghosts, yet these texts were less interested in the objective reality of ghosts than with their wider significance. Fictional representations allowed ghosts to be subtly relocated to safer, sophisticated and more aesthetically pleasing spaces where educated readers could contemplate the meanings of ghost stories from the comfort of their armchairs. As Roger Chartier has insisted, the subtle shifts engendered by novels and extended works of prose and poetry made the practice of reading 'more private, freer, and totally internalized'.[55] In this sense, the reality of ghosts was displaced, domesticated and relocated to the interior imagination – but not rejected. Indeed, the very uncertainty about the real or imagined status of ghosts was essential to the drama and performance of these texts.

Structure

The long eighteenth century is a fresh chronology within which to study the changing status of ghost beliefs and an unusual periodization in which to attempt a cultural history of this nature. The years 1660–1832 are primarily associated with political landmarks in English and subsequently British history, namely the restoration of King Charles II in 1660 and the Great Reform Act of 1832. Although the shape and status of ghost beliefs was certainly influenced by the political settlement of Restoration England, my starting point of 1660 is justified by the religious, social and intellectual changes that accompanied this political watershed, and in which the legitimacy of ghost beliefs was revived as part of myriad attempts to extinguish painful memories of civil war and republican government.

I have covered a period of one hundred and forty years in this study partly due to the nature of the source material available, but primarily to capture for the reader a sense of the non-linear, ongoing and cyclical process by which ghost beliefs and ghost stories were degraded, re-appropriated and transformed in public and private discourses. The theory of survivals articulated by Ronald Hutton is therefore of limited value in explaining the persistence of ghost beliefs post-

1660, which owed less to the dwindling mental landscapes of the sixteenth and seventeenth centuries than to the specific religious, social, political and economic realities of eighteenth-century England.[56] It was the contested cultural atmosphere of the years 1660 to 1800 that made men and women willing and able to negotiate a place for ghost beliefs. Although the evidence presented in this study has some projections into the early nineteenth century, the years immediately following the outbreak of the French Revolution mark a more natural break in the cultural history of eighteenth-century England than the legislative manoeuvrings of 1832.

My focus on English rather than British ghost stories requires justification given the current historiographical trend towards integrating the histories of England, Wales, Scotland and Ireland in a period that, according to Linda Colley, witnessed the forging of the British nation in both political and cultural terms.[57] The first and most practical reason for my concentration on England is due to the sheer volume of ghost stories that circulated in this period. An analysis of British ghost stories in the long eighteenth century is a worthwhile project but one that lies beyond the scope of this present study. The methodological difficulties of synthesizing English, Welsh, Scottish and Irish ghost stories are, however, more foundational to the chosen structure of this study. For much of the period under study here the union of Britons was of a largely political nature and significant differences in the religious and cultural contours of England, Wales, Scotland and Ireland persisted throughout the eighteenth century. Although Linda Colley was right to emphasize the common Protestantism of many Britons as a point of unity, particularly during the period of Protestant ascendancy in Ireland, the vitality of Scottish Presbyterianism as well as Episcopalian and Catholic Highland support for the Jacobite risings of 1715 and 1745 mark important points of disjuncture with the prevailing religious cultures of eighteenth-century England. Since this study emphasizes the links between ghost stories and the specific confessional formations and theologies of English Protestants, there is a danger of drawing too many similarities between the four kingdoms. Furthermore, a British survey may run the risk of obscuring the rich tradition of folk tales that was particularly evident in Ireland and Wales, with the latter maintaining a peculiar hybrid between ghosts and fairies throughout this period.[58] That said, ghost stories from Ireland, Scotland and Wales have been included when they were printed in England and are therefore assumed to have particular relevance. The exchange of ghostly tales within Britain was especially marked in the second half of the eighteenth century, no doubt facilitated by the rapid expansion of printing presses throughout the four kingdoms. The ghost stories of James Hogg are particularly interesting for the late eighteenth and early nineteenth centuries and highlight important cultural affinities within the Border regions, rather than a straightforward division between Scottish and English beliefs and tastes. Nonetheless, this period also witnessed the importation of ghost stories from Europe and from a wide variety of colonial ports, underlining the point that English cultural identity was not simply shaped by a sense of Britishness. Any straightforward analysis of British ghost stories would therefore be somewhat artificial, neglecting the complex processes of cultural formation and oversimplifying important distinctions in the narrative traditions of England, Ireland, Scotland and Wales and their regions.

This text has been organized in a largely chronological fashion stretching from the late seventeenth century to the turn of the nineteenth century. This lengthy time-span incorporates a sense of both continuity and change in the shape of ghost beliefs, and in the shifting form and content of ghost stories. As already stated, this is not a story of progressive disenchantment, and I hope readers will share my own understanding of the non-linear nature of the transformations, recycling and redefinitions to which ideas about ghosts were subjected. Different chapters introduce the different genres of print in which ghost stories surfaced, which reflects the emphasis of this study on patterns of production, circulation and consumption. This approach suggests the points at which particular genres became more influential than others. Chapters have also been organized to juxtapose polemical representations of ghosts with the everyday relevance of these narratives. Chapters 1 and 2 cover the years 1660 to 1700. They should be read as two halves of a whole since they introduce the central dichotomy that runs throughout this study – the ghost story as a desirable material product, but also as a flexible imaginative resource. Chapter 1 examines the rehabilitation of ghost stories within the intellectual context of England's political and religious Restoration. This chapter focuses upon the legacies of the civil war and interregnum, and it identifies a process of de-confessionalization, in which the traditional confessional allegiances of ghost stories were significantly eroded. This process enabled ghost stories to be closely linked to the institutional fortunes of the Church of England, as they were appropriated as vehicles of clerical reform. Chapter 2 examines how and why these clerical strategies may have been successful, focusing on ghost stories within the buoyant marketplace of cheap print. This chapter addresses the question of access to ghost stories, and examines how a variety of authors and publishers constructed ghost stories to persuade and entice readers. Discussion focuses on the material culture of cheap printed ghost stories, the mixed audiences to which they appealed, and the interrelationship of oral and literate cultures.

Chapters 3 and 4 cover the first half of the eighteenth century. Chapter 3 presents a detailed exploration of a ghost story from Canterbury, and the ways in which it was configured in oral communities, in manuscript and in a whole variety of printed texts. This particular ghost story is positioned as an important bridge between local and national cultures, and as a site of debate and exchange between learned and unlearned conceptions of ghosts. This is the only chapter of the book based on a detailed case study, and it is valuable for tracing interpretations of the same narrative over a long span of time. This chapter also addresses the complex relationship between fiction and reality in the eighteenth-century ghost story. Chapter 4 situates reactions to the Canterbury ghost in a wider context, tracing the impact of Enlightenment thought, and assessing the influence of discourses of politeness through the periodical press. These developments are linked to the migration of ghost stories into new fictional spaces. The fit of ghost stories with notions of interiority, the sublime and romanticism are also discussed.

Chapter 5 tracks the fluctuating status of ghost stories through the lens of confessional tension and political change in the second half of the eighteenth century. The role of ghost stories in forging moments of confessional conflict and unity between Methodist and Anglican ministers are explored, alongside the revived relevance of ghost stories in anti-Catholic and loyalist discourses leading up to the French Revolution. The attitudes of other Protestant groups towards ghosts are also traced to provide a more complete picture of the links between ghost beliefs and confessional identities. Polemical rejections of ghost stories are also contrasted with pastoral appropriations at parish level. The final chapter of the book provides a detailed examination of ghost beliefs and ghost stories within everyday life in the closing years of the eighteenth century. Discussion focuses upon the importance of memory, identity and landscape in shaping individual attitudes. The narrative spaces opened up by the physical processes of commercial and imperial expansion are also analysed here. Finally, the fortunes of ghosts are explored within discourses of romanticism and by reference to a growing corps of antiquarian literature which had an important effect upon the views of the polite classes. What emerges from this study is a sense of the flexibility of ghost stories, and the ways that these narratives were adapted to suit a rapidly changing cultural climate. The disjuncture of these narratives with certain trends in eighteenth-century life and thought is undeniable, but at the same time ghost stories complemented the particular themes and problems of English society in these years. Though by no means comprehensive, I hope that the present study will go some way towards reasserting the historical value of ghost stories, and to enhancing understandings of the contested cultural landscapes of English society in the age of reason.

1 RESTORATION HAUNTINGS

On Wednesday, 1 June 1692, a young man, about fifteen years of age, went to his bed. He had no sooner lain down than he heard 'a Hand sweeping on the wall'. Then it came 'with a rushing noise on his beds-head' and 'stroaked him over the face twice very gently'. Opening his eyes he saw before him 'an apparition of a woman cloathed in black apparel'. Following this eerie encounter, other members of his family reported seeing the apparition 'in the same room with a lighted candle'. Perplexed by these unexplained visits, the mistress of this 'Civiliz'd Family' wrote to the editors of the bi-weekly periodical the *Athenian Mercury*. She desired to know 'what should be the occasion of the disturbance' and 'whether it be advisable to ask the question of the apparition?'.[1] Samuel Wesley (father of John), Church of England minister and co-editor of the *Mercury*, advised the woman to speak to the ghost, find out its purpose and discover how it might be satisfied.[2]

We already know that the status of ghosts was highly contested in the religious polemic of post-Reformation England, so Samuel Wesley's advice might appear surprising. His interest in this haunting, however, neatly epitomizes a rehabilitation of ghost stories in Restoration England that peaked in the 1690s, and which forms the subject of this chapter. The years 1660–1700 saw ghost beliefs and ghost stories elevated to public prominence thanks to their congruence with the religious, political, intellectual and social imperatives that followed Charles II's return to the throne. Although the reality of returning ghosts was not universally accepted, the Restoration period produced the most energetic and public defence of ghost beliefs and ghost stories that Protestant England had ever seen.

The distinctive importance of ghost stories in this period will be described under three main headings. First, the increasingly common adoption of ghost stories by Anglican, and especially latitudinarian, ministers will be examined to show how and why these narratives became so relevant to the religious ideologies of the newly-restored Church. When ghost stories were shorn of popish associations, and linked to sound theological tenets, they were allowed to play a prominent role in shaping the most significant religious battle of the long eighteenth century – the struggle for a balance between revelatory and natural religion, between a faith of the heart and one of the head. Second, the intellectual relevance of ghost stories will be explored through the work of Henry More and Joseph Glanvill. The concept of the wandering dead was compatible with the theology of these men, but they were also interested in these relations because of their relevance to natural philosophy, which was one of the most important intellectual developments of the seventeenth and eighteenth centuries. Ghost stories were rapidly becoming legitimate subjects for philosophical inquiry, and they proved invaluable to a fledgling scientific community that was seeking to justify new empirical inquiries into the natural and preternatural worlds. The final section of the chapter again highlights the relevance of ghost stories to contemporary religious discourse, but the focus shifts away from the public stage to examine the pastoral uses to which these narratives were put in parish communities. Discussion will focus on the 1690s, a decade that saw ghost stories employed as weapons in a clerical campaign to stamp out vice and immorality among the laity, and to revitalize Christianity at grass-roots level. This reforming project cut across denominational boundaries, and it suggests that the categories of 'conformist' and 'nonconformist', imposed by the Act of Uniformity (1662), obscure common theological ground among a variety of Protestant believers. Richard Baxter's *The Certainty of the World of Spirits* (1691) will be used to highlight clerical engagement with lay perceptions of ghosts, which filled the pages of John Dunton's long-running periodical the *Athenian Mercury* (1691–7). Taken together, these texts point to the devotional utility of ghost stories; to the shifting priorities of Restoration Protestantism; and to the prominent position that ghosts occupied within the spiritual world-views of the lay community.

Radical Legacies

Those responsible for the public broadcasting of ghost stories in Restoration England were mostly educated men, but their engagement with these narratives served different interests and objectives. What they all shared, however, was revulsion at the religious, political and social turmoil that had been generated by years of civil war and republican government in mid-seventeenth-century England. In many ways the identity of the Restoration elite was forged by the Puritan revolution of the 1640s and 1650s. The events of these tumultuous years provided the immediate impetus for rhetorical engagements with ghost stories.

The execution of Charles I in January 1649 was perhaps the single most dramatic event in almost two decades of disorder and bloodshed. But the mid-seventeenth century also saw the collapse of civil and ecclesiastical authority, with the abolition of episcopacy, press censorship, the church courts and the subsequent emergence of hundreds of independent and semi-independent congregations. Sectarian groups such as the Ranters, Diggers, Quakers, Muggletonians, Baptists, Seekers and Fifth Monarchy Men rejected the authority of Church government in favour of a guiding spiritual light within.

This was no lunatic fringe and many of these idealists were motivated by distaste for the fundamentals of Protestant, and particularly Calvinist, teaching. The avowed infallibility of scripture emphasized by early Protestant reformers led to close and creative readings of the Bible in the hands of freethinking radicals. The Book of Revelation was interpreted literally by the Fifth Monarchy Men, who prepared for the arrival of a new millennium. Others treated its stories as mere allegory, or rejected its authority entirely.[3] However, the most consistent criticism was directed towards the Calvinist scheme of salvation. Psychological torment often resulted from the doctrine of double predestination which lay at the heart of this schema, and which stated that the salvation or damnation of human beings was pre-determined before birth. No amount of good works or faith could change the fate that God had laid down for each individual. The result of this was severe emotional anxiety. Quakers George Fox and Isaac Penington and Fifth Monarchist John Rogers were just some of those who suffered anguished thoughts about what lay in store for them beyond the grave. Such distress led some to thoughts of suicide, and others to doubt the benevolence of God, or eventually to challenge established ideas about the reality of heaven, hell or any kind of life after death. Digger leader Gerrard Winstanley rejected the physical reality of an afterlife altogether. He believed that religion served only a repressive social function, and was designed to distract men from their poor situation on earth.[4] Leveller Richard Overton was also convinced that both body and soul expired at the moment of physical death.[5] Similarly for the Ranters, personal immortality was not an option. Instead, heaven and hell were merely figurative states that corresponded to the pleasures and pains of the physical body. Indeed, the charismatic Ranter Lawrence Clarkson declared that 'In the grave there is no remembrance of either joy or sorrow after'.[6] If body and soul died in the grave, the return of dead souls amongst the living was clearly impossible.

Attacks upon the doctrine of immortality and the post-mortem states of heaven and hell were particularly repugnant strands of the radical manifesto. In 1646 Thomas Edwards condemned no less than eleven heresies relating to mortalism or soul-sleeping in his catalogue of religious heterodoxies known as *Gangraena*. These notions not only undermined established topographies of the afterlife, but they also posed a threat to the accepted moral values and mores of civil society. The rejection of life after death by the Diggers justified the seizure of common lands at St George's Hill near London, where an independent commune was established in April 1649. Similarly, the antinomian beliefs of Ranters allowed them to reject the authority of all moral law, which effectively sanctioned a range of hedonistic excesses enjoyed by members of this group.

The ultimate failure of these radicals to secure enduring social, political or spiritual reformations was less important than attempts to re-imagine the world in which they lived. If England had not been completely turned upside down by 1660, freethinking radicals had left an indelible mark that shaped the priorities of Restoration writers, who were eager to restore peace and stability to civil and religious life. It was against this tumultuous backdrop, and the fierce controversies surrounding the nature of life after death, that clergymen, polemicists and natural philosophers helped to generate interest in ghosts and their meanings.

Ghosts and the Restoration Church

Keith Thomas and Ronald Finucane have tackled Restoration-era ghost beliefs as part of broader chronological surveys, but little has been said about the preternatural world in relation to the institutional fortunes of the Church. The excesses of mid-seventeenth-century England provide the key to the polemical adoption of ghost stories by ministers of the newly-restored Church of England. In the early years of its restoration the Church was internally divided and desperate to re-establish its relevance and authority at the heart of English society. The religious and political orthodoxies of the new regime were fashioned in opposition to the 'enthusiasm' of the 1640s and 1650s. The events of those years did much to reaffirm the value of clerical supervision, theological moderation and religious conformity. In fact these tenets became key priorities for Anglican ministers seeking to forge a new identity for the Church. In many ways, ghost stories interacted with these goals, helping to shape a new theological outlook that comprehended a healthy balance of both reason and revelation. They also served as vehicles through which to attack the twin spectres of atheism and sadducism that were lambasted in pulpit and print as the most monstrous perversions of the Christian faith.

The label 'atheist' was applied not only in its modern-day sense to the denial of divinity, but more regularly to a range of heterodox religious views and displays of licentiousness. It functioned as a catch-all term for people who transgressed the moral and behavioural codes of Christianity. A 'sadducee' denoted anyone who denied the resurrection of the body and the existence of spirits – principles that were perceived as inevitable precursors to the denial of God and Christianity itself. The perceived spread of atheism in Restoration England was greatly exaggerated by contemporaries, who used the label as a rhetorical tool with which to attack their enemies. Nonetheless, there is little doubt that a degree of genuine fear about the spread of irreligion and immorality did exist. The publication of Thomas Hobbes's *Leviathan* in 1651 did little to calm these anxieties, since it

offered firm theoretical foundation to a fluid body of materialist religious philosophies, which rejected notions of immortality, post-mortem punishment and
even the reality of divine intervention.

It was no coincidence then that Anglican ministers were among the most animated supporters of ghost stories in these years. Visions of the dead provided a
particularly dramatic defence against extreme materialist and mortalist philosophies. They also represented visible and immediate proof of divine intervention,
offering assurance of immortality and the reality of an afterlife. Moreover, ghost
stories and ghost beliefs were strikingly absent from civil war sectarianism. The
logic of ghostly appearances clearly did not fit with those who advocated the
death or sleep of the soul in the grave, and even those who maintained belief in
an afterlife and divine intervention shied away from recounting tales of returning spirits. When the Quaker leader George Fox was imprisoned in Launceston
Castle in 1656, he dismissed rumours among his fellow captives that 'spirits
haunted & walked in Doomesdale', declaring that he 'feared noe such thinge for
Christ our preist woulde sanctify ye walls'.[7] In spite of clear interest in the 'sig-
nal judgements' of God, there is little evidence that early Quakers adopted ghost
beliefs as part of their religious world-view, at least on the public stage. Indeed,
historian Rosemary Moore has argued that Restoration Quakers deliberately
distanced themselves from such preternatural episodes in an effort to dissociate
themselves from their civil war forebears.[8] An episode from the late seventeenth
century does however suggest that there may have been a gap between publicly
professed Quaker attitudes towards ghosts and more personal reflections. Farrier
and Quaker convert Walter Harry reported having met with the ghost of former
weaver Morgan Lewis, who wished to reveal the location of some bottoms of
wool that he had hidden in his former house. Harry carried out the ghost's wishes
before commanding him 'in the name of God, that thou trouble my house no
more'.[9] The duty to discharge the wishes of the dead was no doubt more powerful within close-knit community settings, offering an alternative context for the
contemplation of ghostly appearances.

Ghost stories had not then been heavily tarred with the brush of enthusiasm,
which was an accusation levelled at a wide range of preternatural and supernatural events in the mid-seventeenth century. In fact these narratives appeared to
complement a much more moderate religious outlook in the hands of prominent
churchmen. Joseph Glanvill was vicar of Bath and chaplain in ordinary to Charles
II, and he considered ghost stories to offer standing evidence against both atheists and sadducees.[10] In his *Compleat History of the Most Remarkable Providences*
(1697), the vicar of Walberton in Sussex, William Turner, eagerly catalogued
accounts of the wandering dead and other providential phenomena. This was,
he believed, 'one of the best Methods' to refute 'the abounding Atheism of this
Age'.[11] Turner dedicated his book to John Williams, bishop of Chichester, who
may well have approved of his efforts. Turner's publication was moreover a col-

laborative effort, since this collection of providences was begun by the Reverend
Matthew Poole some thirty years earlier.

Ghost stories did more than defend against atheists, however, and churchmen
often credited these relations because they offered proof of the most fundamental
Christian beliefs. 'GOD is a Spirit' argued Turner. To deny that a vital spirit world
existed was to deny that God himself existed.[12] In 1678 Ralph Cudworth was
similarly optimistic about the relevance of ghost stories to orthodox Christian
beliefs when he claimed in his *True Intellectual System of the Universe* that 'If there
be once any visible ghosts or spirits acknowledged as things permanent ... it will
not be easy for any to give a reason why there might not be one supreme ghost
also, presiding over them all and the whole world'.[13] In the same year the Anglican
divine Benjamin Camfield reaffirmed Cudworth's emphasis on the relationship
between ghost stories and the Trinitarian consensus of orthodox Restoration
theology. The denial of spirits, he believed, led inevitably 'to the dethroning of
God, the supreme Spirit, and Father of Spirits'.[14] Ghost stories were thus explicitly
linked to the fundamental Christian doctrines of immortality, resurrection and
the tripartite division of the Godhead – beliefs that remained fundamental to
the Anglican faith throughout this period. Fervent propagation of ghost stories
showed that the religious feeling of the 1640s and 1650s had not disappeared,
but was instead redirected towards the defence of the established Church and
of Christianity itself. Ghost stories were thus adopted by leading figures within
the established Church, and they proved to be crucial weapons in a battle to
encourage religious conformity, and to reassert the value of clerical mediation
and church governance.[15]

Nonetheless, the drive towards religious moderation assumed a number of different forms in which the appropriation of ghost stories was by no means universal.
Samuel Clarke, John Toland, Anthony Collins and the third Earl of Shaftesbury
were leading figures of an amorphous group of thinkers often termed deists. The
most effective antidote to religious fanaticism, they believed, was to advance its
opposite – a sober brand of natural religion. In an attempt to demonstrate the
rational foundations of faith, Samuel Clarke tried to prove the existence of God,
not through Scripture, but by a method 'as near to Mathematical, as the nature
of such a Discourse would allow'.[16] Thomas Burnet's *Sacred History of the Earth*
(1681) included an explanation of the Flood based on mechanical principles,
while John Wilkins held that astronomy proved 'a God and a providence' and
'incites our hearts to a greater admiration and fear of His omnipotency'.[17] Deists
varied in the intensity of their commitment to natural theology. Early adherents
sometimes preserved belief in the immortality of the soul, but rejected revelation,
along with the need for divine intervention. Shaftesbury was one of the more
extreme proponents, condemning religious excess of any kind.[18] Meanwhile John
Toland's provocative *Christianity not Mysterious* (1696) declared that neither
God nor his revelations were above the understanding of human reason.

Deism was never widely accepted in England, and its popularity peaked in the later eighteenth century. Indeed, in the late seventeenth century John Toland's work provoked a number of scathing responses. His text was condemned as the most complete rejection of revelation since Thomas Hobbes's *Leviathan*. Ghosts were naturally denied a place within Hobbes's system, since they furnished vivid manifestations of heavenly intervention and the afterlife of the soul. He described them as mere 'Idols, or Phantasms of the braine' and they were similarly rejected by deist writers.[19] Natural religion began as a logical counterpart to the more emotional, anti-dogmatic faith of the Pietists, yet in the eyes of men like Sir Thomas Browne, Isaac Barrow and John Mapletoft, it went too far in denying agency and mystery to God, and downplaying the spiritual teachings of the Christian faith.[20]

The growth of so-called Cambridge Platonism was another important intellectual movement that shaped the theological outlook of the Restoration Church, along with more positive attitudes towards ghosts. Ralph Cudworth and Henry More were founding members of the Platonist movement, and Joseph Glanvill came to share their convictions during his time at Oxford University. All three men were chief figures in the fervent circulation of ghost stories in Restoration England, since their particular brand of religious philosophy was sufficiently flexible to integrate ghost beliefs with Church doctrine. Platonists accorded less significance to dogmatic truth, ritual and Church government, and emphasized instead the essentials of religion, rather than its external forms. Platonists advocated a simplified moral theology that diluted strict Calvinist orthodoxies, and which comprehended an interest in Arminian theology, which laid greater stress on the value of human agency in faith and worship. These values were also used to amend the rigid schema of predestination, replacing its precepts with a more liberal belief in a dynamic afterlife. The work of More and Glanvill will be discussed in more detail in the following section, but for now it is important to note that the theology of these men, initially labelled 'latitudinarian' as a term of abuse, would go on to achieve much greater prominence within the Church, especially among those who sought to heal the clerical divisions imposed by the terms of the Clarendon Code.

According to James and Margaret Jacob, latitudinarianism became 'the defining ecclesiastical mode of the Whig settlement after 1688', and Richard Kroll similarly labelled it 'a virtual orthodoxy after 1688'.[21] Latitudinarians comprehended a wide spectrum of polity and ways of worship within their theology. According to one of their chief apologists, Edward Fowler, bishop of Gloucester (1691–1714), ghost stories were an important part of this conciliatory outlook. Fowler's *Free Discourse on the Principles and Practice of certain Moderate Divines ... called Latitudinarians* (1670) defended a practical, moral theology that was relevant to the concerns of everyday life. Ghost stories fitted neatly with his approach, and Fowler supplied his friend Henry More with a regular stream of them, many of which were included in More's edition of *Saducismus Triumphatus*. The dissenting physician Henry Sampson approvingly described Fowler as 'a great collector of such storys & others of like importance to prove the Being of Spirits'.[22] The deist apologist Lord Shaftesbury was, however, less complimentary, referring to Fowler as 'a zealous Defender of Ghosts', who was able to 'extend his faith so largely as to comprehend in it not only all scriptural and traditional miracles, but a solid system of old wives' stories'.[23] Fowler did not deny the accusation, but instead underlined the limits of human knowledge about the immaterial world. 'We know not well the System of the Invisible World, the Laws, Permissions, Powers, or Varieties of it; and how easy it is, in certain Cases, for them to play their Pranks, or busy themselves amongst Men'. Nonetheless, Fowler claimed that he was certain 'of both the existence and activity of certain unseen spirits'.[24] The adoption of ghost stories by this cluster of latitudinarian theologians thus brought them closer to mainstream Anglicanism than has previously been acknowledged. These men also shared an interest in natural philosophy, and their experimental pursuits helped to fashion a *modus vivendi* between empiricist philosophies and revelatory religion. The result was the emergence of a more positive relationship between Protestantism and the returning spirits of the dead.

Preternatural Science

The work of poet and theologian Henry More combined curiosity about metaphysics with a healthy appetite for ghost stories. His interest in ghosts was both polemical and personal, and it began at an early age. More was raised as a Calvinist, and he was plagued by fears of damnation as a young boy. He later reacted against the rigid principles of predestinarian thought during his time at Christ's College, Cambridge. In its place, he advanced a more liberal theology that concentrated on moral values and introduced an element of free will into the process of salvation. Along with fellow Platonist Ralph Cudworth, More also sought to reconcile religion with science and faith with reason to steer a middle ground between healthy belief in an active spirit world and utter incredulity.[25] If More's ultimate aim was to redefine theological precepts, his scientific pursuits provided him with the apparatus to achieve this.

Ghosts formed a crucial part of More's vision of a dynamic afterlife. He drew on the vocabulary of Restoration polemicists to refute Hobbes's claim that contemplation of the spirit world was futile by proving that the human mind was indeed capable of knowing immaterial substance. Henry More was among the most advanced thinkers of his generation, and he was one of a number of natural philosophers who believed that the primary role of science was to glorify God by studying his creations on a scale hitherto unknown. English naturalist and botanist John Ray echoed More's thoughts in a series of lectures delivered at

Cambridge in the 1650s, which were later published under the fitting title *The Wisdom of God Manifested in the Works of Creation* (1691). Henry More was convinced that science had the capability to strengthen belief in the existence and benevolence of God by throwing light on the workings of the preternatural world. The existence of ghosts was, moreover, intrinsic to More's religious and philosophical outlooks. There was no saying so true in metaphysics, he claimed as 'No Spirit, No God'.[26] He was particularly excited by the potential of Robert Boyle's air-pump to prove his hypothesis of an 'Immaterial Being that exercises its directive Activity on the Matter of the World'.[27] More's own efforts to support this conclusion would also be achieved by empirical methods.

Henry More investigated and catalogued what he considered to be legitimate ghost sightings, and he was aided in his endeavour by his friend and unofficial pupil Viscountess Anne Conway. Ghosts had to exist, argued More, because so many people had seen them, and often people of unquestionable character – here then was a supreme act of empiricism. Anne Conway nurtured an independent interest in ghosts that stemmed from her unorthodox belief that the universe was composed 'entirely of spirit, in which all creatures are modes of one spiritual substance emanating from God, and in which matter itself is a kind of congealed spirit'.[28] Conway's organic conception of spirit reflected the contracting boundaries between the natural and preternatural realms and, within this mode of thought, ghosts constituted one of the purest forms of this amorphous spiritual substance.

Conway's fascination with this subject led to a blossoming correspondence with Henry More, with whom she regularly swapped tales of ghostly visions. In 1662 both were captivated by the story of Francis Taverner, a porter to the Earl of Donegal in Ireland, who claimed to have seen the ghost of James Haddock – a local man who had died five years previously. Haddock's ghost appeared a number of times on a mission to reclaim his son's inheritance from the usurping grasp of his new stepfather. Conway interviewed Tarverner in person, and he was accompanied by the renowned Anglican divine and spiritual writer Dr Jeremy Taylor, who served as chaplain in the Conway household, and became bishop of Down, Connor and Dromore in 1661. Taylor's involvement in this episode is highly suggestive, since he was a leading latitudinarian clergyman, and was clearly willing to accommodate ghosts within his wide-ranging and heterodox theology.[29] Both Conway and Taylor were so convinced by Tarverner's story that the bishop prepared a special spirit's catechism, with which Tarverner could quiz the ghost about its nature, origin and habitation. Sadly when Tarverner attempted the interrogation the ghost 'gave him no answer, but crawl'd on its hands and knees over the wall again, and so vanished in white with a most melodious harmony'.[30] Despite this disappointment, Henry More was convinced of the ghost's authenticity. Distinguished witnesses had verified the fact, and More considered it a positive omen that Tarverner's horse had taken fright at the approach of the ghost. The sensitivity of animals to the presence of ghosts was a traditional folkloric motif, and More was struck by the 'agonies Horses and Dogs are cast [into] upon their approach'. He therefore judged these reactions 'a good circumstance to distinguish a reall Apparition from our own Imaginations'.[31] Investigations of ghosts thus opened up important spaces for the fruitful exchange of new philosophical learning with more established paths to knowledge, including oral folk traditions. Henry More included Tarverner's account in his 1681 revision of Joseph Glanvill's *Saducismus Triumphatus*. This collection also featured the story of David Hunter, neat-herd to the bishop of Down, a case that was similarly investigated by Conway and Taylor. In 1663 Hunter claimed to have seen the ghost of an old woman named Margaret who charged him to settle 'the charge unpayed at my Funeral' and to persuade her son to forego his dissolute life before it was too late.[32] Again the story came well attested but it also conformed to customary folkloric expectations of the occasions on which ghosts were likely to appear, often to settle unpaid debts and to encourage godly living. These themes will be explored more fully in the following chapter, but for now it is important to highlight the affinities between Henry More's acceptance of ghost stories and more popular conceptions that influenced his own thoughts on this subject. Indeed, More appeared to empathize with run-of-the-mill ghost beliefs when he argued that 'all created Spirits are Souls in all probability, and actuate some Matter or other'.[33] Ghosts were more likely to be souls of the dead rather than angels or demons he claimed, because they had 'more affinity with mortality and humane frailty' and were thus 'more sensible of our necessities and infirmities, having once felt them themselves'.[34] By emphasizing the corporeal qualities of ghosts, Henry More kept them closely tied to the physical world and rendered them worthy subjects of empirical investigation.

In the scientific community Joseph Glanvill joined Henry More in his energetic accreditation of ghost stories. Alongside his pastoral duties in Bath and at the court of Charles II, Glanvill was chief apologist for the Royal Society – the institution that encompassed most of the leading lights of natural philosophy. Glanvill had much in common with More. He was a convert to Platonic thought, shared the same integrated 'religio-scientific' world-view, and positioned spirits at the crux of his theological outlook.[35] 'If the notion of a Spirit be absurd' he wrote, 'that of a GOD and a SOUL distinct from matter, and immortal, are likewise absurdities'.[36] Glanvill was most famous for his defence of ghosts and witches in *Saducismus Triumphatus* (1681), where he joined the chorus of condemnation against atheists and sadducees to establish the validity of his own dabbling with natural theology. Glanvill collected evidence of ghostly goings-on to confirm the vitality of divine providence. But he also aimed to advance a more harmonious Christian outlook which comprehended a healthy balance between reason and revelation. Glanvill's moderation was, however, called into question by his somewhat eccentric ideas about the capabilities of witches, which he thought could fly out of windows and morph into animal form. John Webster took issue with him by dismissing the reality of witchcraft entirely. However, he did not challenge Glanvill's treatment of ghosts. Instead he was willing to confess his own belief in the same because they provided 'a sensible Argument of our Immortality'.[37]

Glanvill's advocacy of ghost stories stands alongside Henry More's contribution as one of the most comprehensive early attempts to apply precise principles of natural philosophy to the study of ghosts. His philosophy of spirits theorized about the vehicles of the soul, aerial casings or bodies that enabled ghosts and other immaterial spirits to travel long distances and so visit friends and relatives still living. Glanvill's theory also enabled scientists to bring ghosts more firmly into the realm of the preternatural than the supernatural. That is to say ghosts were increasingly understood to have quasi-natural or physical qualities that were potentially explicable, rather than representing something that was beyond the scope of nature. Glanvill thus brought a new optimism to 'The LAND OF ESPIRITS', which he considered to be 'a kind of America, and not well discover'd Region' that was ripe for greater human enquiry. Just as knowledge of the physical environment was advanced through experimentation, there was, claimed Glanvill, 'the same way of speculating immaterial nature, by extraordinary Events and Apparitions, which possibly might be improved to notices not contemptible, were there a Cautious, and Faithful History made of those certain and uncommon appearances'.[38]

Glanvill's experiments on immaterial substance began with the pressing of a Linen Bag 'in which some Spirit was moving', but he also developed a consistent methodology for corroborating the authenticity of ghost stories.[39] Glanvill believed that this could be achieved through the interrogation of human testimony and by applying the principle of context – that is, identifying certain typical situations in which the appearance of a ghost was both plausible and credible. This principle of context brought Glanvill and his readers into contact with less scholarly conventions about the activities of the dead, which is usefully illustrated by examining just a few of the stories that he supported in his writing. Glanvill presented well-established philosophical, historical and scriptural rationales for the existence of ghosts in *Saducismus Triumphatus*, but the bulk of his narrative was devoted to practical demonstration of their appearances, which were reported by a variety of people in the course of everyday life. Glanvill remained true to his empirical commitments, and he claimed that these ghosts were 'fresh and near, and attended with all the circumstances of credibility'.[40]

The story of Thomas Goddard, a weaver from Marlborough in Wiltshire, was one such account and it centred on the ghost of Edward Avon who appeared to Goddard, his son-in-law, on a number of occasions. Avon came on well-established errands to settle his debts, to enquire after his family, to reassure his daughter Mary that he was in heaven, and to confess to the murder of a local man more than thirty years previously. Avon had fought with the man over money and ran him through with his sword before burying him in a copse. Accompanied by a mastiff dog and eager to confess his sins, Avon's ghost ushered Goddard to a shallow grave. There he was told to dig for the bones of the murdered man and to expose the crime to the world. In line with Protestant teaching, Avon's ghost did not seek to alter his own spiritual state, but served instead as an example of pious repentance to his family and the local community. Luckily for Joseph Glanvill, Thomas Goddard involved the local authorities, who offered no objection to his story and even instructed him to question the ghost about 'who was confederate with him in this murther'.[41] The participation of town officials strengthened Goddard's testimony, but Glanvill also justified his support for the relation by stating that Goddard was reputed to be an honest and pious man. Glanvill overlooked the fact that Goddard had recently fallen off to the nonconformists, or that he suffered from epileptic fits. These factors, he claimed, did not impair Goddard's external senses, nor could he have gained any personal benefit by fabricating such a story. The ghost materialized for godly reasons, to repent of his sins and to commend the value of moral living. This was then an admirable posture for a ghost to adopt.

Glanvill justified the ghost of one Mr Bower by the same principle of context, even though the only witness to its appearance was a highwayman who was in prison. News of this ghost reached a Surrey magistrate who turned out to be the cousin of the murdered gentleman. The highwayman was questioned under oath, and he was adjudged to have no personal design, having ties neither with the accused nor the victim. Evidence from the ghost was not admissible in court, but the suspicions aroused by the report eventually led to the arrest, trial and conviction of the two men accused. The ghost of Mrs Bretton appeared to recover some land for the poor, and another came to recover possession of a field for his child. The moral righteousness of ghost stories was a recurrent theme, and it gave these tales an important veneer of respectability in public life.[42]

Joseph Glanvill's reasoning formed part of a more general willingness shared by other members of the Royal Society to retain faith in the value of human testimony, despite increasing awareness of its defects.[43] The Royal Society was established in 1660 and, although it would later represent the pinnacle of philosophical achievement, its early members struggled for positive recognition. The Society was, moreover, firmly tied to the ideologies of the establishment, enjoying parliamentary support and receiving a Royal Charter in 1662. The move away from philosophical certainties was then, as Michael Hunter suggests, symptomatic of the Society's eagerness to exercise caution over the extent to which human knowledge could supplant the holy truths of Scripture.[44] Glanvill relied on the theory of *probabilism* to judge the legitimacy of preternatural episodes. That is to say ghosts probably existed because so many people claimed to have seen them, and some were of esteemed character. Nevertheless, Glanvill was not only willing to credit the views of the learned. He was also willing to countenance the testimonies of less illustrious people. The palpable experiences of ordinary men, women and even children justified their relations, 'for in things of Fact', he claimed, 'the People are as much to be believ'd, as the most subtile Philosophers'.[45] Glanvill believed that their reports were by no means inferior because 'the manner of the Narrative is so simple, plain and rural, that it prevents all suspicion of fraud or Imposture in the Relatour'.[46] Glanvill thus created a space for the expression of customary, folkloric conceptions of ghosts alongside more philosophically sophisticated accounts of their activities. In fact, Glanvill's rendition of Edward Avon's ghost appears to be based on a cheap pamphlet, *The Deemon of Marleborough*, published in 1674.[47] The similarities between the two accounts are striking and include vivid descriptions of the 'Clothes, Hat, Stockings and Shoes' worn by the ghost and the reactions of the mastiff dog. Glanvill's most famous case, the 'Drummer of Tedworth', also shared similar linguistic and explanatory structures to a successful black-letter ballad written by the undistinguished Abraham Miles.[48] When presented in different contexts and forms, the same ghost stories could flow through different texts and thereby reach a variety of audiences.

Empirical study of preternatural phenomena by More and Glanvill provided a fresh and legitimate forum for the discussion of ghosts in educated circles. These endeavours also loosened them from negative associations with popery in service of more pressing priorities. The renewed distribution and estimation of ghost stories certainly owed something to the work of these men, but the debt was also reciprocal. The link between ghost stories, traditional Christian doctrines and rejections of religious extremism provided a crucial cloak of legitimacy for new experimental methods that might otherwise have been vulnerable to accusations of materialism and usurping divine authority. In the hands of less scrupulous men, the introduction of too great a degree of reason into religion could be used to question the spiritual truths of Christianity, rather than uphold them. Part of the problem lay in the prioritization of secondary causes by natural philosophers, which was seen to detract from the primary and originating cause – God himself. William Turner understood the delicacy required in advancing the conclusions of empirical enquiries, and in the preface to his book he was careful to recommend that his readers 'look over all these Secondary Causes, and little Instruments that are moved here below, and look up to, and fix his Eye upon the Spring and Original Wheel, that gives Motion to all the rest'.[49] Ghost stories afforded extra protection to natural philosophers by restoring the balance between rational, demonstrable religious principles and the revealed religion of God. Robert Boyle, one of the most eminent natural philosophers of his day, exercised caution by limiting the extent to which God became synonymous with nature. Boyle's attitude fitted well with his support for a ghost story from Masçon in France, to which I will return shortly. Ghost stories were thus used to promote a sensible engagement with natural philosophy, restraining its logical excesses by sustaining links with acceptable strands of Anglican theology.

Political and Pastoral Objectives

The final reason for the public rehabilitation of ghost stories in the late seventeenth century stemmed from campaigns to restore confessional harmony, and to reform the spirituality of lay people. The employment of ghost stories for didactic purposes was not unique to this period, and Peter Marshall has outlined similar processes at work in Elizabethan and Jacobean England. Nonetheless, these early accommodations largely took place behind closed doors, and on an *ad hoc* basis. It was not until the final decades of the seventeenth century that the relationship between Protestantism and ghosts blossomed into one of more thoroughgoing reciprocity, and was consistently acknowledged in public and private contexts. Furthermore, the 1690s witnessed a significant intensification of efforts to amend the religious beliefs and social behaviour of the multitude. Ghost stories played an important role because many clergymen believed, and not without justification, that these visions had a relevance to the daily practice of religious life, and a significant emotional impact on the imaginations of the laity.

I have already outlined how and why ghost stories were co-opted into the service of the Church of England. Yet they were not exclusively shackled to the interests of the establishment. A number of Presbyterian divines took part in this reforming project, and they were happy to promote the devotional utility of ghost stories, along with a few Congregationalists and dedicated laymen. This cross-confessional investment in ghost stories represented an ideological and practical bridge between the ill-defined categories of conformist and nonconformist. It was no coincidence that the main propagators of ghost stories were also committed to realizing a theologically inclusive religious settlement that sought to reincorporate disenfranchised brethren into a united Protestant Church. In this endeavour Henry More, Joseph Glanvill and Anne Conway were joined by the likes of Simon Patrick, Samuel Hartlib and John Beale, who were eager supporters of a vibrant spirit world. As Peter Elmer has suggested, John Beale understood his engagement with ghost stories as part of a broader attempt to break down boundaries between Anglicans and nonconformists by identifying common theological precepts on which they could agree.[50] The unified advocacy of ghost stories was then partly an attempt to promote confessional reconciliation. But a second and more significant motive also rallied these men and women to promote the agency of dead souls – the need to reform lay spirituality.

If ghost beliefs represented a potential solution to religious disunity, they also appeared to highlight escalating trends of lay vice and immorality. 'Irreligion ... hath been still the companion of every Age', wrote Charles Wolseley in 1672, yet "Tis but of late that men come to defend ill living and secure themselves against their own guilt, by an open defiance to all the great maxims of Piety and Virtue'.[51] Wolseley blamed this new-found arrogance on Thomas Hobbes's materialist legacy, correlating his advocacy of freethinking with libertinism and dissolute behaviour. Thomas Bromhall similarly decried 'iniquity, impiety, and dissolute living'. Such immoral behaviour was explicitly linked to the denial of ghosts and spirits in Bromhall's *Treatise of Specters*, since this appeared to be an unmistakable symptom of an irreligious mindset.[52] New legislation against sin and vice lent further support to these outbursts, and in 1691 King William issued a Proclamation 'for preventing and punishing immorality and profaneness'. A request from the House of Commons later that year demanded that the laws were fully enforced, and that the Proclamation be read four times a year following Divine Service.[53] What is more, the regular appearance of departed souls was itself regarded as a sign of divine displeasure about episodes of sin and debauchery. Many clergymen were agreed that instances of ghostly intervention proved that the nation was struggling 'under some providential malaise, punishment no doubt for the sins of its people'.[54]

For Anglican ministers, instances of lay vice were not simply to be blamed upon the supposed spread of atheism. Clerical complaints about irreligion and immorality probably disguised deeper fears that the Church had failed to reassert its influence at parish level despite the official restoration of its supremacy in 1662. Moreover, the status of the Church was reduced to 'established' rather than 'national' following William III's accession. Prospects of religious toleration were distasteful to the High Church party throughout this period, and they loomed ever larger following the concessions of the Toleration Act (1689). The failure of the Church's push for uniformity had effectively killed off any realistic prospect of Protestant unity. The stubborn refusal to recognize the legitimacy of dissenting Protestant groups may well have strengthened the independent identity and resolve of a new generation of Presbyterian and nonconformist congregations. These men and women were disillusioned by the intransigence of the Church, and they no longer sought accommodation within it. They chose instead to focus on strengthening their own congregations, and on attracting new followers. For the hard-line Tory cleric, the prospect of a free marketplace of religion intensified confessional rivalries with dissenters, but it also provided a powerful motivation to engage with the priorities of lay religion to secure their loyalty to the Church.

Nevertheless, the Glorious Revolution of 1688 proved to be a political and religious watershed, and the years after 1689 saw the latitudinarian party reign triumphant within the Church of England. Latitudinarian ministers now represented a stronger force within the campaign to revitalize lay spirituality, and this often took place with the help of their nonconformist counterparts. The theological outlook of the clerics described above emphasized the essentials of religious belief alongside the duties of repentance, piety and holy living. As such, they allowed for more harmonious relations with a large group of dissenters, mainly Presbyterians, with whom they shared common ground. The labels of 'conformist' and 'nonconformist' largely reflected disagreements over the structure of church government, but there was less doctrinal division between these categories than has been commonly supposed.[55] In fact, cross-denominational collaboration and friendships were maintained throughout this period. In the 1690s, clergymen from dissenting and conformist backgrounds worked side-by-side to establish Societies for the Reformation of Manners in London, Westminster and the provinces, 'for the effecting of a National Reformation'.[56] The same collaborative effort was evident in the parallel spread of religious societies, which concentrated on the regeneration of personal religious beliefs instead of promoting the public face of religion. Thomas Bray blamed lay immorality on 'gross ignorance of the principles of the Christian religion', and he sought to improve education by founding the Society for Promoting Christian Knowledge (SPCK) and the Society for the Propagation of the Gospel (SPG) in 1699. Confessional rivalry may have intensified Protestant sponsorship of ghosts to a degree, and some clergymen purposely channelled lay fascination with the dead to secure pastoral loyalty. Nevertheless, cooperation was more characteristic than conflict. Latitudinarian and Presbyterian clergy were united in their concern over spiritual apathy and in their hatred of irreligion and immorality. The circulation of ghost stories and their promotion as pastoral aids was one important expression of this collaboration.

The next section examines some of these tales in more detail, specifically comparing interpretations of ghost stories in the work of the Presbyterian divine Richard Baxter with the bi-weekly periodical the *Athenian Mercury*. Both were published in the 1690s, a period which proved especially fertile for clerical appropriations of ghost stories. Taken together, they highlight the shared affinities between these tales and the dominant concerns of late-Restoration theology. More importantly, however, they emphasize the importance of ghost stories as vehicles through which to engage with the spiritual concerns of the laity. As evidence from the *Mercury* suggests, visions of the dead commanded a dramatic and unique place in the imagination of ordinary men and women.

Richard Baxter's World of Spirits

In 1691 Richard Baxter's *Certainty of the World of Spirits* was first published in England. This tract was the final publication of Baxter's illustrious career and ghost stories were employed here to capture the attention of lay readers, to shape their religious ideas and to encourage them to lead godly lives. Baxter's project was influenced by years of correspondence on the subject of ghosts with Henry More and Joseph Glanvill, and his text provides one of the most illuminating examples of how ghost stories were transformed into effective clerical narratives.[57] Baxter borrowed from the rhetoric of these men to present his work in the language of orthodoxy. His text was, he claimed, a concerted attack upon atheists and sadducees, whose pernicious influence was responsible for the recent upsurge in licentious living. Baxter adopted the language of empiricism to declare that ghostly visitations presented immediate and persuasive evidence that religious sceptics had got it wrong.

Baxter was, however, less interested in the rhetorical value of ghost stories than in their potential as moral exemplars, denouncing acts of immorality in the most dramatic fashion. True to his Puritan roots, Baxter utilized these episodes to shake people out of spiritual lethargy, and to encourage the virtues of a godly life. Baxter allowed ghosts to take an active part in the process of salvation, since they were interpreted as signs from a benevolent God who had a care to purge the sins of the faithful.

The *Certainty of the World of Spirits* extended the potential uses to which tales of the wandering dead could be put in legitimate religious contexts. Baxter was famed for dedication to his flock, and it was for the more enduring devotional uses to which he put ghost stories that his work remains important. Baxter's appropriation of ghosts blended with the renewed popularity of Arminianism among latitudinarians. Baxter described them as 'ingenious Men and Scholars', and his appreciation of their theology was reflected in his attempt to reconcile the idea of a loving and benevolent God with the image of a cruel and vengeful Lord in his discussions of the preternatural world.[58]

Baxter's concern for the spiritual welfare of the uneducated was also shaped by his own theological outlook, and particularly by his Puritan sympathies that were officially outlawed by the Church of England. In this context, Baxter's ghosts must be seen as part of an evangelizing mission, encouraging moral reformation on this side of the grave. Baxter aimed to instil godly principles in his readers. He pressed the need for self-examination, and he encouraged people to nurture an introspective faith to prevent the appearance of evil spirits.[59] Baxter admonished his audience by claiming that evil spirits were more frequently seen than angelic ones. Yet those who were visited by the devil's minions were not to despair, but to look upon these encounters as a test of faith, a call to righteousness by a compassionate God without whose will and permission 'no Spirits can do any thing'.[60] In this sense, Baxter used ghost stories to awaken sinners to the need for repentance – a trademark emphasis of Puritan pastoral activity.

Baxter's treatise included several letters about one such terrifying ghost that haunted the house of Lieutenant Colonel Bowen in Glamorgan. Bowen had risen to prominence in the army during the late civil wars, and his military occupation had brought him into contact with a number of mortalist philosophies, which circulated freely in a profession that was often noted for nurturing freethinking radicals. Bowen's preoccupation with these notions led him to be labelled 'an absolute Atheist'.[61] Baxter declared that he led 'a careless and sensual Life', which was no doubt a reflection of his spiritual degeneracy, since he denied the existence of an afterlife, of God and the devil and accounted 'Temporal Pleasures all his expected

Heaven'.[62] In December 1656 an apparition in Bowen's shape appeared to his wife when in her chamber one evening. The ghost requested conjugal favours, but this godly gentlewoman was not to be fooled since she was lately estranged from her husband and knew him to be in Ireland at that time. Nonetheless, this malicious spirit was not easily deterred and returned to torment the household on several occasions. That this was an evil spirit provoked by Bowen's sins was not hard to fathom, and Baxter underlined the point with descriptions of the spirit's violent antics and by including popular motifs of ghost stories in his commentary. When the spirit appeared, Mrs Bowen felt something 'like a Dog under her Knees' that lifted her from the ground. The candles burned blue at the ghost's approach, and it introduced 'an unsufferable Stench' into the house that was likened to 'a putrified Carcase'.[63] To combat this spirit Mrs Bowen called on others to join her in prayer and when Mr Miles, an Anabaptist minister, and four other godly men answered her plea, the household rested peacefully. Maurice Bedwell, a minister at Swansea, investigated the case. He quizzed Bowen's maidservant, but could find nothing to invalidate the tale since he judged her to be a respectable and pious woman. The opinions of learned and unlearned, clerical and lay, combined to bring this relation to public notice, and because the ghost had assumed the very form and countenance of Bowen, Baxter concluded that it brought a clear message from God that this atheist was headed straight for hell unless he repented.

If Bowen was a lost cause, then a gentleman of rank from London who had succumbed to the sin of drunkenness offered a better prospect for reform. This man received numerous visits from a concerned ghost who knocked at his bedhead every time he lay down drunk. His brother was a sober and pious man and a member of Richard Baxter's congregation. This man resolved to watch his troubled sibling while he slept, and to restrain his hands 'lest he should do it himself'.[64] He could only confirm the actions of this spirit however when a pair of shoes levitated from underneath the bed. Clerical guidance was sought and the sinner was brought before Baxter himself. According to Baxter the ghost was an urgent sign from God that the drunkard must kick his habit before it was too late. God clearly had a care for this man's salvation, and when Baxter asked him 'how he dare so sin again, after such a warning', the gentleman was sobered by his heavenly messenger and could offer no excuse for his wayward behaviour. Baxter reflected on this marvellous providence, but was unsure what kind of spirit would take such a particular care of this man's soul. 'Do good spirits dwell so near us?', he mused, 'Or are they sent on such messages? Or is it his Guardian Angel? Or is it the soul of some dead friend, that suffereth, and yet, retaining Love to him, as Dives to his brethren, would have him saved?'[65] Baxter maintained his commitment to established Protestant teaching on this subject by admitting the regular intrusion of angels and demons into the natural world. However, Baxter's world of spirits also allowed for the return of dead souls amongst the living, which as evidence from the *Athenian Mercury* suggests, was a commonly held belief among sections of the lay population.

Athenianism

The *Athenian Mercury* ran from 1691 to 1697, and it set out to resolve any curious questions that its readers cared to submit. Unlike any other periodical of its generation, the *Mercury* was based around an interactive question and answer format. Readers wrote in with real-life problems and the editors, John Dunton, Richard Sault and Samuel Wesley, addressed them in print. The readership of the *Mercury* is of course difficult, if not impossible, to identify with absolute certainty. Nevertheless, there are clues to suggest that its audience was decidedly mixed. Dunton, Sault and Wesley certainly aimed at a broad social audience, ambitiously claiming that the reason for setting up the periodical was 'to advance all knowledge, and diffuse a general Learning through the many, and by that civilize more now, in a few years, than Athens it self'.[66] The *Mercury* positioned itself in opposition to elitist institutions like the Royal Society, leading McEwen to label it 'an instrument of popular education' thanks to its efforts to popularize learning through broad sections of society.[67] The *Mercury*'s audience was by no means restricted, but its editors sought specifically to engage people with little formal education. This included inquisitive women who wished to keep abreast of new advances in natural philosophy and any curious person who had a burning question to be resolved. Moreover, in an effort to deter intellectual snobbery, the editors preserved reader anonymity for those who feared 'appearing ridiculous by asking Questions'.[68] Those readers who can be identified included Sir William Temple, but the *Mercury* also featured anonymous contributions from maidservants who had managed to acquire a degree of literacy.

The extent to which the *Mercury* can be described as a source of popular opinion does, however, remain unclear. Despite the active participation of readers in shaping the content of the *Mercury*, the editors did not simply reflect the opinions of their readers, but sought to influence, exaggerate or frame them in particular ways to maximize profit. John Dunton in particular was renowned for his commercial acumen, and his numerous publications often catered for a more insalubrious readership, designed to titillate rather than edify. Nonetheless, the commercial success of the *Mercury* suggests that, for those willing to pay a shilling on Tuesdays and Saturdays, this periodical offered something worth reading.[69]

As an Anglican minister and co-editor of the journal, Samuel Wesley answered questions relating to religion and much of his time was spent responding to queries about the topography of the afterlife, the future existence of the soul and ghosts. 'Do the Deceased walk?', asked one reader in issue 29. 'Where go the Souls of Good Men immediately after Death?'; 'Where are the souls of men to

remain till the last day?'; was the soul 'in an active or unactive state' after its separation from the body?[70] These were just a few of the questions put to the *Mercury*
by readers who were clearly unsure what lay in store for them beyond the grave.
Protestant teaching on this subject was ambiguous, and it had seemingly failed to
stem speculation about the exact nature of life after death. These queries also suggest that the religious scepticism unleashed by years of civil war had penetrated
through the social ranks.

Queries concerning ghosts and the nature of the afterlife reflected this social
diversity, with readers identified as gentlemen, gentlewomen and servants alike.
It is clear from their contributions that confusion abounded as to the exact fate
of body and soul following death and, as a result, considerable slippage was envis-
aged between the natural and preternatural worlds. If the souls of the dead could
not be definitively placed, then what was to stop them from returning to earth?
Ghosts continued to haunt *Mercury* readers, sometimes quite literally, throughout the six years of its publication. In fact the journal received so many tales of the
wandering dead that its editors took the unusual step of devoting an entire issue
to reports of their appearances. This was fittingly published on All Souls Night
1691, and according to the editors it served a dual function: first, to reduce 'the
many Proselytes of Sadducism and Hobbism amongst us', and also to give 'great
satisfaction to all our Querists in general'.[71]

Evidence from the *Athenian Mercury* suggests that ministers like Richard
Baxter were in tune with at least some of the religious priorities of lay parishioners, given his emphasis on the relevance of ghost stories to everyday life. The
Mercury's readers were less concerned with the precise theological status of ghosts
than with the messages they brought about individual salvation and the future
state of loved ones. In 1691 the *Mercury* reported the appearance of Mr Lunt's
ghost to his brother in Derbyshire. Having led a sinful life, Lunt now wished to
provide a better example to his relation and asked that his brother 'woul'd go to
one with whom [Lunt] had lived as a Servant, and demand some money which
was due to him'. He was to give it to a woman in the same town 'whom he had
promised marriage to, and got her with child' before deserting both his service
and her. When the ghost offered to reward his brother for his efforts, the man
insisted that he 'would ask nothing'.[72] The tale exemplified the moral fortitude of
this poor man who prized the duties of Christian charity and familial obligation
more than his own personal enrichment. In the style of a parable, ghost stories
were promoted as moral exemplars. They advanced a practical moral theology
which was favoured both by latitudinarian theologians and by Richard Baxter as
a necessary supplement to an introspective faith.

As Peter Marshall and Frederick Valletta have shown, the upheavals of
Reformation and the abolition of purgatory did not stop ghosts from appearing
to the living, and they continued to be invested with important religious and
emotional meanings. Indeed it could be argued that the revised liturgy of post-

Reformation England intensified individual preoccupation with the dead body and its future life.[73] By scrapping purgatory and prayers for the dead, Protestantism officially outlawed an extended process of mourning for the dead in which the living could play an active role. Extra-liturgical comfort was sought and ghosts provided one outlet for expressions of loss by grieving relatives. The *Athenian Oracle*, a spin-off from the *Athenian Mercury*, printed a tale from Smithfield in London where the ghost of Mr Watkinson appeared to his daughter about six months after his death to comfort her during her grieving.[74] This account was also considered a worthy source of reflection by Henry More, who included the case in his own work.[75] Other *Mercury* readers required similar assurance that the dead still remained connected to the living in some way. In June 1691 one reader asked 'Whether separated Souls have any knowledge of the Affairs in this World, and what is to be thought of the Apparitions of the Dead'? In issue 25, another wondered if 'we shall know our Friends in Heaven' and 'Whether the Departed have any Knowledge of, or ever concern themselves with the affairs of their Friends in this Life?'. To this last question, the *Mercury*'s editors clearly recognized the use to which personal anxieties could be put, replying that 'either some departed Souls, have particular Commissions ... or that all of them have a Cognizance of our Affairs'.[76] This response marked an important break with Calvinists of late sixteenth- and early seventeenth-century England, who consistently argued that departed souls had no awareness of events on earth in an effort to discourage idolatrous saint worship. Wesley, Dunton and Sault judged that such queries no longer indicated lingering affection for Catholicism, but instead reflected the desire to cling onto the dead by projecting aspects of social life into the next world.[77]

The comfort that family members and friends took from the appearances of departed souls was also complemented in these years by theological dilutions of predestinarian thought. Fear and despair often resulted from what Joseph Mede termed that 'black doctrine of Absolute Reprobation'.[78] His pupil Henry More 'suffered terribly from the fear of hell', as did Lodowick Muggleton and Samuel Hoard, all of whom developed alternatives to the prospect of eternal damnation.[79] Over the course of the seventeenth century, a number of prominent divines advanced more benevolent ideas of salvation, and thereby responded to the anxieties created by the uncompromising doctrines of election and damnation. Archbishop of Canterbury and latitudinarian John Tillotson promoted a God 'who was not obliged eternally to torment the wicked', and the eccentric William Whiston, professor of mathematics at Cambridge, claimed that wicked souls would be annihilated rather than suffer hell's torments in perpetuity.[80] Isaac Barrow also called upon scriptural evidence to support his theory that souls confined to the fiery pits of hell would eventually be annihilated. Eternal torment, he claimed, represented 'a severity of justice far above all example of repeated cruelty in the worst of men'.[81] For an increasing number of clergymen, the wrath of

God that was so dramatically exercised in the plague visitation of 1665 and the Great Fire of 1666, was gradually tempered by descriptions and examples of his compassion. As a result, returning ghosts achieved greater acceptability as the confessional concerns of the learned intersected with the priorities of the laity.

In October 1691, the *Athenian Mercury* gave a very specific example of how ghosts soothed the anxieties created by an uncertain process of salvation. The journal printed an account from a gentlewoman whose son had taken a wayward path through life. The lady's efforts to reprove her son had made some impact since the young man did eventually reform. But following his untimely death soon afterwards, this pious mother still feared that her son would be denied entrance to heaven as punishment for his sins. Convinced that his repentance had come too late, the lady was 'extreamly afflicted' and 'fear'd he was in Hell'.[82] Her worries were allayed though when just a month later the young man's ghost came to his mothers' bed and reassured her that he was at rest.[83] William Turner was impressed by the details of this story, and it featured in his *Compleat History of the Most Remarkable Providences* (1697). Significantly, Turner recognized the devotional potential of certain ghost stories and thus recommended his treatise 'as useful to Ministers in Furnishing Topicks of Reproof and Exhortation' as well as 'to Private Christians for their Closets and Families'.[84] For Turner, as for sections of the lay community, the precise ontological status of ghosts was less important than the more intimate spiritual and domestic purposes that they served. If a repentant sinner could be welcomed into Abraham's bosom then it gave some hope to ordinary men and women that they might receive a similar reward. Ghost stories soothed the anxieties of the living who feared for the fate of loved ones, as well as providing practical guidance on how to avoid the fires of hell.

If Richard Baxter and Samuel Wesley were convinced that a colourful spirit world lay on the other side of the grave, then they were in good company. Baxter was joined in his attempts to promote the pastoral utility of Restoration ghost stories by a network of clergymen who were similarly keen to promote godliness. Baxter printed tales from John Hodder, minister of Hauke-Church in Dorset, who recounted 'the actings of Spirits in a House, yea, a Religious House of that Country, of which he was himself an Ear and Eye Witness'.[85] Thomas Tilson, minister of Aylesworth in Kent, told Baxter of an apparition at Rochester. As a postscript to his letter, he begged 'that God would bless your pious Endeavours for the Conviction of Atheists and Sadducees, and for the promoting of true Religion and Godliness'.[86] Protestant ministers were also very active in the marketplace of cheap print. A clergyman from Devon was the most likely author of a ghost story from Spraiton that was published in 1683. The adoption of ghost stories as clerical narratives also continued into the early years of the eighteenth century. In 1709, a two-penny pamphlet describing the ghost or ghosts that appeared to Jan Smagge in Canvy Island was followed by a series of scriptural excerpts warning readers against avarice, ambition and pride.[87] In 1712 this was followed by a chapbook detailing the appearance of Edward Ashley's ghost in London. This text was notable because it was accompanied by 'an excellent sermon preach'd by a Reverend Divine of the Church of England on that Miraculous Occasion'.[88]

So why did ghosts play such a key role in campaigns for godly reformation in the late seventeenth century? The answer lies partially in critiques of the forms of Anglican worship that 'failed to move or to satisfy'.[89] Oliver Heywood also singled out the ineffectualness of the liturgy as one reason for the growing popularity of dissenting congregations. The sermon addiction that supposedly characterized this age also relied on the unpredictable skills of individual clergy. One way to engage the lay community and to diversify modes of Anglican worship was to adopt more lively vehicles of religious instruction. Ghost stories fulfilled this objective, and they proved highly successful in dramatizing the familiar moral exhortations that emanated from the pulpit. In 1694 the minister of the Round Church in Cambridge capitalized on a haunting that had captured local attention by making 'a long sermon the next Sunday to his people ... to tell them the whole story of the same'.[90] Similarly the Presbyterian minister Gilbert Rule preached about his encounter with a ghost in a deserted house, which had led him to the skeleton of a murdered man. Rule's speech was apparently so eloquent, that a member of his congregation immediately confessed to the crime.[91] In 1691 a short chapbook told of a dreadful ghost that appeared to John Dyer in Southwark. The frightful forms assumed by the ghost were described with relish, and the visual spectacle of the account was heightened by a crude woodcut of the ghost in its winding sheet. Dyer's tale was given greater reverence however by the appendix of two prayers designed to combat the actions of malignant spirits. Despite the sensational details of the story, the Southwark ghost was judged a worthy vehicle through which to promote the power of divine protection.[92] The following chapter will detail how ghost stories both entertained and edified, and this flexibility ensured the commercial success of these narratives in the competitive marketplace of cheap print. Indeed the years under study here saw ghosts making more frequent appearances in ballads and cheap printed pamphlets than ever before or since, reflecting their prominence in the contemporary imagination.

Widespread appropriation of ghost stories by Anglican and dissenting clergy indicates that ghost beliefs and ghost stories had been effectively de-confessionalized by the final decade of the seventeenth century. One important aspect of this process was to loosen the association between ghost stories, purgatory and popish imposture which was a prominent feature of Reformation polemic in the hands of Protestant apologists like Samuel Harsnett and William Perkins.[93] The political and religious climate of Restoration England was clearly very different from the immediate post-Reformation period. Years of civil war and interregnum did not stamp out fears of popery in England, but they did identify a new enemy that appeared to present a more pernicious and immediate threat – that was atheism in both its philosophical and practical expressions. A few examples will suffice to demonstrate how this new preoccupation helped to strip ghost stories of their popish ties. When Catholic informer Stephen Dugdale was reputedly haunted by ghosts upon his deathbed, his visions were not interpreted as frauds or delusions, but rather as divine punishments for betraying his co-conspirators, and for his poor choice of faith.[94] Similarly, a Jacobite poem from 1690 depicted the ghost of Queen Mary's mother, admonishing her daughter in her bedchamber.

> Can quiet slumber ever close thy eyes?
> Or is thy conscience sunk too low to rise?
> From this same place was not thy aged Sire
> Compelled by midnight-summons to retire?
> Then, with a canting, fulsome trick of state,
> The world was bantered with an 'abdicate';
> Had he been murdered, it had mercy shown
> 'Tis less to kill a king, than to dethrone.[95]

The purpose of this ghost, though allegorical, was to castigate Mary for betraying her Catholic father James II, who was forced to abdicate in her favour. These two examples suggest that Catholic commentators interpreted ghostly appearances in similar ways to their Protestant counterparts – as messengers of divine displeasure sent to punish sinners. The nature of the sin was variable, but the purpose of the ghost was remarkably consistent.

Restoration ghost stories were then released from the anti-Catholic rhetoric of the late sixteenth and early seventeenth centuries. This process allowed the once threatening figure of the ghost to be convincingly reclothed in Protestant attire, and for ghost stories to be more firmly linked to the political and religious ideologies of the establishment than at any time since before the Reformation. Nonconformist clerics like Richard Baxter also made important contributions to this process of de-confessionalization. Eamon Duffy has also demonstrated that ejected Presbyterian ministers like Baxter were extremely active in the marketplace of cheap print. Ghost stories lent themselves to the objectives of these writers who hoped to evangelize and educate the unlearned in the fundamentals of the Christian faith.[96] The best example of this de-confessionalization, however, can be found in the story of the 'Devil of Masçon'. At the start of the seventeenth century a troublesome spirit haunted the house of French Protestant minister François Perrault, and it went on to terrify the whole neighbourhood. Perrault stirred ill-feeling in Masçon when he took possession of his house by law from a local woman. The daughter of this discarded tenant then prayed to God that she could return after her death to take revenge on this troublesome minister.[97] Indeed many of the town's inhabitants believed that the resident ghost was a divine punishment for Perrault's covetousness. The account originally dated from 1612 when the town of Masçon in south-east France was a hotbed of religious conflict between warring Catholic and Protestant factions. The ghost was, however, indiscriminate in its attacks, which led Protestants and Catholics alike to swear the truth of the episode. Robert Boyle was so deeply affected by the case that he asked Peter du Moulin to translate the story into English. Despite his avowed scepticism towards many ghost stories, Boyle admitted that this narrative 'did at length overcome in me all my settled indisposednesse to believe strange things'.[98] Boyle was also able to establish Perrault's good character following a short meeting in Geneva. This personal contact assured Boyle that Perrault's ghost had a legitimate and divinely-inspired cause for its actions since it 'pleased God to bring him [Perrault] into many, and some very extraordinary Tryals' as a test of faith.[99] The divided community of Mâscon was united by attempts to dispel the ghost and this salutary tale came highly recommended by Boyle. It was also reprinted by both Richard Baxter and the *Athenian Mercury*, who credited the relation on the basis of this confessional consensus. It is surely significant that the tale was not printed in England until 1659, when it was pitched into the battle to combat religious extremism. Two further editions were published in 1669 and 1679, reflecting the powerful interest in ghosts that marked these years of religious change.

Conclusion

In terms of the amount of paper consumed by narrators and collectors of ghost stories, the late seventeenth century stands out as a bumper period of publication. According to contemporary commentators, the political, religious and social ills of these years justified the production of a large body of texts defending the legitimacy of ghost stories and publicizing their activities for wide audiences. These texts would be recycled, reinterpreted and reproduced in a variety of forms over the course of the next century. Yet in the short term they testified to a vibrant intellectual and religious culture in which ghost stories enjoyed heightened status thanks to contemporary fears about irreligion, immorality and ungodliness as well as religious and political disunity.

New philosophical pursuits brought ghosts closer to the physical world than ever before. They also created fresh confidence about the utility of ghost stories and the existence of ghosts themselves. By citing ghosts as empirical proof of God's continued intervention in the world, writers like Henry More and Joseph Glanvill positioned ghost stories at the centre of one of the most important cultural debates of the day – that is, the extent to which reasonable religion could supplement revelation. This debate was of course hotly contested and the role that ghosts played within it will resurface periodically over the course of this book. However, in Restoration England, pious reactions against materialist religious philosophies fostered resurgent interest in ghosts and testified to strong belief in an active providential God who continued to rebuke, punish and reward Christians on earth.

Apparitions of all persuasions, angels, devils and departed souls were incorporated into mainstream religious schemas because they served a variety of contemporary purposes. Old theological orthodoxies were increasingly breaking down and ghost stories sat alongside a wide diversity of doctrines, sects and ways of worship that catered for the tastes of a rapidly changing society. The rehabilitation of ghost stories as respectable conduits of religious reformation on the public stage reached its climax in the final decade of the seventeenth century, where they coincided with the foundation of the Society for Promoting Christian Knowledge and numerous societies for the reformation of manners.

Restoration England saw ghost stories more firmly tied to the needs and priorities of the living. These narratives were allowed to serve more intimate domestic purposes, a process which will be more closely detailed in the following chapter. By teaching that deceased souls might yet appear to the living, the work of pastorally-orientated divines like Richard Baxter and Samuel Wesley illustrates the conscious and sustained integration of ghosts into Protestant theology by the close of the seventeenth century. This process of accommodation reflected the shifting priorities of both conformist and nonconformist clergy who sought to engage more vigorously with persistent themes in lay religion in order to cement the relationship between Protestantism and the people. The adoption of ghost stories as clerical narratives by a cross-section of divines was therefore a pragmatic response to a changing climate of religious belief and, potentially, a site of confessional and social unity that could help to heal the internal divisions of an increasingly fragmented Protestant Church.

2 PRINTING THE PRETERNATURAL IN THE LATE SEVENTEENTH CENTURY

'What Age ever brought forth more, or bought more Printed Waste Paper?'[1] In 1681 the pamphleteer who posed this question was struck by the extraordinary success of the cheap print trade in Restoration England – and he was not alone. Historians have confirmed his perception that the years 1660–1700 saw a huge explosion in the levels of production, distribution and consumption of ballads, chapbooks, almanacs, pamphlets and other products of the rich and varied marketplace of cheap print. In the 1660s almanacs sold at an annual rate of between 300,000 and 400,000 copies and an estimated 90,000 chapbooks were purchased in 1664 alone.[2] This revolution in communications was characterized by the sheer volume, variety, distribution and affordability of print. The work of Bernard Capp, Mark Knights and Angela McShane Jones has done much to illuminate this watershed in the early modern print industry. From the 1660s onwards the marketplace of cheap print had never been more sophisticated or so accessible to so many people.

Bernard Capp and Margaret Spufford first demonstrated the importance of ballads, chapbooks, almanacs and jestbooks for tracing the evolution of popular belief, and these initial insights have been enhanced in recent years by important contributions from Tessa Watt, Alexandra Walsham and Peter Lake, who have outlined the complexity of the cheap print market, its modes of distribution and the extent of its impact on wider society.[3] Nonetheless, the Restoration marketplace of cheap print remains relatively unstudied. Those historians that have focused on these years have generally utilized these sources to gauge popular political involvement during the English civil war and the events of 1688. To date, no work has analysed the relationship between cheap print and ghost beliefs.

In this chapter I want to describe how ghost stories also benefited from this thriving industry. My own statistics suggest that the years 1660–1700 saw the production of 42 per cent of all original chapbook and ballad accounts featuring ghosts published in England between 1660 and 1800.[4] Chapbooks devoted to the life of Guy of Warwick and ballads describing the adventures of Robin Hood were perennial favourites, and ghost stories similarly commanded a strong market value. In fact, they popped up at regular intervals in two of the best-selling genres of cheap print – black-letter ballads (especially those centred on love and court-ship) and murder pamphlets or chapbooks. Ghost stories were not a fixed literary genre in this marketplace, but instead the figure of the ghost served as a stock character in these two highly profitable categories of print. I will suggest that the ability of ghosts to cut across these categories had important implications for their longevity in cheap printed publications. Moreover, the association of ghosts with themes of death, love and courtship ensured that these narratives enjoyed an appeal that could transcend chronological and social boundaries, since here were three experiences with which the vast majority of the population could identify.

This chapter will thus consider the role of ghost stories within this flourishing print industry to examine the availability and appeal of these narratives, the mean-ings attached to them in and out of print and the ways in which they may have articulated and shaped the beliefs of ordinary people. As such, this chapter com-plements the arguments of its predecessor; it will place the views of Restoration elites on ghosts in broader economic and social contexts. This exercise seems both useful and necessary, since the more ephemeral products of cheap print had a wider and potentially more varied readership that extended to those further down the hierarchy of wealth. This chapter is thus devoted to the local context of belief, to the people who actually encountered ghosts in daily life and to the ways in which these experiences were made relevant to wider audiences in print. As such, its characters range from household servants and wage labourers, through to yeomen, merchants, magistrates, ministers and country squires. The ghost sto-ries of cheap print did not preclude a more educated readership, and the broad social appeal of these narratives will be a major emphasis in the pages that follow. The chapter is therefore based around a tripartite model of production and con-sumption; beginning with the presentation of ghost stories in oral communities, moving on to the translation of these narratives into printed form and to issues of physical production, and finally discussing the appeal of these stories and how they may have been received by readers when they flowed back into oral contexts. In line with the work of Adam Fox, as well as socio-linguistic theory, this model presupposes a circularity of influences between oral and literate cultures as well as a high degree of social interaction between the lettered and unlettered.

Important debates about the relationship of oral and literate cultures will sur-face regularly since the popularity and distribution of ghost stories highlight the interdependencies of these forms – the drama of ghost stories working best when they were read aloud or performed to an audience. Any attempt to connect the fortunes of ballad and chapbook ghosts to the preternatural beliefs of early mod-ern men, women and children must also involve some consideration of literacy rates to establish who, how many, and what kind of people were able to access these products. Nonetheless, just because people *could* access these texts does not mean that they did: whoever bought anything just because they could afford it? The question of desirability is therefore crucial – who did these texts appeal to and why? Insights from socio-linguistic theory will be used to analyse the material culture of cheap printed ghost stories; their content, form, size, price, imagery and narrative detail – crucial factors that determined the desirability of these tales in a competitive marketplace. Finally, comparisons will be drawn between ghost stories originating in London and those that began life in provincial areas. This geographical dimension had important implications for the nature of the ghost story itself and for its potential circulation.

The Ballad Ghost

Ballads were the cheapest items of print available in Restoration England and they were also the most accessible, constituting just a single page of type, produced in a familiar lyrical format and generally priced between a halfpenny and 2*d*.[5] Based on these estimates, Tessa Watt surmised that cheap print was affordable for most categories of workers in early modern England, from husbandmen upwards. However, even though ballads were cheap, the buoyancy of the trade still relied on high sales. These products were therefore differentiated and commercially focused to appeal to as large a group of buyers as possible. As Angela McShane Jones has pointed out, the black-letter ballad was a well-known brand and people knew what to expect when purchasing them. Ballads were entertaining, moralistic and generally designed to offer something for every taste and pocket. The marketing and sales strategies of leading publishers were highly sophisticated, and so were networks of distribution. Black-letter ballads were peddled across the country, hawked at fairs and markets and sold in thousands on the streets of London.[6] The accessibility of black-letter ballads was further augmented by the use of the familiar gothic type that was reproduced in the cheapest versions of hornbooks, primers and catechisms – texts that formed the basis of the most rudimentary education. In fact the typeface of black-letter ballads suggests that they may well have been purchased to assist in the early stages of reading – for children and adults alike.

The ability to read was, of course, an important factor in assessing how many people were able to engage with ballads and thus with ghost stories, but it was by no means decisive. Estimates of literacy levels in this period give some indication of the potential market for these products and David Cressy has suggested that, in 1640, levels of male and female illiteracy were approximately 70 per cent and 90 per cent respectively.[7] More recently Adam Fox has proposed that by 1700 'England was a society in which at least half the adult population could read print'.[8] Fox's optimistic assessment was based on significant expansion in the provision of formal education and on religious change.[9] More significantly, however, his calculations are also based on a more inclusive definition of 'literacy' or 'literacies', in which reading and/or writing skills are differentiated and equally valued.

The ability to read is of course much more difficult to quantify, but historians agree that this skill was probably widely diffused in these years. This is largely thanks to informal teaching provided by mothers within the home, and by literate members of local communities.[10] Revisionist interpretations have also focused on aspects of elementary and informal education open to the poorer sorts who were much more likely to pick up basic reading skills because they were taught for one year before children began paid work.

Even for those who had no skill in reading or writing, ballads remained highly accessible literary products; their lyrical form ensured that they could and would be read or sung aloud either in the local alehouse, in the home, at market or on the street by professional balladeers. Indeed the use of verse and rhyme in balladry provides one of the best examples of the societal bilingualism that characterized Restoration England.[11] This was a society in which both spoken and written modes of communication were used to carry out the business of everyday life. Indeed the ghost stories of cheap print are prime examples of the circularity and interdependency of oral and literate forms. These tales began in oral communities and depended upon the vitality of verbal storytelling and gossip networks that eventually brought them to the notice of printers and publishers. Once issued in textual form, ghost stories included directly reported speech that was reconverted into sound when read out and performed in the spoken word.[12] More will be said about these performative aspects, but for now it is important to note the myriad ways in which speech, and patterns of verbal interaction, influenced printed ghost stories, thereby appealing to a broad social readership with different levels of proficiency in reading and writing.

The technology of print was clearly very important to the way in which ballads and other cheap printed wares were produced. Sophisticated production techniques alongside the use of cheaper paper lowered overheads, but production also bore a close relationship to demand. The issue of desirability must then be re-emphasized, and a less passive role assigned to the poorer sorts who were able to engage with cheap printed ghost stories and to shape the specific forms and detail included in these narratives. With a few pence to spend on printed goods, they were recognized, and indeed targeted, as powerful consumers in a marketplace driven by commercial gain. Crude comparisons of excess incomes and the price of cheap print must then be accompanied by an analysis of the desirability of ballads alongside other products of the cheap print market. Words and images were intended to be seductive, and were designed to encourage the purchase of ballads and chapbooks as small treats or gifts that could serve as interior decoration, or as educational instruction for peasant households.[13] It is to this question of desirability that I now turn in sketching some of the contexts in which ghosts appeared in the genre of balladry.

John True was a shoemaker from Coventry who won the affection of a local maid named Mease. His love, however, proved inconstant and he betrayed

Susan by courting another woman. This story was narrated in much more dramatic fashion in a black-letter ballad collected by Samuel Pepys entitled *The Two Unfortunate Lovers, or, A True Relation of the Lamentable End of John True and Susan Mease*. Dismayed by the fickle affections of her intended marriage partner, Susan Mease was, quite literally, 'kil'd with loving him' and, after her death, her ghost returned to haunt her betrayer, demanding that 'if e're thou loved'st me dear make hast and come away'. The shock of this appearance proved too much for John, who died soon after; the balladeer left his audience in no doubt about how this tale should be interpreted. The death of these two young lovers was a moral lesson for the young male and female readership that the author assumed would be attracted by this publication. He thus advised 'those that have true loves' to be 'sure unto your friend, / And if you love ... be true unto the end'.[14] A similar message was encapsulated in *A Godly Warning to all Maidens*, another ballad collected by Samuel Pepys. Here a young man named Bateman fell in love with, and proposed marriage to, a woman from Nottingham. However, the engagement was soon broken off by the woman in favour of a carpenter who was 'of greater wealth and better in degree'. On the day of his ex-fiancée's wedding, Bateman 'hang'd himself in desperate sort before the brides own door', and his ghost later appeared to spirit her away from her marriage bed whilst she was expecting her first child. Reconciled to her fate for having broken her oath to Bateman, the young woman conceded that 'Alive or dead I am his right'. This ballad made the moral of the story very clear and directly addressed the reader with the following advice, 'To him that you have vow'd to love, / by no means do refuse; / For God that hears all secret oaths, / will dreadful vengeance take'.[15] This declaration was reminiscent of the last dying speeches of condemned criminals who confessed the error of their ways in order to uphold values of social justice and moral probity.[16] Indeed the primary function of ghosts in ballad and chapbook accounts was as relaters of wrongdoing. Ghosts assumed the role of otherworldly sleuths, and although they were often not the central protagonists, ghosts were an important function of the narrative whereby justice could be served on unpunished murderers and inconstant lovers. The ghost's ability to undertake this role relied on widespread assumptions that ghosts, occupying a liminal position between this world and the next, had access to knowledge that the living did not. As we saw in the previous chapter, this understanding authorized readers and listeners to pay attention to the ghost's revelations and allowed balladeers to link important moral messages to the appearance of ghosts.

Taken together, these two ballads suggest an appreciation of the social and economic realities that determined the choice of marriage partner in this period, but they also display an idealistic strain that prioritized true love over material wealth. Margaret Spufford has argued that love was the primary reason why young people from humble backgrounds entered into marriage.[17] The ghost thus interacted with contemporary social mores and had an important role to play in upholding ideals of marital love. Women have been increasingly recognized as important consumers of cheap print and publishers clearly made an effort to tailor accounts to female interests. The ghosts of popular courtship ballads may have appealed to women because they allowed readers to indulge deep emotional feelings. They offered advice on the proper conduct of courtship and marital relations, and they provided some informal regulation of these fragile affairs with the possibility of public censure awaiting the inconstant lover. Indeed as discussed in Chapter 6, these concerns persisted throughout the eighteenth century and ensured the continued relevance and appeal of the courtship ballad.

The Suffolk Miracle was another black-letter ballad that offered an idealized vision of early modern courtship. Here a wealthy and ambitious farmer separated his daughter from her chosen marriage partner because he believed that she could aspire to a more prosperous union. The farmer sent his daughter to live with her uncle and, as a result, her husband-to-be 'mourn'd so much' that 'for love he dyed'. The young woman was ignorant of his death until the ghost of her beloved appeared before her, and she was apparently so grieved by the sight that she died soon afterwards. The ghost was not the central protagonist in this story but it was the representative of social and amatory justice; following its appearance the narrator went on to give the following warning to his readers, 'Part not true love you Rich men then, / but if they be right honest men, / your daughters love give them their way, / for force oft breeds their lives decay'.[18] This kind of ballad may have appealed to contemporary audiences in a number of ways. Although black-letter ballads were an essentially conservative medium that made no direct challenge to the social order, poorer folk liked to indulge in criticisms of the wealthier sections of society and often claimed the moral high ground. In *The Suffolk Miracle* the ghostly narrative represents a romanticized and idealized version of marital relations. The virtues of honesty, loyalty and devotion are here prized above riches and social status. Such a message may well have appealed to a more humble, and possibly male, audience, who had little money to offer in the marriage market. By shifting the emphasis to the personal qualities of the characters involved, this ballad promoted a scenario in which the poor man could compete on an equal footing with his social superiors.

The ballad ghost can then be seen as a tool of social criticism, sometimes directed against the middling sorts and wealthier sections of society. However, the relevance of these themes was not restricted to the lower tiers of the social ladder. This particular meaning of ghosts was recognized further up the ranks, pointing to a mixed social readership for many courtship ballads. The ideal of true love and distaste for betrayal and oath-breaking were just as prominent in ballads featuring characters of middling and upper-class background. *The Leicestershire Tragedy: or, The Fatal Overthrow of two Unfortunate Lovers* neatly illustrated this point when the bleeding ghost of a yeoman's son appeared after being usurped by a young squire in the affections of his beloved, Susana Lynard. The sight of the ghost so frightened Susana that she fell into a fever and quickly died, justifying the narrator's warning to 'See that you are not false in Love, / for there's a righteous God above'.[19]

Just because yeomen and squires featured in these narratives does not mean that these were the people to whom they exclusively appealed. Other factors, however, suggest that a different kind of audience was targeted as compared with the tales of John True and young Bateman. *The Leicestershire Tragedy* was a white-letter ballad – a less familiar typeface that was often used in political satire and one that usually signified a more learned audience than black-letter ballads. Moreover this ballad was accompanied by two woodcuts depicting the figures of a gentleman and gentlewoman of fashion. Indeed, as Angela McShane Jones points out in her excellent study of ballads in this period, the ballad market was highly sophisticated, with publishers deliberately adapting typography, format, content and imagery to suit the tastes of different consumers.[20] The material form of *The Leicestershire Tragedy* combined with its content shows that this ballad may well have attracted wealthier readers. The ghost ballad had the potential to cut across social boundaries, and this was in part due to the flexible meanings attached to souls of the dead. Ghosts were uniquely able to dish out post-mortem punishments for sins of inconstancy that may have otherwise gone unpunished. This prominent association ensured that ballad ghosts integrated with a topic of near-universal concern, ensuring a powerful prominence in the imagination.

The scenarios in which ghosts appeared in courtship ballads were sometimes improbable and even allegorical, and the genre of balladry was itself characterized by blurred boundaries between the real and the fictional. Nonetheless, the use of named characters, biographical details and real-life locations all served to bring some kind of social and economic reality to bear on these accounts and to introduce a degree of plausibility to the appearance of ghosts. These were not simply the romances of chivalric tradition filtering down into popular tradition, but inventive new appropriations of ghosts that were relevant to the experiences of ordinary folk and which articulated a range of contemporary concerns about daily life. As Lennard Davis notes in his discussion of the complex relationship between factual and fictional literary representations, the chivalric romance was 'the contrary of the ordinary world, making possible the idealized vision'.[21] Although ghostly ballads displayed idealistic strains, they also corresponded to lived reality, comparable in some ways to a seventeenth-century soap opera. Ballads highlighted a range of scenarios with which ordinary men and women could identify and the reader was thus drawn in by 'the actual possibility of being involved in the scene one reads about'.[22] Ghosts appeared in familiar settings, in homes and gardens, and they spoke to real-life dilemmas. Ghost stories also featured characters that could be met in the course of everyday life: shoemakers, carpenters, yeomen and squires. The inclusion of context and dense narrative detail in reports of ghosts was also crucial in disabling the separation of logic from rhetoric that is characteristic of more academic or abstract forms of writing. The composition of ghost stories and their configuration as factual fictions suspended disbelief. This technique also limited scope for reader scepticism, thereby extending the appeal of these narratives.[23] The contention that the second half of the seventeenth century saw the distancing of learned audiences from the cheap print market may then be a little premature; the very fact that many of the ballads described above owe their survival to Samuel Pepys proves that the gentry certainly partook of the cheaper products of the print industry. Ghostly ballads were easily affordable, readily available and simply one of a range of literary products from which consumers were able to choose.

Murder Revealed

The connection of ghost stories with themes of mortality was another key context in which ghost stories retained interest for readers of cheap print. The ghosts of cheap print fame appeared time and again following death of an untimely or unnatural kind, and often to expose the vile crime of murder. Murder was conceived as an infringement of divine authority, for only God had the power to give life and to take it away. The exposure of killers by avenging ghosts thus fitted neatly within contemporary ideas of providential intervention and also satisfied deeply-held principles of social justice, expressing feelings of moral outrage engendered by this heinous act.

Black-letter ballads and murder pamphlets or chapbooks recognized and courted widespread fascination with death and particularly murder. As expressions of horror but also of curiosity, ghost stories were again positioned at a crossroads where the paths of learned and unlearned beliefs met. Publishers and printers churned out multiple versions of the same stories with formats and prices to suit every interest and pocket. Although not as cheap as black-letter ballads, chapbooks were highly affordable commodities. They were usually no more than eight pages in length and often included decorous woodcuts, with prices ranging from 2*d*. to 6*d*. Margaret Spufford has argued that by 1664 chapbook production was already more significant than ballad production. If chapbooks were readily available, does it follow that they were desirable? In 1681 Justice Scroggs hinted at the esteem in which these publications were held by suggesting that even the very poor clamoured to get their hands on them. They would 'deny their children a penny for bread' he claimed, but 'will lay it out for a pamphlet'.[24] In March 1680 a black-letter ballad and a short four-page chapbook appeared for sale with breaking news of murder in Holborn, London. Just two days after the alleged discovery of human remains on 16 March, the chapbook came hot off the press and drew in readers with the compelling title *Great News from Middle-Row in Holbourn or*

A True Relation of a Dreadful Ghost. The chapbook narrated the appearance of Mrs Adkins's ghost, a former midwife who had died six months previously. Her ghost 'with gastly Countenance ... belching flames of Fire' suggested her fate in the afterlife, and so it was little surprise when she visited a maidservant in the house she formerly occupied to reveal the concealed bones of children that she had murdered. Her ghost was unable to rest until she had confessed her crime and requested a decent burial for the babes, and so she instructed the maid to search 'under the Tiles in the hearth' and to bury what she found beneath. Human bones were unearthed that were conjectured to be those of 'Children Illegitimate, or Bastards' – that is according to local rumour at the Cheshire Cheese, the Holborn inn where these remains were somewhat gruesomely displayed. The opinions of 'divers Chirurgions' backed up the ghost's claims by concluding that the bones had lain undiscovered for many years.[25]

A mixed social audience is suggested by the form and content of this chapbook. The ranks of the labouring poor might be happy to accept the word of a maidservant, but the opinions of surgeons may have held more sway with the professional sorts of London. The tone and language used by the author also placed a heavily moralized and religious spin on events, diluting the sensationalism of the murder and its spectacular discovery. 'The great God', who thought that such a 'Monstrous Crime' should be exposed for all to see, justified the appearance of the ghost. At the close of the narrative, the reader is reminded that even in death there is no escape from the consequences of sin. 'Murther bears a lasting stain and clogs the Conscience of the Guilty soul', causing restless spirits to be 'forced about the Earth' and 'to wander up and down until they have made known those Crimes the Party represented in those thin and Airy forms did in their Lifetimes act'. To reinforce the religious portent of the ghost, the narrator finished with a quote from the Psalmist David: 'Great and wonderful art thou O Lord, and dreadful to be feared in Heaven and Earth'.[26] The frontispiece of this chapbook advertised the appearance of a 'GHOST' in the largest typeface, drawing the reader in with gruesome details of murder. The reader was, however, both observer and participant in this narrative. The curiosity aroused by elaborate details of the event drew the reader into the scene, permitting the author to establish a broader moral purpose, warning the reader that worldly sins will not escape divine punishment. The combination of graphic details of murder and the more serious undertones of the story were designed to titillate the audience, whilst simultaneously reinforcing a moral conviction that murder would not go unpunished. This narrative was then a composite text, which satisfied an appetite for ribaldry, but also for the exemplary punishment of sinners.

The linguistic and interpretive structures used in this chapbook are reminiscent of Richard Baxter's approach to ghost stories in his *Certainty of the World of Spirits*. As I suggested in the previous chapter, learned men and women were familiar with the products of the cheap print market and they were aware of how

these narratives could shape the values of wider society. This awareness lay behind
clerical and reformist efforts to overlay cheap printed wares with devotional narratives, and although the emphases of these messages had changed from the fervent
Protestantism favoured in the mid-seventeenth century, the method remained
the same.[27] Indeed, evidence from the ghost stories of ballad and chapbook fame
shows that these endeavours were not misplaced since they highlight an important, if complex connection between ghost beliefs and religious sentiment.

*A Strange, but True Relation of the Discovery of a Most Horrid and Bloody
Murder* expressed this link most explicitly when its author declared that 'the grand
Concernments of Religion, and Interests of Mankinde, as to their future estate'
depended 'upon the belief of Invisible Powers'.[28] God sent the ghost that appeared
in this chapbook to expose a usurping executor, and the characters involved in
the narrative clearly recognized that it was only through religious supplication
of some kind that the ghost could be put to rest. They were uncertain, however,
of the most effective method, and when some neighbours and local gentlemen
heard of this haunting they advised the executor to repent his sins but also 'to
take councel of some Minister what to do to be rid of so great a disturbance'.[29]
In a similar vein, a murderer from Lincolnshire who tried to lay the ghost of his
victim by employing a conjurer was unable to banish his nemesis because it was
sent by divine authority.[30] Ballad accounts also acknowledged God's agency in
conjuring and dispelling ghosts. When a poor maidservant from London was
confronted with a 'pale and dreadful' ghost, the author of the single-page ballad *A
True and Perfect Relation from the Faulcon* noted that 'the maid cry'd out O Lord,
/ I heartily do pray / That by the power of thy word, / Chase this same fiend away'.
When she repeated the words once more and lifted her hands towards heaven, the
ghost 'Quite banisht out of sight'.[31] When a ghost appeared before a farmer in his
orchard one night, his automatic reaction was to address the visitor in the name
of Jesus Christ. Since the farmer had not made clear the specific religious lesson
to be drawn from the text, the ballad author did it for him in the closing lines.
'Therefore lets fear the Lord on high, / That we may be of the flock with Christ
/ And then we need not fear to dye, / Our souls no doubt will be at rest'.[32] The
practical model of devotional behaviour recommended by ballad and chapbook
ghosts encouraged moral reformation, repentance, good deeds and prayer, some
of which might have a beneficial impact upon the individual process of salvation.
The learned authors encountered in Chapter 1 did not acknowledge the direct
effect of godly living on the fate of individual souls, but they did suggest that
this practice was a step in the right direction. Thus, although the emphases were
slightly different, there was considerable overlap between the moral theology
advanced in high places through the medium of ghost stories and the interpretations put forward in cheap print. As Bernard Capp has suggested, ballad writers
'generally ignored the theological distinction between saving grace and the good
works that would accompany it'.[33] In contrast to the writing of learned authors,

there was little sense of panic in the ghost stories of cheap print about the spread of atheism, but there was a shared understanding of the particular usefulness of ghost stories in devotional contexts. The ghost narratives of cheap print advanced a similar disapproval of licentiousness whilst acknowledging a more organic and fluid connection between the workings of God and the activities of ghosts. As will become clear in the chapters that follow, these understandings were less politicized and thus the popularity of ghost stories was less restricted to specific time frames.

Learned engagement with the ghosts of ballads and chapbooks can also be demonstrated in less obvious ways. Political satirists revealed sound familiarity with the well-established forms and metaphors of these narratives, often using them for satirical effect.[34] However, a less irreverent approach was suggested in a number of white-letter ballads that adopted the trope of the returning ghost as a vehicle to voice political discontent, to make accusations or to express a sense of social injustice. A pamphlet entitled *Mr. Ashton's Ghost* was published in 1691 and claimed 'Upon the Word of a Ghost' that Mr Ashton, otherwise known as the Earl of Essex, had been unlawfully murdered.[35] *Bradshaw's Ghost*, a twelve-page chapbook published in 1659, featured the ghost of King Charles I and it was specifically designed as a warning from beyond the grave about the fate of rulers who abused their royal powers and prerogatives.[36] The years of political and religious unrest that accompanied revelations of the Popish Plot and the Exclusion Crisis also furnished a large number of politically-minded ghosts. *Sir Edmundbury Godfreys Ghost* was one of a series of pamphlets that used the truth-telling figure of the ghost to accuse Catholic traitors of murdering this prominent Westminster magistrate who was found strangled and stabbed near his home in London on 17 October 1678. Sir Edmundbury Godfrey had met with Titus Oates shortly before he was killed, fuelling rumours of a murderous Catholic conspiracy. A pamphlet entitled *Garnets Ghost* went even further by specifically identifying the murderers as a private cabal of Jesuits.[37] Of course the ghosts that featured in these pamphlets were not real, but by appropriating the trope of the righteous ghost they acknowledged the authoritative voice with which these figures spoke.[38] Representations of ghosts at the top and bottom end of the cheap print market demonstrate that these figures were understood as revealers of truth by broad sections of English society.

A New Ballad of the Midwives Ghost was a second version of the Holborn tale of murder encountered earlier, appearing for sale in 1680 from the press of the highly successful printer Thomas Vere.[39] This account was a follow-up to the original ballad of *The Midwives Ghost* that also came from Vere's printing house in the same year, such was its success that a second run was authorized almost immediately. Thomas Vere was a prominent figure in the cheap print industry and, in partnership with Francis Coles, John Wright and William Gilbertson, he printed a series of ghostly ballads including the top-selling *Lamentation of Dell's Mistris*,

A Godly Warning to All Maidens, *A True and Perfect Relation from the Faulcon* and *Hubert's Ghost* – a satirical white-letter ballad that catered for a very different consumer. Vere knew the print market inside out, and so his involvement with ballad ghosts is highly significant. The decision to print a ballad was never an easy one, since it represented a hefty investment for many publishers. Partnerships were often formed to share the costs involved, and this was particularly marked when expensive woodcuts were to be included. In the case of *The Midwives Ghost* and *A New Ballad of the Midwives Ghost*, Thomas Vere was sufficiently confident of the profit to be gained that he stood the cost of printing on his own.

The form and simple style of this ballad indicated that a less literate audience was aimed at by both author and printer, as compared with chapbook treatments that used more sophisticated language and rhetorical structures. The typeface was black-letter, and the page was dominated by the woodcut of a female ghost in winding sheet, as reproduced in Figure 1 below.

The action of the ballad was described in rhyming couplets and was set to the verse of '*When Troy Town, &c.*'.[40] It therefore catered for those with a rudimentary reading ability, for those who might hear the tale set to music in the street and for those who might hear a group reading in the local alehouse. However the story was received, the essentials remained the same as the chapbook treatment. Revulsion was expressed for the untimely death of the children, for the midwife as an unnatural murderer of the innocents in her charge, and for the improper burial of the infants under the hearth. The ballad did, however, present these details in a different way, including techniques suited to oral performances as well as private readings.

The ghost of Mrs Adkins took a speaking role here, declaring her purpose 'to let the World to know my Crime, and that I am most sorry for't', and she was also permitted to address a direct warning to the reader, 'desiring Midwives to take heed, how they dispose their Bastard-breed'. The ballad devoted more time to sketching the character of the maidservant (with whom an unlettered audience might more readily identify), and directly reported speech was used to establish her honest character and thus the credibility of her story – according to local opinion, she was 'a religious maid'.[41] This highly detailed account, combined with the use of dialogue in the text, emphasizes the suitability of this narrative for reading audiences, but also for those who would hear it read aloud. Both the ballad and chapbook versions of this story give details of the children's remains at the Cheshire Cheese inn. Both accounts also drew on the language of empiricism by encouraging sceptical readers to seek verification of the details by speaking to the regulars at the inn. The truth value of the spoken word was here prioritized over the written text.

Reports of this murderous midwife offer a prime example of how ghosts could migrate across different print categories and between different social audiences. This was also one of the cross-over ballads identified by Angela McShane Jones,

Figure 1. Woodcut of female ghost in winding sheet, in *A New Ballad of the Midwives Ghost* (London, 1680). Reproduced with the kind permission of the Bodleian Library, University of Oxford.

which told the same stories but appeared in both black- and white-letter form. The white-letter version, *The Bloody Minded Midwife*, told essentially the same story as that narrated in *The New Ballad of the Midwives Ghost*, but the style and sophistication of language was adapted to suit different tastes. This ballad was presented in simple form, without woodcuts, biographical details or dialogue and was probably destined to appeal to a more restricted audience. This case study thus suggests that the readership of ghost stories in the marketplace of cheap print was inherently mixed. Readers may have approached these texts for slightly different reasons, but the same ghosts were able to capture the interest of wide sections of society through revelations of secret murder and by confirming the moral virtue of the reader by condemning murderers and other wrongdoers.

Strange and Wonderful News from Lincolnshire provides another example of the widespread appropriation of ghosts as otherworldly detectives. From the very beginning of this four-page chapbook, the author clarified the general purpose of ghosts, who 'Groan out absconded horrors, and are often Instrumental made to the discoveries of Vilianous Exploits'.[42] The story centred on William Carter, a gentleman who lived near the town of Stamford in Lincolnshire, and who had arranged for the murder of his younger brother Thomas. Carter's crime was motivated by avarice, one of the seven deadly sins, as he aimed to usurp his brother's portion of the family inheritance. Before the gruesome details of the crime were related in full, the villainy of Carter's crime was established by a description of the fratricidal plotter who was 'by Nature of an extravagant wild temper'.[43] The author of this piece also likened Carter to the scriptural figure of Cain who murdered his brother Abel.

Underlining the importance of oral forms of communication and of local opinion, the conspiring William tried to pre-empt the suspicions of his neighbours by telling them of his plan to send his brother to Cambridge University, where he was to study divinity. Believing he was on his way to Cambridge, Thomas mounted his horse and set off, but he made it only to a nearby wood before he was set upon by three ruffians disguised as highwaymen. Thomas was shot from his horse and run through with a sword. For this act, the perpetrators were promised the sum of £10 each by William Carter. Lacking any witnesses to the crime, William seemed home and dry so the discovery was left to 'the dictates of Providence' (perhaps shorthand for local gossip networks) and there followed 'a certain rumor spread about the place, without a known Author, that there had been a dreadful Ghost seen in Mr. Carters Yard'. Carter's household was the most obvious source of this rumour since thereafter 'the Servants had strict charge not to reveal to any of the Neighbours any such disturbance'.[44] With an insider's view of the Carter household, it seems probable that William's crime had been discovered by one of the servants, who, motivated by a sense of social injustice, circulated reports that the ghost of Thomas Carter had appeared to his killer with fresh bleeding wounds – this detail served to reinforce existing suspicions that Thomas had met with a sticky end. Further knockings, groanings and laments were heard for two or three nights, after which the neighbourhood again grew suspicious and reports of the ghost spread afresh. William removed to another house but was pursued by the ghost until he finally employed a man 'that pretended to Astroligy' to conjure the ghost down, but all to no avail.[45] The murdered youth again appeared to William, this time on horseback, showing the wounds from which he had died and telling the conjurer that, notwithstanding his own proficiency, he would be unable to lay his spirit until his blood was avenged. The ghost accused William and his three accomplices of murder, finally eliciting a confession from William before a local magistrate, whereupon he was committed to the county jail.

This ghost therefore upheld the might of heavenly authority and, along with the midwife's ghost, satisfied ideals of social justice by ensuring that the offender was punished, allowing the local community to reaffirm customary ideas of the dignified way to die. Such concerns paid little heed to social difference, indeed the account reinforces a sense of common purpose within the community with the revelation of Thomas Carter's murder assured by curious neighbours, household servants and local officials all working together. Furthermore, the centrality of the spoken word in this narrative again supports the notion of societal bilingualism from which ghost stories profited, with oral reports rapidly translated into print. The suspicions of lowly servants were taken seriously and their reports were endorsed in 'a Letter to a Gentleman of very good Quality in London', by which means this account came to be printed in London and to which local men of 'good Repute and Fame' were willing to sign their names.[46] Carter's ghost was plausible thanks to heavy contextualization of the circumstances that provoked its appearance and due to local knowledge of William Carter's character. In this account ghosts were conceived as opponents of unlawful killing by different sections of society, pointing to a shared set of meanings surrounding the appearance and purpose of ghosts.

Invention and Appropriation

The tale from Lincolnshire supports the proposition of both Malcolm Gaskill and Laura Gowing that supernatural evidence was employed by the poorer sorts 'as a popular strategy deployed in order to influence and engage the authorities' and as a way for 'the powerless to expose secrets and misdeeds' in early modern England.[47] This section will reinforce and build upon these conclusions, by focusing upon the creative social and economic usages to which ghost stories were put. It will become clear from the following examples that such tactics were not just monopolized by the poorer sorts, but extended through the hierarchy of ranks. Only a deep-seated and widespread belief in the reality of ghosts made it possible for men, women and children to manipulate ghost stories for such practical ends.

A chapbook that unravelled a mysterious murder in Exeter provides a prime example of how ghost stories could be fashioned by humble folk to bring accusations of murder against members of the local community, and thereby damage the reputation of prominent individuals. *The Wonder of this Age: or, God's Miraculous Revenge against Murder* was published in 1677 but its story began seven years earlier, when the body of a man was discovered in a local inn. Buried under the kitchen floor of this establishment, his demise violated cultural ideals and practical rituals surrounding death, and prompted official investigations into the heinous crime.[48] The killing had taken place almost thirty years earlier and, although the victim's corpse had by now 'mouldered away to Dust', his linen cap had been fortuitously preserved and bore the distinctive initials of the deceased man. This 'occasioned much Discourse' in the local area 'because the two Letters answered to the Name of a Person that had heretofore kept that House'. Local memory and gossip were crucial factors in reconstructing the pieces of this jigsaw of sin, especially since the victim was not thought to be a local man traceable in town records, but was instead a stranger 'from beyond the Seas' who had taken rest at the Inn. Despite the discovery of the victim's corpse, however, there was insufficient evidence to bring any formal accusations of murder and, as the chapbook's author explained, the case 'proceeded no further at that time, than certain muttering Surmizes; everyone guessing, as his Fancy led him'.[49]

Seven years later new life was breathed into the case when another stranger took up residence at the inn and reported having seen 'a Ghost or Apparition, in the Form of a Man, and by his Habit, (being Embroidered Cloaths) resembling a Gentleman'. According to this testimony, the ghost spoke the following words to him, disclosing details of his death, 'Thirty Years ago was I barbarously Murthered in this house for my Money: Part of my Body hath been found, but my Blood is not Revenged; I Charge you to acquaint the Magistrates that the thing may be Examined'. Unsure of how to proceed, the percipient delayed spreading news of his experience until the ghost appeared for a second time, demanding why he had not performed his request. The man protested that his hesitation in engaging a magistrate was because 'he was poor; and to make out and prosecute the business Effectually, would be Chargeable'. The ghost replied that he need not want for money, for in the kitchen was hidden a sum of £80. The man continued to protest however by reasoning that 'if he took any persons on suspition, he had not witnesses to prove it against them; and if he should Charge them, and they were Cleared, they might sue him'. Still insistent on revenge, the ghost promised that 'God will raise up Witnesses: and rather than fail, I will appear, and make the Murderers Confess it'.[50] Neatly illustrated here were the very real concerns that faced those on a meagre wage who wished to action lawsuits. This man was acutely aware of the potential pitfalls involved in initiating legal proceedings and the ghost may well have functioned as a form of insurance or protection to save him from the cost of an unsuccessful prosecution or an ensuing libel suit since he could not be identified as the primary accuser. The ghost was thus a convenient ally in cases where material evidence of a crime was insufficient to secure a conviction.

Rumour and gossip were highly effective in casting suspicion upon people whose crimes had gone unpunished by law. By framing charges of murder or wrongdoing in a narrative context, ghost stories helped to attract a much wider audience who were perhaps more willing to take seriously the allegations of the poor or those with little social standing. Such was the case with the Exeter ghost that roused the interest of local officials, who interpreted it as a providential sign that an offence had been committed. This was most clearly demonstrated when the poor man fell seriously ill soon after his encounter with the ghost. Near to death, he called on a local minister to whom he related every circumstance; the minister was so convinced by the story of the ghost that he urged the sick man to report the experience to a magistrate, something he did just a few days after his recovery. The magistrate was sufficiently persuaded of the truth of his claims to order the examination of two maidservants who worked at the inn at the time of the murder. One of them recalled the gentleman who wore the embroidered clothes and his mysterious disappearance. This investigation was still in progress at the time of publication but, even if it did not result in a conviction, the ghost story was plausible enough to set the wheels of the legal system in motion.

In 1692 the ballad of *The Duke's Daughter's Cruelty* was printed by order of John Deacon at his print works in Guiltspur Street, London.[51] This ballad was licensed and registered with the Stationer's Company, and it displayed similar themes to the Exeter case, including wicked behaviour, unlawful killing and heavenly retribution. Yet this ballad went further still by presenting a shocking example of the corruption of upper-class morality. I have already noted the popularity of ballads that focused on the moral failings of the wealthier social ranks, and which clearly enunciated concepts of righteousness and justice. This ballad was a case in point. The story centred upon the young daughter of a Yorkshire nobleman, who had a secret affair with her father's clerk. The unfortunate woman fell pregnant, and to conceal her shame she murdered her newborn babes (for she had twins). The innocent children were stabbed in the heart with a penknife, and a grave was hastily dug for them in the forest. When the woman returned to her father's house, however, her victims' ghosts appeared before her 'as naked as e're they was born'. Taking a speaking role, the children condemned her murderous deed, declaring, 'O Mother, O Mother for your sin / Heaven-gates you shall not enter in'. The moral message as well as its intended audience was made clear in the final lines, 'Young Ladies all of beauty bright / Take warning by her last good-night'.[52] The ballad was printed in roman-letter typeface, and it may well have attracted the notice of the better sorts. It is more likely, however, that the presentation and form of *The Duke's Daughter's Cruelty* reflected changes in the ballad production process. By 1700 black-letter typescript was increasingly supplanted by roman-letter. But, far from losing touch with their traditional market, publishers retained black-letter headings to convey continuity, and to let readers know what kind of ballad this was. The title of John Deacon's ballad was indeed produced in black-letter script and set to a lively new tune. Deacon's willingness to publish ghost stories was also significant, since he formed one of the group of London men known collectively as the 'ballad partners', alongside Philip Brooksby, Josiah Blare and John Back. These men had been apprentices of Wright, Clarke, Passinger and Thackeray, and they commanded a virtual monopoly of ballad printing in Restoration England until the lapse of the Licensing Act in 1695 opened production to a wider market.[53] John Deacon also published the ballad of *The True Lover's Ghost* in 1671 and in partnership with Brooksby, Blare and Back he invested in *An Answer to the Unfortunate Lady*, in which an avenging ghost was the star character. Ghost stories were clearly a good investment, and in the consumer-driven world of balladry, a good return was clearly expected from a vibrant consumer market that devoured these accounts with alacrity.[54]

Ghost stories thus provided a space for the active agency of the more marginalized social groups in early modern England and a means by which the suspicions of less wealthy men and women, and sometimes children, could compete on a stronger footing with their superiors. Ghosts, primarily understood as God's messengers, were emblematic of unspoken truths and were commonly expected to uphold principles of social justice. Narrative structures could thus have important public consequences and allowed local and national concerns to be effectively connected. As will become clear in Chapters 3, 5 and 6 these themes resonated throughout the eighteenth century and were deeply woven into the cultural fabric of English society.

Ghost stories were, however, configured in a variety of different ways and often for less dramatic purposes than to expedite accusations of murder. They could operate on a more informal level that did not involve the collusion of local officials. These practical uses were made clear in ballads and chapbooks, but they were also laid out in other published and unpublished works that were less noted for presenting an ambiguous mixture of factual and fictional events. In his collection of antiquities and popular superstitions, Royal Society man John Aubrey described how ghost stories were sometimes used as a tactic to secure occupancy. 'It is certain' he wrote 'that there are Houses that are haunted, tho not so many as reported, for there are a great many cheats used by Tenants'.[55] In 1680 the Yorkshire antiquary and Royal Society member Abraham De La Pryme recalled that a great house near his childhood home remained perennially unoccupied 'by reason of the great disturbancys that had been there by spirits ... of whome there are many dreadfull long tales'.[56] In his *History and Reality of Apparitions* Daniel Defoe would later remark 'how many houses have been almost pull'd down' on account of rumours that ghosts inhabited them.[57] The prospect of living in a haunted house was thus an unattractive one. A resident ghost might well have proved a deterrent to alternative occupants or helped to ward off rent increase by grasping landlords. The invention of a ghost in such scenarios is however less significant than the belief that such tactics could be successful. Similarly, the chapbook entitled *A Strange but True Relation of the Discovery of a Most Horrid and Bloody Murder* included the story of a ghost that haunted a rich and greedy executor who attempted to usurp the fortune of two young orphans. The ballad of *The Rich Man's Warning-Piece; or, The Oppressed Infants in Glory* told how a ghost came to punish a rich farmer from Reading who murdered two young children in his charge to get his hands on their inheritance money. This ghost was one of many that were explicitly understood to embody values of social justice and equity. The readers of this ballad were also clearly identified by the author, who issued them with the following warning: 'You rich men all that do in London dwell, / Give ear unto this story which I do tell, / And be content with what the Lord has gave, / To wrong the Poor besure you no way Crave'.[58] Restoration ghost stories can therefore be understood as part of a policy of resistance against the incursions of social superiors. But they were also weapons used to secure social and economic survival more generally. These narratives might then be included as a miscellaneous item in the 'economy of makeshifts' identified by Olwen Hufton.[59] In this context, ghost stories shed light on the otherwise invisible preoccupations, fears and fantasies of the poorer sorts.[60] The language and familiar narrative structures of these texts could be manipulated by more marginalized social groups to negotiate power and authority.

This antagonistic trend should not be overstated, however, since this strategy also worked in the opposite direction. A case in point is provided by *An Account of a Most Horrid and Barborous Murther and Robbery, Committed on the Body of Captain Brown*. The murder of prosperous Captain Brown near his hometown of Shrewsbury made for sensational reading, since it was his own servant who had killed him.[61] The servant owed Captain Brown the large sum of £50 in rent, and it was this debt which appeared to provoke the attack. Captain Brown was seized one night by the servants and his accomplices. His head was chopped off, thrown in a sack, and his body was unceremoniously buried in a nearby hop field. Lacking any witnesses to the crime, the Captain's ghost reportedly appeared before two gentlewomen of his acquaintance, and to another gentleman from the same village. This ghost again confirmed already existing suspicions that the servant had been complicit in his master's murder. The ghost alerted the authorities to the servant's guilt, and he was eventually apprehended and sent to Shrewsbury prison before his victim's body was unearthed and given a more dignified burial. The characters in this tale, along with the scenario itself, may well have spoken to the interests of both the middling and upper sorts. A second report of the ghost published in 1694 noted that a servant had killed his master for love of money and that 'an apparition made some signs of this murder to some of his friends'.[62] On a more informal level, Daniel Defoe described how a miserly gentleman spread the false rumour of a ghost to deceive some credulous country folk into completing expensive excavation work on his property. These makeshift labourers appear to have been encouraged in their toil by the promise of discovering hidden treasure.[63]

Ghost stories highlight elements of social, economic and interpersonal conflict, yet this was not their primary function. If ghost stories had a job description it would be of a more generic kind, to punish dishonesty and sin, which were principles upon which most members of society were agreed. Within this remit, conflicts and accusations could arise between servant and master, landlord and tenant, but also within families and between husbands and wives – something that will be more fully explored in the following chapter. These narratives could be appropriated for highly specific purposes by manipulating established meanings of ghosts. The cases already described indicate that a wide range of people were sufficiently familiar with the meanings commonly attached to ghosts, with the contexts in which they were generally expected to appear and with the narrative conventions used to frame successful accusations. This kind of knowledge was sustained by the products of the cheap print industry, which helped fashion perceptions of ghosts in wider society. More creative usage of ghost stories was then a notable theme in ballad and chapbook accounts from the later seventeenth century. As noted in Chapter 1, this was partly due to the fact that Restoration ghosts had been stripped of confessional allegiance. This process validated their entry into print, or occasionally into formal legal proceedings. Ghost stories were not of course universally condemned as Catholic forgeries before 1660, but their appearances outside of purely religious contexts proliferated in the final decades of the seventeenth century. This was due in large part to the volume of stories churned out by the printing presses, which helped to link ghosts more intimately to the trials and tribulations of daily life. The domestic concerns of ghosts testify to the fact that many of these tales began life in oral communities. Ordinary people must then be credited with a crucial role both as producers and consumers of this body of literature.

The Geography of Ghost Stories

Evidence from cheap printed accounts has so far revealed no clear-cut pattern in the social distribution of ghost beliefs. Ghost stories that originated in regional centres beyond London reinforce this conclusion, and they also highlight fruitful interaction between learned and unlearned folk who shared overlapping interests in ghostly phenomena, though perhaps for different reasons. Regional accounts position ghost stories as an important site of cultural exchange, while also highlighting the different contexts in which both characters and readers became involved with these narratives. The first thing to note about regional ghost stories was that the vast majority featured the formal examinations and depositions of local magistrates. This was certainly a more pronounced feature of regional ghost stories, where the very act of printing represented a process of negotiation between lettered and unlettered, and between oral and written modes of communication. The physical process of print production in regional centres, or lack thereof, made this more distinct than in London accounts. With the lapse of the Licensing Act in 1695, London lost its printing monopoly and permanent presses were established on a wide scale throughout England and Scotland.[64] These changes led to numerous reprints of older chapbook and ballad accounts that were produced in new forms and distributed to fresh audiences. These years also saw a shift from the production of black-letter ballads to slip ballads, which were shorter, usually illustrated and allowed publishers to produce three different ballads on one sheet of paper, thus maximizing space and lowering the production costs of cheap print even further.

Prior to 1695, however, regional ghost stories had to pass through London before they could be enshrined in print and peddled in the marketplace. Many regional ghost stories must then have remained in oral communities, but those that did make it into print most often featured revelations of murder, which necessarily engaged the participation of local officials. Magistrates and church officials were often made up of the middling sorts and it makes sense that these people figure more prominently in regional ghost stories. In this guise, such men can be identified as important mediators between local and national cultures. These were the people most likely to possess advanced literacy skills and, as I will suggest below in the case of Isabel Binnington, they were among the first to hear news of the latest ghost sightings and were well positioned to spread it to friends and acquaintances through networks of correspondence.

The case of the Exeter ghost discussed previously underlines the circularity of oral and written representations of ghosts that characterized regional reports. News of this particular ghost was 'common discourse' in the town according to the author of *The Wonder of this Age*, who claimed that 'many Whole-sale Men' heard of the affair from neighbourhood gossip 'at the last Fair at Exeter'. Nonetheless, the printed version of this story was based on 'Letters to divers worthy Persons in London; as by the Information of several credible People, lately come from the Parts wherein the Thing was transacted'.[65] Another chapbook based on this tale, and perhaps directed at a more educated audience, also reached the printing presses of London after the story was 'taken from the mouth of a civil person that lived very near the place where this fact was committed, and came to Town on Fryday night last'.[66] The geographical space separating regional centres from metropolitan printers was an important factor in determining whether oral reports of ghosts reached wider audiences. This physical gap could be bridged, however, by visitors to the capital, or through networks of private correspondence which were commonly used to transport ghost stories across the country.

A Warning Piece for the World, or, A Watch-Word to England provides a good example of this process in action. In 1655 the ghost of a gentleman 'in bright and glittering armour' appeared before William Morgan, a farmer near Hereford, and to his shepherd John Rogers. The two men were so amazed by the event that they immediately told passers by 'what they had seen and heard', and news of the ghost soon spread around the whole village. The author of this chapbook account neatly described how the report came to be published when he assured his readers that

> the certainty of this hath been confirmed by divers Persons about the City, who have read Letters from good hands to justifie the same, which Letters have been said to be signed by the hands of the Church-wardens, and the rest of the Masters of the Parish which came as true and certain Newes to London, to be put in Print, to the end that all Men and Women that hear of it, may repent and amend their sinfull Lives.[67]

The translation of this report into print is significant for a number of reasons. First, it shows that the ghost excited the interest of important sections of the Exeter community; second, it demonstrates that audiences existed in London for the reception of these narratives; and third, it highlights the importance of physical proximity and / or accessibility to the London printing presses.

The Examination of Isabel Binnington of Great-Driffield, and *A Strange and Wonderfull Discovery of a Horrid and Cruel Murther* add further weight to this conclusion.[68] Both were short printed chapbooks, approximately eight pages in length, and they told how a ghost, eager to avenge his murder, visited a young Yorkshire woman named Isabel Binnington in 1662. Isabel was most likely a servant, and she had only recently moved to the East Riding when the ghost first appeared in her house. It visited a number of times and claimed to be the restless spirit of one Robert Elliott, a Londoner who had been robbed and murdered by three women whilst sleeping in Binnington's house fourteen years earlier. To corroborate the ghost's story, Isabel dug up some loose mould from under the floor, and underneath she discovered a pile of human bones along with a stake that had been driven through the victim's corpse.[69] The ghost revealed an elaborate biography to Isabel, vividly describing the circumstances of his death and details of his killers. Isabel's testimony therefore stuck to the familiar narrative conventions met with in the Exeter report, associating the ghost with sudden death, robbery and murder. Familiarity with this tried and tested narrative formula may well have helped to persuade the magistrates that Isabel's testimony was authentic. Local magistrate Thomas Crompton was sufficiently convinced of it that he instructed Isabel to address the ghost the next time it appeared and to ask it the names of the murderers. These details are included in the original deposition, which was included with the pamphlet. Isabel's evidence also led to further excavations after magistrates made inquiries in neighbouring parishes where the ghost claimed his murderers now lived. The legal implications of Isabel's testimony ensured that it reached the ears of local officials, and this legal context was an important area in which the interests of more illustrious personages could overlap with those of a humble maidservant. Ghost stories thus provided opportunities for knowledge exchange between different social groups.

The production, circulation and reception of ghost stories in London provide a somewhat different picture from the process encountered in regional accounts. Reports of ghosts which originated in London were more likely to achieve wide circulation, and they are more likely to appear on the historical record – largely thanks to physical proximity to a large number of printing presses. This geographical advantage also ensured that a different type of ghost appeared in these stories, one that was less reliant on learned mediation and which suggests a more direct relationship between ghostly gossip on the streets of London and the products of the printing press.

The Rest-less Ghost: or, Wonderful News from Northamptonshire and Southwark was an eight-page chapbook published in London in 1675. It told the story of a ghost that appeared to William Clark, a maltster from Hennington in Northamptonshire. The ghost claimed to be the spirit of a man murdered 'two hundred and sixty seven years, nine weeks and two days ago'.[70] Greed was the motive for the killing. The ghost claimed that his head had been chopped off by someone who coveted his estate. This ghost had once haunted the place where he had formerly lived in Southwark, but an exorcism performed by a Catholic friar had prevented him from appearing again until now. This account decried the sins of murder and avarice according to the conventions of the ghost narrative already set out. But it seems that the story was only printed after William Clark journeyed to London in person at the ghost's request on 10 January 1675. Since the alleged killing had taken place such a long time ago, there was no chance that the perpetrator could be brought to justice, and so the relation was of no immediate relevance to the local authorities. This report was therefore based on William Clark's personal testimony, and on the report of the Northamptonshire messenger who told the story at the Castle Inn without Smithfield-Bars. William Clark evidently followed him there since the frontispiece advertised that this relation was 'taken from the said Will. Clarks own Mouth, who came to London on purpose, and will be Attested and Justified by Will. Stubbins, John Charlton, and John Stevens, to be spoken with any day, at the Castle Inn'.[71] This chapbook made no claims to learned authority, and Clark's testimony seems to have spread to the printing press via gossip from the local alehouse. Smithfield-Bars housed a particularly dense concentration of inns and probably enjoyed a vibrant culture of gossip and storytelling in which Clark's story was likely to have spread quickly. Clark's ghost also appeared in a ballad named *Strange News from Northampton* which was printed by Richard Burton. This ballad came replete with woodcuts of the ghost and was most likely based on the spoken word, rather than on written reports.[72]

Spatial dimensions were crucial to the way that this tale was produced and disseminated. After all, the site of the ghost's appearance at Southwark and its narration at the Castle Inn were just a stone's throw from the print-works of Richard Burton in Horseshoe Lane, Smithfield. The chapbook and ballad versions of this story both identified the Castle Inn as an important site of dissemination, and strong local interest in the case was presupposed by the author of the chapbook, who noted that the story was well known on the south bank of the Thames. Burton's ballad may well have circulated outside of London, but its author clearly anticipated that a local audience would form a strong part of his readership. He therefore addressed the account to 'friends and neighbours' and explained where the town of Hinnington was actually located for those unfamiliar with Northamptonshire.[73]

In 1691 a Southwark sawyer named John Dyer was also haunted by a dreadful ghost, the story of which was narrated in a short chapbook.[74] The author of the account interviewed Dyer in person, along with some of his friends and acquaintances. This tale also presupposed a good deal of local knowledge, mentioning a series of locations and characters including 'Barnaby-street' and 'Mr Mealing the Brewer' that would hold little relevance for readers outside of the Southwark area. Moreover, the story may have satisfied local curiosity since Dyer was a well-known figure, having lately kept 'a Victualling-House at the Sign of the *Blew-Coat* in *Deadman's place* in *Southwark*'. The 1661 ballad *A True and Perfect Relation from the Faulcon* displayed similar characteristics. It described how the ghost of Mr Powell, a baker from Southwark who had died some five months before, appeared to his maidservant Joan and looked 'sometimes like a goat ... and sometimes like a Catt'. Again, knowledge of the geography of London lent greater familiarity to the tale since the ghost was spied 'Close by the faulcon' which the author claimed was a familiar local landmark in Southwark. Nonetheless the author clearly intended his song to reach a wider audience, and he declared his intention 'To let the nation know' about this peculiar preternatural event, and his dramatic account included a series of woodcuts as well as lively dialogue.[75] Significantly, this ballad was found among the collections of famous antiquarian Anthony Wood. Along with the likes of Samuel Pepys and John Aubrey, Wood provides a good example of another context in which the ghost stories of cheap print could reach a more educated audience – through the practice of collecting, a much-neglected phenomenon in the historiography of early modern England.

If these ghost stories were in some ways targeted at local audiences, they also contained messages that were more widely applicable, namely condemnations of murder, sin and moral laxity. Reports based on oral testimony and hearsay could, however, find their way more easily into print in London than in provincial areas. The sites of many London ghost stories were very close to the printing houses that churned them out. Moreover, the taverns and inns that aided their dissemination were also condensed into a relatively small area of the city. The vast majority of these activities were clustered around St Paul's Churchyard and usually extended only as far north as West Smithfield and as far south as Southwark. Printers of cheap ghost stories were almost without exception based within this lively community of gossip and print. William Gilbertson was based in St Paul's Churchyard itself, John Wright worked out of Old Bailey, Philip Brooksby was to be found at West Smithfield, John Deacon on adjacent Giltspur Street, Benjamin Bragg on Paternoster Row and James Roberts on nearby Warwick Lane. The physical layout of London was therefore crucial in determining the character of many ghost stories, and in maximizing the role played by ordinary men and women as producers and consumers of this literature. The everyday experiences and beliefs of such people could find their way into print more easily in London, and helped to shape the marketing strategies and products of the cheap print industry.

Production and Performance

This chapter has so far examined some of the reasons why ghost stories were told, how they were presented in ballads and chapbooks, why they were appealing, and some of the ways in which they were distributed. This section returns to the final part of the tripartite model set out previously, namely to modes of performance and reception. The reception of ghost stories, as with many texts, is notoriously difficult to reconstruct with precision. Some broad speculations can, however, be presented based on the material production of texts, and upon the ways in which printers, publishers and authors *expected* ghost stories to be read. It is only too clear from the way that ballads and chapbooks were constructed that they were meant to be performed, to be read out, sung or discussed among friends, family and neighbours.

Those who had not seen a ghost in the flesh could vicariously enjoy the experience at second hand through stories that employed lively narrative detail, dialogue and dense contextualization. The importance of contextualization cannot be overstated in this formula since the rich descriptions offered by both percipients and printers of ghost stories established plausibility. This literary technique also enabled testimonies like that of Isabel Binnington to engage the imagination of local officials. Dense narrative detail was of course central to the way in which speech communities functioned. The ghost stories of cheap print reflected these characteristics, and appear heavily influenced by oral modes of communication, often including direct speech and conversation between the main characters of the text. By incorporating these aspects, writers, printers and publishers began the process of reconverting the written word into speech. This practice was vital and it suggests that the producers of ghost stories recognized the centrality of oral performance to their endeavours. Walter Ong provided a succinct explanation for this technique when he observed that 'the written text, for all its permanence means nothing, is not even a text, except in relationship to the spoken word. For a text to be intelligible, to deliver its message, it must be reconverted into sound.'[76] The oral performance of ghost stories was particularly appropriate because speech contains qualities well suited to dramatic reconstructions of events, such as intonation, pitch, stress and tempo, all of which translate badly into print.[77] Socio-linguist Dick Leith has emphasized the persuasiveness of oral performances, characterizing conversation as a form of physical behaviour, and a convincing one at that since it makes use of the eyes, head, hand gestures and body language to convey authenticity and meaning.[78]

The experience of listening to ghost stories was further augmented by the use of music in balladry, which complemented broader cultural emphases on lyrical forms and song. In contemporary educational practices, children learned their alphabet with a hornbook and usually 'in a sing-song, forwards and backwards'.[79] Ministers and churchmen also relied on the spoken word to communicate important religious messages. Catechisms were not simply tests of memory, since they required children to learn written texts. He or she also had to perform the dialogue, with the minister putting questions to the child, who responded verbally. Liturgical practice further emphasized the centrality of oral communication to elements of contemporary religious culture. Easter communicants and intended marriage partners were expected to 'say by heart' the crucial prayers and precepts – they were not required to read them.[80] Faith was also reinforced by regular sermons, which were extremely popular in these years, and which provided a dramatic performative quality to religious practice. In addition, the Church of England provided textual aids for parishioners through publications of the Bible, Psalters and prayer books, many of which were abridged, simple and illustrated. Parallels can again be drawn with cheap printed ghost stories that very often included lively woodcut illustrations. Figure 1 was the most common woodcut image to be found in the texts examined here, and this stock figure appeared in the ballads of *The Midwives Ghost*, *Strange and Wonderful News from Northampton-shire*, *A True and Perfect Relation from the Faulcon*, *A Godly Warning to all Maidens* and *The Lamentation of Dell's Mistris*. In chapbook publications, similar woodcuts were also reproduced in *The Rest-less Ghost*, *A True Relation of the Dreadful Ghost Appearing to one John Dyer* and notably in *Lord Stafford's Ghost*. The latter work was a political commentary that used the execution of the Earl of Strafford as a warning to Catholic conspirators in the highly-charged atmosphere of suspicion that followed rumours of a Popish Plot in 1678.[81] Figure 2 below shows a similar, though slightly more sophisticated, image of a ghost that appeared in *The Wonder of This Age*.

Images like these were directly relevant to the text and they added meaning to it. In all such illustrations the ghost appeared in familiar guise, bursting out from its winding sheet. The ghost also held a lighted faggot in one hand. Before the repeal of the heresy laws in 1559, convicted heretics were made to carry faggots as a sign of sin, but also to encourage repentance. If they failed to recant, the faggot was used to light the fire at the execution ground. The depiction of faggots

Figure 2. Woodcut of male ghost in winding sheet, in *The Wonder of This Age: or, God's Miraculous Revenge against Murder* (London, 1677), p. 6. Reproduced with the kind permission of the William Andrews Clark Memorial Library, University of California.

in Restoration woodcuts no longer symbolized heresy, yet these icons retained symbolic value as emblems of social and divine justice. Just as the heretic was punished for transgressing the religious laws of the kingdom, so the ghost carried a lighted faggot to announce its mission of vengeance, and to reaffirm its mandate as the righteous nemesis of murderers, sinners and oath-breakers. In this guise, faggots functioned as signs of religious legitimacy, which were designed to connect with the spirituality of the masses.

Faggots may have also served a more mundane function, however, to allow ghosts to see where they were going since they almost always appeared at nighttime. The crescent moon depicted in the top corner of spectral woodcuts reaffirms a point made in contemporary reports. This might seem a strange proposition to the modern reader. Yet, as these woodcuts suggest, visual depictions of ghosts from this period show that they were imagined in less abstract terms, and were closely related to the state of the physical body at the moment of death. Ghosts were depicted as flesh and bones, with the prominence of the winding sheet serving to associate ghosts with the practical rituals of death and burial, and to suggest their affinity with the temporal world.

Woodcut depictions of ghosts also rarely bore any distinguishing features that identified them as particular individuals. This may have been due to the expense involved in such images, and in practice woodcuts were often shared among many printers and publishers.[82] However, this lack of individuality also points to the broader purpose of these images, as a visual *memento mori*, or general reminder of the fragile condition of the human body. Art historian Nigel Llewellyn has demonstrated the centrality of print and pictures in the mortuary culture of early modern England. He has also emphasized the role that these images played in preparing people for physical death by confronting them with vivid images of bodily dissolution.[83] Curiously, woodcuts are missing from Llewellyn's list, and the significance of these images has also been neglected by those engaged in the social history of death. Cheap printed woodcuts of ghosts could by no means compete with the artistic excellence of Robert Walker, John Souch and Thomas Stothard, but they deserve consideration alongside these esteemed painters as part of the diverse repertoire of mortuary images designed to inspire thoughts of individual mortality.[84] These crude images of ghosts deserve greater historical attention, if only in terms of the sheer scale of their distribution. Such depictions were among the most familiar and accessible images of death that were available in these years, especially for those who pasted ballad and chapbook images on the walls of their homes as domestic decoration. The illustration shown in Figure 3 reinforces the similarities between woodcut ghosts and those ghosts that were actually imagined by early modern men and women.

A seventeenth-century reader of Pierre Le Loyer's *Treatise of Specters* sketched this ghost next to the title-page of the text, and it is strikingly similar to the iconographical images already encountered.[85]

Figure 3. Reader's sketch of a ghost (artist unknown), in P. Le Loyer's *Treatise of Specters or Straunge Sights, Visions and Apparitions Appearing Sensibly unto Men* (London, 1605). Reproduced with the kind permission of Cambridge University Library.

The material production of cheap printed ghost stories thus ensured that written accounts of ghosts could be brought to life through lively verbal performances
and dramatic visual imagery that were designed to add deeper meaning and lend
authenticity to the text. The reminiscences of adult male writers who tended to
recall ghost stories from their childhood also suggests that these strategies were
effective in engaging the attention of readers. A history of memory therefore
offers one possible way of explaining the prominence of ghost stories in the early
modern imagination. For now it is important to recognize that the medium of
cheap print was itself crucial in sustaining the popularity and relevance of ghost
stories to wide audiences.

Conclusion

Ghost stories were not a fixed literary type in Restoration England. Instead these
figures performed as character actors in different categories of cheap print – the
two most prominent were murder pamphlets and courtship ballads. The compelling association of ghosts with death, love and marriage, rites of passage in
which everyone would at some time participate, had its origins in social life. The
products of the cheap print industry both reflected and elaborated these familiar
expectations. As such the written and spoken words were inextricably intertwined,
and mutually reinforcing. Printed ghost stories lent authority to oral narratives,
and they also spread them to fresh audiences. This reciprocal process therefore
had important implications for the longevity of ghost stories in the marketplace
of cheap print and in the imaginations of early modern people. By drawing on
real-life ghost sightings, ballad and chapbook accounts helped both to construct
and to propagate established conventions, contexts and narrative frameworks in
which the appearance of ghosts made sense to readers. Wide dissemination of
these narratives also allowed ghost stories to be appropriated and manipulated by
different social groups for highly specific purposes. Cheap print thus highlights
the increasing affinity between ghost stories and the daily trials of the living as
they were laid open to more creative usage.

Flexible configurations of ghost stories found their beginning in widespread
understandings of ghosts as opponents of wrongdoing. Men and women from
a variety of social backgrounds were authorized to take ghostly revelations seriously because of the idea that God sanctioned their messages. The idea of ghosts
had important, if ambiguous connections with lay religious life. As Chapter 1
described, these associations were exploited by a number of Protestant ministers in these years. The process of printing the preternatural was also a socially
inclusive activity, since it brought together discussions of ghost stories in oral
communities, correspondence and formal depositions. The product which even-

tually appeared on the open market was therefore the culmination of a process of interaction and exchange between several different interest groups.

The ghost stories of ballad and chapbook fame also acknowledged the value of oral testimony in verifying spectral episodes, and in bringing these tales to wider prominence through print. These narratives were a vehicle through which ordinary men and women could make their voices heard. Familiar narrative structures and received knowledge of ghosts could therefore be used by a wide spectrum of the population to capitalize on such appearances. The middling and upper sorts also adapted these narratives for similar purposes, but their interest in ghost stories incorporated a variety of other reasons including legal obligation, empirical curiosity, religious conviction, antiquarianism and pure entertainment. There was, however, enough interest among the better-educated sorts to sanction a whole range of more sophisticated print products that featured ghosts in prominent roles.

The ghost stories of cheap print were able to cut across social and spatial boundaries, and they could also overcome chronological divides. This chapter has focused on the ghost stories of cheap print in Restoration England because of the high volume that were published in these years, the sophistication of production techniques and the overlapping interest in ghosts in high and low places. Nonetheless, despite the claims of some historians that the popularity of cheap print was dying out towards the start of the eighteenth century, these narratives continued to be reprinted in large numbers. In contrast to the political ghosts discussed above, ghosts in ballads and chapbooks did not rely on political crises to secure an audience. Instead they benefited from the underlying and long-term interest of readers. By interacting with the events of everyday life, many of the tales met with here were recycled, and became familiar to new generations of men, women and children. Aside from the immediate interest excited by news of murder, these stories were not very topical, and in the case of ballads they were often undated. This temporal imprecision ensured a wider distribution, a longer shelf life and a cheaper price for such tales because they were old. The ghost stories of cheap print thus had the ability to outlast many other narrative types, largely thanks to the ubiquitous moral message inscribed in these texts. The following chapters will demonstrate how cheaply-printed reports of preternatural activity were able to meet with the new challenges and changing genres of eighteenth-century life and literature.

3 A NEW CANTERBURY TALE

There were 2 Persons, intimate Acquaintance, one call'd Mrs Bargrove, the Wife of an Attorny near St. George's Gate in the City of Canterbury, and the other Mrs Veal, who lately lived at Dover, where Mrs Bargrove lived formerly, and contracted their Familiarity.[1]

On Satterday Sept. 8 last Mrs Bargrave being in her little house alone She heard a little kind of a Rustle (It had just struck 12 at noon) & looking towards ye Door in came Mrs V[eal] with a Wrapping Gown & held it together with her hand to across, an handsome suit of Night Cloaths & hood & Silk handkerchief tyed about her neck.[2]

This Gentlewoman was much overjoyed at ye sight of Mrs Veal, and went to salute her, but she rushed by her, and sat herself down in a great armed Chair, and fel into discourse of severall things yt had hapned when they lived together at Dover.[3]

Mrs Bargrave sat down beside her and told Mrs Veal she had been in a sad Humour just before she came in yes said Mrs V[eal] I perceivd it by your eyes is it noe better with you and your Husband then it used to be to which Mrs B[argrave] Replieing noe Mrs Veal there upon undertook to Comfort her by giving her hope that in a little time it wold be other wais and then fell into some religious Discourses and Exhortations and seeing a book lie in the Window asked Mrs B: what Book it was she said it was a book they two had taken great delight in Reading in at Dover it was Drelincourts Discourse against the fear of Death Mrs Veal Replied it was an exelent Book and full of truth.[4]

After this, She desired Mrs Bargrave to write a Letter to her Brother, and tell him, she wou'd have him give Rings to such and such; and that out of a Purse of Gold that was in her Cabinet, she wou'd have Two Broad-pieces given to her Cousin Watson.[5]

Then she [Mrs Veal] said, she would take her leave of her, and walk'd from Mrs Bargrave in her View, 'till a Turning interrupted the sight of her, which was three quarters after One in the Afternoon.[6]

On Monday morning [Mrs Bargrave] sent to Mr Watson's to enquire after Mrs Veal ... They were surprised at her enquiring for Mrs Veal, and said, they were sure by their not seeing her, that she could not have been in Canterbury ... In the mean time Capt. Watson came in, and told them of preparations making in town for the funeral of some person of note in Dover. This quickly raised apprehensions in Mrs Bargrave, who flew away directly to the undertakers, and was no sooner informed it was for Mrs Veal, but she fainted away in the street.[7]

Mary Veal died following a sudden fit at twelve noon on Friday, 7 September 1705 – one day *before* Margaret Bargrave had conversed with her friend in her Canterbury home, and seen her with her own eyes. Little had Margaret suspected that the familiar face that sat opposite her in the comfortable chair had not been the person of Mary Veal, but her ghost instead. The details given above are snippets from the most famous ghost story of eighteenth-century England, and they have been pieced together from the surviving reports of Mary Veal's ghost that circulated in the first half of the century. They range from private correspondence to newspaper articles and commercialized versions of the story. This chapter is based on this rich diversity of sources, the characters involved in them and the people attracted by them.

This chapter has a three-tier structure to appreciate the complex social and cultural meanings of ghost stories in these years. Initially, the local context of the narrative will be investigated. Why was this story produced? How was the ghost understood within the town of Canterbury? And why did a range of local notables take Margaret Bargrave's relation seriously? Margaret Bargrave's ghost story had very particular meanings in its original domestic setting, not least as a vehicle through which to publicize her marital problems and mistreatment at the hands of her husband. The directions given by Mary Veal's ghost for the disposal of her modest estate also provoked tensions within the Veal family and in the wider community.

The second strand of this chapter extends out from the milieu of the parish to examine this Canterbury tale through the eyes of two prominent natural philosophers. This emphasis reveals a complex affiliation between early modern ghost stories and the principles of experimental philosophy. The third layer of my story concentrates on how and why this narrative transcended its original domestic context to achieve national fame over a longer period of time. The chapter will trace the complex evolution of both private and public reactions to this tale, and to ghost stories in general over the first half of the eighteenth century. It will do this by focusing on the broader meanings of the story, the channels through which it circulated and the ways in which it was adapted for multiple audiences. Key questions address how Mary Veal's ghost was interpreted across social and chronological boundaries; what means were employed to test the veracity of the relation; and how, and by whom, it was discredited by the middle of the eighteenth century.

During this process of reconstruction a wide variety of characters will be allowed to speak, from the maidservant who lived next door to Margaret Bargrave to prominent Royal Society figures, and even to Queen Anne herself. The chapter therefore positions ghost stories as facilitators of social interaction that emphasize the fluid, though complex connections between local and national cultures. Margaret Bargrave's testimony also provides a first-rate example of how ghost stories could lend authority to female voices, especially when set within a providential context, and used familiar narrative conventions. These kinds of stories allowed female domestic troubles to be aired in public spaces and in print. They exposed the misdeeds of men, and rallied support for women in distress.

Although this ghost story has been relatively well documented, most treatments have centred on the contribution of Daniel Defoe, who may have penned the most famous rendition of the tale in 1706, entitled *A True Relation of the Apparition of one Mrs. Veal, the Next Day After her Death, to one Mrs. Bargrave, at Canterbury*. Academic interest in the story has been largely confined to literary scholars, interested in the story for what it reveals about the elusive character of Defoe and the significance of his early work.[8] His literary renown has tended to overshadow the intrinsic historical merit of the story itself and no work has yet examined this tale for what it says about changing perceptions of ghosts in these years. Nonetheless, the association of Defoe with the ghost of Mary Veal and his propagation of ghost stories more generally in *The History and Reality of Apparitions*, raises important questions for this study. First, Defoe was acutely aware of his audience and he catered for a broad middle ground of educated opinion that wished to preserve the authenticity of *some* ghost stories whilst disassociating themselves from more vulgar accounts. Second, experts on Defoe have usefully pointed out the intricate mix of 'fact' and 'fiction' that he employed in his work. I want to suggest here that *A True Relation*, though purporting to be a true and authentic relation of the event and being corroborated by a number of other accounts, helped to partially redefine the ghost story as a fictional entity. In an age that was beginning to enforce the ideological and practical separation of 'fact' from 'fiction', this work transgressed these not yet very firm boundaries, and the controversies that surrounded its publication foreshadowed and perhaps eased the subsequent incorporation of ghost stories into novels and Gothic fictions of the later eighteenth century. Accounts of Mary Veal's ghost are thus invaluable for the level of insight they offer into the local context of ghost stories and the particular meanings attached to them, for identifying a broad range of interest groups that were willing to countenance the appearance of ghosts, for highlighting the interaction of local and national cultures and for showing how the genre of ghost stories itself developed and changed over the course of the period.

Breaking News

News travelled fast in Canterbury and the first extant report of Mary Veal's ghost was penned just five days after Mrs Bargrave encountered it. The account appeared in a letter dated 13 September 1705 from 'E. B.' at Canterbury to an unknown lady. E. B. had chosen this occasion to write because there had occurred 'such an extr. Thing in ys town, that I can't omit giving ye relation'.[9] The report itself adhered to the well-established pattern of ghost stories identified in the previous chapter, whereby the spirit of someone lately deceased appeared to loved ones to reveal wrongdoing, or to settle worldly affairs. In this case, the ghost broadcast the abuse of Richard Bargrave towards his long-suffering wife, and publicized details of Mary Veal's personal bequests. The novelty of the relation for E. B. almost certainly arose from the physical proximity of the author to the scene of this wondrous event, and the letter prioritized the knowledge of the local parish about the central characters involved.[10]

E. B. gave an impressive account of Margaret Bargrave's life and circumstances, and of her acquaintance with Mary Veal. Margaret Bargrave (née Lodowick) was an attorney's wife who had formerly lived in Dover, and it was there as a child that she had first met Mary Veal, and the two had become friends. Mary's father had taken little care of his children and she sometimes turned to Margaret's family for want of food and clothing. Mary and her brother William had also lodged with Margaret and her husband, Richard Bargrave, for a time before William was appointed to the Customhouse at Dover. It was at this point that Mary, who kept her brother's house, was forced to move away from the neighbourhood. The improvement in Mary's material fortunes contrasted sadly with those of her friend, whose comfortable situation in Dover deteriorated soon afterwards when Richard Bargrave was removed from his job for drunken and careless behaviour. The Bargraves were forced to move to Canterbury, to a much smaller house and with a significantly reduced income. Margaret's mistreatment at the hands of her husband was common knowledge in the parish of St Mary Bredin, and in the neighbouring parish of St Margaret, which was separated from Margaret Bargrave's house by just a few yards.[11] On the day that Margaret Bargrave claimed to have seen Mary's ghost, her husband had returned home drunk and shut his wife out of doors. As E. B. wrote, the virtuous Mrs Bargrave 'not being willing to expose him & disturb ye neighbourhood walk'd & Sate on ye steps all Night'.[12] When she was let back into the house the next morning she had contracted a fever and had to go straight to bed. The honest character of this neglected wife stood in stark relief to that of her drunken and abusive husband and served to support her testimony that she really had seen a ghost.

E. B.'s description of Mary Veal hinted at her incorporeal nature, she 'look'd very pale', refused to eat or drink anything and asked Margaret to write her list of bequests and send it to her brother.[13] Nonetheless, E. B. never questioned the essential nature of the spirit that appeared – was it for example an angel or a demon? Such metaphysical detail apparently held little relevance for the author, or for the recipient of the letter. Instead E. B. identified the ghost as the returning soul of Mary Veal by the familiar nature of her demands. The ghost was concerned for the welfare of Margaret Bargrave, and was also desirous to document the personal bequests of Mary Veal's property. The ghost also articulated anxiety about improper burial, since Mary's parents reportedly had no stone over their grave. This detail appeared exclusively in E. B.'s letter and firmly cemented the understanding of this ghost in terms of the worldly concerns of Mary Veal, and the customary practices and preparations carried out before death.

This correspondent was probably a close neighbour of Margaret Bargrave, and the truth of the ghost was clearly to be found in her personal credit rating, and in oral reports of the event that circulated in the parish. E. B. did not have the relation first hand, but heard it instead 'from every body that comes in' and particularly from one who 'had it from Mrs B's own mouth'.[14] Furthermore, E. B. was not alone in crediting the authority of local opinion, since significant sections of Canterbury society similarly prioritized the good reputation of Margaret Bargrave. All 'speak well of her', noted E. B., '& my Lady Coventry's Chaplain & other of ye clergy have been wth her and I don't find any disbelieve here'.[15]

A letter sent from Canterbury on 9 October 1705 presented a similarly gossipy account of Mary Veal's ghost and its author, Lucy Lukyn, claimed that she had it from Margaret Bargrave herself. The letter briefly touched on the spiritual discussions of the two women, who had taken to reading Charles Drelincourt's *Christian's Defence Against the Fears of Death*. This led Mary's ghost to reflect, from a position of privileged knowledge, that 'ye things of the other World are not as we here think them'. Her ghostly status was further suggested by her physical appearance – 'Mrs B[argrave] sayes she had ye strangest Blackness about her Eyes she ever saw'.[16] Nonetheless, details of the heavenly conversation enjoyed by the two women were far less prominent here than in many later accounts of the ghost. Lukyn was mainly concerned to establish the purpose of the ghost, along with the good character of Margaret Bargrave, as the surest proofs of the ghost's authenticity. The letter was written to Lukyn's aunt who lived outside of Canterbury and, as with E. B.'s letter, the ghost sighting proved a spur for this correspondent to re-establish contact with her relation, to whom she had neglected to write for some time. The tone of the letter was familiar, and it showed a close acquaintance with Margaret Bargrave's affairs. Lukyn described Bargrave's marital trials and her long-term acquaintance with Mary Veal. Mary's personal bequests to her immediate kin also featured prominently – Mary's cousin, Margaret Watson, was to have 'a suit of mourning, if not her best gown and petticoat and severall other things she had in a Cabinett'.[17] Lukyn's letter personalized the ghost to fit in with local knowledge of Margaret Bargrave and her affairs, in a similar way as the letter from E. B. had done. Lukyn, however, can be more easily identified than E.

B., being a prominent member of Canterbury society and the eldest daughter of Paul Lukyn, a notary who was well known in the town. At the time of writing she was around twenty-five years old and lived in St Mary Bredin. It seems that her acquaintance with Margaret Bargrave was personal, but it was most likely cemented by the Lukyns' friendship with the Oughtons, another local family of note.[18] Indeed, although Margaret Bargrave had lately been reduced in material circumstances, she came from good stock. Her father, John Lodowick, had been a respected minister in Dover, and she enjoyed the friendship of influential families following her move to Canterbury. Mary Veal also had impressive family connections. Her brother William was controller of the Customs at Dover and she had formed a close acquaintance with Robert Breton, a wealthy man from Dover who gave her an annuity of ten pounds. These connections may well explain how details of the ghost reached Lady Coventry's chaplain, George Stanhope, dean of Canterbury, and other prominent figures. Moreover, the fact that Lucy Lukyn took reports of the ghost seriously, and supposed that her kin might share her interest, highlights the socially diverse nature of ghost beliefs, which allowed the tale to spread beyond the parish boundaries of St Mary Bredin.

Astronomical Connections

Fluid correspondence networks were vital in maintaining links between local and national cultures, and the letters of E. B. and Lukyn show that reports of ghost sightings flowed easily through these channels. E. B.'s letter from Canterbury benefited from these lines of communication, and it probably owes its survival to the illustrious hands into which it had fallen by the winter of 1705. As an interesting aside, the original manuscript letter can now be found in the scientific correspondence of John Flamsteed, founder of the Greenwich Observatory, and the first astronomer royal of England.[19]

Flamsteed was appointed to his post by Charles II in 1676, and he had impressive credentials. Flamsteed studied at Cambridge University, he was ordained a clergyman in 1675, and he became a fellow of the Royal Society in 1677, being a member of its Council from 1681–4 and again in 1698–1700. Flamsteed also enjoyed the favour and patronage of high-ranking aristocrats and government officials including Sir Jonas Moore, master of the Royal Ordnance. Flamsteed's scholarly interests included meteorology and optics, which as Chapter 4 will make clear, often inspired fascination with ghost stories in these years. Nonetheless, in the scientific world, John Flamsteed is best remembered for his painstaking astronomical work which culminated in the *Historia Coelestis Britannica* in 1725 – an encyclopaedic work cataloguing more than three thousand stars and their positions in the night sky.[20]

Flamsteed may well have become embroiled in the affair of Mary Veal's ghost to satisfy his own intellectual and personal curiosity. In fact he had much in common with those men who energetically supported ghost stories in Restoration England. Flamsteed confessed to reading romances as a child, which often left an indelible mark on the imagination. His library included numerous texts by latitudinarian divines, and he clearly believed that exchanges between the material and immaterial worlds took place, having visited the famous spiritual healer Valentine Greatrakes for medical treatment in August 1665.[21] Nonetheless, whatever Flamsteed's own thoughts on the matter may have been, it seems that his initial interest in the Canterbury ghost was sparked by his wife, who assisted him in his observations, and who was most likely the lady to whom E. B. had written in September 1705. Flamsteed spread news of the affair among his learned acquaintance, but he made no further enquiries until he received the following letter, dated 31 October 1705.

> Sir,
> I was asked the other day by a very great person if I had heard anything of the story you showed us in your letters about the apparition at Canterbury. I said I had, and mentioned the letters that you had. I also added that I believe I could procure a copy of them, which I beg you would do me the favour to send me by the penny post (direct for me at my house in St. James Palace), with what you know of the credit of the persons concerned. I shall not give copies to any person, but them I mention; nor shall it be published by my allowance. In doing this you will extremely oblige.
> Sir, your most humble servant.
> Ja Arbuthnot[22]

The letter was penned by Dr John Arbuthnot, Scottish mathematician, author and physician to Queen Anne at the time of writing.[23] Arbuthnot was elected a fellow of the Royal Society in November 1704, and it is likely that he formed an acquaintance with John Flamsteed shortly afterwards, as he helped to supervise the Royal Society's investment in Flamsteed's star catalogue. Arbuthnot's royal appointment, combined with his literary and scientific interests, ensured that he moved in highly privileged circles. Chief among his acquaintance were Tory statesman and first Earl of Oxford, Robert Harley, writers Jonathan Swift and Alexander Pope and famous natural philosopher Sir Isaac Newton. It seemed moreover that Arbuthnot enjoyed a particularly close relationship with his royal patient. Jonathan Swift referred to Arbuthnot as 'the Queen's physician and favourite' in a letter to his beloved 'Stella';[24] Peter Wentworth told Lord Raby that Arbuthnot was 'a very cunning man, and not much talk't of, but I believe what he says is as much heard [by the Queen] as any that give advise now'.[25] The scheming Duchess of Marlborough went even further by suggesting that Arbuthnot and the Queen were conducting an adulterous sexual relationship. She claimed that 'Her Majesty was met going to his [Arbuthnot's] chamber alone by a boy of the kitchen, at Kinsington'.[26] Whatever the truth of Arbuthnot's relationship with Queen Anne might have been, it was clear that they had formed a bond more significant than that of merely employer and employee.[27] Anne was said to engage Arbuthnot in regular conversation, and so it is likely that he was familiar with her personal interests. It seemed that Mary Veal's ghost formed one subject of these discussions in the autumn of 1705. The 'very great person' to whom Arbuthnot referred in his letter to Flamsteed and who had expressly requested more information about the Canterbury ghost, was Queen Anne herself.[28]

Following this royal request, Flamsteed set out to investigate the ghost story in earnest, and on 3 November 1705 he wrote to his trusted friend and amateur scientist Stephen Gray. Gray lived and worked in Canterbury and he had collaborated with Flamsteed on a number of astronomical observations.[29] Gray is best known for his work on electricity but, until he was elected a fellow of the Royal Society in 1732, Flamsteed provided his main link to legitimate scientific enquiry. Gray was not part of the scientific elite in 1705, and despite brief employment at an observatory at Trinity College, Cambridge (backed by Isaac Newton), he was forced to supplement his income by painstaking work in the family business, as a dyer in Canterbury's thriving silk manufacturing industry.[30] Stephen Gray was in an ideal position to fulfil Flamsteed's request to examine the truth of Margaret Bargrave's claims, since he was based in the very town where the ghost had caused so much controversy.

Experimenting with Ghosts

Stephen Gray was not only in the ideal location to fulfil John Flamsteed's assignment, his scientific background and links to the Royal Society also made him the ideal investigator. The truth of Mary Veal's ghost was, after all, to be tested with the painstaking precision and empirical rigour used by Restoration scientists. During the course of his experimental career, Robert Boyle developed a coherent set of principles and conventions for establishing *matters of fact*, and his collaborator Robert Hooke systematically catalogued them as standard procedures for the conduct and verification of experiments within the Royal Society. Boyle's schema aimed at objectivity and transparency, and he demanded that *facts* were produced in sterile, controlled surroundings. The fact itself also had to be agreed by a collective group of qualified witnesses. To fulfil these stringent requirements, the methodology of fact-making involved three technologies: material, literary and social. As Steven Shapin and Simon Schaffer have illustrated in respect of Boyle's air-pump experiments, his *material* technology referred to a physical apparatus used to test a hypothesis; his *literary* technology was usually a report illustrating how the experiment had been carried out and detailing its results; and the *social* technology referred to the expertise, moral probity and qualifications of the experimenter, and those who were called upon to acknowledge the authenticity of the fact. Stephen Gray and John Flamsteed were very familiar with these methodologies, and it was this empirical framework which they applied to test whether Mary Veal's ghost could be categorized as a matter of fact. Yet this was to be no mean feat, since the first of Boyle's three technologies – his material apparatus, did not exist in this particular instance. Mary Veal's ghost, if it had indeed appeared – was by definition an *immaterial* spirit, and therefore impossible to verify or disprove by physical examination. Nonetheless, Gray and Flamsteed were able to put Boyle's social and literary technologies to considerably greater effect – a process which involved close collaboration with the inhabitants of St Mary Bredin.

John Flamsteed's original letter to Stephen Gray no longer survives, but the bones of it can be reconstructed from Gray's response, which was sent from Canterbury on 15 November 1705. Flamsteed seems to have insisted that Gray verified the authenticity of the Canterbury ghost by making enquiries into Margaret Bargrave's character from among her personal acquaintance. In other words, Gray and Flamsteed agreed with the letters of E. B. and Lucy Lukyn that the credibility of this ghost story depended on the personal credit of the chief witness. But how was this credit to be measured? Shapin and Schaffer have rightly pointed out that, in the scientific community, the personal credit of witnesses was closely allied to social rank or, to put it in their words, to the 'social and moral accounting systems' of Augustan England.[31] Margaret Bargrave's character was thus to be tested by the same criteria as legal witnesses in courts of law: how knowledgeable was she, and how faithful in delivering her testimony? Margaret's family, friends and neighbours thus held the key to the truth of the affair. For the duration of Stephen Gray's enquiries, the parish of St Mary Bredin would be transformed into an experimental laboratory.

Specifically, John Flamsteed wished to know if Margaret Bargrave was 'a serious Person not given to any thing of levety', and whether she was 'affable open and free or Close and Cunning in her Conversation'.[32] To complete his task, Gray conducted an interview with the chief witness, and he gathered information from people, especially clergymen, who knew Margaret Bargrave when she lived at Dover and in Canterbury. All of them confirmed that she was 'a Religious Discreet Witty and well accomplished Gentlewoman'. Gray also judged her to be 'Generally open Affable and free in her Conversation'. Having passed this first test, Margaret Bargrave's credibility was also subject to the respectability of her family. Gray noted his approval when he discovered that she was the daughter of Reverend John Lodowick, Minister of St Mary the Virgin in Dover *c.* 1670–98, and that she was 'seen often to frequent the Divine Servise of the Church'.[33]

In Stephen Gray's written report to John Flamsteed (his literary technology), Margaret Bargrave's religious devotion testified to her honesty and stood in stark contrast to that of her violent husband, who had once beaten her 'for being soe silly' as to receive the Sacrament. Indeed, the irreligious, immoral and drunken conduct of Richard Bargrave further strengthened the testimony of his downtrodden and virtuous wife. His behaviour also ensured that Stephen Gray regarded Margaret Bargrave's detractors, her husband among them, with a degree of suspicion.

Richard Bargrave was in fact a main player in a group of Canterbury folk who scorned reports that Mary Veal's ghost had ever visited the neighbourhood. William Veal claimed that the ghost was a fake because, when he opened the cabinet mentioned by his sister's ghost, there were no gold pieces to be found inside as she had claimed. The fact that William Veal had opened the cabinet in the presence of several witnesses, however, underlined the fact that his personal reputation was on the line if his sister's ghost was believed to be authentic. The ghost had after all accused William Veal of being untrustworthy. He had neglected his parents' tombstone, and seemed unfit to distribute his sister's goods as she had wished. William and his friends thus went on the offensive, and they endeavoured to quash reports of the ghost, and to sully Margaret Bargrave's character at the same time. He spread reports that nobody had seen Margaret in the street at the time that she was said to have bid farewell to Mary Veal. More damning, however, was the accusation that Margaret had a propensity to report the houses in which she had lived as being haunted. William Veal's connections ensured that these rumours spread beyond Canterbury and, upon hearing this conjecture, John Flamsteed demanded that Gray discover whether his Canterbury experiment had been thus contaminated.

Nevertheless, Stephen Gray's exploration of the objections to Margaret Bargrave's story added further weight to it, rather than casting suspicion upon her testimony. In keeping with Boyle's prescribed literary techniques in documenting experiments, Gray's openness assured the reader of the investigator's neutral stance, since he was not omitting any evidence that could potentially contradict his hypothesis. Gray's admissions were equivalent to the documentation of failed experiments in the laboratory, and this amounted to what Shapin and Schaffer have called 'the literary display of a certain sort of morality', which allowed the reader to trust the narrator and to add plausibility to his claims.[34] What is more, Gray's mention of William Veal's objections allowed Margaret to put her side of the story, and to underline once again her own moral probity in contrast to that of her detractors. William Veal's main objection – that she made a habit of seeing ghosts – was in fact a misunderstanding provoked by the adulterous exploits of her wayward spouse. Margaret went in search of her husband one evening after he had been out hunting. She tracked him down to a public house a few miles outside Canterbury, and discovered him in the garden. Upon her arrival she saw a woman speedily climbing over the garden wall. Unable to account for this vision, Margaret 'said she thought it to be an Apparition, but they afterwards found it to be an ill Woman that was want to use that house'.[35] When Margaret told her husband what she had seen, Stephen Gray noted that he did nothing to contradict his wife's belief that she had seen a ghost, 'being Glad of the opertunety of soe Pretty a Delution to Conceal his Rogery'.[36] Gray also commented that Margaret Bargrave's embarrassment at finding her husband in such company had understandably prevented her from relating the more salacious details of the episode to him. He had nonetheless discovered them from another source.

Richard Bargrave was no doubt anxious to salvage some respectability following the exposure of his scandalous treatment of his wife, and so he joined William Veal in trying to discredit her testimony. He declared, in true Calvinist fashion, that his wife had never met with the ghost of Mary Veal, but had instead been 'discoursing with ye Devil'.[37] Richard Bargrave's doctrinal precision was, however, unlikely to carry much weight since, as Bernard Capp has suggested, the kind of abuse to which he subjected Margaret Bargrave was increasingly condemned in the late seventeenth and early eighteenth centuries. Wife-beating in particular came to be seen as barbaric, especially among the middling sorts who subscribed to new values of civility, and who formed a good proportion of Margaret Bargrave's acquaintance.[38] Richard Bargrave was moreover guilty of more than just wife-beating. He had committed all three of the primary abuses of marriage identified by Capp in early modern England – violence, adultery and failure to provide for one's spouse.[39] In addition to cavorting with prostitutes, his reckless and drunken behaviour at Dover had reduced the Bargraves' economic circumstances and forced their removal to Canterbury. Margaret Bargrave was clearly resentful of her situation, and she referred to her Canterbury home as an 'old hole' on a number of occasions.[40] The ghost story that Margaret Bargrave told thus allowed her to broadcast her sufferings and to condemn her husband for his part in bringing them about.

In 1700 a ghost story from the journal of Cassandra Willoughby served a similar condemnatory purpose. This relation shows that Margaret Bargrave was far from alone in choosing a ghost story within which to frame accusations of spousal abuse, since the intervention of this divine nemesis lent greater authority to common rumour and gossip. Willoughby told the story of a local woman whose husband beat her as she lay critically ill with a fever. The husband's fit of violence was motivated by a fancy that his wife had hidden some money in the house which he was anxious to uncover before she died. The wife passed away soon afterwards, but before she died she begged God to allow her to take revenge upon her husband. On the third night after her death, her ghost appeared and beat her husband so terribly that he was covered with blood from head to toe. The attack was so ferocious that the man survived his wife by just a few days, although he managed to crawl to his neighbour's house to tell them how he had come by his injuries.[41] This story revealed the physical vulnerability of wives within the home, but it also articulated a strong thirst for vengeance, which was sanctioned by the local community judging by the lack of sympathy afforded to this violent husband.

For women who were largely unprotected by law from marital violence and neglect, it was a common response to formulate a narrative strategy to expose spousal misdeeds. Ghost stories formed an important part of this repertoire and these preternatural tales were often effective in securing the condemnation of abusive men among friends and neighbours who intervened to express disapproval. Bernard Capp and Laura Gowing have shown that this task often fell to other local women, and it is notable that both E. B. (probably a woman) and Lucy Lukyn expressed sympathy with the plight of Margaret Bargrave. The following section also describes the testimony of the next-door neighbour's maidservant, who verified Richard Bargrave's unacceptable behaviour. In so doing, she authenticated Margaret Bargrave's claims that she had seen and spoken with the ghost of Mary Veal at the time she claimed. Indeed, the common expectation that female friends would step in to publicize male abuse may well have lent a more general credibility to Margaret Bargrave's testimony. Mary Veal was after all Margaret Bargrave's closest friend, and her ghost appeared just as she was 'weeping and bewailing her self upon the account of her afflicted Condition'.[42] Mary's ghost spent a long time consoling her friend and offering assurances that her miserable situation would not last much longer. Indeed, when Margaret Bargrave was interviewed years later in 1714, she interpreted the ghost's promise of deliverance as a reference to her husband's death in 1707.[43] Mary Veal's appearance thus conformed to a set of familiar social practices, whereby women rallied together to expose marital abuse and to regulate spousal relations – all within a familiar framework of providential intervention.

Assiduous documentation of Margaret Bargrave's domestic woes therefore added further authority to Stephen Gray's report, since the inclusion of heavy circumstantial detail offered a sense of verisimilitude to the reader. This technique was analogous to the emergence of literary realism in late seventeenth- and eighteenth-century literature, and it allowed readers to become virtual witnesses to the story, to weigh up the evidence on offer, and to reach their own conclusions about the authenticity of Mary's ghost.[44] Yet the production of Gray's report relied upon a close and fertile engagement with Margaret Bargrave's friends, neighbours and acquaintances. Indeed, rather than revealing an essential disjuncture between the rigour of Gray's empirical method and the naivety of local opinion, this engagement revealed a common set of assumptions and expectations regarding the appearance of ghosts that closely mirrored the interpretations attached to the ghost by Margaret Bargrave's friends and neighbours.

Although Gray's report was to be digested by the crème de la crème of polite society, his explanations of Mary Veal's ghost did not conflict in any significant ways with the account given by E. B. Gray was similarly unconcerned about the metaphysical status of the ghost, and he considered that Margaret Bargrave really had met with the ghost of the recently deceased Mary Veal. The physical state of the ghost was for Stephen Gray, as for E. B. and Lucy Lukyn, a further sign that Margaret Bargrave had truly encountered her friend's ghost. She was unable to carry out simple human tasks such as drinking tea and reading, and she tried to cover her face with her hand to disguise her weary appearance. The materiality of the ghost was a well-established component of traditional ghost lore, and this clearly resonated with Stephen Gray's understanding of ghosts, and perhaps with his learned acquaintance. By including the ghost's demands about the distribution of her property, Gray's report endorsed the customary role of ghosts in reminding the living of their duties towards the dead. The substantial overlap between Gray's empirical criteria and what might be termed the naive empiricism of the other Canterbury witnesses may seem surprising at first glance. But it is explicable if we adhere to Michael McKeon's assertion that concerns about historicity and truth were central components of popular and elite narrative cultures in seventeenth- and eighteenth-century England. Producers and consumers of cheap print were accustomed to evaluating different accounts of the same event, and they had developed a healthy sense of scepticism that was catered for in the narrative-style of cheap printed literature.[45]

Nonetheless, Stephen Gray's focus on the divine mission of Mary Veal's ghost did set his account apart from those written by the other Canterbury witnesses. Gray placed particular emphasis on the religious conversations enjoyed by Margaret and Mary, focusing on the message of spiritual consolation delivered by the ghost. Gray noted approvingly that Margaret and her ghostly visitor discussed the 'Discourse on friendship' by Anglican divine John Norris, as well as 'Drelincourts Discourse against the fear of Death', which the ghost claimed was 'an exelent Book and full of truth', giving sound notions of 'death and Eternety'.[46] This aspect of Gray's narration placed Mary Veal's ghost within a broad providential context, and within a familiar narrative framework in which ghosts intervened to chastise sinners or to encourage faithful members of the lay community. Gray's spiritual focus was clearly understood to add greater authority to his tale, and indeed John Flamsteed had expressly requested that the ghost was investigated in such terms.

The pious message brought by Mary Veal's ghost may well have given a more respectable gloss to Margaret Bargrave's relation, just as her personal devoutness had confirmed her respectability in the eyes of Stephen Gray. Nevertheless, the main thrust of his account was based on circumstantial gossip, which he gathered from credible witnesses within Canterbury itself. Gray judged that local assessments of the character, family background and piety of Margaret Bargrave provided the most faithful guide to the truth of the case. Indeed, his report implicitly recognized that the power to credit or discredit this ghost story rested with the people of St Mary Bredin. This community of believers included prominent churchmen who flocked to hear Margaret Bargrave's testimony, the 'sober men' of the town and the neighbour's maidservant whose testimony was invoked by Gray. This maid had been at work in the yard on the day of the ghost's appearance, and she testified that she 'heard Somebody talking very Pleasantly with Mrs Bargrave'.[47] Her mistress surmised that it was unlikely to have been Richard Bargrave, since he was 'not use to be soe pleasant with her', whereupon the maidservant confirmed that she had heard the voices of two women that afternoon, although she had not been close enough to make out the details of their conversation.

Just as the ghost was strengthened by the opinions of the local community, so the ghost in turn testified to the strength of that community as a source of authority and a powerful repository of knowledge. This ghost provided Canterbury with a voice, and one that resonated as far as Queen Anne herself. Richard Bargrave's sinful conduct was exposed for all to see, and William Veal's dishonesty was uncovered for the benefit of Mary Veal's inheritors. Yet these voices did not go unmediated. Indeed the very nature of Gray's commission denoted a refusal to accept the ghost story based solely on the second-hand reports of Margaret Bargrave and her supporters. Reflected in Gray's task then was the epistemological shift taking place in wider society, which privileged first-hand knowledge, eye- and ear-witnessing over accepted tradition. The attempt to test the accuracy of E. B.'s letter therefore identifies John Flamsteed and Stephen Gray as men of their time, applying new empirical methodologies to establish the authenticity of ghost stories.

In the final lines of his letter to John Flamsteed, Stephen Gray reflected that 'upon the whole Consideration of all Circumstances I Cannot say those that doe not believe Mrs Bargraves Relation to be true are altogether without Reason yet I think the Arguments for the truth of it are of much Greater validity then those against it and am Inclined to believe that Mrs Bargrave did Realy Converse with the Apparition of her Deceased friend'.[48] Gray's decision to support Margaret Bargrave's testimony based on her good reputation and (in true Boylean fashion) on the opinions of esteemed witnesses is highly suggestive. His endorsement proved that networks of natural philosophy were not uniformly opposed to the idea of returning ghosts, and that empirical methodologies favoured by the Royal Society could in fact work in tandem with oral report and gossip to authenticate such episodes. The desirable credentials of trusted witnesses in gentlemanly science did not only consist of those of superior social rank. The virtues of prudence, experience and worldliness were also prized, and these were qualities that could be acquired without bookish learning or formal education.[49] Furthermore, the intellectual rigour that Gray and Flamsteed employed to verify Mary Veal's appearance opened up this particular ghost story to much wider audiences than it might otherwise have attracted. Gray's empathy with Margaret Bargrave's marital plight also positions ghost stories as highly effective outlets for public expressions of domestic discontent. As such, they provided opportunities for marginalized groups to negotiate power and authority in public spaces.

Nonetheless, if ghost stories offered a vehicle for ordinary men and women to broadcast wrongdoing to wider audiences, this practice was increasingly mediated by considerations of rank. The concept articulated by David Lux and Hal Cook that gentlemanly science operated through 'open networks' rather than 'closed circles' highlights how many natural philosophers were by no means ashamed of engaging with the notions of those beyond a narrow intellectual elite. On occasion they could even engage with the ideas of 'Midwives, Barbers', and '"old women" down the street'.[50] However, these ideas and opinions did not stand on their own merit. The evidence of the next-door neighbour's maidservant was materially significant in confirming the reality of Mary Veal's ghost, yet her testimony only gained wider authority through Stephen Gray's endorsement, alongside more eminent witnesses from Canterbury. The discourse of empiricism could be flexible, but it was not without limits. This theme is explored in greater depth in the following chapter, but this ghost story is a prime example of how the second-hand opinion of Stephen Gray carried more weight in educated circles than any of the acquaintances he made at Canterbury. In line with Boyle's stipulated qualifications for creditable witnesses of facts, Stephen Gray's intellectual pursuits and impressive social connections ensured that his opinion in this matter was prioritized over those from more humble backgrounds. The chain of correspondence that linked E. B., Lucy Lukyn, Mrs Flamsteed, John Flamsteed, Stephen Gray, John Arbuthnot and Queen Anne was based on a shared fascination with Mary Veal's ghost, but it also reflected a strict social hierarchy. Ghost stories clearly had the potential to link local, national and courtly cultures, but such episodes often relied on the endorsement of men and women of good stock.

Public Responses

So far attention has centred on responses to the Canterbury ghost through networks of private correspondence. This evidence denoted fairly positive belief in the reality of Mary Veal's ghost, or at least conceded the possibility that she may have appeared as Margaret Bargrave described. But what is to be made of those accounts that were intended for a wider audience? The first published account of the affair appeared in *The Loyal Post* on Christmas Eve 1705.[51] It told a similar story to those accounts already described, albeit in abbreviated form. Noteworthy, however, were the introductory and concluding sections of the article, which were expressly constructed to verify the truth of the story. The author articulated a need to distinguish this particular ghost story from less reputable tales. From the very start, he claimed that this relation was 'better attested than things of this Nature generally are' and so hoped that it would not be unacceptable.[52] This cautious opening anticipated a potentially negative response from readers of the *Loyal Post* who were accustomed to receiving news about foreign and domestic affairs from this erudite publication. To include a ghost story in the pages of this sober newspaper seemed a potentially hazardous move. By claiming credibility for the story in the public domain, this journalist was well aware that he might risk his own reputation and that of the *Loyal Post*.

Such caution highlights an important problematic in perceptions of ghost stories at the start of the eighteenth century, that is the contested epistemological status of these narratives as fact or fiction, or, in Lennard Davis's terminology, as 'news' or 'novel'.[53] As highlighted in the previous chapter, elements of both reality and fantasy coexisted in the ghost stories of early modern ballads and chapbooks. This interaction was characteristic of both genres and, rather than proving an unworkable tension, this fusion often added to their drama and appeal. However, growing emphasis on empirical knowledge was gradually spreading outwards from the field of natural philosophy into the arts. Combined with the introduction of the Stamp Acts of 1712 and 1724, the way in which ghost stories were conceived, and the publications in which they featured, changed dramatically. The Act of 1712 was a tax on news, and it resulted in printers separating the factual – i.e. 'news' – from the fictional – defined as history and literature – in an attempt to save money. Ghost stories fell between these two stools and, as the next section sets out, the concern to drive a wedge between these two categories had a significant impact on reactions to our Canterbury ghost story. This was especially true for reactions to *A True Relation of the Apparition of one Mrs. Veal*, which would have long-term implications for the status of ghost stories in the later eighteenth century.

The journalist at the *Loyal Post* was aware of these shifting definitions, and he seized every opportunity to establish the respectability of Mary Veal's ghost, of the chief witness, and other interested parties. 'There are many Persons in Town', he insisted, 'that have Letters giving an account of a remarkable Passage that happned lately in the City of Canterbury, Several Letters thereof from Persons of Good Credit have reached our hands, besides Relations we have had by Word of Mouth'.[54] The concluding paragraph further reinforced the trustworthy nature of the relation, in which Margaret Bargrave and Mary Veal were described as 'Persons of Reputation, and Many Juditious Persons have taken the Pains to inform themselves particularly of the Matter. More especially, Mr Paris the Minister of St Andrews. Dr Boyce and other Eminent Persons, both Clergy and Layety: To all whom Mrs Bargrove gives the same Relation, not varying in a Tittle.'[55] No mention was made of the maidservant, or of suspicions that Margaret Bargrave had a tendency to see ghosts. For readers of the *Loyal Post*, authority lay with the interpretations of eminent supporters of Margaret Bargrave, and it was only through their eyes that Mary Veal's ghost could function as a legitimate item of news. This journalist trod a delicate line between figuring Mary Veal's ghost as a newsworthy item and preserving the credibility of the tale. This fine balancing act led him to apologize for the lack of 'Scruple or Caption' that would have further safeguarded the reputation of the newspaper.[56] A fundamental tension was thus revealed; the construction of the article acknowledged strong currents of scepticism among readers of the *Loyal Post* and a desire for 'fact', yet it also catered for persistent fascination with ghosts. The flood of oral and written reports received by the *Loyal Post* clearly showed that ghost stories continued to attract widespread public interest, but governmental pressure on factual publications increasingly limited the appearance of these narratives in such genres. As a result, ghost stories were increasingly relocated to the periodical press, to novels, drama and poetic verse.

The ghost of Mary Veal played an important part in this gradual migration, and the version of this Canterbury tale that most clearly epitomized the tension between the factual and fictional status of this ghost story was also the most celebrated. *A True Relation* first appeared on 6 July 1706, and it may have flowed from the pen of proto-novelist and literary chameleon Daniel Defoe.[57] This chronicle was by far the most meticulous account of Mary Veal's dramatic appearance, and its heavy use of circumstantial detail, lively dialogue and creditable witnessing was designed to persuade readers that this episode was 'Matter of Fact and attended with such Circumstances as may induce any Reasonable Man to believe it'.[58] The writing style clearly owed a debt both to the ghost stories of cheap print fame and to the empirical method of Restoration scientists. But this account also added something new to the mix – suspense, detail and length.[59] The average ghost story at the turn of the eighteenth century was relatively short. Most chapbooks devoted just eight pages to these stories, and Joseph Glanvill's tales in his *Saducismus Triumphatus* were around two pages in length. In ballads, ghost stories ran to just a single folio sheet, and in John Aubrey's *Miscellanies* they were little more than a paragraph long.[60] By contrast this ghost story ran to fourteen pages, and the ghost stories that Defoe recounted in his *History and Reality of Apparitions* averaged around six pages in length.[61] The extra word count in *A True Relation* was taken up by careful scene-setting, and by a minute description of the ghost's physical appearance. The author employed dialogue, verisimilitude and a description of physical actions to add depth to his characterization. He also assumed an active editorial role, interjecting at points in the story to comment on the wider moral and spiritual significance of particular passages, and on the credibility of the story in general.

These techniques were particularly effective in the lengthy description of the spiritual conversations between Margaret Bargrave and the ghost. The author included discussions of death, immortality and the afterlife, and he lingered over the reference to '*Drelincourt's Book of Death*', which the ghost declared to be 'the best ... on that Subject was ever Wrote'.[62] The work of William Sherlock (*A Practical Discourse concerning Death*) was also mentioned, along with two Dutch books, but Mary Veal's ghost confirmed that Drelincourt 'had the clearest Notions of Death, and of the Future State, of any who have handled that Subject'.[63] In this important passage, the author also made claims about the broader moral and spiritual significance of Mary's ghost, namely as a spiritual comforter to her afflicted friend. The ghost spoke in a 'Pathetical and Heavenly manner', and assured Margaret Bargrave that the afflictions she suffered at the hands of her husband were 'Marks of Gods Favour'. Her virtue, patience, and religious devotion would be recognized in heaven.

> One Minute of future Happiness will infinitely reward you for all your Sufferings. For I can never believe, (and claps her Hand upon her Knee, with a great deal of Earnestness, which indeed ran through all her Discourse) that ever God will suffer you to spend all your Days in this Afflicted State: But be assured, that your Afflictions shall leave you, or you them in a short time.[64]

In this author's skilful hands, Mary Veal's ghost articulated hopes of salvation, personal immortality and heavenly reward, as well as undying friendship – all of which had relevance for a wider readership as well as for Margaret Bargrave herself. This was moreover a friendly ghost, and it brought with it a message of divine benevolence, which complemented the shifting religious emphases of prominent theologians. 'If the Eyes of our Faith were as open as the Eyes of our Body', declared the ghost, 'we should see numbers of Angels about us for our Guard'.[65] Defoe's *History and Reality of Apparitions* reflected his optimistic conviction that angels were the most common type of spirit, since 'almost all real Apparitions', he claimed, 'are of friendly and assisting Angels, and come of a kind and beneficent Errand to us'.[66] Defoe would clearly have numbered Mary Veal's ghost among these protecting angels, and his preface reinforced the universality of the account even more clearly. It was intended to confirm that 'there is a Life to come after this' and to inspire reflection

> upon our Past course of Life we have led in the World, That our Time is Short and Uncertain, and that if we would escape the Punishment of the Ungodly, and receive the Reward of the Righteous, which is the laying hold of Eternal Life, we ought for the time to come, to turn to God by a speedy Repentance, ceasing to do Evil and Learning to do Well.[67]

Defoe clearly located the ghost story within the rhetorical canon elaborated by Restoration divines to claim respectability for his tales, and he linked the appearance of ghosts with calls for moral and spiritual reformation. This strategy also characterized *A True Relation*, and publication statistics suggest that it was a successful approach. On the open market *A True Relation* went on to become by far the best-selling version of the affair, and the best-selling ghost story in eighteenth-century England. The text was widely affordable, relatively short and lacking illustration. The typeface was also simple and accessible, with dialogue highlighted in italics, and raw publication figures indicate that the narrative enjoyed a wide and long-lasting appeal. By 1719 it had reached its ninth edition and had already been published around the kingdom in London, Edinburgh and Coventry.

Nonetheless, by 1720, a number of critics suspected that this text served a more sinister purpose. Suspicions were provoked after *A True Relation* was prefixed to Charles Drelincourt's *The Christian's Defence Against the Fears of Death* – the same text that was given a post-mortem recommendation by the ghost of Mary Veal. Drelincourt was a French Protestant minister from Paris who first wrote this text as a devotional aid in his native tongue in the mid-seventeenth century. Marius D'Assigny believed that Drelincourt's advice on how to prepare for, and deal with, death would prove popular across the Channel, and so he translated the text, where it was first published in England in 1675. This book, which was nearly four hundred pages in length, had already run through four English editions before 1705, but it was given a boost by the famous ghost of Mary Veal. After all, who better to comment on the accuracy of Drelincourt's otherworldly speculations than one who had experienced them at first-hand? The revised text, with *A True Relation* acting as preface, subsequently ran through an impressive twenty-two editions before the end of the eighteenth century. The preface claimed that Mary Veal's ghost was 'of Universal Use', and that it was intended to be 'an easie Purchase' to reach the widest possible audience.[68] It seemed to many that the author's true purpose had now been revealed, namely to promote the sale of his own work, and of Charles Drelincourt's devotional text, by exploiting, and perhaps even fabricating, the Canterbury ghost.

Doubtless there was money to be made from this venture, but advertisements of Drelincourt's text at the beginning and end of *A True Relation* only served to intensify suspicion of the author's motives. Critical responses to this publication strategy were often damning. In 1732 *The Universal Spectator* accused the author of *A True Relation* of fabricating the story for his own 'temporal interest and advantage'. In 1734 the same publication reinforced this sceptical stance with the following commentary.

> There is scarce a little Town in all England but has one of these old Female Spirits appertaining to it, who, in her High-Crown Hat ... clean Linnen and a red Petticoat, has been view'd by half the Parish. This Article of Dress is of mighty Concern among some Ghosts; wherefore a skilful and learned Apparition-Writer, in the Preface to Drelincourt on Death, makes a very pious Ghost talk to a Lady upon the important Subject of scowring a Mantua.[69]

The Penny London Post added to this chorus of disapproval in 1726 when it parodied the association of Mary Veal's ghost with *The Christian's Defence*.[70] Despite the fact that both Stephen Gray and Lucy Lukyn had mentioned Drelincourt in their reports of the ghost, and that Margaret Bargrave herself had confirmed her positive opinion of it, *A True Relation*'s blunt advertisement roused suspicions about the truth of the apparition itself. The ghost of Mary Veal had been given its most public expression in *A True Relation*, but as a result it was now branded a 'fabulous legend', designed to create profit for a money-motivated author who prostituted his pen for financial gain.[71]

The construction of *A True Relation* also played an important part in the author's condemnation. His account proved divisive partly because it claimed so convincingly to be an absolute and incontrovertible fact, thereby duping a wide public audience who purchased the narrative with alacrity. The title-page advertised the relation as true, and the preface confirmed that it was 'Matter of Fact, and attended with such Circumstances as may induce any Reasonable Man to believe it'. What is more, the chief witness could hardly be faulted since she was a woman of known virtue, honesty and piety. In contrast to Stephen Gray's account, the author of *A True Relation* left out any evidence that undermined the credibility of Margaret Bargrave's testimony. He ignored the night she spent locked in the cold washhouse, the fever she had contracted, and he made no mention of her previous encounters with ghosts, nor of the contradictory stories 'raised by her Husband and the Beans his companions'.[72]

If these omissions were intended to reinforce the impact of *A True Relation*, they conflicted with increasing demands for the separation of fact from fiction that have already been described. For a number of educated commentators, *A True Relation* blurred these boundaries to an unacceptable degree, both in terms of content but also in form, since the length, detail and literary techniques employed gave the account the air of a short fictional tale, rather than a news report. If written by Defoe, both the timing and the construction of *A True Relation* establish this text as an important bridge between his career as a journalist and political commentator, and his transformation into an accomplished novelist. McKeon's work on the rise of the novel demonstrates that this was in fact no great leap since the relationship between fact and fiction in this inherently mixed genre was highly ambiguous, and it left spaces for ghosts to appear.[73] Furthermore, Lennard Davis posits that a piece of writing can only be deemed fictional 'if there is no resemblance between literature and life'.[74] Just as *A True Relation* presented Mary Veal's appearance in the most realistic way possible, so the essence of the eighteenth-century novel was to present fiction in the most realistic way. *A True Relation*, and Defoe's subsequent work, therefore helped to negotiate a place for ghosts within this new literary form. J. Paul Hunter has described how Defoe's use of the supernatural influenced the pattern of his later novels. In *The Farther Adventures of Robinson Crusoe*, the central character confirmed the ambiguity with which ghosts were conceived in these years. 'I know not to this hour whether there are any such things as real Apparitions, Spectres, or Walking of People after they are dead, or whether there is any Thing in the Stories they tell us of that Kind'.[75] *A True Relation* thus marked an important watershed in the history of ghost beliefs and ghost stories. The form of this narrative and the reactions it provoked helped to shift the genre of ghost stories more decisively into fictional spheres. As a result, this relation eased the assimilation of ghost stories into novels, verse and works of gothic fiction in the later eighteenth century.

Nonetheless, if this work helped to sustain the long-term prominence of ghost stories by relocating them into fictional spaces, this process was gradual and uneven. In the immediate term, *A True Relation* was advertised as, and primarily understood as, a true history. This was explicitly recognized by the correspondence of John Flamsteed, Stephen Gray and John Arbuthnot, and also by public commentaries that protested at *A True Relation*'s perversion of the story through its realistic pretence. Many of these responses make sense if the criticism levelled at the narrative is understood not only against a background of epistemological transition, but also as a series of personal attacks on the author's sales strategy, rather than on the legitimacy of the Canterbury ghost itself.

In 1722 the bookseller Thomas Luckman declared that *A True Relation* was penned 'to answer a lucrative purpose', but his comments were in fact designed to promote a new version of this tale that he was publishing, and that he wished to dissociate from that which had gone before.[76] Luckman's publication was written by one Reverend Payne and it first appeared for sale in 1722. Payne's narrative again demonstrates the flexibility of this particular ghost story as a powerful vehicle of religious instruction. It was published following a personal interview between himself and Margaret Bargrave, which took place seventeen years after the ghost had appeared. In spite of Luckman's protestations, this new tale implicitly recognized the quality of *A True Relation*, and borrowed heavily from its themes and style. The prefatory comment provided by the publisher established the purpose of the text, which was to appropriate Mary Veal's ghost as evidence of God's providential activity – a familiar reason for clergymen to adopt and promote ghost stories. Luckman also included a thorough condemnation of *A True Relation* to establish the credibility of Payne's account, and he insisted that 'The story as prefixed to a former edition of Drelincourt's treatise on death, was a very imperfect, confused, and mutilated one, which the Bookseller had picked up without consulting Mrs Bargrave'. This version, he claimed, had 'made the fact itself to be entirely disbelieved by some, and done no honour to the excellent piece to which it is joined'.[77]

It was true that the author of *A True Relation* had not received his account directly from Margaret Bargrave. Yet when she was asked in 1714 'whether the matters contained in this narrative are true', she replied that, despite one or two circumstances that 'were not described with perfect accuracy', she was generally satisfied that 'all things contained in it … were true as regards the event itself or matters of importance'.[78] This evidence, combined with the fact that Reverend Payne's account differed only in emphasis rather than detail from *A True Relation*, strongly suggests that the credibility of its author was under suspicion, rather than the ghost of Mary Veal. Indeed, in a similar vein to the earlier text, Reverend

Payne's account focused attention on the spiritual message of the ghost, who assured Margaret Bargrave that her afflictions were part of God's plan 'to try and perfect you; for God does not afflict willingly, nor grieve the children of men'.[79] Payne was not the only clergyman who retained support for the Canterbury ghost story. He was joined by esteemed Anglican divine and author George Stanhope, who served as chaplain in ordinary to King William and Queen Mary before his installation as dean of Canterbury in March 1704.[80] Stanhope's belief in Margaret Bargrave's testimony was such that William Veal failed in his attempt to make him disbelieve the story. Veal was reportedly so piqued by Stanhope's attitude 'that when he came to Canterbury to be married by him, that he was married by another'.[81]

Payne's account also showed that the devotional context of ghost stories identified by Restoration theologians still had relevance for eighteenth-century audiences, and his narrative was itself prefaced to a new translation of Drelincourt's *Christian's Defence* in 1766. Indeed the intimate association with Drelincourt may well have provided a respectable context for this ghost story. Drelincourt's pious text aimed 'to promote the Salvation of Souls' by taking the reader through the three stages of natural, spiritual, and eternal death.[82] A series of reassuring passages instructed the reader how to prepare for physical death by leading a righteous life, by regularly contemplating death and by assenting belief in God's providence. The pastoral concern of this devout Protestant minister was also manifested by the series of prayers concluding each chapter, which offered practical guidance on how to deal with the death of a loved one as well as how to contemplate personal mortality.[83]

The explicit link between Mary Veal's ghost and discourses of death and immortality was further witnessed in the preface to the fifth edition of *The Christian's Defence*. In this version, Marius D'Assigny recommended Drelincourt's book as an aid 'to Divines in Funeral Sermons, in Visiting the Sick, the Poor, and Afflicted' and he declared it fit 'to be left as Legacies to surviving Friends at Funerals'.[84] D'Assigny justified the attachment of *A True Relation* by insisting that 'God may condescend that a departing Soul, or its good Angel in its stead, may appear' to 'witness the Happiness of Heaven, the Torments of Hell, and the Immortality of the Soul'.[85] This was precisely the context in which Mary Veal's ghost was configured, and this serious and contemplative accent, emphasized by the author of *A True Relation*, Payne and Drelincourt, gave philosophical validity to this ghost story, and allowed it to function as an important aspect of contemporary mortuary culture.

The Ghosts of Defoe

Ian Bostridge and William Burns have described how the language of supernatu-
ralism was increasingly challenged as an ideological support of Church and State
in the early decades of the eighteenth century.[86] Amidst intense Tory–Whig fac-
tionalism, the literary, poetic and philosophical contexts in which ghosts were
configured grew in significance. Daniel Defoe's *History and Reality of Apparitions*,
written twenty-one years after *A True Relation*, both recognized and catered for
these changing cultural preferences. This lengthy tome was no doubt written for a
very different audience than *A True Relation*, and here Defoe spent two-thirds of
his text simply telling ghost stories. This was a consummate act of empiricism, in
which Defoe employed sheer weight of evidence to verify the existence of spirits.
He described countless ghost stories with Boylean techniques of empirical reportage, evaluating conflicting accounts and judging credibility according to the fame
and credit of the witnesses involved. If this technique added greater legitimacy
to Defoe's endeavour, he was also forced to preface these accounts with complex
metaphysical speculations about the make-up of the spirit world. Whereas *A
True Relation* never challenged the idea that Margaret Bargrave had met with
the returning ghost of Mary Veal, Defoe here drew an important linguistic distic-
tion between *ghost* and *apparition*. He poured scorn upon the very notion of a
ghost, which he claimed was a clumsy, ignorant and doctrinally incorrect term,
which should be substituted with the more sophisticated notion of *apparition*,
or *guardian angel*. Defoe advanced a slight variation on conventional Protestant
definitions of spirits as angels or demons, and he elaborated a third possibility.
Ghosts, or apparitions as he now preferred to term them, were in fact a 'middle-class of spirit' that belonged to a body of 'detach'd angels'. These spirits were
'allow'd to act and appear here, under express and greatly strain'd Limitations'.[87]
Defoe's linguistic discrimination was highly significant, since it reflected a process of social differentiation from which many vulgar ghost stories had suffered
in the opinions of polite society during the early years of the eighteenth century.
In order to preserve an air of respectability (and no doubt to help sales of his
latest book), Defoe insisted that his apparitions were 'not such as are vulgarly
called Ghosts that is to say, departed souls returning again and appearing visibly
on earth'. These spirits were not even what 'our Northern People' called 'a Ghest'.
Instead they were rather 'spirits of a superior and angelick nature'.[88]

As George Starr has rightly commented, Defoe's rejection of ghosts as defined
in the *History and Reality of Apparitions* was more in line with the author's own
dissenting religious convictions.[89] However, it is unwise to conclude from this
that Defoe had simply ceased to believe in ghosts; that he was only now able
to show his true opinions; or that he could never have written *A True Relation*.
It is notoriously difficult to pin down Defoe's own views on ghosts, witches or
any other supernatural phenomena, and his work may well tell us more about

his audience than about the man himself. The *History and Reality of Apparitions* recognized the politico-religious conflicts of its day. The text was relayed in an acceptable, empirical style, and in a distinguished language. It therefore represented an attempt to reclothe ghosts in a more legitimate guise, to render them acceptable to fashionable opinion, and to satisfy the attendant desire for social distinction. Indeed, the book was almost four hundred pages long, hard-bound, and it included a number of quality illustrations. The author gave time and space to complicated, philosophical definitions of apparitions, which were noticeably absent from Defoe's earlier publication. It is not unreasonable to assume therefore that Defoe's target market was likely to have been quite different – well-heeled, and with the purchasing power to splash out on luxury items of literature. Judging by the publication success of the *History and Reality of Apparitions*, Defoe was right to think that a significant audience existed for the consumption of apparition narratives, and his book was reprinted in 1735, 1752, 1770 and 1791. Individual ghost stories from this work were also incorporated into collections of supernatural phenomena well into the nineteenth century.[90]

By following the tenets of Defoe's more formal, less sensational text, respectable readers could indulge a private fascination with apparitions, whilst laying claim to a complex metaphysical conception of the spirit world. Yet, aside from this philosophical change, Defoe's apparitions were almost indistinguishable from the *ghosts* or *ghests* of the vulgar. They could after all 'take up the shape of a living or a dead person', and they were even allowed to assume 'the very cloaths, countenances, and even voices of dead persons'.[91] Defoe's work also supplied a series of images to accompany his reports. His apparitions were, without exception, fleshy and life-like, and they were highly reminiscent of the ghosts met with in cheap printed literature – except perhaps that they wore finer clothes.

What is more, Defoe's new brand of apparition appeared on missions to uphold moral virtue, and to expose sin and wrongdoing. Defoe therefore firmly connected his spirits to the social and religious discourses that were used to explain why ballad and chapbook ghosts materialized. These explanations were also remarkably consistent with the story of Mary Veal's ghost. Defoe recounted the story of an alleged murderer who was forced to confess his crime in court when 'he saw the murther'd person standing upon the step as a witness'.[92] Also included was the apparition of a clergyman who sought to prevent an illicit sexual liaison between a young gentlewoman and a wealthy but disreputable suitor.[93] This apparition was sent to prevent the young lady from prostituting her virtue, and at the close of the narrative Defoe remarked that 'Be it a parable or a history, the moral is the same'.[94] Defoe's justification of his storytelling again highlights significant cross-over between the traditional motifs of early modern ghost stories and the principles of the experimental community. Just as the ghosts of cheap print were authorized by the social and moral purposes for which they appeared, so the credibility of such tales was strengthened by what Simon Schaffer has termed the '*moral probability*' of the events in question.[95]

For Defoe, the ability to prove whether an apparition narrative was based on a real-life event took second place to the moral lessons with which they were infused. It was on this basis that Defoe recommended these tales for serious public contemplation. In a decade that witnessed the collapse of the South Sea Bubble, and which Defoe himself described as tainted by 'usury, extortion, perjury and blood', such lessons seemed very apposite.[96] Defoe's shift of emphasis from the historicity or truth of ghost stories to their moral utility was highly significant. Defoe's emphasis made his work particularly important for easing the transition of ghost stories into new fictional genres over the course of the eighteenth century. According to Defoe, the wider moral and allegorical meaning of ghost stories alone justified their narration. At the close of the *History and Reality of Apparitions*, he therefore insisted 'upon the moral of every story, whatever the fact may be, and to enforce the inference, supposing the story to be real, or whether it be really so or not, which is not much material'.[97] He went on to conclude that it was a guilty conscience that made ghosts walk and, having captured the attention of his learned readers, he interspersed his colourful narratives with forceful commentaries on the evils of social injustice. Defoe railed against corrupt landlords, cheating tradesmen and wealthy oppressors, lamenting that

> tis not a thing of the least concern to us to have the cry of the poor against us, or to have the widows and orphans, who we have injur'd and oppress'd, look up to heaven for relief against us, when they, perhaps have not money to go to law, or to obtain or seek remedy against us in the ordinary way of justice. I had much rather have an unjust Enemy draw his Sword upon me, than an injur'd poor Widow to cry to Heaven for Justice against me; and I think I should have much more Reason to be afraid of the Last than the First, the Effect is most likely to be fatal.[98]

This embittered outburst was reinforced by the words of Job, who declared 'Ye shall not afflict any Widow or Fatherless Child: If thou afflict them in any wise, and they cry at all unto me, I will surely hear their Cry'.[99] At the end of this diatribe Defoe apologized for his digression, promised not to do it again, and continued with his respectable explications. This passage clearly identified Defoe's intended audience as landlords, employers and the governing classes, who Defoe believed were neglecting their duty of Christian charity to those less fortunate than themselves. Ghost stories and/or apparition narratives were thus timely reminders of the consequences of moral corruption, and Defoe clearly approved of the way they were used to regulate social abuses.

By positioning moral virtue at the centre of his preternatural tales, Defoe's work foreshadowed the commentaries of men like Joseph Addison and Richard Steele who preserved the legitimacy of some ghost stories by linking them to the ethical standards of civil society and to gentlemanly values. Defoe's *History and Reality of Apparitions* thus furnishes a valuable example of how ghost stories could retain relevance in polite society if they were packaged in the right way. The publication success of this text testified to the continuing appeal of ghosts or apparitions to the learned imagination, while also identifying the increasing division between the acceptable and unacceptable face of ghost stories that was largely defined by the social location of knowledge about the preternatural world.

Conclusion

Responses to the ghost of Mary Veal highlight the relevance that ghost stories retained in local contexts and also in wider public discourse in the first half of the eighteenth century. Stephen Gray's application of experimental principles to the puzzle of Mary Veal's ghost represented a conscious search for a new, non-partisan way of writing about such phenomena. Yet his conclusions also register important affiliations between ghost stories and the networks of the new science. This Canterbury tale underlined the fact that the most reliable source of knowledge about ghost stories existed at grass roots level, with those who were acquainted with the main protagonists, and for whom the purpose and timing of the ghost made most sense. For John Flamsteed and Stephen Gray the local community held the key to the authenticity of Mary Veal's ghost. This community knew the ins and outs of Margaret Bargrave's affairs and character, and they were thus able to determine the credibility of her testimony. The story also implicitly affirmed the authority of traditional ghost lore and oral report, although they had to be mediated by more eminent supporters to gain wider acceptance. Nonetheless, this episode reveals considerable overlap in styles of authentication between the parishioners of St Mary Bredin and the fellows of the Royal Society. Furthermore, the corroboration of Mary Veal's ghost through experiment, first-hand testimony and reliable witnessing – the key facets of empirical enquiry – underlines the fact that John Flamsteed and Stephen Gray were figuring themselves as practitioners of Enlightenment ideals. As Jonathan Barry has eloquently demonstrated in his explorations of eighteenth-century Bristol, empirical discourse was sufficiently flexible to lend support to preternatural beliefs, alongside more tangible natural phenomena.[100] The story of Mary Veal's ghost also identifies ghost stories as important vehicles for addressing the issues of marginalized groups in early modern England. This was particularly true for women, both married and unmarried, and from a wide spectrum of social backgrounds. Margaret Bargrave's testimony showed that women were able to manipulate widespread belief in the providential meaning of ghosts to expose the often turbulent nature of gender relations, to contest mistreatment and abuse at the hands of men and to inflict punishment on those who transgressed the accepted boundaries of the moral and Christian communities. Ghost stories must then be recognized as important narrative strategies whereby women could assert power and authority. The fascination provoked by Mary Veal's ghost also had the potential to connect local and national cultures. It is only by acknowledging widespread belief in the existence of ghosts that we can understand how the domestic trials of a Canterbury housewife came to attract such illustrious attention. Widespread curiosity about the workings of the invisible world thus enabled Margaret Bargrave's story to participate in important cultural and intellectual debates surrounding the reality of ghosts and the configuration of ghost stories as true histories or fictions.

Nonetheless, the career of John Arbuthnot most clearly illustrates the increasingly problematic interpenetration of private and public narratives surrounding ghosts. Arbuthnot's private letter to John Flamsteed admitted the possibility that Margaret Bargrave really had met with Mary Veal's ghost. It also established Arbuthnot's own curiosity about the event. Furthermore, the sale catalogue of Arbuthnot's personal library that was printed after his death in 1779 supplies further evidence that Arbuthnot may have been motivated in his enquiries by a private fascination with ghosts. The catalogue included the 1605 translation of Pierre Le Loyer's *Treatise of Spectres*, Lyttleton's *Dialogues of the Dead* and William Sherlock's *On a Future State*.[101] Moreover, as the following chapter details, Arbuthnot's interest in ghost stories may have been strengthened by his philosophical pursuits, and particularly by his interest in environmental pathogens.[102] There is, however, strong evidence that Arbuthnot did not wish to broadcast his views in public. He promised not to give copies of Flamsteed's letters to any person, nor would they be published by his authorization. Arbuthnot here signified a desire to keep this communication strictly behind closed doors. Arbuthnot's private curiosity about ghost stories was difficult to spot, since it contrasted quite markedly with his satirical appropriation of ghost stories in a political squib of 1712 entitled *The Story of the St. Albans Ghost, or the Apparition of Mother Haggy*.[103] The ghost story could thus be configured both as a satirical joke and as objective reality, even from the same pen. Arbuthnot's example therefore typifies an important discrepancy between the apparent scepticism surrounding ghost stories that surfaced in the world of letters, and the nature of private, individual belief.

The chorus of scornful commentaries about preternatural tales, and particularly *A True Relation*, must be attributed in some degree to the epistemological crisis which was taking place in England at the turn of the eighteenth century. Michael McKeon has rightly identified in these years a 'major cultural transition in attitudes toward how to tell the truth in narrative'.[104] By transgressing the boundaries between the realms of fiction, journalism and empiricism, *A True Relation* highlighted the instability of these categories, and consequentially proved controversial. However, the partial disjuncture between public discourse and private conviction identified above provides a more convincing explanation for the seeming paradox that *A True Relation* and the *History and Reality of*

Apparitions were commercially successful in a sea of consumer scepticism. These texts indicate that between the extremes of intense credulity and utter denial of the credibility of ghost stories there lay a middle ground of interest that has been largely overlooked. Defoe appealed to this middle ground by altering the vocabulary of ghost stories, and by sketching his apparition narratives in the language of empiricism. Defoe also downplayed the reality of ghost stories, and instead emphasized the moral and philosophical value of these narratives, which ensured that his writing retained appeal for respectable audiences. It was still feasible then to justify the telling of ghost stories in public life, if they were framed in acceptable ways. More crucially for the long-term fate of ghost stories however, Defoe's writing played a prominent role in the gradual shift of these tales into more firmly defined fictional spaces. This process had important implications for the way in which ghost stories would be presented to eighteenth-century audiences, and inevitably for the ways in which they would be perceived. However, this process of fictionalization was slow and patchy. The following chapter will illustrate that ghost stories refused to be easily defined in the first half of the eighteenth century. Discussions surrounding the nature of ghosts and the meanings to be taken from them continued to form hot topics of debate for natural philosophers, social commentators, poets and novelists alike.

4 GHOST STORIES IN THE PERIODICAL PRESS, *c.* 1700–*c.* 1750

Broadening out from our Canterbury haunting, this chapter examines how ghosts were represented in one of the fastest-growing print media of the eighteenth century – namely the periodical. My spotlight falls on this burgeoning set of publications in the first half of the eighteenth century for a number of reasons. First, periodicals differed in both content and style from the sermons, treatises, ballads and chapbooks looked at so far. Periodicals offered news items, official statistics and bills of mortality, but they were also accompanied by topical essays, reviews, articles and poems that spoke to new trends in economic, social and cultural life. This eclectic content was sometimes copied from other publications, or it was produced by the editors of these publications. For the most part, however, it was supplied by loyal readers and occasional correspondents, who used the periodical as an open forum for cultural and intellectual debate. This mixed mode of production constituted what Michael MacDonald and Terence Murphy have termed 'a kind of collective popular literature' that reflected a wide variety of cultural practices, attitudes and beliefs.[1] Periodicals were priced cheaply at one penny, and they were available at daily, weekly and monthly intervals. As such, periodicals offered a unique space in which ideas and information could be rapidly and regularly exchanged, and where the burning issues of the day could be discussed, digested and disputed. This literary genre also connected readers in both the metropolis and the provinces. The broad geographical spread of periodicals, combined with their periodicity and dynamic mode of production, forged a new sense of intimacy and common identity among a diverse set of readers.

This sense of intimacy and identity was further heightened by the role assumed by editors such as Joseph Addison, Richard Steele and Edward Cave, who were respectively the editors of the *Spectator*, *Tatler* and the *Gentleman's Magazine*. These men did not simply reproduce the views of their readers, but they actively sought to shape them. These publications were therefore tools of social and educational instruction as well as sources of entertainment. They kept readers up-to-date with the latest advances in natural philosophy and literature, whilst usefully suggesting how readers should respond to them. Periodicals thus created an identity of interests among readers, and they helped to define acceptable norms of behaviour, lifestyles and attitudes that permeated polite society. This advice was of course more readily available to those people who had the money and the time to keep abreast of intellectual trends, literature and the arts. Through the pages of periodicals, readers were given the vocabulary with which to engage in debate about politics, art or theatre, and in so doing they were able to distinguish their superior taste from the coarse opinions of the less educated.

Historians are agreed that periodicals commanded great authority over their readers, so did ghost beliefs and ghost stories complement or compromise the cultural sensibilities expressed therein? The answer is of course a mixture of both. Readers were presented, for example, with new challenges to the authenticity of ghost stories by reports of the latest advances in optical research. The drive for social distinction which was implicit in the periodical genre meant that the sensationalized ghost stories of cheap print were increasingly rejected due to the lowly status of their authors. This is, however, a story of endurance and adaptation as well as erosion. Periodicals subjected ghost stories and ghost beliefs to a process of refinement but not to outright rejection. Ghost stories appeared in these publications at frequent intervals in these years because they fed into a number of important cultural debates. These included the nature of the soul and its post-mortem location, the survival of individual personality in the afterlife, epistemological contests between ancient philosophy and modern empiricism and the continuing debate about how far human reason could supplant revelation as the guiding principle of religious life. Periodicals emphasized the patchy acceptance of purely naturalistic explanations of the world by printing, and often promoting, intellectual counter-currents. The historical correlation between enlightenment and the anti-marvellous will also be qualified by illustrating the role played by ghost stories in the periodical press. It will become clear in the following pages that ghost stories made a very real contribution to developments in natural philosophy and medicine.[2] Ghosts also featured prominently in more pessimistic, poetic reflections on the fragility of human life, and the decay of the natural world. As James Carson suggests, the concept of 'enlightenment' itself must be expanded to incorporate those urges to illuminate phenomena that sat on the margins of human knowledge and included such topics as 'ventriloquism, somnambulism ... and reanimation of the dead'.[3] Periodicals therefore offered a varied menu of conceptual models and epistemological frameworks that allowed for both the authentication and rejection of ghost stories.

This chapter is divided into three main sections, and it will examine three different types of periodical: interactive periodicals, essay periodicals and general periodicals or magazines. This is intended to reflect the evolving format of the periodical genre, and to incorporate a sense of chronological change. The wide circulation of periodical literature in these years will be an important focus, along with the practical challenges that faced the print industry, and which shaped the content of its products. Finally, regional periodicals will be contrasted with those produced in London to highlight the geographical diversity of reactions to ghost stories.

The Interactive Periodical

Chapter 1 described how John Dunton's *Athenian Mercury* became one of the most successful early periodicals. It was also the first to introduce a question and answer format to address the interests and to resolve the anxieties of its readers. The *Mercury*'s content was based around the contributions of its audience, but it was also shaped by processes of editorial selection, which were no doubt dictated by the commercial marketplace of print. A chief editor who was renowned for producing titillating and sometimes salacious material may well have prioritized sensational and entertaining topics over more mundane queries.[4] Nevertheless, the interactive style of the *Mercury* still promoted more dynamic participation from its audience than any of the other periodical types that feature in this chapter. Little or no space was given over to editorials, essays, poetry or financial news in the *Mercury*. Its interactive voice was in fact less tied to the news content of the publication than most periodicals and magazines have been up to the present day. As Janice Winship points out, twentieth-century women's magazines encouraged the mutual exchange of ideas and interests, but the terms of this communication were largely shaped by the magazines themselves, and by the dictates of genre. The eighteenth-century periodical genre was only formalized after the Stamp Acts of 1712 and 1724, long after the *Athenian Mercury* had ceased publication.[5] The *Mercury*'s readers were not just readers. They were also producers, who enjoyed greater freedom to pose metaphysical questions about the existence and nature of God, and about the mysteries of the invisible world. As a result, ghost stories and queries about the make-up of the preternatural world were especially prominent here. Ghost stories also featured heavily in spin-off publications such as the *Athenian Oracle*, which ran through four volumes in the first decade of the eighteenth century. Readers of the *British Apollo*, another interactive-style periodical, were similarly confused about the precise nature of the afterlife. In submitting such queries to the *Mercury* and the *Apollo*, periodical readers were engaging with very topical issues. The fate of body and soul beyond the grave was a subject that preoccupied both divines and educated laymen in the late seventeenth and early eighteenth centuries. They were prompted to speculate about these subjects by unorthodox descriptions of the last day, and diverse topographies of the afterlife, which drew on natural philosophy to challenge accepted biblical traditions about eternal life and the end of the world.[6]

The case of John Asgill illustrates the contentious nature of these theological dilemmas at the turn of the eighteenth century. In 1700, Asgill, an MP, lawyer and amateur theologian, anonymously published an eccentric tract entitled *An Argument Proving, that According to the Covenant of Eternal Life Revealed in the Scriptures, Man may be Translated from Hence into that Eternal Life, Without Passing Through Death*. Asgill applied empirical principles to his study of scripture, and he surmised that there was no consistent biblical law dictating the inevitability of death. He argued that the mortality regime which dominated contemporary thought had not reigned supreme before Adam's transgression in the Garden of Eden. As a result, the 'Legal Power of Death' had been satisfied by Christ's sacrifice on the cross.[7] Within Asgill's novel schema there was no place between death and resurrection, and no notion of the soul's immortality. It is no surprise then that it was condemned. The same fate awaited Henry Dodwell's 1706 *Epistolary Discourse, Proving, from the Scriptures and the First Fathers, that the Soul is a Principle Naturally Mortal*. Dodwell contended that humans had forfeited immortality after the Fall, but this notion was scorned by a host of philosophers including Thomas Milles, Samuel Clarke and John Norris.[8] Besides these specific rebuttals of Dodwell's treatise, Lawrence Smith, Catharine Trotter, James Taylor and William Reeves all went on record in the first decade of the century to defend established notions of immortality and resurrection. Joseph Addison also reiterated his belief that the promise of future rewards and punishments was 'the Basis of Morality, and the Source of all pleasing Hopes and secret Joys'. Addison's interjection confirmed that preoccupations with post-mortem existence extended beyond a narrow theological sphere.[9]

Unseen things in general and the concept of ghosts in particular were useful for defenders of resurrection theology. These men came out in force following the radical claims of John Locke and the third Earl of Shaftesbury that the soul, and therefore personal identity, was separable from the human body.[10] Humphry Hody spoke for a number of divines and philosophers when he rebutted Locke's claims, and insisted instead upon the material re-embodiment of the soul after death. Hody's 1694 *Resurrection of the Same Body* voiced a highly materialistic conception of the post-mortem state, and a short tract written by an anonymous 'Divine of the Church of England' in 1706 went a step further. Christian teaching on the soul's immortality and the resurrection of the flesh was, he argued, 'evident and consequential upon the Truth of Apparitions'.[11] By 'apparitions' this author made it clear that he was referring to 'souls departed'. These spirits were not only able to appear amongst the living, but they actively wished to do so since they retained an emotional connection with those they had left behind. This divine dismissed the scriptural objection from Revelation 14:13 that blessed souls were at rest. Although they were freed from their labours and sorrows, he argued, they did not rest 'from their *Duty* and *Service*'.[12] But he did make some concession to orthodox Protestant teaching about spirits. Departed souls were seen as analogous to ministering angels, and they were sent forth by God to assist those who would be saved.[13] This tract clearly had rhetorical intent, but it also continued a well-established body of literature and philosophy, both ancient and modern, that insisted on the materiality of resurrected bodies.[14] According to this particular author, the promise of immortality and resurrection was most forcefully articulated in the modern age through the figure of the ghost. As such, ghosts provided unique visual and imaginative assurances of the continuation of personal identity after death. Ghost stories thus sat at the crux of a range of contemporary theological, philosophical and cultural discussions about mortality, immortality, resurrection and identity. Queries to periodicals about if, how and in what circumstances ghosts might return from the dead must then be seen as important manifestations of these broader debates.

In January 1709 the *British Apollo* printed a question from a gentleman who identified himself only as 'E. G.' He wanted to know 'if 'tis Possible for a Soul once Imparadis'd in Heaven to Return again to it's Body, and dwell again on this Earth'.[15] It is unclear whether E. G. favoured the concept of an animated spirit world, and the response that he received was similarly non-committal. The *Apollo's* respondents admitted the possibility that souls may return to earth, but they cautiously set out the reasons why this might not take place. The editors of the *Apollo* were interrogated more rigorously in May 1708 by a correspondent who enquired about the whereabouts of deceased souls. The editors had denied any agency to departed souls, which the correspondent claimed was a direct contradiction of 'the Ancient Fathers, Origen, St. Hilarie-Victorinus Martyr, Novatianus and St. Augustin' to name just a few.[16] The *Apollo* dismissed this correspondent's reliance on ancient authorities, which they claimed were far from infallible. The contest between the authorities of the ancients and moderns was a recurrent debate running throughout the periodical literature of the early eighteenth century. The outcome of this clash would have serious implications for the credibility of ghost stories, which were so often endorsed because of scriptural and classical precedents for the reappearance of departed souls.

If the *British Apollo* appeared to mistrust ancient authorities, the *Review* offered a more optimistic perspective. The *Review* borrowed from the successful format of the *Athenian Mercury* by introducing a question and answer section for correspondents to express opinion. This proved so successful that a regular supplement, *Advice from the Scandalous Club*, was founded to respond to the enthusiastic influx of letters in greater length and detail. The third issue, published in November 1704, dealt with the question of 'Whether there be any other Beings besides matter?'.[17] This query was one of a number of similar questions received by the *Review* concerning the distinction between body and soul, the nature and location of the spirit world and the existence or location of heaven, hell or some other middle place. The *Review's* response came perhaps from Daniel Defoe, who was chief editor at this time and who, as we already know, maintained a healthy interest in ghosts during his career. 'Our Converse with the World of Spirits', declared the editor, 'is a thing in our Opinion very certain and if farther search'd into, might serve very much to illuminate this Affair'. The doctrine of spirits, he claimed, 'demonstrated much of a future Existence, and perhaps might discover a great many Niceties we are not yet Masters of'.[18] This encouragement to study the workings of the spirit world echoed the endeavours of those natural philosophers and intellectuals encountered in Chapter 1, who saw the work of the Almighty carried out by ghostly appearances. The reality of a world of spirits appeared to give comfort to a number of the *Review*'s readers who displayed anxiety and doubt about the immortality of the soul. 'If there is a World of Spirits' argued the editor, 'if there are Discoveries made of a Conversation between Spirit Embodied, and Spirit Uncas'd; if there are Appearances from that Enlightned State, then the Spirit lives after the Prison is broke; and the Case of Flesh and Blood being laid down, the Soul is yet a Being'.[19] The questioning of an immortal state, and the confused status of body and soul emphasized by readers of the *Review* were persistent themes in the intellectual and theological debates of the first half of the eighteenth century. The *Review*'s editor clearly thought these reflections were symptomatic of growing currents of scepticism about preternatural phenomena. But, in contrast to the *British Apollo*, he railed against those who refused to believe anything that they could not verify for themselves. Turning the tables on the doubters, the editor threw down a challenge to those who wished to prove his philosophy wrong. If there was no immortal state, if there were no such things as ghosts, then let the sceptics resolve 'what is the meaning of Visions, Foresight, Forebodings of Evil or Good, and whence such things come; if not from some Sympathetick Influence of Spirit unembodied'?[20]

Illusions and Delusions

Eighteenth-century England witnessed a whole series of responses to this challenge. In natural philosophy, medicine and the fine arts, the term 'enlightenment' had both metaphorical and literal meaning. In its metaphorical sense, 'enlightenment' referred to any number of attempts to shed light on previously unknown qualities of the natural and spiritual worlds. This intellectual fervour inspired attempts to categorize ambiguous or shadowy substances, to make visible the invisible and thereby dispel the darkness of human ignorance. The uncertain status of ghosts was therefore a problem to be solved. Robert Boyle and Joseph Glanvill began the empirical drive to gain greater knowledge of ghosts, and enquiries into the essence of preternatural phenomena continued apace in the early eighteenth century, with the aid of important new technologies that enhanced the physical act of seeing. The publication of Newton's *Opticks* in 1704 accelerated the prioritization of visual knowledge among natural philosophers, who described the eye as a 'noble organ' whose workings were to be revered.[21] Newton's work was groundbreaking. He laid bare the mechanical workings of the inner eye, and described how myriad images could be produced by reflections and refractions of light. Advances in optical technology were doubtless encouraged by Newton's work, and a range of specialist equipment became increasingly available to consumers, ranging from reflecting and refracting telescopes, to microscopes and spectacles. Astronomers made particularly effective use of these new instruments and in 1738 professor of astronomy Robert Smith published his *Compleat System of Opticks*. In this text Smith described experiments with glasses, light and shadow, and he gave a technical explanation for double vision.[22] We have seen that astronomer royal John Flamsteed headed investigations into the ghost of Mary Veal, and his interest in the case may have been strengthened by the optical instruments installed in the new Royal Observatory at Greenwich, which effectively reduced the cognitive gap between the celestial and the terrestrial.

Greater awareness of the properties of vision also highlighted its distortions and defects, which had a significant and largely negative impact on the credibility of ghost stories. For many empiricists, substance and bodies had acquired a new transparency. They were less an organic entity in flux between the natural and preternatural worlds than an 'abstract arrangement of light and colors'.[23] In *A Sketch of Opticks*, topographer John Donovan noted the 'uncertain information' given by his eyes, and he marvelled at the 'astonishing appearances' that could be produced by looking-glasses and strategically placed mirrors.[24] Robert Smith also described for his readers how bodies could be distorted and made to appear transparent 'by applying any substance to a hole, through which some light is immitted into a dark room'.[25] This experiment was refined over the course of the eighteenth century, and it eventually had important implications for the faking of ghostly appearances, to which I will return. Reported sightings of ghosts could now be dismissed as optical illusions or tricks of the eye. This was especially so, argues Barbara Maria Stafford, because eighteenth-century England was obsessed with the visual. As a result, the evidence of the eyes was increasingly associated 'with falsification', and with the creation of 'fraudulent apparitions'.[26] Philosophers could now look under the skin, inside the human body and the mind. In so doing they discovered a new set of reasons, and indeed a new vocabulary with which to deny, or at least complicate, the existence of ghosts.

The Essay Periodical

The visualization of knowledge outlined above was not restricted to the laboratory or observatory. In fact, a wide range of publications disseminated information about optics to a large audience. Some of these texts were more penetrable than others. John Shuttleworth's *Treatise of Opticks*, for example, was written in accessible language, but it included a number of complex mathematical diagrams to illustrate his explanations. *The Young Gentleman's Opticks*, written by Edward Wells, was more modestly sized, and it contained a more comprehensible explanation of optics. Both texts discussed the several defects of sight, and they introduced readers to theories of double vision, transparency, illusion and to instruments of correction such as microscopes, telescopes and spectacles.[27] Spectacles or 'visual glasses' could now be purchased from specialist shops like 'The Archimedes and one Pair of Golden Spectacles', which was run by George Sterrop in St Paul's Churchyard, London. Visual aids became more technically sophisticated, more widely available and more affordable than ever before.[28]

The title of Edward Wells's text suggests that the principles of optics were now an important component in the educational repertoire of every educated young man. Joseph Addison reinforced this sentiment in 1721, when he discussed 'the discoveries they have made by glasses'.[29] There was now no excuse to be deceived by optical illusions for those who could afford it. Given the link between optical knowledge and the credibility of ghost stories, Addison's views were particularly important because he was chief editor of the *Spectator* – one of the most successful periodicals of the century. Three thousand copies were published in 1712, and by 1767 the copyright value of the *Spectator* was estimated at a prodigious sum of £1,300. Addison's biographer Peter Smithers concluded that this publication enjoyed 'a fame and popularity unknown to any former periodical publication'.[30] The *Spectator*, along with other essay periodicals like the *Tatler*, was concerned to mould the manners, morals and tastes of its readers. In so doing, it continued the reforming tendency of earlier publications like the *Athenian Mercury*, but it aimed at a more exclusive audience. The *Spectator* included features on opera, theatre, contemporary literature and book reviews, which mainly appealed to the leisured classes who had the time and resources to keep up with these pursuits. Elements of direct reader participation were more limited here, as the editorial essay came to supplant the question and answer format that had proved so successful in the *Athenian Mercury*. Joseph Addison thus had considerable power to shape the content of this serial publication, and the opinions of his readers. Samuel Johnson recommended that 'Whoever wishes to attain an English style, familiar, but not coarse, and elegant, but not ostentatious, must give his days and nights to the volumes of Addison'.[31] Dudley Ryder openly confessed that he read the *Spectator* 'to improve my style and manner of thinking'.[32] Familiarity with the *Spectator* therefore served as a tool of social distinction.[33]

On Thursday, 8 March 1711, the *Spectator* ran the story of an 'Antiquated *Sybil*' who was 'always seeing Apparitions, and hearing Death-watches'. Joseph Addison claimed that she gained an audience by playing on 'the Horrour with which we entertain the Thoughts of Death (or indeed of any future Evil) and the Uncertainty of its Approach'. Addison drew on the language of lunacy in condemning this idle talk, and he argued that an 'old Maid, that is troubled with the

Vapours' was particularly wont to indulge this dangerous habit of storytelling. These musings were believed to damage the nerves of people with a sensitive disposition or 'melancholy Mind', who were distressed by tales of returning ghosts.[34] The link between ghost stories and melancholy had a long rhetorical history, but the discovery of the nervous system in the eighteenth century gave medical legitimacy to this stereotype for the first time. Thomas Willis coined the term 'neurology' in the late seventeenth century, and he also formulated 'a doctrine of weak or unhealthy nerves'. Willis was later succeeded by Scottish physicians Robert Whytt and George Cheyne, who specialized in 'internal medicine', that is to say in psychological disorders and delusions caused by frayed nerves.[35] The tendency for children to believe wholeheartedly in ghosts could also be explained in neurological terms, because their tender nerves were easily excited. The physiological make-up of children was perceived to make them more susceptible to terrifying stories. Here then was the medical corollary of John Locke's theory of social conditioning. The practice of nursemaids telling ghost stories to their young charges was rejected on the grounds that children were unable to distinguish truth from fiction. As a result they would be susceptible to credulous beliefs as adults.

The physician A. F. Sticotti further reinforced the idea that females, especially old ones, were particularly prone to believe in ghosts. The fantastical and the imaginary, he argued, governed women because 'they are not occupied with anything solid'.[36] The Parisian physician Samuel Tissot underlined these conclusions still further, by positing that women 'were plagued by a hypersensibility'. They also suffered from 'the vapors', which led their minds to imagine 'chimeras at every instant'.[37] Newton's work on optics reported that 'the humours of the Eye by old Age decay', so that the object in view would almost certainly 'appear confused'.[38] And in 1753 the author of *Observations On the Use of Spectacles* wondered 'how forlorn' the latter part of life might prove 'unless Spectacles were at Hand to help our Eyes'.[39] It is little wonder then that the credibility and testimony of old women was frequently regarded with suspicion and disbelief. In many ways, the leading lights of enlightened philosophy reified traditional stereotypes of credulous people, and they provided a new vocabulary with which to marginalize them, and to attack ghost stories. In 1711 Joseph Addison reinforced these tropes still further. His fictional character Sir Roger de Coverley was amused by his servants and aged mother who believed that his country estate was haunted. Sir Roger represented the ideal of gentility recommended by the *Spectator*, and it was he who finally 'dissipated the Fears which had so long reigned in the Family' by employing his chaplain to exorcize the supposed ghost.[40] Thanks to Addison, readers of the *Spectator* were familiar with advances in natural philosophy and medicine. These developments gave readers the tools with which to distinguish their ideas about ghosts from the vulgar expressions of the multitude.

Pleasures of the Imagination

Despite vocalizing distaste for certain kinds of ghost stories, the *Spectator* did not dismiss them out of hand. In fact Joseph Addison confessed that 'we are sure, in general there are many Intellectual Beings in the World besides our selves, and several Species of Spirits'. To prove his point he called on the 'general Testimony of mankind', and upon classical philosophers such as Lucretius who expressed certainty that 'Men have often appeared after their Death'.[41] Reference to ancient texts was a well-established method of defending ghost stories, but at the time of writing it usefully illustrates the mixture of epistemological authorities that were credited in polite society. Historians have often underestimated the reverence with which classical and scriptural texts were viewed in the eighteenth century, preferring instead to focus on emerging empirical research. In fact this body of literature continued to form the core of gentlemanly learning and pedagogy.[42] Joseph Addison held the classics in great admiration, and he recommended them to his readers, artfully blending traditional modes of thought with up-to-the-minute intellectual trends.

It was partly due to this reverence that Addison constructed moral scaffolding to legitimate the circulation of ghost stories in the *Spectator*. On Wednesday, 13 June 1711, Addison warned his readers against 'a continued Course of Voluptuousness' or an indulgence of worldly passions. Such traits did not fit with the gentlemanly ideal constructed by the *Spectator*, and they also had negative long-term consequences. When 'obscene passions' are indulged by the mortal body, wrote Addison, 'they cleave to her inseparably, and remain in her for ever after the Body is cast off and thrown aside'. 'It is for this Reason', he continued, 'that the Souls of the Dead appear frequently in Coemitaries, and hover about the Places where their Bodies are buried, as still hankering after their old brutal Pleasures, and desiring again to enter the Body that gave them an Opportunity of fulfilling them'.[43] Addison believed that the prospect of a restless soul that was unable to find peace after death was the most effectual vision to extinguish immoral passions. Visions of ghosts were therefore invoked to assist in the shaping of polite moral conduct. The *Tatler* appropriated ghost stories in a similar way, and it was published by Addison's great friend and collaborator Richard Steele. On 30 March 1710, an article described the voyage of Ulysses to 'the Regions of the Dead', where he encountered 'a prodigious Assembly of Ghosts of all Ages and Conditions'. The author described the physical and moral deformities of these ghosts in great detail to provide a lesson 'for the Amendment of the Living'. One ghost, for example, told how he had broken his neck 'in a Debauch of Wine'. This was used 'to inspire the Reader with a Detestation of Drunkenness', and to deter his audience from indulging in similar social evils.[44] Although the author was not telling a ghost story comparable to that of Mary Veal, he recognized that the idea of ghosts could intersect with the priorities of polite literature when firmly allied to the concerns of daily life and supported by a respected authority. The encouragement of human morality was necessary for the smooth functioning of social life, and this was a principle to which Steele and Addison were particularly attached. Addison censured the sceptics by declaring that 'If any Man think these Facts incredible let him enjoy his Opinion to himself, but let him not endeavour to disturb the Belief of others, who by Instances of this Nature are excited to the Study of Virtue'.[45] Both Addison and Steele believed that it was for the public and personal good that ghost stories were preserved as moral exemplars. With this in mind, Addison believed that 'a Person who is thus terrify'd with the Imagination of Ghosts and Spectres' was 'much more reasonable, than one who contrary to the Reports of all Historians sacred and prophane, ancient and modern, and to the Traditions of all Nations, thinks the Appearance of Spirits fabulous and groundless'.[46] Addison's arguments provide a useful reminder of the moderate path that the *Spectator* steered between extreme credulity and extreme scepticism. Accusations of atheism and vain frivolity were just as damaging as those of enthusiasm, and the sensible reader should seek to avoid both by a sensible engagement with ghost stories.

The syncretism of empirical and customary paths to truth was, moreover, part of a wider social vision shared by groups like the 'Scriblerians'. This collection of literary masters featured some of the most celebrated writers of the age, including John Arbuthnot, Jonathan Swift, Robert Harley and Alexander Pope. Through parodies and satires published under the fictional name of 'Martin Scriblerius', these men took it upon themselves to condemn the kind of narrow mentality that took the application of reason to unreasonable lengths by converting 'every trifle into a serious thing' and reducing all to system.[47] In 1722 *The Universal Library: or Compleat Summary of Science* similarly deplored the 'Misbelief' and 'Vanity' that had served to 'put out the inward Eyes' of the intellect. It went on to outline an organic theory whereby a combination of bodily moisture and 'appearing Affections' allowed departed souls to return to earth.[48]

Preternatural Poetry

The *Tatler* and the *Spectator* used ghost stories to check the extremes of natural philosophy, atheism and deism. They were also employed in support of correct moral conduct, but these publications placed them at the centre of new aesthetic and imaginative pleasures. Medical explorations inside the cavities of body and brain were mirrored in the fine arts and literature by the discovery of interiority, and by growing awareness of the unconscious mind. The brain was increasingly identified as the seat of human knowledge, behaviour and feeling. As a result, artists, poets and prose writers now sought to stimulate human passions, not through coarse bodily pleasures, but by stirring the pleasures of the imagination.

The fleshy, bloody and real-life ghosts of chapbook fame were thus dismissed by essay periodicals, and ghosts were relocated to the internal space of the imagination.

In March 1710 Richard Steele's *Tatler* began its thrice-weekly issue by reflecting that 'A Man who confines his Speculations to the Time present, has but a very narrow Province to employ his Thoughts in'.[49] 'For my own Part' it continued, 'I have been always very much delighted with meditating on the Soul's Immortality, and in reading the several Notions which the wisest of Men, both ancient and modern, have entertained on that Subject'.[50] This essay included classical accounts of returning ghosts, and he also cited the following verse from John Dryden to confirm the aesthetic value of the spirit world.

> Ye Realms, yet unreveal'd to human sight,
> Ye Gods, who rule the Regions of the Night,
> Ye gliding Ghosts, permit me to relate
> The mystick Wonders of your silent State.[51]

For the author of this essay, contemplation of 'that Half of Eternity which is still to come' did not characterize a fantastical or unruly mindset, but was instead the mark of an elevated Imagination.[52] Joseph Addison was similarly impressed by the drama that ghost stories created. He regarded them as invaluable tools for the poet because they raised 'a pleasing kind of Horrour in the Mind of the Reader'.[53] John Locke's model of human memory also explained why ghosts tended to fix so firmly in the imagination – because they were associated with the basic human emotions of pleasure or pain. The comments of Addison and Locke anticipated Edmund Burke's 1757 *Philosophical Enquiry into the Origins of our Ideas of the Sublime and Beautiful*, in which he recommended that the mind was regularly exercised with apprehensions of danger and terrifying images. Representations of ghosts in poetry, drama and fiction display clear elements of the 'sublime' as defined by Emma Clery and Robert Miles as 'an apprehension of danger in nature or art without the immediate risk of destruction',[54] or by Edmund Burke as a 'state of the soul, in which all its motions are suspended, with some degree of horror'.[55] The awe, reverence and fear that dramatists and poets aimed to incite in their audiences only worked because the precise ontological status of ghosts was uncertain. As such, ghost stories hovered on the elusive boundary between fact and fiction. The dramatic impact of the fictional ghost would be lost if an audience could not entertain at least the possibility that the dead might be able to return from the grave.

The high quality of verse produced on this topic certainly aimed to provoke such 'sublime' ideas, which were at once pleasurable and painful. Joseph Addison argued that English poets were best suited to producing this kind of verse because 'the English are naturally fanciful, and very often disposed by that gloominess and melancholy of temper, which is so frequent in our nation, to many wild notions and visions'. Indeed 'it is impossible', he continued, 'for a Poet to succeed in this who has not a particular Cast of Fancy, and an Imagination naturally fruitful and superstitious'.[56] Addison here identified a strong native tradition of ghostly fictional writing that owed a debt both to individual belief in the existence of ghosts and to a rich cultural tradition of narratives stretching back through the ages. 'Our forefathers', he wrote, produced an infinite number of these tales, so much so that in former times 'there was not a village in England that had not a ghost in it, the churchyards were all haunted ... and there was scarce a shepherd to be met with who had not seen a spirit'.[57]

Eighteenth-century readers would be familiar with these narrative traditions because they were kept alive 'in legends and fables, antiquated romances' and in the lively oral traditions of 'nurses and old women'.[58] Familiarity with Shakespearean drama was also the epitome of good taste and literary sophistication in these years, and Shakespeare's ghosts came highly commended by Addison. 'There is something so wild and yet so solemn in the speeches of his ghosts', he noted, 'that we cannot forbear thinking them natural ... if there are such beings in the world, it looks highly probable they should talk and act as he has represented them'.[59] Addison admired Shakespeare's ability to engage the superstitious part of his reader's mind, and he praised the 'noble extravagance of fancy' that conjured up such convincing apparitions. There was clearly an element of national pride in Addison's admiration for spectral fiction, and it may be partly due to his public endorsement of this way of writing that ghosts became increasingly prominent in poetry during the course of the eighteenth century.

Joseph Addison admired the solemnity of ghostly soliloquy, and this also influenced the work of the so-called Graveyard School of poetry that rose to prominence in the mid-eighteenth century, which included men like Thomas Gray, Edward Young, Robert Blair, James Hervey and Thomas Parnell. Collectively, the work of these men aestheticized fears of death and of ghosts. They urged readers to embrace the theme of human mortality and to confront the vulnerability of the human condition. Thomas Parnell's 1721 *A Night Piece On Death* invoked the image of a ghost rising from the grave to voice the central message of his poem, crying 'Think, Mortal, what it is to dye' as it burst out from its shallow grave.[60] Parnell was aware of the dramatic impact that this device would have on the imagination of his readers, 'How great a King of Fears am I!' continued the ghost, 'They view me like the last of Things: / They make, and then they dread, my Stings'.[61] In line with the sentiments of the *Tatler* and the *Spectator*, Parnell used this iconic figure to discourage attachment to material wealth and social status, emphasizing a traditional view of death as a social leveller. Parnell, however, clearly disapproved of the emotional attachment with which people regarded ghosts. He forced his revenant into an act of self-denial, and reprimanded the reader for conjuring up spirits of the dead.

Fools! If you less provok'd your Fears
No more my Spectre-Form appears
Death's but a Path that must be trod
If man wou'd ever pass to God.[62]

If Parnell wished to dilute fears of returning ghosts, then James Hervey's *Meditations Among the Tombs* (1756) deliberately nurtured them. Hervey's work presented the vision of a skeletal body bursting from its grave to warn the living of their ultimate fate. Hervey deliberately echoed the words of Samuel's apparition in I Samuel 28. This was the most oft-cited example of a departed spirit return-ing to earth, and the only biblically attested case. Hervey allowed his audience to indulge the possibility that ghosts might be real, and to draw links with the work of Joseph Glanvill and A. L. Moreton (alias Daniel Defoe), who had recounted this example in great detail. Hervey's preface declared that his purpose was simply 'to remind my Readers of their Latter End', and to invite them 'to set, not their Houses only, but, which is inexpressibly more needful, their Souls, in Order'.[63] It is significant that Hervey chose to sting his readers into action by conjuring the vision of a ghost, and this literary device was clearly well considered. The ghost's 'solemn warning, delivered in so striking a Manner must strongly impress my Imagination' claimed Hervey, 'A message in Thunder would scarce sink deeper'.[64]

Warnings to set one's house in order, to renounce the sins of the soul and to give up attachment to the material world were by no means new. In fact, they ech-oed the tradition of the *ars moriendi* literature, which taught early modern men and women how to prepare themselves for death, and how to die well.[65] Similar themes were also prominent in theological works such as Isaac Barrow's *Practical Discourses upon the Consideration of Our Latter End* and Josiah Woodward's *Fair Warnings to a Careless World*.[66] Ghost stories played an important role in Woodward's cosmology. They provided tangible evidence of a future state, while also emphasizing the subordination of the natural world to divine power. Writers of the Graveyard School similarly emphasized the brevity of human life through the medium of ghosts, but they promoted a more secular and aesthetic narrative by neglecting to connect ghosts to specific devotional practices. Robert Blair's evocative poem *The Grave* was littered with descriptions of the wandering dead. 'Light-heel'd ghosts' and 'grisly spectres' were 'Rous'd from their slumbers' to frighten those that passed through Blair's graveyard.[67] The poet's descriptions of ghosts were horrifying. He was revolted by both the vision and the putrid smell of the corpse, leading him to mourn the separation from life and the departed joys that death entailed. In contrast to religious appropriations of ghosts, Blair emphasized emotional attachment to human life. Rather than welcoming death as a passage to heavenly joy, he considered instead that it must 'be an awful thing to die'.[68] Nonetheless, Blair's ghosts also offered psychological comfort by refut-ing the prospect that nothing existed after death. The poet's anxiety about the extirpation of individual personality sustained a terrified fascination with ghosts. This also led him to describe how bodies would be restored to their rightful owners in the afterlife. Blair's poem thus lends support to the cult of individualism identified by Clare Gittings in the eighteenth century, and which was characterized by an emotional affection for the earthly body, and revulsion of death. Lucia Dacome has also identified similar themes in medical and theological debates over re-embodiment, which surfaced in the *Spectator*.[69] More significantly however, the recurring figure of the ghost among the Graveyard poets supports a more fundamental argument advanced by Gittings. In spite of growing knowledge of the natural world and advances in medical wisdom, there was little evidence to suggest that anxiety about death was diminishing.[70]

The aestheticization of ghosts instead indicates that a process of *abjection* may have been underway in these years. Abjection literally means to reject or to cast out, but Julia Kristeva's elaboration of this concept identified the abject as something that elicited negative human reaction – in this case horror, because it reminded people of a sickening or unthinkable reality.[71] The displacement of the human corpse or ghost was a prime example of abjection, because images of decay and dissolution represented traumatic reminders of individual mortality. The treatment of ghosts by the Graveyard poets and in Gothic fictions reminded readers of this inevitability, whilst diluting the harsh reality of death by projecting ghosts into a fictional or imaginative space. The abjection of ghosts was further supported by the epidemiological theories of environmentalists that were similarly characterized by fear and revulsion of the corpse. John Arbuthnot and Robert Boyle were among the first to develop the idea that putrefying dead bodies transmitted dangerous pathogens, and were a major cause of disease.[72] The dead were believed to harm the living both physically and psychologically. Environmentalists therefore drew up plans for the physical separation of the dead through the relocation of burial grounds to the outskirts of towns, and the construction of extramural cemeteries.[73] Despite Philippe Ariès's work on the mortuary culture of this period, it is unlikely that these preventative measures were brought about by a widespread change in attitudes.[74] Ruth Richardson has documented the often violent resistance to the relocation and re-interment of the dead in these years.[75] A more convincing explanation is James Riley's assertion that public health initiatives lay behind proposals to separate the dead from the living.[76] However these ideas came about, they suggest that the physical process of death still incited fear and revulsion on both the conscious and unconscious mind. Theories of miasma, along with the Graveyard School of poetry, thus provide an important counterweight to the general optimism about the human condition associated with Enlightenment philosophies. These themes have been under-explored in the historiography of the eighteenth century. They must, however, be embraced more fully if we are to gain a more rounded understanding of the cultural influences and beliefs that remained current in this period. Certainly the genre of poetry should not be neglected, since poems accounted for 47 per cent of all published literature, making it the most frequently published genre in England by quite some margin.[77] Poems were second only to sermons in terms of distribution and consumption, and they were far more widely available than learned treatises on natural philosophy that more often dismissed the reality of ghosts.

Ghosts on the Stage

On stage, ghostly performances were limited by a growing preference for domestic or natural theatre. The celebrated David Garrick achieved fame by perfecting a more natural style of acting, before he assumed management of the Drury Lane Theatre in 1747. Garrick was one of many who advocated the theatrical depiction of human life. The impulse to limit man's contemplation to the tangible physical world, and to spread realistic representations of life, was characterized by the inclusion of dense circumstantial detail. This emerging tradition of realism also culminated in a new literary genre, which was additionally influenced by the natural philosopher's dogged empiricism. The novel set out to dramatize the mundane episodes of domestic life, and to reduce the cognitive space in which man's imagination could and should usefully function.[78] This genre was exemplified by the work of Samuel Richardson and Henry Fielding, and its success owed much to its appeal among a growing readership of professional people, who appeared to have little time to indulge fascination with the invisible world.

Once again, however, this process of naturalization was incomplete, and it sat alongside a number of artistic counter-currents that sought to restrain the narrow rationalism that was steadily creeping into fictional productions. It was in this context that ghosts retained support from playwrights such as Gabriel Odingsells, from novelists like Henry Fielding, and from the polite periodical.[79] In April 1711, the *Spectator* noted the unique impact that ghosts had on a theatre-going audience, 'A Spectre has very often saved a Play, though he has done nothing but stalked across the Stage, or rose through a Cleft of it, and sunk again without speaking one Word'.[80] The Irish-born actress George Anne Bellamy recognized this important role, and she took care to perfect the art of 'fainting on the appearance of the ghost' since it was something that she was often required to perform to distract audiences during her successful career on the London stage.[81] The effect created by the theatrical ghost was similar to that of the Graveyard poets. Ghosts prompted deep-seated emotional reactions, making 'the Hearts of the whole Audience quake' while conveying 'a stronger Terrour to the Mind than it is possible for Words to do'.[82]

Joseph Addison put his faith in the dramatic potential of ghosts to practical use in 1715 when his play *The Drummer; or, The Haunted-House* was first published.

The play was based on a real-life haunting – the case of the Drummer of Tedworth that was famously investigated by Joseph Glanvill in the 1660s, and was eventually exposed as a fraud. Addison chose this episode carefully, since it allowed him to raise the possibility of spirit activity for his audience without admitting to the reality. As Richard Steele pointed out in 1712, this distinction was an important one since the theatre-going public was made up of two kinds of people, 'those who know no Pleasure but of the Body, and those who improve or command corporeal Pleasures by the Addition of fine Sentiments of the Mind'.[83] Here again was an example of the process of abjection outlined above. This was an art based on suggestion, in which ghosts were projected into safer fictional spaces and specifically linked to aesthetic values. The enjoyment of these tales was no longer a stigma, but instead acted as a badge of social distinction. In Addison's opinion, depictions of ghosts on the stage did not merit opposition, especially 'when they are introduced with Skill, and accompanied by proportionable Sentiments and Expressions in the Writing'.[84] Addison further acknowledged the warm reception given to these fleshy and gratuitous figures when he observed that 'there is nothing which delights and terrifies our English Theatre so much as a Ghost, especially when he appears in a bloody Shirt'.[85]

Henry Fielding voiced similar reasons for including ghosts in his plays. The *Tragedy of Tragedies, or The Life and Death of Tom Thumb the Great*, included a pivotal role for the ghost of Tom's father, Gaffer Thumb, who warned King Arthur to beware the impending rebellion by his subjects. When the King threatened to slay him, Gaffer's ghost was expressly identified as a returning soul from beyond the grave, replying 'I am a Ghost, and am already dead'.[86] Gaffer's ghost was an important plot device, but Fielding also used his appearance to launch a broader defence of theatrical ghosts in a footnote to Gaffer's speech:

> Of all the Particulars in which the modern Stage falls short of the ancient, there is none so much to be lamented, as the great Scarcity of Ghosts in the latter. Whence this proceeds, I will not presume to determine. Some are of opinion, that the Moderns are unequal to that sublime Language which a Ghost ought to speak. One says ludicrously, That Ghosts are out of Fashion; another, That they are properer for Comedy; forgetting, I suppose, that *Aristotle* hath told us, That a Ghost is the Soul of Tragedy.[87]

Fielding's affection for ghosts was based on an attachment to classical authority. This affection was associated with the *Spectator*, *Tatler* and with the Scriblerians, but was also foundational to gentlemanly education. Yet Fielding did not confine his ghosts to the established genre of plays, since he also allowed them to shape his novel writing. In *The History of Tom Jones*, the eponymous hero sought revenge against Ensign Northerton, who had assaulted Tom with a glass bottle. Tom was left half-dead with blood pouring from his head, and when he ventured out after midnight, Fielding gave his hero the following description:

He had on, as we have said, a light-coloured Coat, covered with Streams of Blood. His Face, which missed that very Blood, as well as twenty Ounces more drawn from him by the Surgeon, was pallid. Round his Head was a Quantity of Bandage, not unlike a Turban. In the right Hand he carried a Sword, and in the left a Candle. So that the Bloody *Banquo* was not worthy to be compared to him. In Fact, I believe a more dreadful Apparition was never raised in a Church-yard, nor in the Imagination of any good People met in a Winter Evening over a Christmas Fire in *Somersetshire*.[88]

Fielding drew on the images and vocabulary used to depict fleshy chapbook ghosts, and he sent Tom's 'ghost' on a familiar mission of revenge. An unfortunate sentinel who was confronted with the sight of Tom was brought to his knees, and Fielding noted, perhaps with a wry smile, that 'his Hair began gently to lift up his Grenadier Cap'.[89] The sentinel was convinced that Ensign Northerton had murdered Tom, and now his ghost had returned to demand vengeance – at least that is the story he told to a gathering of men and women who roused him after he fainted. Fielding's ghost was not real, yet his description evoked the same blood-thirsty fascination which surfaced in the annals of cheap print. Yet by employing the distancing techniques of comedy and stereotyping, Fielding separated Tom's ghost from those 'real' ghosts that proved so controversial in polite discourse. In this respect Fielding's work prefigured the technique of the 'explained supernatural' that literary critics generally associate with the work of Gothic novelist Ann Radcliffe.[90]

Fielding's indulgence was reinforced in the following chapter of the novel, which contained an explanation of the art of novel writing and outlined his views about the acceptable role of the marvellous within this genre. If unchecked, the marvellous was simply the stuff of romance. But if it was mixed with a dose of the probable and mundane, then it became convincing, even poetic. Fielding endorsed the views of Alexander Pope, who believed that 'the great Art of all Poetry is to mix Truth with Fiction; in order to join the Credible with the Surprizing'.[91] The category of the marvellous, itself, however required greater refinement before it could be safely absorbed into the novel. 'Elves and Fairies' were dismissed as mere 'Mummery', and Fielding declared that 'The only supernatural Agents which can in any Manner be allowed to us Moderns are Ghosts'.[92] In Fielding's opinion, John Dryden had successfully defended the use of spectres in heroic poetry. To those who objected that ghosts should be exorcized from verse because they were 'unnatural', Fielding countered 'tis enough that, for ought we know, they may be in Nature: and what ever is or may be, is not, properly, unnatural'.[93] Fielding thus defended the literary use of ghosts on the grounds that the status of these figures was ambiguous, almost unknowable, and because they excited the interest of readers. His observations paralleled those of Joseph Addison, who believed there was enough probability in the idea of returning ghosts to make them credible. It was unwise therefore to 'look upon the representation as altogether impossible'.[94]

Ghosts appeared less frequently in the essay periodical than in the pages of interactive publications like the *Athenian Mercury*. But from the evidence on offer here, it seems that learned readers of these publications still found reasons to pay attention to ghost stories. Indeed, in many contexts it was considered morally, religiously and socially justifiable – perhaps even necessary – to place limits on the potential of human wisdom to supersede or dismiss the unknown. Ghost stories provided an important means to achieve this by highlighting the vulnerability of the human body to death and decay – inevitable processes that were beyond the control of natural philosophy. The *Tatler* and *Spectator* functioned as tools of social criticism, and they clearly objected to a narrow rationalism that marginalized ghosts as vulgar nonsense. These periodicals refined the contexts in which ghosts could appear as well as the meanings that could be safely attached to them. This said, ghosts continued both to instruct and to entertain educated men and women. They were made indispensable to campaigns for the independence of the individual imagination, and they fed into ideas of the sublime that flourished in the Romantic writings of the later eighteenth century.

Magazines

By the mid-eighteenth century ghosts still haunted the periodical press, albeit less frequently. Since the very existence of these publications relied on their ability to keep abreast of current opinions and controversies, the continued appearances of ghosts suggests that they had yet to be successfully exorcized from private reflections. The *Gentleman's Magazine, or, Monthly Intelligencer* was founded by Edward Cave in 1731, and it was the first periodical to adopt the name 'magazine'. This title gave expression to the distinctiveness of this monthly publication, which was the first 'general' periodical of its type in England. The *Gentleman's Magazine* included a series of articles and essays which were assembled from books, pamphlets and a vast array of other sources. This eclectic composition reflected the persistent demand for variety from readers and subscribers, and the editors of the *Gentleman's Magazine* took pains to ensure that they were satisfied. In 1732, October's issue offered 'Prices of Goods; Grain; Stocks, in London', 'Monthly Bills of Mortality' and a list of 'Births; Deaths; Marriages; Promotions; &c.'. More in-depth features included weekly essays 'Of Apparitions; Coffeehouses; Fortune-telling; Ambition; Dress; Flattery; Virtue and Nobility'.[95] Far from revealing a progressive distaste for tales of the wandering dead, this month's essay 'Of Apparitions' seemed to be grappling with the same issues that its predecessors struggled with at the turn of the century. Did ghosts really exist, and should they retain relevance in Enlightenment England?

In January 1731 the *Gentleman's Magazine* tempted its readers with the story of William Sutor, a farmer from Craighal in Scotland. The report had lately been published in Edinburgh, but it found its way south of the border thanks to the report of 'a Gentleman of unexceptionable Honour and Veracity'.[96] In December 1728 Sutor was working in the fields with his servants when he heard 'an uncommon skrecking and noise'. After investigating the disturbance, the workers fancied they saw a dark-coloured dog but, since it was dark, they concluded that it must have been a fox. Sutor was often in the same spot where he had first seen the animal, and he was visited by the dog several times over the next two years. He thought little of these episodes until one Monday in November 1730 when he was returning home at sunset. The dog passed by as usual but, before he disappeared, it spoke the following words, 'Within eight or ten days do or die'.[97] The next Saturday evening as William was at his sheepfold, the dog appeared again, and this time it asked Sutor to meet him at a certain spot of ground within half an hour.

Sutor resolved to investigate further and so visited the appointed spot. When the dog appeared before him, Sutor demanded 'In the name of God, who are you?'. The voice replied 'I am David Sutor, George Sutor's Brother: I killed a Man, more than 35 years ago, at a bush by East the road as you go into the Isle'. William Sutor was startled by this revelation, and he wondered how it could be true since 'David Sutor was a Man, and you appear as a Dog'. The animal then explained, 'I killed him with a Dog, and am made to speak out of the mouth of a Dog: and I tell you to go bury these bones'.[98] This request was no doubt familiar to William Sutor (and to readers of the magazine), since discoveries of secret murder and requests for decent burial were well-established motifs of the folk ghost story. Sutor did as he was asked, and he returned the next day to dig up the ground, whereupon he discovered a number of human bones. It was not long before news of this episode reached other members of the community and Sutor was soon joined in his task by 'the Minister of Blair', 'the Lairds of Glasdoon and Rychalzie' and 'about 40 or 50 people who had convened out of curiosity'. In place of a winding sheet, the remains of the dead man were wrapped in fresh linen, and put in a coffin before being interred that same evening in the churchyard of Blair. The account concluded with a postscript from members of the local community who listed their names in support of the tale, and who recalled that the alleged murderer, David Sutor, had 'listed for a Soldier, and went abroad about 34 or 35 years ago'.[99]

With revelations of concealed murder, buried bones and anthropomorphism, this tale was brimful of recognizable folkloric themes that had been associated with ghosts since time immemorial. Its publication in the mid-eighteenth century testified to the resilience of traditional conceptions of ghosts, but its inclusion in the *Gentleman's Magazine* may have had a more complex subtext. This narrative, unlike other discussions of ghost stories that appeared in this periodical, showed no signs of the rigorous scrutiny or empirical tests that were often applied to these narratives. Although the story boasted an impressive list of witnesses, it was unrefined, and therefore unreliable. Moreover, there may well have been an element of abjection involved in recounting this tale – that is geographical abjection, since the story originated from a backwater of the British Isles, far removed from the taste and sophistication of London. As we will see in the case of the Cock Lane ghost in Chapter 5, this tale may well have attracted greater opposition had it originated in the capital.

An essay printed in October 1732, entitled 'Of Ghosts, Daemons, and Spectres', was more characteristic of the suspicion with which ghost stories were publicly viewed by contributors to the *Gentleman's Magazine*. This essay was printed anonymously, but the reforming agenda of the author was clear from the outset. This was a thinly-veiled attempt to denigrate ghost stories as the amusements of the vulgar. The essay set out the reasons why polite readers should be mistrustful of ghost stories. In so doing the author borrowed heavily from the rhetoric of enlightened philosophers, physicians and fashionable wits. 'Some Spirits or Ghosts' claimed the author, 'owe their Existence only to a distemper'd Imagination'. Others could be blamed on the 'early Errors of Infancy'. The rest could be ascribed to 'a motley Mixture of the low and vulgar Education'.[100] The author here revealed a general antipathy towards the poorer sorts, who seemed clearly at fault for implanting 'traditionary Accounts of *local Ghosts*' in the minds of the general population. On this point the author went further still by elaborating a distinct hierarchy of ghost stories. Along with the apparitions at 'Verulam, Silchester, Reculver and Rochester', the 'Daemon of Tidworth' was labelled a vulgar ghost even though Joseph Glanvill, a respected Anglican churchman, had famously sponsored this ghost at the time of its alleged appearance. The 'Story of Madam Veal' was similarly relegated despite the fact that people from all sections of society had credited the truth of this episode. It seems likely then that this author's attempts to deny the legitimacy of ghost stories comprised a frustrated attempt to reform the errors and credulity of his peers, who were still captivated at some level by the possibility of wandering spirits. Indeed, the author recognized that he faced an uphill struggle.

> If our Reason sets us above these low and vulgar Appearances, yet when we read of the Ghost of Sir George Villers, or the Piper of Hammell, the Daemon of Moscow, or the German Colonel, mentioned by Ponti, and see the Names of Clarendon, Boyle &c. to these Accounts, we find Reasons for our Credulity, 'till at last we are convinc'd by a whole Conclave of Ghosts met in the works of Glanvil and Moreton.[101]

According to this judgement, it was less the *idea* of ghosts that was problematic than the authority with which they were presented. The ghost of Sir George Villiers enjoyed the patronage of Edward Hyde, Earl of Clarendon, who first presented the story in his *True Historical Narrative of the Rebellion and Civil Wars in England*, reprinted in 1702. Daniel Defoe's inclusion of the same tale in the *History and Reality of Apparitions* further suggested that the story retained contemporary interest for the polite audience at which his book was pitched. Robert Boyle had vouched for the authenticity of the Devil of Masçon, and consumer demand ensured that Joseph Glanvill's *Sadducismus Triumphatus* was reprinted in 1700 and 1726. The healthy publication statistics of these texts underline the continued importance of patronage and credit networks in shaping personal opinion about ghosts.

Nevertheless, the role played by medical, scientific and astronomical learning in reshaping responses to ghost stories cannot be neglected, and it was in the *Gentleman's Magazine* that these influences were most striking. In November 1747 an essay in the magazine offered a natural explanation for some strange visions seen in Cumbria by Win Lancaster's servant on Midsummer Eve, 1735. The servant reported that he saw 'the East side of Souter-fell, towards the top, covered with a regular marching army for above an hour together'. However, there was no other witness present to corroborate the sighting, and when the servant relayed his experience to friends and acquaintances 'he was discredited and laugh'd at'. That is until two years later, again on Midsummer Eve, when Win Lancaster himself saw several gentlemen 'following their horses at a distance' in exactly the same spot. At first he assumed they had been out hunting and 'pay'd no regard to it', but after ten minutes he looked again and noticed that the gentlemen now 'appeared to be mounted, and a vast army following, five in rank, crowding over at the same place, where the servant said he saw them two years before'. He then called on his family to confirm that this was no optical illusion, and upon arriving at the spot they 'all agreed in the same opinion'. The excitement of seeing these apparitions again died down until the Midsummer Eve preceding the Jacobite rebellion of 1745. On this occasion twenty-six people convened at the spot 'who all affirm they then saw the same appearance'. Some of the company who were eager to discover the cause of the vision climbed the mountain the following day 'through an idle expectation of finding horse-shoes', but upon investigating 'they saw not the vestige or print of a foot'.[102]

The narrator of this tale was reluctant to attach a supernatural explanation to these uncanny visions and yet the whole story was peculiarly resistant to logical explanation. A 'lambent agitated meteor' might be blamed for these ghostly visions, he argued, but how could it 'affect the optics of so many people'? And why did it appear on three separate occasions, on the same day, and in the same spot? As discussed previously, optical research had a clear impact on the way in which people thought about ghosts. Yet, in spite of this knowledge, there seemed to be a clear pattern to the visions at Souter Fell that defied the logic of coincidence. The author's confusion was deepened further by his acquaintance with the chief witnesses who, he claimed, 'could have no end in imposing on their fellow-creatures, and are of good repute in the place where they live'. The author was unable to discount the story based on personal reputation, and it seemed highly unlikely that all twenty-six of them had been deceived by an optical illusion. This

author reluctantly confessed that the issue was 'at present beyond my philosophy to explain'. He sought assistance therefore from his fellow readers, and he
appealed to 'such as will give themselves the trouble of enquiry'.[103]

In the December issue of 1747 a reply was published, but it offered no new
philosophical or optical explanations whereby to explain away the reported
visions. Instead this author attacked the need 'to deny the facts, by accusing
the relators of falsehood, folly, or credulity, or impute them to other causes'.[104]
Why he asked, did the narrator seek to naturalize such visions? 'Might he not
truly answer, that they were a company of spirits, confined for a time to inhabit
material bodies of different forms and textures?' Where, he demanded, 'is the
absurdity in supposing it possible for some spirits to appear for a short time in
bodies still more refined, and capable of what shape they please, and when?'.[105]
The Universal Library concurred with this opinion, and it offered a physical
explanation of how this process took place. Souls of the dead were able to cloak
themselves in 'a Sidereal or Elemental thin Body' and return to earth therein, so
long as the body of the deceased retained moisture. When the moisture drained
away 'the Apparition or Ghost does grow weak, and at last vanish'.[106] Applying
organic understandings of the natural world to life after death could thus validate
the existence of ghosts. Having forcefully presented his case, the author finished
with the following postscript. 'It is pleasant to observe that, notwithstanding the
endeavours to discredit the being of spirits, there is hardly a person in England (I
believe I may say the world) but hath either heard or seen one himself, or been
acquainted with those that have: and if this was rightly attended to, such apparitions would be reckoned no more supernatural than it is to see an American
or East-Indian; the one being as much a work of creation as the other'.[107] This
debate neatly encapsulated the fragmentation of learned opinion about the reliability of ghost stories in these years, and the contestation of purely naturalistic
explanations of the world. Astronomical research into the effects of meteors and
growing knowledge of the science of optics were just two means by which natural philosophy narrowed the contexts in which ghost stories remained credible.
Nevertheless, intellectual trends could also provide new justifications and contexts to confirm their legitimacy.

Dreaming of Ghosts

In February 1739 John Walker from Gloucestershire wrote to the *Gentleman's
Magazine* with a story from Bristol. It was in this provincial centre that a clergyman's wife relayed tidings of her daughter's death to other members of her family
whilst in a dream. This account was quickly followed by the story of a gentleman who claimed to have seen his own apparition. In 1722 *The Universal Library*

commented on the increasingly common appearance of ghosts in dreams, and it attempted to explain the mechanics of this phenomenon.

> It is far easier and familiar for the Deceased Souls to communicate their Secrets to their Living Friends in Dreams ... for Men in Dreams are nearer unto the Condition of departed Souls than when awake, and therefore they can with ease and great familiarity discourse and reveal their Minds unto them ... the Souls of Strangers do sometimes make Application to such sympathising Souls of the Living, whilst the Body lies asleep and reveal great Secrets, or foretell them of things sometimes good, and sometimes evil that are likely to befall them.[108]

The bookseller William Owen recounted one such instance in his *Warning Piece Against the Crime of Murder*. A poor woman from Bristol, whose husband had left town in search of work, discovered that he had been robbed and murdered after his ghost appeared to her in a dream. The crime had been committed by a publican with whom the poor man had lodged whilst on his way to London. She related the dream to a local minister, who judged it a sign of providential intervention. He informed a local magistrate and the publican was investigated and eventually executed for the crime.[109] Religious visions had for hundreds of years presented themselves in dream sequences, but the reported incidence of ghosts encountered in dreams increased noticeably in the eighteenth century. The ghost-in-dream scenario was popular among the poorer sorts whose testimony might otherwise be discounted. If a ghost was encountered during sleep, the individual was considered less likely to be guilty of fraud and more likely to be the recipient of some divinely-inspired message from beyond the grave. Such inspiration was claimed by a number of Methodist supporters who commonly met with visions of departed souls in dreams.[110] The generation of ghost stories by Methodists will be discussed in more detail in Chapter 5, but for now it is important to note that the ghost-in-dream scenario became an increasingly acceptable way to frame a ghost story thanks to developing theories of the unconscious and the idea of interiority in many aspects of eighteenth-century intellectual life. Heavy emphasis on the consciousness of man was typical of much seventeenth-century philosophy, and especially in the work of Descartes. But this was challenged in late seventeenth-century England by Cambridge Platonist Ralph Cudworth, who engaged with abstract ideas of the unconscious mind in his 1678 *True Intellectual System of the Universe*. In 1690 fellow Platonist John Norris declared that 'we have many ideas of which we are not conscious', and John Locke's *Essay Concerning Human Understanding*, first published in 1689, was among the most influential of texts to examine the properties of the unconscious mind.[111] Locke saw no connection between the thoughts produced whilst sleeping and those conscious ideas that could be confirmed by the human senses. In Locke's view, personal identity resided in the conscious mind, and so an individual could not be accountable for the wanderings of his/her mind when asleep. It therefore followed that people could not be blamed or ridiculed for the visions they saw in dreams.[112] This radical detachment of the unconscious mind from the human senses was, however, subjected to more intense scrutiny in the following years. Physicians specializing in sleep research surmised that the involuntary movements and thoughts that took place evidenced 'an inner mental vision' that was 'superior to mere physical sight.[113] Growing confidence in the powers of the unconscious mind also problematized John Trenchard's argument in his *Natural History of Superstition*, that 'Spirits and Apparitions' encountered in dreams were false images that could not be relied upon because the mind was cut off from 'the Organs of sense.[114]

By the 1750s, evidence of the eyes was regarded with much greater distrust, since these organs were too easily tricked. Sight also became commoditized by traders who deliberately set out to pervert it by perfecting the art of optical illusion. In the second half of the eighteenth century, a series of sight-related toys came into fashion – optical boxes, magic lanterns and kaleidoscopes – and they were designed both to deceive and to entertain the eye.[115] By 1796 *Gale's Cabinet of Knowledge* confidently described how to fabricate the appearance of a ghost. The trick involved positioning an inverted portrait of a familiar person under a door. When the portrait was illuminated, it would reflect off a large concave mirror and form a most convincing apparition for an unsuspecting dupe entering the room.[116] *The Laboratory* informed readers how a Camera Obscura could be used to conjure up an imaginary ghost, which was a trick practised by fortune-tellers to make a profit from 'credulous and ignorant people.[117] Terry Castle went even further by describing how the psychological tendency to see the ghosts of loved ones foreshadowed inventions 'such as the magic lantern, photography, cinematography, television and holography.[118] Given that the physical eyes were so easily cheated, a ghost that was seen by the inner eyes assumed greater credibility since the faculties of reasoning and deceit were disabled. In 1791 an English clergyman considered dreams to be 'of equal authority with the Bible'. He also suggested that 'the experience that many men have of significant dreams and night visions' had 'a more powerful effect on their minds than the most pure and refined concepts.[119] The German physicist and mathematician G. C. Lichtenberg recommended that dreams and unconscious thoughts be recognized as intrinsic parts of human life. He claimed that 'we live and feel just as much in dreams, as in waking, the one is as much a part of our existence as the other.[120] As Lancelot Whyte has argued, the unconscious mind was thought to link the individual with the universal and the organic.[121] Ghosts were part of this realm and thus, by relocating ghosts to an interior space, the networks of natural philosophy worked to authenticate the reality of ghosts rather than to undermine them.

Regional Reports

I have known many a Country Lady come to London with frightful stories of the Hall-House being haunted, of Fairies, Spirits, and Witches; that by the time she had seen a Comedy, play'd at an Assembly, and ambled in a Ball or two, has been so little afraid of Bugbears, that she has ventur'd home in a Chair at all Hours of the Night.[122]

This extract from *The Drummer* continued a well-established rhetorical tradition of early modern times. This was a tradition that blamed the melancholic, the lunatic, the garrulous old wife and credulous country folk for nurturing fears of ghosts. As we have seen, these tropes were strengthened by philosophical and medical advances, but they were also exploited by the wealthier residents of the capital. These people increasingly fashioned themselves in opposition to provincial cultures to reify London as the cultural heart of English society. This metropolitan drive for cultural distinction was evidenced in contemporary periodical literature, and it was the corollary of the social and economic dominance of London, which was soon to become the financial centre of the world. Fed by immense trading profits from the Americas and the Indies, the wealth of the city expanded on a daily basis, as did its population. Wealthy entrepreneurs were increasingly drawn to the bright lights of London and they brought their money with them, patronizing new trends in theatre, literature, music and the arts to suit their new lifestyle and establish a place in fashionable society.

In the pages of the *Tatler*, the *Spectator* and the *Gentleman's Magazine*, London was depicted as the epitome of good taste, rationality and distinction – a far cry from the supposed ignorance and credulity of regional centres. I have already indicated that London was by no means free of ghostly activity, and it often generated a number of hauntings that will be explored at greater length in Chapter 5. But how reliable was the projected image of credulous provincial society? This section explores contrasting representations of ghosts in regional publications that rolled from the provincial presses in the first half of the eighteenth century. The cities of Norwich and Newcastle have been selected because of their strong traditions of religious dissent, their distance and distinctiveness from the capital, and their reputations as advanced centres of literacy and printing. Norwich was especially noted for its concentration of printers, booksellers and coffee-houses, and for establishing the first provincial city library in England as early as the 1630s.[123] Given its isolation among the sprawling rural communities of East Anglia, one might expect to find tale upon tale of ghostly activity in the Norwich press. However, a fruitless search through periodicals and news media of the day proved this expectation to be largely unfounded. There was in fact surprisingly little said about ghosts in the printed media of this substantial market town.

A few newspaper items did, however, shed light on how people perceived ghosts in this region. In 1708 Henry Crossgrove published *The Accurate Intelligencer*, which contained 'Answers to a Number of Curious Letters Never yet Publish'd in the Norwich Gazette, Being a very choice reserve of such questions as were too long or improper to be inserted in a News-paper'.[124] Among the queries sent in by curious readers of the *Gazette* was a letter from a gentleman whose friend claimed to have seen a ghost. This man's wife had lately passed away, and on the third night after her burial 'he saw her sitting by the Parlour Window in her usual Posture and Dress'. The querist was convinced of the truth of his friend's account, but he ventured to get a practical explanation about how this could occur. He therefore asked Crossgrove, 'if Persons that appear so are then in their Graves? Or if not, how do they get out?' The need to imagine the dead in a physical location suggested that this gentleman may have shared a materialistic conception of death and the afterlife that characterized many readers of the *Athenian Mercury*. If this ghost had returned to comfort her grieving husband, it was logical to conclude that the dead remained sensitive to the emotions of the living. This correspondent went on to quiz Crossgrove about 'whether Persons have Knowledge of Matters acted here after they are dead'?[125] John Dunton's *Essay Proving we Shall Know our Friends in Heaven* supported this idea, as did Henry Curzon, who argued that persistent affection for loved ones after death was 'the chief General Cause of Apparitions of Souls departed'.[126]

The letter also replicated the confusion about the spiritual status of the dead that appeared in London periodicals, asking 'if you think such are happy Spirits that appear to us after they are Dead'. This gentleman's desire to know if his friend's wife was saved or damned was no doubt inspired by his personal affection for the lady. But if she numbered among the elect, her conduct whilst living could prove a useful guide for those friends and relatives left behind who were clearly impatient to receive Crossgrove's thoughts on the matter. Some educated men and women from Norwich thus continued to invest meaning in ghostly appearances because they engaged with issues of death and salvation. The reluctance to admit the separation of body and soul at the moment of death was a very traditional argument for the existence of ghosts. Persistent curiosity about the future condition of the soul may have sustained the impact of ghost stories (as it did in London), but evidence from the *Norwich Mercury* also suggests that the city was not untouched by sceptical thought on this issue.

In February 1752 the *Norwich Mercury* presented one of the most important new challenges to the status of ghost stories in this region, at least among the middling sorts who made up a large proportion of the *Mercury*'s reading public. A letter entitled 'The Fruits of Enthusiasm' was printed, from an anonymous gentleman whose family had been reduced to misery because of the rebellious acts of his once loyal cook Margery. Margery began to misbehave at morning and evening prayers, when 'she mutter'd to herself incoherent stuff, so that those who kneeled by her, could hear nothing but Sweetest Jesus! Loveliest Lord! Dearest Spouse!'. Soon after, the gentleman lamented that John the Butler had joined Margery in her defiance and refused to say 'Amen' at the end of each prayer. These disruptions caused division within the household until the gentleman eventually dismissed them to perform their devotions alone. Despite this concession, the gentleman's letter told how Margery's behaviour continued to deteriorate. Several dinners were spoiled by her negligence, her appearance began to be 'ragged and dirty', and her poor mother, whom she had always helped to maintain, was abandoned to the workhouse where 'she soon died with Sorrow and Grief'.[127]

Some time afterwards, Margery was heard screaming from the privy at the bottom of the garden. The noise was so terrible that Sarah the chambermaid was sent to investigate. However, she returned to her master with an ashen face, confessing that she dare not go to Margery because 'she fear'd meeting her Ghost as it should come from her Body'. The butler was next dispatched to enter the privy, and upon his return he reported that Margery 'was dead'. Instead he had 'met her Apparition with a Pair of Eyes as big and of just such a Colour as our Warming-pan Lid, and that in running away he looked back behind him, and saw her ascend into Heaven, for Sir, says he, she was a pious dear Soul, and had the Spirit'. However, before the gentleman had time to respond to reports of Margery's demise, she appeared before him, whereupon all the servants took fright and were taken away for blood letting to relieve their distress. After examining the case, reports of Margery's demise proved rather premature. She was not about to meet her maker but had instead been taken by the 'inner spirit' that commanded her to sing 'one of Mr. Wesley's Hymns'. The servants' visions of Margery's ghost were presented as ridiculous delusions by the gentleman, whose letter was principally an anti-Methodist satire, and it formed part of a more general polemic against the spread of Methodism in Norwich.[128] When Calvinist Methodist James Wheatley arrived in Norwich with his congregation in 1751–2, religious tensions ran so high that riots ensued, led by the Tory Hell-Fire Club.[129] At the time this letter was published, Norwich was gripped by anti-Methodist feeling and ghosts were thus being made central to a cultural conflict of pressing importance in Norwich, becoming embroiled in angry rhetoric and tarnished as products of enthusiasm.[130]

In spite of this furious disavowal, ghosts continued to be both credible and relevant in other areas of Norwich life at this time. In May and June 1752, the weekly advertisements in the *Mercury* included a publication notice for *A Warning Piece Against the Crime of Murder*.[131] The preface identified the contemporary relevance of the work. It was claimed to be a direct response to 'the horrid and unnatural crime of murder', which 'has within a very few Years last past become much more frequent in this kingdom, than it was ever before known to be'.[132] This publication coincided with official anxieties about the frequency of murder in these years that culminated in the Murder Act of July 1752. As a deterrent to would-be killers, this legislation introduced harsher penalties for those convicted of this most heinous of crimes.[133] Since human powers of detection had failed to discover the perpetrators of many of these crimes, the value of ghostly revelation again came to the fore.

The *Warning Piece* included many wondrous discoveries of murder, three of which were solved by ghosts who returned to condemn their killers. Having secretly drowned his pregnant wife in a pond, William Barwick thought he had escaped punishment until his wife's ghost was raised to make the discovery. The victim's ghost appeared to her brother-in-law Thomas Lofthouse, who reported his suspicions to the Lord Mayor of York. Barwick later confessed to the murder and was sentenced to death at York Assizes.[134] A soldier who fled to the army after murdering his master also figured in the *Warning Piece*. He was forced to confess his crime, however, by 'somewhat like a headless Man' that continually haunted his bedside.[135] Finally, a man put on trial for murder was confronted by the ghost of his victim in the courtroom. The material evidence against the defendant was too circumstantial to secure a conviction and so divine justice roused his victim's ghost to incite a confession from the guilty man. He was eventually sentenced to death and 'hanged in Chains at the Place where he declared the Murder was committed'.[136] The *Warning Piece* was printed in twelve numbers, each containing three half sheets and priced at a modest 2*d*. It was thus accessible to a wide audience and was sold by bookseller William Owen at Temple Bar in London as well as in Norwich.[137] As was the case in London, the status of ghost stories was contested in Norwich but retained legitimacy in certain contexts, especially when allied to moral reflections.

If the Norwich press offered only snippets of social commentary about ghosts, the Newcastle press was even less forthcoming, although the *Newcastle General Magazine* was more fruitful. It was printed monthly and included editorial essays, news from London, poetry, book reviews and general advertisements. In September 1747 an article discussed the doctrine of the immortality of the soul. Despite the attention that this subject had received from 'Men of Genius and Application in all Ages', the author of this piece was unsurprised 'that so little Satisfaction has been hitherto obtained'. He remained undecided about the nature and properties of the human soul after death, but no ghosts were found to accompany his conjectures. Apart from a few poetic offerings about 'inchanted Grounds' and complaints about the 'idle Stories' of servants, ghosts were noticeably absent from this magazine in the first half of the eighteenth century.[138] Of course this silence does not mean that the reading public of Newcastle no longer thought about ghosts, but indirect references to these preternatural episodes are found only infrequently in the monthly book notices on the back page of the magazine. In February 1748 the register of new books included *Revelation, and not Reason, nor yet Enthusiasm, the Criterion in Religion*, and the poetry section for the same issue advertised two volumes of Edward Young's *Night Thoughts on Life, Death, and Immortality* at a price of 4*s*.[139] Direct mention of ghosts came in a satirical ballad entitled *Lovat's Ghost* advertised at 6*d.* in May 1747, and a similar pamphlet named *Scelas's Ghost* was included in the July issue of 1748. The ghosts in both of these publications were highly figurative, and they served to reinforce general principles of morality rather than advancing claims for the real existence of these creatures.[140] This was reminiscent of treatments of ghost stories in the *Tatler* and *Spectator*, and the *Newcastle General Magazine* may have been influenced by these periodicals, alongside the *Gentleman's Magazine*, which enjoyed national circulation. Readers in Newcastle and Norwich were thus able to share in metropolitan opinions of ghosts as well as forming views of their own in line with regional priorities.

Conclusion

Ghost stories stood in complex relation to readers of periodicals in the first half of the eighteenth century. Many of the editors of these publications had clear reforming agendas and they used periodicals as a platform to shape the manners and opinions of their readers. Some chose to laugh ghosts out of countenance, but this was by no means a straightforward process of disenchantment. This was partly due to the personal beliefs of men like Edward Cave, proprietor and editor of the *Gentleman's Magazine*, who informed Samuel Johnson that he had once seen a ghost. Joseph Addison and Richard Steele did not admit to such a personal encounter, but they did value ghost stories for promoting self-regulation and moral virtue. The early decades of the eighteenth century saw such values increasingly prioritized by writers like Daniel Defoe. The moral lessons taught by Defoe's ghosts in his *History and Reality of Apparitions* were firmly set within the context of corruption and malpractice associated with episodes like the collapse of the South Sea Bubble in 1720.

Addison's support for ghost stories did, however, come with important qualifications. His discussions of these narratives were often displaced into fictional contexts from where Addison and his readers could admire the aesthetic value of ghost stories without consenting belief to those real and crude ghosts of chapbook notoriety. In this guise, however, ghost stories still had an important role to play in polite society. Ghost stories, whether real or imagined, were good for thinking with. They spoke to contemporary moral dilemmas, but also to an emerging cultural emphasis on the cultivation of the mind as the proper object of man's perfection. Musings about the contours of an invisible world had a crucial role to play both in shaping artistic endeavours and in defending the pleasures of the imagination from philosophers who wished to limit individual contemplation to natural, knowable phenomena. The dramatic effect of ghosts in poetry and prose relied upon the very ambiguity of these figures. The apparent tensions in these accounts between fiction and reality, pleasure and pain were later elaborated in explanations of the sublime, and in the genre of Gothic fiction – two of the most influential cultural forms of the later eighteenth century.

Despite this continuity of interest, however, ghosts did appear less frequently in periodicals as the century wore on. Had people simply become less willing to believe in these narratives or were there other factors at play? Currents of scepticism did undoubtedly erode the credibility of ghost stories. They now required greater supporting evidence, moral scaffolding and respected witnesses to gain wide acceptance. Nevertheless, the apparent decline of interest in ghosts may also be partially explained by the evolving nature of the periodical genre itself.

At one level, the periodical's commitment to literary realism and empiricism ensured that ghost stories were subjected to ever greater scrutiny. Emphasis on corroborative witnessing and circumstantial evidence meant that these narratives were boiled down to the essential facts, rather than devoting time to plot and character development – something that was not conducive to an impression of verisimilitude. The abridgment of these tales also afforded little opportunity for the wider moral implications of ghost stories to be drawn out, thus restricting their value in this print genre. Though ghost stories did not appear in periodicals on a daily basis, the serialization of these tales from across the British Isles may well have created the impression that ghost stories were common occurrences. The implications of this process are difficult to measure, but the apparent multiplication of ghost stories in periodicals may well have destroyed some of the mystique associated with these strange and unusual episodes, prompting readers to uncover man-made explanations for such appearances.

The empirical epistemology utilized by periodicals and newspapers, combined with the Stamp Acts of 1712 and 1724, meant that the boundaries between fact and fiction became more rigidly marshalled. Tales of the wandering dead occasionally surfaced in periodicals from the later eighteenth century, but many others were gradually relocated to different literary genres, and crucially to an interior imaginative space that was increasingly reified by new medical research. Heightened interest in the workings of the human imagination and its unconscious expressions allowed ghost stories to resurface in Gothic fictions of the later eighteenth century. The popularity of these texts was especially marked among the leisured classes, and it was encouraged by the material production of reading chairs and bookstands for the home –which now often incorporated a private library.[141] The marketplace thus promoted new reading practices that allowed ghost stories to be relocated to domestic spaces and to the individual imagination, which helped to redefine the boundaries between fantasy and reality, and to limit public discussions of these narratives in leading periodicals.

The relationship between ghost stories and enlightened philosophy was similarly complex in periodical literature. New optical, neurological and astronomical vocabularies helped to expose many ghost stories as illusion. Yet a persistent desire to understand the nature and movements of departed souls can be traced, with enquiries into the nervous system, psychological disorders and dreams, and in technological developments such as the magic lantern. The public marginalization of ghost stories should not be overstated then, since in the course of this chapter alone we have seen how ghosts continued to feature in theatre, comedy, drama, poetry, novels, satire, newspapers, historical narratives, medical treatises, theological tracts and educational discourses to name just a few. Undoubtedly, these ghosts were conceived in different ways, but in whatever guise they appeared, they influenced both the content of the narratives in which they featured and the forms that they took. Ghosts were central to the Graveyard poets, and they had the power to shape this genre as well as being shaped by it. Important parallels then might be drawn with Jacques Derrida's *Specters of Marx*, which continued to haunt a new world order that had proclaimed the passing of the communist moment and the death of Marxism itself.[142] The idea of ghosts, like the ideas of Marx, refused to go away. Ghost stories were good to think with because they provided a unique imaginative path to unconscious, invisible worlds. Despite attempts to transform the reality of ghost stories by cutting them off from empirical substantiation and objective 'proof', they survived as a kind of disembodied knowledge, being reinterpreted and recycled into new, more abstract contexts. Such manipulations and survivals were only made possible because ghosts retained profound personal and emotional significance, because they were embedded in deep structures of belief.

5 CONFESSIONAL CULTURES AND GHOST BELIEFS, *c.* 1750–*c.* 1800

If public explanations of ghost stories were shaped by principles of natural law, medicine and discourses of politeness, they also continued to be bound by spiritual directives. But how did these narratives fare in the second half of the eighteenth-century when the intellectual ferment of the Enlightenment had fundamentally altered the theological landscape? Gospel truths had fallen under the inscrutable gaze of empirical philosophers, and liberal theologians began to ask new questions about the nature of God and his relationship with the natural world. Were the miracles described in the bible now explicable by the laws of nature? Was Christian emphasis upon divine supernatural intervention now outmoded? Many Protestant reformers of the sixteenth and seventeenth centuries had insisted that signs, wonders and miracles should be consigned to the apostolic age, but Enlightenment medicine and philosophy now offered a way for such episodes to be empirically tested. Questions like these began a new phase in persistent debates about the correct balance between reason and revelation in religious life. This chapter investigates how perceptions of ghost stories altered in accordance with these new emphases, and whether any discernible connection between patterns of ghost belief and confessional identity can be traced. The analysis here works on two levels. The first concerns how publicly-professed attitudes towards ghost stories shifted in line with confessional conflict, which fluctuated in response to intellectual, political and cultural change. The second level examines links between this public discourse and more private reflections about the appearance and meaning of ghosts. At issue here are the ways in which ordinary parishioners made sense of these extraordinary episodes; how their responses were conditioned by religious affiliation; and whether their interpretations influenced the way in which clergymen, theologians and philosophers responded to ghost stories. Reactions to ghost stories in these years also throw new light on existing historical debates about the vitality of eighteenth-century Anglicanism, the relationship between clergy and parishioners, and relations between the established Church and dissenting groups. The chronology of this chapter coincides with the rapid spread of evangelical Methodism from the 1740s, which partly explains why interpretations of ghost stories were such contentious issues in Methodist and Anglican communities. This focus also reflects the circulation of ghost-related texts in these years, which was dominated by Methodist, Anglican and other Protestant apologists. The confessional rivalry which marked this period helps to explain diverse responses to one of the most famous ghost stories that eighteenth-century England encountered.

Fanny Lynes of Cock Lane

On 10 July 1763 Richard Parsons and his wife were brought to trial before chief Justice Lord Mansfield at the Court of King's Bench, Guildhall. With them was their maidservant Mary Frazer and Methodist sympathizer the Reverend John Moore, who was assistant preacher at St Sepulchre's and rector of St Bartholomew the Great in West Smithfield. All four stood accused of conspiracy and, after a trial lasting just one day, they were each found guilty of plotting to 'take away the life of William Kent by charging him with the murder of Frances Lynes by giving her poison whereof she died'.[1] These criminal charges were brought following the exposure of the most sensational ghost story that London had ever known, and Richard Parsons, the drunken parish clerk of St Sepulchre's, was its most unlikely orchestrator. In a narrow alley in the shadow of St Paul's Cathedral, Parsons had played host to an apparition who famously accused wealthy stockbroker William Kent of having murdered his fiancée Fanny Lynes. Kent and Lynes had lodged with Parsons for a short time at his house in Cock Lane in 1759. But he had quarrelled with them after Kent threatened to bring a lawsuit against Parsons to recover a debt of twelve guineas. Kent and Lynes moved out of Parsons's house and Fanny died soon afterwards, giving Parsons the perfect opportunity to secure his revenge. Parsons reported that a ghost, nicknamed 'Scratching Fanny', haunted his house, and that it was none other than the disturbed soul of Fanny Lynes who had been poisoned by Kent as she lay on her sickbed in February 1760. John Moore seemed genuinely convinced of the ghost's authenticity and, following a series of public séances held at the house, news of Scratching Fanny, and of William Kent's crime, spread rapidly across London. In so doing, the story engaged the attention of the capital's most wealthy and renowned citizens, as well as the poorer sorts who flocked to the house in Cock Lane night after night. No fewer than eight newspapers and four magazines covered the story and such was the consternation it produced that Lord Mayor Samuel Fludyer was forced to intervene.[2] Fludyer ordered an independent inquiry to discover whether the reports were true. As a result, the ghost was eventually exposed as a fake, with Richard Parsons condemned as a fraudster who had maliciously set out to ruin the reputation of his former tenant. John Moore was dismissed from court with a reprimand, but he was ordered to pay £600 to Kent in compensation. Mary Frazer was sentenced to six months in Bridewell prison, and Mrs Parsons to one year. The most severe sentence was reserved for Richard Parsons, who was to serve two years in prison, and was ordered to stand three sessions in the pillory. This very public sentence was unusual, but highly appropriate for a man who had excited such extraordinary curiosity in the early months of 1762.[3]

The case of the Cock Lane ghost will be explored in more detail shortly, but it is important at this stage to establish the wider significance of the affair. First, wrangles over the authenticity of Scratching Fanny position ghost stories as persistent sites of cultural contestation well into the second half of the eighteenth century. Second, widespread support for the accusations levelled by the ghost reveal a neglected aspect of London's history in this period, which was the apparent groundswell of belief in the interventions of ghosts. Third, the authority given to Scratching Fanny's revelations by the support of Methodist minister John Moore points to the complex position of ghosts within a matrix of confessional tensions and rivalries. In the immediate term, the authenticity of the ghost became a struggle between Methodist ministers and Anglican clergy to establish superior religious authority. Yet any sharp division between Methodist credulity and Anglican disbelief is overly simplistic. In spite of the public discrediting of the Cock Lane ghost, and vociferous opposition to the enthusiastic excesses of early Methodism, ghosts were abandoned neither by Anglican clergy nor by their parishioners. In fact it was largely thanks to the efforts of churchmen in spreading preternatural reports that ghosts were reinvested with important theological meanings in a period of severe social, religious and political dislocation. Reactions to the Cock Lane affair, and to similar ghost stories in these years, thus highlight the neglected significance of revealed religion and particular providences in historical assessments of late eighteenth-century religion and spirituality.

In January 1762, the London daily newspaper the *Public Ledger* first published news of Scratching Fanny in a series of articles detailing the downfall of Fanny Lynes. This young woman from Norfolk had fallen in love with William Kent and followed him to London where, claimed the newspaper, she was persuaded by Kent to take on the role of his wife. Although no marriage had taken place, Fanny soon fell pregnant with Kent's child. At Kent's insistence the couple masqueraded as man and wife to conceal their illegitimate union, but they were forced to pass through a number of temporary lodgings as and when the deceit was discovered. One of these lodgings belonged to Richard Parsons. Kent and Parsons quarrelled over money, and William and Fanny were forced to move to a nearby jeweller's at Bartlett Court in Clerkenwell.

So far the story was straightforward, but those who later became embroiled in the lurid affair hotly disputed what happened next. All were agreed that Fanny Lynes died soon after she left Parsons's house on 2 February 1760, and that she was laid to rest in the vault of St John's, Clerkenwell. It was, however, the manner of her death that sparked bitter controversy. William Kent would maintain that Fanny had fallen sick soon after she had been forced to move out of Cock Lane, and that he called Dr Thomas Cooper to treat her illness on 25 January 1760. Fanny was now in the late stages of her pregnancy, and she supposed that she had gone into premature labour after developing acute pains in her back. However, further examination revealed that she had contracted a virulent strain of smallpox from which she would never recover. William Kent was extremely grieved by the sudden death of his fiancée according to a local clergyman who visited Fanny in her final hours, and he claimed that he had never seen 'a grief more expressive than in Mr. K'.[4]

This is a very different tale from that told by Richard Parsons and the *Public Ledger*. The newspaper claimed that William Kent had cried crocodile tears at Fanny's funeral, since it was he who had lured her to London, compromised her virtue, and eventually murdered her to get his hands on her inheritance by administering a fatal dose of red arsenic. Fanny Lynes's family also supported this version of events after Kent was given absolute control over Fanny's estate in a will written just a few months before her death.[5] The articles in the *Public Ledger* painted a damning picture of William Kent, and they complemented Richard Parsons's attempts to ruin Kent's reputation in local credit networks, which had little prior knowledge by which to judge the conduct of this litigious newcomer.[6] Thanks to Parsons, William and Fanny's illicit relationship was exposed, and this shocking tale of sexual immorality was made worse still when it became known that Fanny was the sister of Kent's dead wife. Conventions of public morality had been transgressed, and from reports of his lewd behaviour with his dead sister's wife it seemed that William Kent might indeed be capable of murder.

Parsons circulated rumours that Kent had murdered his so-called wife before 1762, but his mutterings initially fell on deaf ears. However, in the closing months of 1761 he hit upon the idea of employing a higher authority to advance his cause. He then told a group of local clergymen, John Moore chief among them, that his house had for some time been disturbed by strange scratchings and knockings. Parsons claimed that he was unable to identify any natural cause, and he asked Moore to investigate since he feared some otherworldly agency was at work. John Moore was an early Methodist convert and a follower of John Wesley. When Richard Parsons related his scandalous story of William and Fanny, Moore seemed convinced that the restless ghost of the dead woman was behind the disturbances. Even if Kent had not killed Fanny, John Moore believed that 'these visitations must at least be considered as a judgment on him'.[7]

Moore's particular interest in the case can be attributed to his confessional allegiance. Ever since John Wesley felt his heart warmly embraced by the Holy Spirit in 1738, growing numbers of Methodist converts claimed to have a special affinity with the invisible world. These claims drew criticism from devotees of the mechanical theory, which held that the natural world was self-regulating and had no need for intervention from external forces. Nonetheless, historians have rightly claimed that the evangelical emphasis of early Methodism had some kinship with the spirituality of ordinary men and women, which initially enabled this new brand of Protestantism to gain a foothold among the people.[8] John Moore clearly included ghosts within his theological world-view, and he sought to capitalize on this particular tale to advance the Methodist cause among the labourers of industrializing London, and also among more prominent figures such as William Legge, Earl of Dartmouth. Support for the ghost showed that large sections of the capital's population still preserved a space for the direct intervention of God in the world. What is more, ghosts had a well-established reputation for punishing sinners. It was therefore entirely plausible that the disgruntled ghost of Fanny Lynes had received divine permission to expose William Kent for his vile deed.

John Moore held nightly séances in Parsons's house to communicate with Fanny's ghost and he met with particular success in the chamber of Elizabeth Parsons. Elizabeth was Richard Parsons's twelve-year old daughter, and she had formed a special bond with Fanny during her stay in Cock Lane. It made sense then that Elizabeth was one of the few people who claimed to have actually seen Scratching Fanny, and she described the appearance of a woman 'without hands, in a shrowd'.[9] To further legitimate his enquiries, Moore called on Reverend Thomas Broughton, lecturer at St Helen's, Bishopsgate Within and All Hallows, and secretary of the Society for Promoting Christian Knowledge (SPCK). Like Moore, Broughton was a Methodist convert, and this group had promised financial contributions to aid the ghost's supporters. As a result, this affair rapidly became an important case upon which the efficacy of Methodist faith was to be publicly tested. Parsons and Moore carefully managed the media spectacle that ensued, and Mary Frazer acted as an impromptu medium. It was Mary's job to quiz the ghost and to interpret the knocks that came in response – one for yes and two for no. Before a large audience in February 1762, Mary emerged as the ghost's chief interrogator. The ghost communicated with her via a series of knocks, and it soon emerged that Fanny's spirit had returned to accuse William Kent of poisoning her.

The diverse make-up of the crowd that gathered at Cock Lane was highly significant and this narrow alley was temporarily transformed into a space where the labouring poor, curious maidservants and men, women and children from all social backgrounds literally rubbed shoulders with one another, and with the crème de la crème of fashionable London society. Newspapers clearly thought this remarkable and reported that 'The clergy and laity, the nobility and commonalty ... continue their nightly attendance upon the invisible agent'.[10] Author and politician Horace Walpole described his visit to the most celebrated haunted house in London's history in a letter to his friend George Montagu. It was a cold and rainy winter evening, 'yet the lane was full of mob, and the house so full we could not get in it'.[11] Walpole was, however, admitted into the house when he revealed that his distinguished companions were none other than the Duke of York, Lady Northumberland, Lady Mary Coke and Lord Hertford. Once inside, the group waited for some ghostly action until past one o'clock in the morning, and Walpole later reported that a strange kind of knocking was heard behind the wainscot in Elizabeth Parsons's bedchamber.[12]

Walpole went on to parody ghosts in his gothic creation *The Castle of Otranto* (1765) and, as Emma Clery has suggested, he appreciated the Cock Lane affair as aesthetic spectacle rather than objective reality. Nonetheless, his correspondence provides an important glimpse of the genuine social interaction occasioned by this particular episode. William Legge, Earl of Dartmouth, moved in similar social circles to Walpole but, as a Methodist sympathizer, Dartmouth entertained the very real possibility that Fanny's ghost had been sent on an important providential mission. At the same time, currents of scepticism were well catered for in cheap printed wares. A broadside ballad entitled *Cock-Lane Humbug* mocked the disruption that Fanny's ghost had caused in London. Local taverns and street vendors also profited from the flood of visitors to the area, and local hawkers exploited them by selling the best viewing positions in and around Richard Parsons's house. Even Walpole and his companions were obliged to line the pockets of these canny men. Richard Parsons himself had told James Franzen, landlord of the Wheat Sheaf, about the ghost, and Franzen was one of the few who claimed to have seen Scratching Fanny. Little wonder then that Franzen's tavern made huge profits, 'the credulous swallowing down with his beer his tales of terror'.[13]

The ghost of Fanny Lynes undoubtedly had novelty value, but the question of its authenticity was central to more serious matters. William Kent's defence against accusations of murder now relied on the exposure of this ghost. John Moore had similarly staked his own credibility and that of his Methodist peers on the truth of it. The case was referred to Lord Mayor Sir Samuel Fludyer in the hope of reaching a satisfactory conclusion to the affair. Fludyer was initially reluctant to get involved since his predecessor Sir Crisp Gascoyne provoked an angry mob in 1753 following his intervention in the Elizabeth Canning affair.[14] Nonetheless, Fludyer did order an independent investigation to bring an end to the media circus, although he refused to arrest William Kent for murder, or to detain Richard Parsons for fraud. Stephen Aldrich, Anglican minister of St John's Clerkenwell, headed up the investigation, and he was joined by the Earl of Dartmouth, the bishop of Salisbury and seasoned investigator of supernatural phenomena John Douglas, hospital matron Mrs Oakes, eminent physician George Macaulay and Samuel Johnson – the great essayist and conversationalist who nurtured a lifelong fascination with ghosts.[15] Under Aldrich's direction, the ghost was revealed as a fraud after Elizabeth Parsons was seen making knocking sounds on a wooden board. Some members of the committee claimed that the noises were nothing like those previously heard at Cock Lane, but Elizabeth's actions turned the tide of opinion in William Kent's favour. The committee therefore concluded that

Elizabeth had 'some art of making or counterfeiting particular noises, and that there is no agency of a higher cause'.[16]

The committee's resolution was published in the *Gentleman's Magazine*, but this was not sufficient for William Kent, who commissioned journalist and novelist Oliver Goldsmith as his chief apologist.[17] Goldsmith's literary prowess was put to good use as he attempted to restore Kent's battered reputation in *The Mystery Revealed*, a short pamphlet first published in 1762 and selling for 1s. Goldsmith's account contained a highly romanticized version of William and Fanny's courtship. This was designed to tug at the heartstrings, and to pardon Kent's moral lapses for the middle-class reader who could both sympathize with his predicament and afford to purchase this topical text. Kent also sought redress through the courts, and he filed suit against Parsons and his co-conspirators, which, as we know, resulted in Parsons's imprisonment and public humiliation in the pillory. Yet, in spite of Kent's legal vindication, London opinion remained divided, and when Parsons appeared in the pillory he was spared any abuse. A collection was instead taken up for him by the supportive crowd, and a public subscription was also organized on his behalf. Lord Mansfield's judgement may have followed the letter of the law, but it did not fit with customary notions of right and wrong. In spite of his drunkenness, Richard Parsons was a popular man of previous good character, and Fanny's ghost had created as much sympathy for him as scorn. For the stranger William Kent it was a different story. No formal charges were brought against him, but Fanny's ghost ensured that a question mark would always hang over his reputation. His innocence was still being questioned in 1850 when J. W. Archer reopened the coffin of Fanny Lynes. Inside he found female remains, but could discern no trace of the smallpox that had reportedly carried her off.[18]

Despite the fame of this extraordinary episode, the historical significance of the Cock Lane affair has been somewhat neglected. Douglas Grant produced a comprehensive narrative of the event, Andrew Lang discussed the case in his attempt to trace a heritage for nineteenth- and twentieth-century ghost stories and Keith Thomas dealt with the episode in two short sentences.[19] Reactions to the ghost have yet to be inserted into wider historical debates about the status and meaning of ghost stories, and the relevance of the tale for assessments of eighteenth-century spirituality has been likewise overlooked. The Cock Lane affair was clearly a *cause célèbre*, but how did it shape wider perceptions of ghosts in these years? Emma Clery believes that the affair marked a watershed in attitudes towards ghosts, and towards the supernatural more generally. It was the Cock Lane fraud, she argues, that effected the commodification of the ghost as an amusing figure of satire and spectacle in consumer London. The epistemological status of ghosts was soon to become irrelevant, since they existed only to titillate and entertain, to be bought and sold on the open market. For Clery, Cock Lane was also a landmark event that saw ghosts 'freed from the service of doctrinal proof', and incorporated into a process of fictionalization from which they would never escape.[20] Valuable as these observations are, the eagerness to provide a genealogy for the rise of gothic fictions has arguably led to an underestimation of the extent of genuine ghost belief in the second half of the eighteenth century. Moreover, the preceding chapters suggest that the Cock Lane episode was merely the latest in a long line of ghost stories which had been adapted or commoditized for pecuniary purposes. The fictionalization of ghost stories was also a patchy and ambiguous process. A number of publications that satirized ghost beliefs in the wake of the Cock Lane affair implicitly demonstrated that the fact or fiction of ghost stories remained a contested issue. What is more, these texts had been designed to counter a series of alternative offerings that sought to capitalize upon the sudden explosion of interest in ghost stories, including new editions of Charles Drelincourt's *Christian's Defence Against the Fears of Death*, and two editions of Daniel Defoe's *Secrets of the Invisible World Laid Open*.[21]

The laughter that was heard in and around Cock Lane in 1762 can therefore be interpreted in a number of different ways. First, the satirical parody of ghost stories must be viewed in part as a literary tactic or trope, which formed part of a well-established rhetoric of spoof that was used to attack miracle claims and anything else that offended the prevailing philosophical fashions.[22] Second, public ridicule of the Cock Lane ghost was fairly restrained before Stephen Aldrich's committee declared it to be a fraud. It was only then that fashionable London set out to minimize the embarrassment to its reputation by parodying the ghost as a figure of fun, as a product of vulgar credulity and Methodist enthusiasm which the educated had never taken seriously in the first place. William Hogarth revised his engraving *Credulity, Superstition and Fanaticism* to include the Cock Lane ghost in 1762, Joseph Addison's satire *The Drummer*, based on another famous ghostly imposture, enjoyed a new lease of life in the 1760s, and Charles Churchill ridiculed the episode (and Samuel Johnson) in his poem *The Ghost!*, published in 1762. By laughing ghosts out of countenance, fashionable society sought immunity from the widespread credulity that had pervaded the capital. It was David Hume after all who claimed that popular delusions were much more likely to succeed amongst ignorant people or in remote countries 'than if the first scene had been laid in a city renowned for arts and knowledge'.[23] Hume's claim was, however, more optimistic than realistic. Charles Coote's *History of England* highlighted the damage that the Cock Lane affair had done to London's reputation when he made reference to the ghost in between descriptions of great military victories. For Coote, the episode represented 'strong proof of the credulity of the English populace' and he observed that 'the delusion operated with considerable effect; and superstitious terrors were widely propagated'.[24] Reverend John Adams was more forceful in his condemnation of the London crowd in 1762, whose conduct was proof 'of their blind superstition'.[25] Moreover, Scratching Fanny was one of a great many ghosts that haunted the capital in the late eighteenth century.[26]

When reactions to a wide range of ghost stories are explored in greater depth, and over a longer chronological period, it becomes clear that the boundaries between the natural, preternatural and supernatural were far from settled by the 1760s. Assorted responses to the Cock Lane affair show that a wide variety of opinions co-existed about the meaning and authenticity of ghost stories. Cock Lane also demonstrated that responses to ghost stories were bound up with questions of religious authority. These narratives had an important part to play in intra-Protestant struggles for authority over doctrine, forms of worship and devotional practice. Nevertheless, if the polemical association of ghost stories deterred public declarations in favour of these narratives at moments of political and religious tension, it was a different story away from the heated world of public comment and posture. Anglicans and other Protestant dissenters encouraged limited, yet fruitful engagements with the preternatural world as part of their pastoral strategies, and as such they identified important areas of crossover and common interest.

Methodist Ghost Stories

In 1762 an anonymous pamphlet called *Anti-Canidia: or, Superstition Detected and Exposed* was published in London. It set out to free mankind from 'the tyranny of superstition', and to fell the 'mighty Colossus' of ghost beliefs that had lately caused such uproar in the capital.[27] The author was prompted to write this lengthy tract by 'the contemptible *wonder* in Cock-lane, that has lately made so much *noise*; and the *more wonderful* attention paid to it, even by some persons of rank and character'. The affair was clearly no laughing matter for this particular author, who attacked ghosts in the interest 'of *pure* religion' and '*for* the honour of God and Providence'.[28] The variety of religion favoured here was reasonable, and it was heavily influenced by the notion of a self-sufficient universe, in which religion was bound to the ordinary laws of nature. A contemporary analogy likened God to a watch-maker whose creation ticked along by itself, under supervision, but without constant interference from its inventor. Rational or reasonable Protestantism thus carried with it a particular view of providence, and one which was heavily influenced by the confidence of Enlightenment philosophies. Public endorsement of prodigies, miracles and wonders was similarly discouraged by the ferocious Tory–Whig battles of the early eighteenth century. Party publicists from both sides tried to tar their opponents with the label of superstition, hoping to conjure up negative associations with civil war sectarianism and Jacobitism.[29] On the public stage at least, the emerging dominance of reasonable religion characterized by latitudinarianism was closely tied to philosophical and political fashion. Many argued that, since mankind was now set on the path to perfectibility, it was unnecessary, even offensive, to suggest that God still needed to intervene to chastise sinners and to encourage the faithful through visions and miracles. Peter Annet's *Supernaturals Examined* declared that God would not violate the natural laws which he had set down, and this was reinforced just a year later by David Hume's seminal work *Of Miracles*.[30] Signs and wonders that were made to serve trivial and insignificant ends were often termed 'particular providences', and they offended the dignity of a more transcendent conception of divine providence. The Cock Lane fraud was a case in point, and the ghost of Scratching Fanny was deemed a fabrication, which only served to satisfy a sinful lust for revenge. Those who favoured such a theological outlook could not justify the interruption of nature for such a particular and trifling providence as this, nor could they tolerate Methodist support for such wonders. Ironmonger and theological writer William Sturch represented the views of many Unitarians when he confined revelation to the morally debauched period of the early Church. Supernatural communication was useful then only to awaken people to the preaching of Jesus. For Sturch even the gospel miracles were questionable because they relied on the vagaries of human testimony.[31]

By 1750 sceptics had much to complain about. Methodist encounters with the supernatural had been widely published in the early years of the movement, because they both reflected and advertised the success of the evangelical cause. There is no denying, however, that some of these episodes were more than a little incredible, and they exposed early converts to accusations of wild enthusiasm. In June 1756 John Wesley published an account from a Dublin clergyman, which told how the ghost of Richard Mercier had lately appeared to his fiancée after he had been struck dead by a mistimed church bell.[32] In 1789, the official Methodist publication, the *Arminian Magazine*, related the tale of Mrs Brown, who had seen a flash of light in her house, and heard the footsteps of 'a heavy man in loose slippers'.[33] She was unable to account for the meaning of this episode and so deferred to Wesley's expertise on the subject. If Mrs Brown's case was perplexing, then the experiences of a woman from Sunderland were even more difficult to decipher. Wesley himself admitted that the case of twenty-two-year-old Elizabeth Hobson was one of the strangest he had ever encountered, yet that was no grounds on which to dismiss it out of hand.

Elizabeth Hobson had seen more than her fair share of ghosts for such a young person. Her experiences had begun in early childhood, when she frequently saw apparitions of her neighbours just before or just after they had died. 'I observed all little children, and many grown persons, had a bright, glorious light round them; but many had a gloomy, dismal light, and a dusky cloud over them.' Elizabeth clearly had a gift for deciphering the spiritual reward of the ghosts that appeared to her, and at the age of twelve or thirteen the spirit of the wicked family lodger visited her all aflame. Four years later, after the death of her beloved uncle, Elizabeth prayed to see him one last time. He dutifully appeared before her, and in the guise of a guardian angel. He was dressed in a white shining robe and accompanied by 'delightful music', and he took care to nurture Elizabeth through her grief by appearing at her bedside for almost six weeks. Next, Elizabeth claimed to have seen the ghosts of two more loved ones. The first was her fiancé who had lately died at sea, and the second was her brother George who had been drowned along with the crew of his ship in 1763. The ghost of a third sailor, John Simpson, also visited Elizabeth. This ghost declared that he could not rest until she had vowed to take care of his orphaned children. This ghost also brought an assurance of Elizabeth's future salvation when he told her that 'where I am, you will surely be' before he disappeared accompanied by sweet music. Thus far Elizabeth's narrative was eventful, yet inoffensive. In 1767, however, she put her affinity with the spirit world to a more lucrative purpose after inheriting a house in Sunderland from her grandfather, John Hobson. Elizabeth employed an attorney to recover possession of the house from her aunts but, finding them stubborn, she claimed to have been visited by the ghost of her ancestor, who was 'an exceeding wicked man'.[34] His ghost told Elizabeth that if she wished to evict her ageing relatives from the house, she must sack her present attorney Mr Dunn in favour of Mr Hugill from Durham.

Elizabeth was ultimately successful in her legal suit, but her financial windfall raised questions about the reliability of her testimony. As we have already seen, the authenticity of ghost stories, alongside other seemingly miraculous happenings, could be allowed to stand if there was sufficient evidence to back them up. It was on this basis that Samuel Johnson, who was no enemy of ghosts, rejected Hobson's story when he heard it in London.[35] John Wesley also insisted upon the empirical verification of signs and wonders, yet he could not be persuaded to discount the story so easily. Elizabeth's visions were attended with enough circumstantial detail to make them plausible, and her narrative was an edifying tale that could be put to effective devotional use. Wesley publicized her relation in the *Arminian Magazine*, which boasted higher circulation figures than even the *Gentleman's Magazine* in the later decades of the century. Wesley also provided a running commentary to Elizabeth's narrative for the benefit of his readers. He drew parallels with biblical passages, and highlighted the salient lessons to be learned from Elizabeth's encounters with the invisible world. If Wesley's choice of evidence was variable, his purpose in spreading these accounts was highly consistent. In accordance with Richard Baxter's thoughts on the subject, Wesley believed that encounters with the invisible world might teach us to admire the 'frame of divine government', 'to confirm Believers against temptations to doubt of the life to come', to prove the immortality of the soul and future judgement, and to inspire love for a God that sent divine messengers to preserve the faithful.[36] Many churchmen, including Wesley himself, argued that the gospel miracles should be sufficient to relay these messages to the laity. Yet, in practice, Wesley believed that a little more help was needed if his evangelical preaching was to gain a hearing among the people.

Wesley set out the Methodist recipe for a successful sermon in his 'Serious Address to the Preachers of the Gospel of Christ'. Preachers were to take care 'that dry speculations and schemes of Orthodoxy, do not take up too large a part of your discourses', and he insisted that 'something practical' was brought into every sermon. Wesley was supremely aware of his audience, and a key ingredient in the successful sermon was the conversion narrative, something that related 'the first awakenings of the conscience of a sinner, by some special and awful providence'. The preacher had an obligation to speak from his or her own experience, or 'from the Experience of Christians who have passed through the same trials'. This would make it clear 'that religion is no impracticable thing'. It was believed that this sort of instruction would 'animate and encourage the young Christian that begins to shake off the slavery of sin, and to set his face toward heaven'.[37] Methodists were not renowned for doctrinal innovation, but they were famed for identifying innovative ways to bring religion to the people. According to Wesley's formula, ghost stories provided a way of bringing the gospel to life.

Nonetheless, Wesley's interest in the preternatural was personal as well as practical, and ghosts fitted neatly with his theological outlook. The activity of guardian angels was one of Wesley's favourite topics. The divine agency of these spiritual messengers harmonized with strands of Arminianism, which emphasized the benevolence of God rather than his wrath.[38] Wesley was also happy to admit that God intervened in the world on a regular basis, since he did not conform to the idea that man was a perfectible being. That said, Wesley was a man of his time, and wherever possible he insisted upon the empirical verification of the wonders to which he lent his support. Wesley's theology therefore admitted both reason *and* revelation. In this he was not alone, since the roots of his evangelicalism can be traced back both to High-Church Anglicanism and to the puritan values of the seventeenth century.[39]

Wesley's appropriation of ghost stories was not a new departure for a Protestant minister either. We have already seen how the religious and political priorities of Restoration England had overridden early Protestant insistence on the cessation of miracles. With the help of natural philosophy, leading churchmen such as Henry More, Joseph Glanvill and Richard Baxter adopted familiar ghost narratives, and inscribed them with spiritual and moral principles to reinvigorate parish religion. John Wesley serialized Baxter's work for a new audience in the 1780s and 1790s, and he adapted the moral of each tale to suit contemporary concerns about the spread of consumerism, materialism and secularization. Despite the rhetoric of his enemies, Wesley's engagement with the invisible world in general, and with ghosts in particular, was part of a rich Protestant tradition that can be traced back to the early years of the Restoration Church.

Methodism's critics were not all drawn from the margins of rational religion of course, and one of the most outspoken opponents of the early movement was George Lavington, bishop of Exeter. He accused Methodists of inciting dangerous passions among the populace by the crude adoption of signs and wonders from the invisible world. Lavington adopted the familiar language of Augustan Tories and High Churchmen, and he identified Methodism as the same unruly disease that had gripped England during the years of civil war, causing anarchy in Church and State in the 1640s and 1650s. In *The Enthusiasm of Methodists and Papists Compared*, Lavington adopted a tried and tested rhetorical formula, attacking the Methodist 'pretence to Inspiration', and comparing 'the Extravagant freaks of Methodism' to 'the Fanaticism of the Romish Church'.[40] Lavington's lengthy tract was a particularly damning indictment of Methodism because it was first printed just four years after the Jacobite invasion of 1745. This event produced the most vehement outbreak of militant anti-Catholic sentiment since the century had begun. Ritual pope-burnings were carried out on the streets and they took ideological justification from the bishop of London and his clergy, who delivered sermons encouraging 'a just Abhorrence of Popery'.[41] Meanwhile, cheap ballads and pamphlets played on fears about Catholic usurpation and the suppression of British liberties. Anti-Catholic tensions reached a peak in the 1740s amidst fears of a political crisis, and against the backdrop of war with Spain and the fall of Robert Walpole in 1742. Early Methodist converts did in fact number among the most vehement opponents of Catholicism, but in the climate of paranoia that followed the Jacobite invasion of 1745, Lavington was able to fashion Methodists as crypto-Papists, who represented a threat not only to the Church, but to the social and political establishment itself.[42]

Whilst Lavington's anti-Methodist rhetoric may well have drawn upon genuine concerns about political instability, his attack was also motivated by the confessional rivalry which characterized persistent Anglican attacks upon Methodists in the early years of the evangelical movement. This conclusion is reinforced by closer inspection of Lavington's attitude towards ghosts. Lavington articulated Anglican fears that Methodist reliance on the guidance of the Holy Spirit promoted a more direct relationship between God and the individual. Such a theological model encouraged dangerous anti-clerical sentiment, and Lavington went on to rail against the 'impulses, impressions, feelings, impetuous Transports and Raptures' which the Methodists had the nerve to ascribe 'to the extraordinary interposition of Heaven'.[43] Lavington devoted considerable space to debunking episodes of supposed witchcraft, yet he was more guarded in his dismissal of ghosts and apparitions. He conceded that ghost stories still had 'some pretension to a Divine direction' in certain contexts.[44] Lavington revived a well-worn Protestant argument used to authenticate providential signs when he argued that on rare occasions ghost stories 'may sometimes come from God' even though many were undoubtedly 'counterfeits and impostures'.[45] The author of *Anti-Canidia* also agreed that if a ghost story 'was for the reclaiming of a sinner, and to save but one soul from everlasting perdition; it might be a cause worthy of divine interposition: and consequently in some degree credible'.[46] In other words,

Lavington's condemnation must be read as a conditioned response to intra-Protestant struggles for authority, rather than as an innate aversion towards ghost beliefs and the stories through which they were expressed.

There was, moreover, a brand of Methodist ghost that inspired reverence rather than ridicule from a variety of confessional groups. An entry in John Wesley's journal for Sunday, 28 March 1736 related the story of Peter Wright, the servant of one Mr Bradley. The young man spoke to Wesley on his sickbed (though Wesley took care to note that Wright was 'perfectly sensible' in spite of his illness). Peter told him that on Thursday night around eleven o'clock he heard a voice calling his name. When he looked up, his chamber was filled with light and he saw 'a man in very bright clothes stand by the bed, who said, "Prepare yourself, for your end is nigh"'. Wesley was eager to put this apparition to pastoral use, and so told Wright that 'The advice was good, whencesoever it came'. It was with delight no doubt that Wesley wrote how the apparition subsequently transformed Peter Wright's behaviour. Just a few days later 'his whole temper was changed as well as his life, and so continued to be till, after three or four weeks, he relapsed and died in peace'.[47] Peter Wright's experience was convincing because it was familiar, and parallels could easily be drawn with the lives of the saints. Peter Wright's tale was essentially a 'conversion narrative', which enjoyed a rich biblical tradition, most famously associated with the life of Mary Magdalen. The acceptability of Peter Wright's relation was strengthened by the weight of the gospel, and by the fact that it bridged the gap between particular and general providences. Although Wright benefited personally from the intervention of the apparition, the subsequent publication of his experience served a broader purpose, namely to reinforce the value of a pious life to society at large. Ghost stories allowed clergymen to emphasize the value of a practical, moral Christianity, and this was a message with which Anglicans also identified.

Ghosts, Loyalism and the Church of England

Despite George Lavington's vicious attacks upon John Wesley, the two men shared a common aim – to fulfil the objectives of the early eighteenth-century High-Church movement for moral reformation and parochial renewal. It was the methodology employed to achieve this end, rather than the end itself, which caused disagreement. Whilst Lavington hoped to reach his goal by sober methods of persuasion, Wesley was willing to adapt revelatory episodes for the purpose. But if Lavington's formula excluded the use of ghost stories, a number of his fellow churchmen did not agree. Archibald Cockburn was a firm believer in ghosts, and he defended their place in his theological outlook as evidence of the soul's immortality, and as paragons of virtue.[48] Cockburn commended tales of returning souls as signs of God's infinite compassion, since 'He leaves it not solely to Faith to conduct us to the Eternal World, but stoops to the low Reach of Human Faculties, and gives us a sensible Evidence of a State that's distant from our Senses. Heaven and Hell are invisible under these our Mortal Circumstances, and therefore from thence he sends Inhabitants, to bring them often into our Remembrance.'[49] Following Cockburn's example in 1747 was a new six-penny pamphlet from the London presses entitled *An Account of the Apparition of the Late Lord Kilmarnock to the Reverend Mr. Foster*. This pamphlet resembled those described in Chapter 2 in both size and form. It most likely appealed to a mixed audience since the main character was the ghost of the infamous William Boyd, fourth Earl of Kilmarnock, who was sentenced to death for high treason in July 1746 for his part in the Jacobite invasion. Foster attended the disgraced peer in his final hours to urge his repentance, following his capture at Culloden. Foster was unsatisfied by Kilmarnock's speech on the scaffold, and so he penned a lengthy account of the conversation he claimed to have had with Kilmarnock's apparition on the morning after his execution. Kilmarnock's ghost appeared chastened by his crimes, and he dutifully appeared to Foster to warn all 'noe to postpone their everlasting Concerns to their last Days'.[50] The ghost went on in the manner of a preacher, declaring 'that Jesus Christ is the w[a]y of Truth, and the Life, and that no Man cometh to the Father but by him'. 'Dare not', he continued, 'attempt to find out a new Way to Heaven: Good Works will follow all Men into Heaven, for none can go there without them'.[51] The words of the Catholic traitor were now used to underline the righteousness of the victorious British nation and the triumphant Protestant faith.

Another dialogue between an Anglican clergyman and a naval captain was appended to this pamphlet. Having lately arrived from Jamaica, the captain had read about Foster's meeting with the ghost (after first hearing it read from a manuscript), and he was overjoyed at news of Kilmarnock's beheading. The clergyman then engaged in a lengthy conversation with the captain during which the cleric recited the articles of the Church and the Book of Common Prayer. The clergyman then went on to relate that, on the same day that Kilmarnock's ghost appeared to Foster, he too was visited by the ghost (whom he knew personally when living) whilst in his garden. The ghost gave the cleric 'a small Paper Book in Octavo. The Writing was plain, and of an azure Colour, shining exceeding bright' and it contained the account of the ghost's conversation with Foster. The clergyman was given divine permission by the apparition to publish the account for the use it might have in bringing sinners back to the path of righteousness. This extraordinary tale was similar to Wesley's account of Peter Wright, and the author made full use of not one, but two conversion narratives. Not only was Kilmarnock delivered from his sinful ways, but the naval man was also transformed by the tale and declared that 'I have been an Infidel hitherto as to Apparitions'. Yet he was now confirmed in his faith, and he went on to promise that 'I shall think more of Jesus Christ than ever I did before in all my life'.[52] In contrast to the alleged instability promoted by Methodist engagement with the invisible world, Kilmarnock's ghost was now allowed to service the needs of the political and religious establishment.

The anonymous author of this pamphlet capitalized both financially and spiritually on the notoriety of Kilmarnock, and on the patriotic taste for military victories and bloody executions. He was not alone in using the marketplace of cheap print to communicate important religious messages. In 1764 he was joined by another minister, this time from Northampton. *The Ghost, or A Minute Account of the Appearance of the Ghost of John Croxford* was written two years after Cock Lane, and it was later published as the follow up to *A True and Circumstantial Relation of a Cruel and Barbarous Murder*. The first twelve-page pamphlet told of the shocking murder of peddler Thomas Corey, who had his throat cut before being stabbed in the head after an argument about the price of the stockings he was selling. The killing took place at a house of ill repute in the parish of Guilsborough, kept by Thomas Seamark, who had been recently executed for highway robbery. After Corey was stabbed, his body was stripped and his clothes were taken upstairs where the Seamark children lay in bed. Corey's corpse was then cut into little pieces and buried in different parts of the house. Three men were convicted of this gruesome killing, but the chief villain and the man who allegedly struck the fatal blow was John Croxford, a twenty-three-year-old tailor from Brixworth. Croxford was executed in 1764 and his body was taken to Holloway Heath and hanged in chains on a specially-erected gibbet. Many locals objected to this harsh sentence, however, since Croxford never confessed his part in Corey's murder, though he did admit to a string of petty offences. The opinion of the crowd was divided at the scaffold and protestations of innocence from all three convicted men 'brought many over to a full persuasion of their Innocence, and left others to half between two Opinions'.[53] Ann Seamark, wife of the executed Thomas, was chief witness for the prosecution. It was on her evidence, and that of her ten-year-old son, that Croxford's conviction was secured. Seamark's honesty was brought into question after the execution, and a public row ensued in which she was attacked as a traitor and a liar. This was the background then to the publication of *The Ghost* by a churchman who seemed determined to defend the justice of Croxford's sentence, and to champion Anne Seamark's role in his downfall.

It was on 12 August 1764 that the ghost of John Croxford first appeared to this clergyman. The scene was highly appropriate, since he had just returned to his study after instructing his parishioners in scripture. He was reading St Paul's Epistle to the Corinthians on the resurrection of the body, when all of a sudden he was confronted by 'the perfect form and appearance of a Man'.[54] The ghost bid the cleric not to be scared, and he immediately confirmed that he came on a divine mission and could do nothing 'but by the immediate permission of GOD'. The ghost identified himself as John Croxford, 'PRINCIPAL and RINGLEADER'

of the gang that had murdered Thomas Corey. He declared that 'he was particularly appointed by *Providence* to undeceive the world, and remove those Doubts
which the solemn protestations of their innocence to the very Hour of Death had
raised in the Minds of all who heard them'. When the clergyman asked the ghost
why he had denied his part in the murder, he answered that, aside from being
drunk on the scaffold, he and his accomplices had entered into a sacramental vow
never to tell a soul. They had sealed this macabre pact by 'dipping their Fingers
in the Blood of the deceased and licking the same'.[55] According to the ghost, the
guilty men believed that they would literally get away with murder because Anne
Seamark's husband had been confederate in the killing. Her evidence would
have been inadmissible, had she not been widowed shortly before the trial took
place. The clergyman wisely asked the ghost for some firm proof following these
extraordinary revelations, and so he was told to dig in a certain spot of ground.
Here he found a ring belonging to the unfortunate pedlar, which bore the fateful
words 'HANG'D HE'LL BE WHO STEALS ME – 1745'. The discovery of the
ring not only persuaded the author that he 'had the full use of both my Senses and
Reason' when the ghost had appeared to him, but it also convinced him of his
obligation 'to communicate to the World the Particulars of the Whole'.[56]

This story was bound to capture the imagination of its readers since it contained murder, grisly pacts and buried treasure – all the classic ingredients of a
popular folkloric ghost tale. Nonetheless, the pamphlet may also have appealed
to a more discerning audience. It was of a substantial length, incorporated Latin
quotations, and was priced at 1*s*. Moreover, the author was not just interested in
lining his own pockets with the profits of publication, since he mixed the familiar
motifs of the ghost story with a strong dose of moral and religious rhetoric. The
author drew his readers in on the title-page with the promise of a 'GHOST', and
then he set about preaching on the perils of vice and immorality that were infect-
ing the nation in 'an Age of Dissipation'.[57] The author made clear that it was only
with God's assistance that private and public debauchery could be defeated, and
it was in this context that this very particular intervention was offered up for public consumption. The author firmly linked John Croxford's ghost to 'wonderful
Providence'. He went on to contest new linguistic expressions that had come to
dilute, or to provide secularized alternatives to this term, 'What we call Fortune,
Chance, or Fate here below has a different Name above & is term'd the Power,
the Wisdom or Providence of GOD'.[58] This narrative was intended to 'reform
the Vicious ... quicken the spiritual sluggard, persuade the Diffident, and encourage the Virtuous in a steady perseverance of the Duties of Religion', and John
Croxford's ghost was a timely reminder of the punishment that awaited sinners
if they strayed from the path of virtue.[59] Obedience to the Church was central to
the achievement of virtue, and only by respecting the Sabbath and the ministrations of the Church would John Croxford's fate be avoided. This pamphlet was
first published just two years after the Cock Lane episode, and it provides a use-

ful reminder that ghosts had yet to be loosed from doctrinal service. Croxford's repentant spirit reaffirmed the symbiotic relationship between Church and State, and it linked religion to principles of national virtue.

Both Methodist and Anglican ministers sought to reinforce the authority of Protestantism in an age of apparent secularization and also to promote a practical, moral theology as a prerequisite to salvation. Ghost stories were an important medium through which to achieve both ends. As Linda Colley has argued, anti-Catholic sentiment was an important means of self-definition for British Protestants in the eighteenth century, and a source of unity for Protestant denominations in the face of a common enemy.[60] A Methodist ghost story printed in the *Arminian Magazine* in the 1780s expressed a strong sense of patriotism centred on the defence of the Protestant faith. In 1754, the house of John and Ann Lambert of Winlington, Newcastle, was greatly disturbed by the ghost of Henry Cooke, who had lived there until his death in 1752. Strange noises were heard in the house for about two weeks before Ann Lambert saw a man dressed in his burial clothes at one o'clock in the afternoon. The ghost frightened her so much that Ann persuaded her husband to move to another house in the neighbourhood. However, the Lamberts could find no respite. After just a few days the couple reported having seen the head of a very pale man as they lay in bed one night. The ghost next appeared at the foot of the bed. He was dressed in the clothes that he had worn when alive, and he was immediately identified as the disturbed spirit of Henry Cooke, a notorious Catholic recusant. The revelation of Cooke's Catholicism went a long way towards explaining the violent antics of the ghost that followed over the next year. The Lambert children were dragged kicking and screaming from their beds, the cat was murdered, Ann Lambert was stamped on by the ghost, who came dressed 'in a surplice and white wig', and in December 1755 Ann saw the ghost 'in the likeness of a brown and white calf; it grew bigger and bigger till it was the size of a middling horse, then it leapt into the bed and struck her three times'.[61] The details of this encounter were clearly sensational, but its purpose was only too apparent, namely to connect Catholicism with the devil, since nobody could have mistaken the ghost of Henry Cooke for a benevolent spirit.

In periods of political crisis, ghost stories expressed feelings of anti-Catholicism and Protestant patriotism, which highlighted commonalities rather than conflicts between different Protestant denominations. The timing of Henry Cooke's ghost was highly significant, and it represented one expression of the huge outpouring of loyalist and anti-Catholic feeling produced by the Jacobite invasion of 1745–6. The political threat posed by Catholicism was at its height between 1688 and 1746, when it was explicitly linked to Jacobitism. The Young Pretender's claim to the British throne was also most vigorously supported by Catholic France and Spain in these years. With these nations newly resurgent on the European stage from the 1730s, anti-Catholic sentiment reached a peak, and it cut across social, political and religious divides. A two-page ghost story published in 1758 fitted this model of Protestant patriotism, with the ghost of Admiral Edward Vernon referring to French Catholics as the 'treach'rous foes' of Britons. The ghost also lamented the failings of British commanders during the Seven Years' war, upon which 'proud Gallia builds her fame'.[62] Nicholas Rogers described Vernon as 'the Britannic bane of the great Catholic powers'.[63] An account from 1757 described the appearance of Admiral John Byng's ghost, and it displayed similar patriotic qualities and linked belief in ghosts to the true religion of Britain.[64] A number of ghost stories from the mid-eighteenth century thus support Paul Langford's claim that anti-Popery was an 'expression of national unity'.[65]

Nonetheless, the death of James Edward Stuart ensured the security of the Hanoverian succession. The Pope recognized George III as King of Great Britain in 1766, and as a result the nature of anti-Catholic feeling changed. This was especially evident among politicians and enlightened intellectuals, who were willing to make concessions to Catholics both at home and abroad to secure loyalty to the Crown, to cement imperial policy in the colonies, and to further commitments to religious toleration. However, this periodization of anti-Catholic feeling should not be too categorically enforced. The Gordon Riots of 1780 suggest that a latent groundswell of Catholic hatred persisted, especially among the poorer sorts, and that it could erupt in moments of crisis.[66] Ghost stories were also re-adopted as vehicles of anti-Catholic polemic in the 1790s, which again positions these tales as the shared resources of different confessional groups that could be used to uphold the legitimacy of Church and State against the threat of French invasion.

If the political menace of the Catholic faith was diluted after 1766, evidence indicates that theological objections to Catholicism remained strong among Anglicans, and especially among Methodists. A new edition of John Tillotson's *Discourse against Transubstantiation* was published as late as 1797, and a ghost story serialized in the *Arminian Magazine* for 1785 explicitly denied any association with Catholic beliefs surrounding the fate of the dead in the afterlife.[67] It may also be significant that a number of eighteenth-century ghosts displayed angelic qualities. As we saw earlier, Elizabeth Hobson was visited by her uncle in the guise of a guardian angel, and Daniel Defoe's *History and Reality of Apparitions*, reprinted in 1752, 1770 and 1791, compared the qualities of angels and apparitions of the dead. The increasingly blurred metaphysical distinction between angels and departed souls during the eighteenth century may well have been an important differentiating feature of Protestant ghost stories, deflecting any association of departed souls with a middle state of purgatorial trial.[68]

Changing notions of anti-Catholicism thus heavily influenced the way in which Anglicans and Methodists responded to ghost stories. Yet members of several denominations also articulated common concerns for moral reformation through their engagement with these narratives. Bishop Fisher of Exeter declared that Christianity was a gospel of social action, with the moral code of Protestantism termed 'the common possession' of all.[69] This consensus is unsurprising given that John Wesley's theological roots grew from the same preoccupations that influenced many Restoration churchmen. The importance of a practical, moral Christianity was not only championed as a means of engaging with the ethical instincts of a disaffected population, but also as a unifying force for Protestant denominations, who could work together to achieve a common goal. Indeed, a number of Presbyterian ministers joined the chorus of voices seeking to negotiate a *via media* between reason and revelation in religious life. For Alexander Webster, supernatural revelation was an aid to repentance and amendment.[70] In 1764 Webster's colleague John Leland penned *The Advantage and Necessity of the Christian Revelation*. In it he drew analogies between the moral bankruptcy of the ancients and the public vice and corruption with which he was surrounded.[71] In a society such as this, Leland prioritized episodes of divine intervention to admonish sinners and to urge repentance. John Wesley similarly laid great store on the need for godly reformation to smooth man's path to heaven. His publication of ghost stories was designed to shock men and women out of spiritual lethargy. Wesley was no doubt also familiar with his father's appropriation of preternatural episodes in the *Athenian Mercury*, which served a similar purpose.[72] As we have seen, these accounts were mostly published in the 1690s, and they coincided with Samuel Wesley's participation in a broader clerical project for moral reform in this decade. A drive to reinvigorate Christian life began in earnest in 1690s England and gave rise to the Society for Promoting Christian Knowledge (SPCK; 1699) and the Society for the Propagation of the Gospel (SPG; 1701), along with numerous societies for the reformation of manners. Although their theological outlooks differed, both John and Samuel Wesley were concerned with the moral and spiritual welfare of the people and both went on to preach sermons for the reforming societies.[73]

The fruits of this campaign were realized in the eighteenth century, which saw 'the flourishing of practical Christianity' in England.[74] The drive to inject new vigour into parish religion was especially needful as the century wore on. Clergymen feared that imports of luxurious foreign goods would inevitably distract the populace from religion and lure them into habits of vanity and dissipation. The author of John Croxford's ghost story condemned Bernard Mandeville's *Fable of the Bees* for celebrating private vices, and others feared that the dawning industrial age would produce a nation of atheists and libertarians. To stem this tide of immorality the SPCK published bibles and other religious literature at a prolific rate. Societies for the reformation of manners also tried 'to regulate public morality by exhortation' in an effort to win back the loyalties of parishioners.[75]

Archbishop of Canterbury Thomas Secker was determined that the Church would learn from the traumas of the seventeenth century, and that it would find new ways to engage with the laity. Secker was famed for his pastoral zeal and he told one clerical assembly that 'We have in fact lost many of our people to sectaries by not preaching in a manner sufficiently evangelical'.[76] To remedy the situation, Secker taught his clergy how to deliver a sermon effectively and he also proposed a compromise between the principles of rational religion, where man might aspire to knowledge of God through his own efforts, and a revelatory faith where God could still intervene to teach more direct lessons to the faithful. Bishop Butler's *Analogy of Religion* anticipated Secker's blueprint for reform in 1736 when he sought to bring the works of revelation and nature closer together. The idea of a transcendent divine providence was by no means out of step with the religious culture of Hanoverian England, and William Gibson has gone so far as to call it 'a corner-stone of eighteenth-century Anglicanism'.[77] The legitimacy of both Church and State had also been consistently expressed in providential vocabulary since the Glorious Revolution, and the accession of William III was justified as an act of supreme providence. Similarly, the defeat of the Jacobite rebels in 1745, and Britain's escape from the revolutionary turmoil of 1790s Europe were also proclaimed as benevolent judgements on the chosen Protestant nation.[78] Within this framework, the concept of divine superintendence was complemented by instances of particular favour bestowed upon this favoured land. Avenging spirits occasionally appeared on the battlefield to serve heaven's justice upon Catholic traitors and to strengthen belief in the glorious destiny of Protestants.[79] Sermons compared Britons to the ancient Hebrews trying to escape the bonds of popery with the assistance of God's grace.[80] Secker's emphasis on the revelatory aspects of religious faith complemented, rather than conflicted with, certain aspects of Anglican religious culture. This also provided a platform for clergymen to communicate with their congregations.

The nature of Protestant doctrinal struggles in these years provided a further incentive for Anglican apologists to highlight the devotional and spiritual implications of ghost stories from the 1750s and 1760s. Persistent conflicts over the degree to which reason should supplant revelation in religious thought were brought into focus once more by Church of England clergyman Francis Blackburne. Blackburne provoked controversy with his liberal theological principles and his refusal to subscribe to the Thirty-Nine Articles. But it was his adherence to mortalism, or the idea that the soul slept between death and resurrection, which caused widespread friction among his peers. Blackburne's heterodox belief that the soul was naturally mortal had been popular among the radical religious sects of the civil war. The memory of those tumultuous years combined with a dogged Anglican faithfulness to the Holy Trinity ensured that Blackburne's *No Proof in the Scriptures of an Intermediate State* (1755) and his *Historical View of the Controversy concerning an Intermediate State* (1765) were roundly condemned.[81] Bishop William Warburton denounced Blackburne's historical view of immortality, and he was joined by scores of clerics and laypeople who offered defences of revealed religion. Prominent among them was Grantham

Killingworth, whose treatise *On the Immortality of the Soul* defended the validity of supernatural revelation through the example of John's vision of Christ under the altar. Killingworth upheld St Paul's interpretation of the apparition as a visualization of faith and hope in God.[82] If Killingworth offered an over-arching defence of revealed religion, Lancashire curate and schoolmaster of Middleton Richard Dean embraced this concept more wholeheartedly. In 1767 Dean published *An Essay on the Future Life of Brutes*, which firmly established his belief in a world marked by specific instances of direct providential intervention.[83] It was no coincidence that he was also a firm believer in the providential role of returning ghosts.[84] A desire to build upon such principles may well have motivated layman John Norris to establish a professorship of revealed religion at Cambridge University. Plans for the endowment dated back to 1767, but the position was finally created in 1770, funded by Norris's private estate at Bromholme Abbey in Norfolk.[85] Continuing this trend in 1778 was Benjamin Caulfield's *Essay on the Immateriality and Immortality of the Soul*. Caulfield insisted that it was heretical to suggest that God worked only by general laws of providence, since there was overwhelming evidence that particular providences continued to be experienced by ordinary men and women. In fact miraculous episodes and ghostly appearances were to be accounted 'particular and extraordinary deliverances' sent by God to demonstrate his goodness and mercy. Although God was indeed the watch-maker, this author considered it only common sense that 'the watch does sometimes want both to be wound up, and to be repaired'.[86] Although earlier Calvinist understandings of providential signs and wonders were clearly prominent in this text, this was no straightforward repudiation of the Protestant mantra that miracles had ceased. Those who maintained the possibility of divine intervention in mid-eighteenth-century England did so in the language of enlightened empiricism and civic humanism. Many argued that, although most reported wonders could be explained by natural means, a few choice episodes might still be ascribed to a higher authority if attended with substantial evidence. Not everyone chose to utilize ghost stories to preserve a balance between the marvellous and matters of fact in religious life. Some preferred to confine miracles and visions to the apostolic age, while others defended the holy mysteries of God from Socinian and deist attack by 'clear and natural arguments'.[87] Nonetheless, the preoccupations of theologians and philosophers ensured that ghost stories could be called upon as potentially valuable resources for Protestant apologists seeking to secure the faith from extremist attacks. The drive to find a compromise between the extremes of enthusiasm and materialism arguably resulted in a new Protestant orthodoxy, which was characterized by a carefully-constructed balancing act between the tangible and mystical elements of Christianity. When ghost stories could be verified within empiricist models of authentication, this theological compromise provided an important air of respectability for the telling and retelling of ghost stories, both in parish and in print.

If Anglican, Presbyterian and other dissenting commentators were united by their concern for moral reformation, they were sometimes divided by confessional rivalries that were intensified by the need to retain the loyalty of their congregations. Following the Toleration Act of 1689, parishioners could legally worship outside the Church of England, and Archbishop Secker's call for greater clerical activism was no doubt a response to the competitive marketplace of religion that had emerged. If the Church of England was to keep up with its sectarian rivals then spiritual truths had to be packaged and communicated in effective ways. Success could be achieved through lively sermons and cheap religious tracts that were expressed in plain language and accessible to the common man.[88] John Wesley and his brother Samuel devised a series of pioneering techniques to enliven Methodist worship, and music was to prove a crucial medium for attracting followers. Wesleyan theology was played out in hundreds of widely-published hymns and ballads, which were targeted at specific interest groups, including children. John Wesley banned organs from Methodist chapels in case they drowned out the voices of the congregation. The lyrics, he believed, 'intensified the emotion of Methodist worship', and expanded the ways in which Wesley could spread the Methodist gospel.[89]

Thomas Secker was reared as a dissenter himself, and he realized that he had much to learn from the Methodists. Secker was envious of their evangelical methodology, and he sought to imitate it within the Church of England. He demanded that something be done 'to put our psalmody on a better footing', because 'the Sectarists gain a multitude of followers by their better singing'.[90] If clergymen could reach their parishioners through song, then they also did it through print. Cheap pamphlets and short collections of ghost stories provided a particularly lively and engaging way of grabbing the attention of readers, and a number of conformist clergy went on to pen these accounts.[91] These collections preserved an important balance between instruction and entertainment and often followed the pattern of a familiar conversion narrative or parable with which an audience could readily identify. The success of these endeavours, however, ultimately relied on the reception of the narratives at parish level. Did the lay community invest ghosts with religious meaning, or were they just fodder for local gossip and titillation? A case from Harbury in Warwickshire helps to shed some light on this complex issue.

On Sunday, 4 May 1755 Richard Jago, vicar of Harbury in Warwickshire, preached a sermon in the parish church, 'On Occasion of a Conversation said to have pass'd between one of the Inhabitants, and an Apparition, in the Church-Yard belonging to that Place'.[92] Few details of this encounter survive, but the conversation supposedly took place on the previous Thursday night. The event caused such excitement in the local community that Jago seized this opportunity to turn the apparition to some useful pastoral purpose. It was his intention, he wrote, 'to adapt the present Occurrence, not building on any fanciful Notions, or disputable Arguments, but on the fundamental Principles of Reason and Revelation'.[93] For this serious and committed minister, the apparition constituted an important call to repentance for the people of Harbury. The vicar felt that those who believed the apparition to be of supernatural origin were guilty of lax morality, since God only intervened in such dramatic fashion to chastise the most degenerate of sinners. It was these people to whom Jago was preaching when he chastised those 'that are *slow* and *heartless* when ye are summon'd to attend the Duty of Public Prayer' and those 'that can loiter about the Doors of this holy Place, when the Service is begun'.[94] He reminded them 'that *Revellings* and *Drunkenness* are inconsistent with this holy Calling, and that they who do such Things shall not inherit the Kingdom of God'.[95] Jago thus manipulated the interest caused by the apparition to regulate the behaviour of his wayward congregation.

It was not only Jago who invested the event with spiritual meaning. The parishioners of Harbury turned out in unusually large numbers to hear the vicar's sermon on this subject, which had been the topic of so much speculation. The congregation looked to Jago for guidance about the meaning of the apparition, and he took full advantage of the opportunity to edify his congregation. Jago was somewhat circumspect, however, in giving a more general assent to supernatural wonders. Extraordinary providences were useful supports to the faith, but they were no substitute for the authority of Scripture, or for regular sermons and instruction by the parish minister. In this Jago was joined by Joseph Williams of Kidderminster, who acknowledged the link between ghost belief and lay spirituality. But Williams also regarded this as a sign of weak faith that could be overcome by trusting 'in the promises, the power, and the presence of God and Christ'.[96]

Richard Jago was clearly attracted by a more transcendent idea of providence, and the local literary circle in which he circulated may well have fortified this interest.[97] Nonetheless, Jago was willing to subdue his own scepticism to win over his flock, and the Harbury ghost had furnished an ideal opportunity to do just that. On this particular Sunday in May, Jago reminded the occasional sermon attendees in the crowd that 'God requireth your public Worship of him, and your thankful Use of his Ordinances', in the hope that his sermon would have some lasting impact and 'may be a Means of bringing them here again, even into the Courts of the Lord's House upon a better Principle!'.[98] Jago's move was astute, and it was likely to have made some impact on his parishioners given the rich tradition of haunting and superstition in this rural county. The ghost of Squire Newsham, a dissolute young man ruined by a gambling addiction, was believed to haunt Chadshunt House after his death in 1760 and the Reverend Augustus Fent was reported to have seen the ghosts of 'two kneeling women dressed in grey cloaks' in St Lawrence's Church in Napton.[99] Richard Jago prioritized the spiritual and moral welfare of his parishioners before his own philosophical beliefs, claiming that 'what makes such things proper, and sometimes necessary is owing to Circumstances peculiar to a Minister, and his own Congregation, which can never affect others exactly in the same Manner, especially if the Occasion be somewhat singular in itself, as the present was'.[100]

Jago's sermon was first and foremost a considered response to local circumstance. But he clearly believed that the Harbury apparition had something to offer to wider audiences, and so his work was published in 1755. Indeed, Jago's words may well have engaged those people that James Ramble encountered in his tour of northern England. For them, the idea 'that persons departed visited the upper regions again' was 'a part of their creed'.[101] When news of a ghost circulated in the parish, Ramble described how 'the church-yard was filled with numbers from all parts' who had gathered to watch two local parsons attempting to lay the ghost through prayer. Ramble noted with some disdain how this episode ensured that the two churchmen were 'hailed for their sanctity, and adored for their authority over the realms of darkness'.[102] Ramble's experience was far from isolated, and the implicit link that he identified between the power of exorcism and clerical status was reproduced many times. Reflecting on the late eighteenth-century ministry in 1826, Reverend Richard Polwhele recalled that 'some of the rusticated clergy used to favour the popular superstition by pretending to the power of laying ghosts. I could mention the name of several persons whose influence over their flocks was solely attributable to this circumstance'.[103] When John Atkinson became the minister of Danby in 1850 a local woman was put out when he told her that he could not lay the ghost that haunted her house. She clearly understood the job description of the clergyman to include mastery of the spirit world and complained that 'if I had sent for a priest o' t' au'd church, he wad a'deean it. They wur a vast mair powerful conjurers than you Church-priests'.[104] A report given to the vicar of Gateley, Robert Withers, further underlined the fact that many parishioners interpreted the appearance of ghosts within religious and providential schemas. This particular report related how the ghost of a deceased parishioner, Mr Taylor, appeared to his friend Mr Shaw to warn him of his imminent death, and that of another local man named Orchard. When Orchard died as predicted, Shaw sought the advice of Reverend Withers, amongst whose correspondence the report survived.[105] Reports of ghostly visions could then play a significant role in binding together incumbents and parishioners.

Aside from these specific instances, Richard Jago's work would also have gained a wide audience due to the fact that sermons were a very popular medium in eighteenth-century religious life, with demand often outstripping supply. They were the most important literary genre, with an average of three new sermons published each week. Readers also appeared to study these texts with a degree of diligence that they did not extend to other texts.[106] Sermons were printed individually, in collections and in newspapers and, as Anthony Russell suggests, those penned by eminent divines enjoyed huge sales.[107] John Tillotson's sermons were best-sellers, and twelve-volume editions of his *Works* were reprinted nine times before 1752. His *Twenty Discourses on the Most Important Subjects* was published in 1763 and 1779, and his individual sermons were still being printed as late as 1797.[108] Tillotson's sermons proved popular because they were concerned with preaching the virtue of morality and common-sense religion, rather than complex doctrinal formulations. These were themes with which the common man could identify. Contemporary handbooks also taught that 'energetic and colloquial preaching', that took into account the interests of parishioners, was 'the most generous, and likely method of winning souls to God'.[109] Jago's sermon fits this model of preaching, and it is highly significant that the Harbury apparition was incorporated within this genre, and thereby assimilated within the religious culture of Anglicanism. Jago's adoption of the apparition was also considered and rational, and he justified his work by emphasizing the civic purpose to which the proceeds of publication would be put. All profits would be used to fund the Free-School at Harbury, a project which coincided with similar philanthropic efforts in these years to educate the poor, and to improve society as a whole. Civic humanists could scarce object to the Harbury apparition when it served the greater good of the local community.[110] The school would be allowed to stand as a material testimony to the persistent belief in ghosts in Warwickshire and would foster 'a true Sense of Religion, and Humanity' for future generations.[111]

Augustus Toplady, vicar of St Olave, Jewry, similarly preached on the possibility of ghosts and apparitions for charitable purposes. More specifically, he wished to collect money for his parochial school. In a sermon preached in his parish church on Sunday, 29 October 1775, Toplady insisted that there was nothing absurd in the philosophy of apparitions. 'I do not suppose', he continued, 'that one story, in an hundred of this kind, is true. But I am speaking, as to the naked possibility of such phaenomena. And this I am satisfied of.'[112] Toplady regarded the Cock Lane ghost as a scurrilous yarn, yet the exposure of this episode had not dampened his 'stedfast and mature belief, not only that there are unembodied spirits; but also that, upon some special occasions, unembodied spirits and disembodied spirits have been permitted, and may again, to render themselves visible and audible'.[113] For Toplady, disembodied souls commanded a logical place in orthodox Trinitarian theology. Furthermore, the idea of ghosts could hardly be considered unreasonable, when 'God the Holy Ghost' was conceived as 'an unembodied spirit', which shared some kinship with the 'disembodied spirits' of 'glorified souls of the departed elect'.[114] Toplady's descriptions of the spirit world were designed to entice money from the pockets of his parishioners, but they also formed part of wider attacks on Unitarian heresies that were gathering pace in these years, and which denied the tripartite division of the godhead. Toplady's sermons indicated that ghosts were intimately associated with the workings of the Holy Ghost. By encouraging belief in the activities of lesser spirits, Toplady found an expedient way to defend the Trinity from attack, and to fortify the faith of his parishioners. The priorities of lay spirituality could thus shape the contours of parish life. In certain circumstances, local reports of returning ghosts could also influence wider philosophical debates about the relationship between the natural and invisible worlds.

Rational Dissent, Revolution and Revelation

Clergymen played crucial roles in sustaining the credibility of ghost stories. Their published accounts also provided an important channel through which the idea of ghosts could influence local and national audiences. However, if clerical appropriations of ghost stories identified common ground between several Protestant denominations, Unitarian dissenters did not share these interests. Scientist Joseph Priestley was one of the most outspoken Unitarians of his age and in the 1790s he launched a robust attack upon the legitimacy of ghost stories. The idea that the souls of the departed could return to earth was anathema to Priestley, because it implied the existence of a 'separate conscious state' after death upon which he believed a 'whole fabric of superstition' had been built.[115] Priestley believed that the idea of ghosts had its origins in pagan philosophy, and he identified it as one of the corruptions of the Christian faith in his *History of the Corruptions of Christianity*. Unitarians denied the Trinity and the invisible workings of the Holy Spirit. As such, the prospect of a future life was to be found only in the gospel, and specifically through recognition of Christ's humanity on the cross.[116]

True to his convictions, Priestley took issue with a ghost story from Lincolnshire, the events of which dated back to 1716, but which were only published in the 1780s. The story concerned a ghost named 'Old Jeffrey' that haunted the rectory at Epworth in Lincolnshire, and it achieved public notoriety primarily because the incumbent of Epworth at the time was none other than Samuel Wesley, father of John. The alarm was first raised in the Wesley household on 1 December 1716 when the children and servants of the house 'heard at the door of the Dining room groans like a person in extremist at the point of death'.[117] The noises continued for a number of weeks, and explanations varied as to the cause. The mistress of the house, Susanna Wesley, believed that the house was infested with rats, and she sent for a horn to scare them away. Nevertheless, the rest of the household were convinced that the disturbances were raised by a ghost sent to torment them.

Old Jeffrey was the name of a man who had died in the rectory some years before, and his ghost plagued the Wesley household almost every night for the next two months. Jeffrey was variously heard walking about the house 'like a man in a long night gown', slamming doors and jangling latches. He also came in many guises. Servant Robert Brown thought he sounded 'like the gobbling of a Turkey-cock', whilst something 'like a badger, only without an head' was spotted under one of the beds.[118] When Samuel Wesley and his wife went to investigate the noises one night, they heard a sound that resembled a large pot of silver being poured at their feet at the bottom of the staircase, and were later advised to dig there for treasure. Old Jeffrey's ghost became very violent in the nursery, but he reserved his strongest objections for the master of the household. In his journal, Samuel Wesley recorded that he had been violently pushed by the spirit no less than three times.

The Epworth haunting was one of the best-documented ghost stories of its day, and it seems that the entire Wesley clan, including the servants, were convinced that the ghost was real. Samuel Wesley Junior was the first to take an interest in the case after his mother told him of the disturbances in a letter of 12 January 1717. John Wesley later joined him to investigate the affair and the pair gathered reports from mother, father, from siblings Suky, Emilia, Molly, Nancy and Kezia, from servant Robert Brown and from Joseph Hoole, vicar of nearby Haxey, who was asked by Samuel Wesley Senior to expel the spirit from the rectory.[119] Irrespective of age, sex, education or confessional loyalty, all were ready to attest the truth of the case, and to confirm the providential nature of the haunting.

Susanna Wesley became convinced that the ghost had some providential purpose either to announce the death of one of her children, or, as she later thought, to portend the death of her brother, who had disappeared whilst working for the East India Company. Samuel Wesley Senior was unsure of Old Jeffrey's motivations, but he firmly believed that the ghost was sent on a divine mission, and hoped that God would put an end to the disturbances in good time. John Wesley believed that the ghost was a judgement upon his father 'for his rash promise of leaving his family, and very improper conduct to his wife in consequence of her scruple to pray for the prince of Orange as King of England'.[120] Samuel and Susanna Wesley had separated for a year just prior to the haunting on account of Susanna's Jacobite sympathies. Although John Wesley conceived a very specific meaning behind the Epworth haunting, he and his brother Samuel also recognized the more general import of the narrative for wider audiences.

John Wesley believed that the episode would prove a firm support to the faith of Methodists by demonstrating the particular care that God took to chastise and reward his followers. The whole story was thus serialized in the October, November and December issues of the *Arminian Magazine* in 1784. Joseph Priestley chose to address this particular ghost story because it gained so much publicity. Priestley himself confessed that it was 'exceedingly lively and entertaining; so that this is perhaps the best authenticated, and the best told story of the kind, that is any where extant'.[121] However, his motivation was also linked to the intimate association of the narrative with the early Methodist movement of which he wholeheartedly disapproved. John Wesley was aged just thirteen when Old Jeffrey tormented his family, and the episode proved a formative influence on his spiritual convictions. Wesley became convinced that the hand of God had providentially intervened to punish his family, and Joseph Priestley believed that it was this ghost that led Wesley to become 'strongly tinctured with enthusiasm, from the effect of false notions of religion very early imbibed'.[122] By attacking the credibility of Old Jeffrey, Priestley sought to discredit the evangelical cause, and to further the interests of rational dissent. Yet his work also underlined the point that ghost beliefs were foundational to eighteenth-century Methodism.

The sixty-seven-year time lag between the actual haunting, its publication in the *Arminian Magazine*, and Joseph Priestley's opposition to it, can be explained by the disorientating events of the 1780s and 1790s. Priestley's objections to Old Jeffrey surfaced at the same time that he proclaimed his support for the ideals of the French Revolution. Events in France did much to promote the radical religious cause in England, and the push for parliamentary reform in the early 1790s, but this benefit was short-lived. As events in France became increasingly bloody, Britain experienced the rapid growth of militant loyalism that strengthened conservative reaction against dissent.[123] Loyalist clubs and societies sprang up across Britain, and this activity was motivated by a variety of factors. Some came out in defence of county rather than country, and others to protect British trading interests. But these practical concerns were also accompanied by ideological motives, and most notably by naked Francophobia and a revival of anti-Catholic sentiment.[124]

Philosophical objections to the French Revolution were nurtured in both press and pulpit, and they were designed to stem the tide of radicalism from spreading across the channel. Moreover, as Harry Dickinson suggests, the values of the revolutionaries in France were generally depicted across the channel as 'an assault on Christian morality and ecclesiastical authority'.[125] The Church of England played a crucial role in rejecting these principles, and in fashioning British morality and Protestant spirituality as the very antithesis of French ideals. High Church Anglicans such as George Horne, William Jones and George Berkeley defended the privileges of the established Church. Samuel Horsley launched a doctrinal defence, and he condemned Joseph Priestley's anti-Trinitarian views as heretical and destabilizing.[126] These conservative ideologies also filtered into popular loyalist traditions, and the violence directed at Priestley in 1791 suggests that his religious and political views were not widely shared.[127] Moreover, as Boyd Hilton has argued, the moderate evangelicalism that dominated British political thought from 1784 to the 1840s rejected the 'religion of humanity' in favour of one that was more providentially inspired. The mundane activities of economic and social life were thus played out in 'an arena of great spiritual trial and suspense'.[128]

Long-standing opposition to the extremes of rational religion and the revolutionary events in France thus combined to promote the political value of revealed religion, in which the public legitimacy of ghost stories was again, albeit briefly, reasserted. We have already seen how Augustus Toplady's sermon of 1775 used scriptural and contemporary reports of ghosts to launch attacks upon Unitarian precepts. What was also significant about this sermon, however, was that it was not published until 1793. This followed the declaration of war between Britain and France when supernatural rhetoric was increasingly employed to reinforce political and religious orthodoxies. Richard Watson defended the virtue of revealed religion in pulpit and in print, and in 1795 the Reverend John Whitaker, a prominent critic of Arianism, published *The Real Origin of Government, deriving the State from Revelation, not Natural Religion.*[129] It was in this context that ghost stories were adopted as conservative vehicles of loyalist propaganda that stressed the value of public and private morality and political and religious fidelity.

A pamphlet narrating the appearance of Major George Sydenham's ghost illustrates how ghost stories fitted with these new priorities, and it clearly set out the punishments for immorality and irreligion when it was reprinted for a new audience in 1788. Sydenham and his friend William Dyke were religious sceptics, and they had made a pact that whoever should die first would return from the dead to tell the survivor whether or not there was a God and whether the soul was immortal. Sydenham had the misfortune to die first, and true to his word his ghost came to Dyke's bedside and declared 'I am come to tell you that there is a God, and a very just and terrible one, and if you do not turn over a new leaf, you shall find it so'.[130] The evils of religious profanity were further reinforced by a second providential narrative attached to this pamphlet. This related how a blasphemous and licentious young gentleman was struck dead by lightning. Two of the squire's dissolute companions died soon afterwards, and another fell into a trance in which he caught a glimpse of hellish torments and heavenly joys. When he awoke, he felt obliged to tell his story 'to several Divines, desiring that it might be published as a warning to other wicked persons'.[131] The distinctive piety of middle-class evangelicals like Hannah More also demonstrated the interaction of spiritual concerns with religious and political priorities. As such, they helped to link up personal holiness and morality to 'new concepts of public probity and national honour'.[132] In so doing, the pious discourse of evangelical reformers authorized the publication of narratives such as *The Wonderful Apparition of Mary Nicholson*. Published in Durham in 1799, this single-page narrative told the story of Mary Nicholson, who was executed for theft, and of her ghost that came to repent her sins, and to urge others to do the same. The author recommended this account as essential reading 'To the pious christian', for whom Mary's example 'ought to strike deep into the heart and mind'. The relation also provided a timely reminder 'that God's judgments were upon the earth'.[133] The narrative concluded in apocalyptic fashion with thunder and lightning accompanying the departure of Mary's ghost.

The link between ghost stories and conservative reactions to the French Revolution was more firmly established in a short pamphlet of 1793. *An Account of a Most Horrid, Bloody, and Terrible Apparition* was written by 'a Most Holy Person'. It gave an account of a meeting in the parish of Shotts in Scotland where a group of conspirators were talking 'of overthrowing the government, established by GOD in this country, and in its place establishing a diabolical plan, by which those who were the greatest thieves, or the most atrocious murderers, would be the sole rulers of the land'. The author's disapproval was manifest from the language used, and the pamphlet went on to draw very obvious parallels with contemporary events in France. The abhorrent plans of this motley crew were derailed, however, by the sudden appearance of 'a most hideous spectre, with a visage as white as snow, his hair clotted with blood, and clad in a white winding-sheet'. 'Let it be a warning', declared the ghost, 'against all seditious attempts; and remember, That the powers which be, are ordained of GOD; whosoever therefore resisteth the power, resisteth the ordinance of GOD; and they that resist, shall receive to themselves damnation'.[134] With this the ghost disappeared in a cloud of fire, and those who witnessed the spectacle fell to their knees and immediately prayed to God for forgiveness. The reality of this spectre was unimportant compared to the meanings with which it was invested.

The Church of England had been a close ally of the political establishment throughout the eighteenth century, but in the revolutionary context of 1792–3 this role assumed heightened significance. Anti-revolutionary propaganda painted the French as atheists, republicans and anarchists, everything that British apologists abhorred. Since the Restoration of Charles II in 1660 ghost narratives on the public stage had been fashioned in opposition to atheism, republicanism and extremism. The early modern ghost narrative was then an ideal vehicle through which to recommend the values of loyalty, patriotism, morality and religiosity. In the context of national crisis, ghost stories were just one of a number of polemical devices employed to dilute the extremes of rational religion and political radicalism.

Ghost Belief and Confessional Identities

Examination of the connections between Anglican and Methodist attitudes towards ghosts has been largely motivated by the weight of public comment from these two camps which circulated in print. Yet the attempt to outline how interpretations of ghosts were shaped by particular confessional outlooks prompts the question of what other denominations made of these episodes. What, if anything, were Catholics, Quakers and Baptists writing about ghosts in the second half of the eighteenth century? If the rhetoric of Anglicans, Presbyterians, Unitarians and deists is to be believed, we might expect to find English Catholics peddling frivolous stories of ghosts at every opportunity. William Hogarth's *Credulity, Superstition and Fanaticism* (1762) depicted a chaotic scene wherein a group of Methodists were thrown into fits of delusion by tales of wonders, miracles and ghosts, including the apparition narratives of Joseph Glanvill and the Cock Lane ghost. This was of course a satirical attack upon Methodism, but Hogarth also insinuated that latent Catholic superstition lay behind these Methodist excesses by depicting the preacher George Whitfield at the centre of the engraving, with the shaven crown of a Jesuit.[135] George Lavington similarly associated the origins of so-called Methodist superstition with crypto-papism. But was this empty rhetoric, or were these men right to draw such close connections between Catholicism and ghost beliefs?

In 1754 Catholic priest and hagiographer Alban Butler was appointed chaplain to Edward Howard, ninth Duke of Norfolk, but this cleric was more celebrated for penning a number of important theological treatises including *The Moveable Feasts, Fasts, and Other Annual Observances of the Catholic Church*. In this piece Butler adopted a markedly circumspect attitude towards reports of returning ghosts, remarking that 'we cannot deny extraordinary Warnings to have been sometimes received by that special Order of Providence, in Visions of just departed souls, nor does it seem impossible, but some holy Souls may, by a like extraordinary Appointment of God, communicate Thoughts to living Minds on Earth, but such Effects fall not under the ordinary Course of Providence, and depend not on the mere Will of any Souls'.[136] Visits of souls departed were not impossible for Butler, but they did undermine the philosophical precepts of those who denied the necessity for excessive divine ministrations. In common with many of his Protestant counterparts, Butler's reflections on the invisible world suggested a healthy knowledge of empirical philosophy, which required firm verification of visions and wonders before assent could be given to them. His reflections also highlighted the diluted emphasis upon purgatory in eighteenth-century Catholic discussions of ghosts.

Nevertheless, it is difficult to assess how far Butler's work mirrored wider Catholic sensibilities, or how far it truly reflected his own private beliefs on this topic. A few further examples may help to shed light on this matter. Joseph Berington was one of the best-known Catholic priests and writers of his day. He served as chaplain to Thomas Stapleton of Yorkshire between 1776 and 1782, and he was a firm supporter of Catholic emancipation. His hopes for political conciliation with the Protestant state may well have prevented his thoughts on ghosts from entering the world of print. In a handwritten and highly incendiary tract simply titled 'On Ghosts', Berington insisted that belief in the returning souls of the dead was not only outdated, but that it was a particular manifestation of the 'puritanical age of superstition' that reigned in England in the mid-seventeenth century.[137] Berington reversed the Protestant rhetoric that linked Catholics to bouts of uncontrolled enthusiasm, and instead insisted that the multiple visions (or delusions) of ghosts that Protestants continued to report were symptoms of a 'corruption in morals & licentiousness in religion'.[138] As for ghost stories in Catholic times, Berington was disposed to look more favourably on such visions, which he claimed were 'usually pleasing' and were put to good use in inspiring hopes of future salvation amongst the faithful.[139] He was careful, nonetheless, to date these visions to pre-Reformation Catholicism, as he wished to project a respectable image for the reformed Catholic faith. Although Berington appears to have kept his reflections on this subject to himself, the polemical intent of his work was highly reminiscent of his Protestant adversaries, who used accusations of superstition and credulity to attack their opponents. A different perspective was highlighted, however, by a private letter from Richard How of Apsley Guise in Buckinghamshire to his friend William Tomlinson in 1745. How's correspondence featured two ghost stories, one of which came from an unnamed Lady of his acquaintance, who was also a Roman Catholic. The first narrative, which was spread by the son of a Northamptonshire farmer, was exposed as a fraud by How's friend Mr Bonell, whose speciality was to explode supposedly wondrous tales of this kind. The following chapter will explore this episode in more depth, but the ingenious Bonell also provided a natural explanation for the second vision, in which the ghost of the young pretender Charles Stuart seemed to appear in a portrait to this Catholic gentlewoman and her acquaintance in Edinburgh.[140] A gathering of officers, gentlemen and ladies in a room close to the port saw a ship, which was said to be carrying the body of Jacobite conspirator Lord Kenmure. The gentlewoman then observed that 'If King James (young pretender) did but know the miserable catastrophe he had brought on so many noble families, sure he would weep tears of blood'.[141] At that moment, the lady looked at his portrait, and she saw three drops of blood on it which greatly alarmed both her and the assembled company. Confusion was deepened when the Lady tried to wipe off the blood with a white handkerchief, but no blood was to be seen. When Bonell heard the tale he quickly surmised that the dampness that was visible on the picture was likely to have arisen from the sea, and that it had a tendency to stick on pictures and mantle-pieces. The appearance of blood was simply created by the reflection of the officer's red coats. Despite the religious affiliation of this gentlewoman, no special condemnation was reserved for her mistake. In fact, Richard How's letter merely illustrated how both Protestants and Catholics were equally susceptible to optical illusion. The lady's story was of sufficient interest to allow it to flow easily through correspondence networks as an intriguing curiosity. When this story is placed alongside the evidence from Alban Butler and Joseph Berington, there appeared no simple dichotomy between Catholic belief and Protestant scepticism upon the issue of ghosts. This conclusion is hardly surprising since, in the ordinary course of life, Christians on both sides of this confessional divide speculated about the meaning and possibility of such episodes, often reaching the same conclusions.

As for Quaker attitudes towards the inhabitants of the invisible world, it is difficult to discern a distinctive viewpoint, since there is a notable silence in the archives on this subject. The absence of comment is in itself very suggestive, and it may well support the views of Rosemary Moore, who has argued that Quakers deliberately eschewed involvement with ghosts, or any other miraculous episodes, to procure a more respectable image amongst rival Protestant groups.[142] Indeed, the eighteenth century is generally known as the quietist period of Quaker activity. These years were a far cry from the early enthusiasms of the 1650s and 1660s, when Quakers tried to emulate biblical wonders such as raising the dead and healing the sick. These years were also far removed from the world of early leader George Fox, whose claims of miracle-working caused offence to those who believed he portrayed himself as a Christ-like figure. Indeed, Fox's journal shows that he understood his own curative powers, along with those supposedly worked by his fellow Quakers, as signs of divine favour and authority – something that was anathema to the established Church as well as to other Protestant dissenters. The memory of persecution that early Quakers suffered during both interregnum and restoration may well have persuaded later converts to steer clear of controversy in the years following the Toleration Act. Jane Shaw has, however, discovered that some former Quakers continued to be involved with acts of healing in the opening decade of the eighteenth century.[143] For the later part of the century, there is very little to go on. A handwritten collection almost certainly produced by William Awmack entitled 'Letters, Dreams, Visions and other Remarkable Occurrences of some of the People called Quakers' (1788) was marked by the absence of any ghosts. An angelic vision appeared before Samuel Spavold in 1754, and the Quaker minister John Churchman admitted to a similar apparition in one of his dreams.[144] The lesson he drew from it, however, was one of racial tolerance rather than providential intervention.[145] The particular domestic purposes to which ghost stories were routinely put may also have been less appealing to Quakers, who preferred to put their faith in more transcendent mystical wonders. Even in the heyday of Quaker miracle-claims, reports of ghostly visions were the exception rather than the rule. Indeed, as we saw in Chapter 1, George Fox himself declared that he did not subscribe to that particular belief since God would protect him from such visions.[146]

Nonetheless, an episode from 1791 suggests that a similar divergence existed between public and private Quaker reflections upon ghosts. On 6 July 1791 the young Lydia Tanner attended a 'meeting of the people called Quakers' in her native village near Sidcot. At approximately half past eleven the meeting was interrupted by Mary Neads, who lived in the cottage adjoining the meeting house. Bursting through the door, Neads exclaimed, 'For mercy's sake, do ye come out, or old Joany Beacham's things will be all broke to pieces!'.[147] The local schoolmaster and Quaker John Benwell attended the scene of the uproar with other members of the congregation, and the cause of the alarm was soon revealed to be a troublesome spirit. This particular ghost was thought to be Joan Beacham's late husband George, who had died about three months previously. His ghost now seemed intent on destroying his old home, tipping over chairs and pails of water, and throwing plates and jars from the shelves. Joan's maidservant was frightened out of her wits, forcing her mistress to send for the parish parson to read prayers. Parson Jones insisted that John Benwell leave the house since he refused to take off his hat. Yet following Jones's ministrations, the disturbance appeared to sub-side.

Witnesses who had been present at Joan's house were clearly convinced that something unnatural was afoot. John Clark investigated local responses to the affair some years later, and he interviewed John Benwell, who declared that 'It was very extraordinary, and I never could account for it'.[148] Others were more imaginative, and the most convincing explanation put forward was that George Beacham had left orders with his wife for his body to be buried in one of his own fields, 'or else in the church porch with a tinder box and flint in his coffin'.[149] Before he died he told her that if she did not carry out his wishes he would trouble her by coming again. Joan Beacham had indeed gone against her husband's wishes, and she had him buried instead in the churchyard at Winscombe. This place of burial may well have offended the religious and personal sensibilities of George Beacham, which forced him to carry out his threat. There were certainly confessional tensions in the village, which were typified by the encounter between Benwell and Parson Jones. Further weight was lent to this explanation by local recollections that the deceased was 'an eccentric old man ... who was looked upon by many as a wizard'.[150] Joan Beacham's servant also remembered having seen the ghost of her old master on the very night of his funeral. He was sitting on top of the roof and 'was dressed exactly as he used to be and having on his red cap'.[151] It seems then that local memory and the circumstances surrounding George Beacham's death were the most powerful explanatory forces at play here. Nobody present at the time shared John Clark's subsequent interpretation that the disturbance had been caused by electrical activity in the house. Indeed, irrespective of religious persuasion, the authenticity of George Beacham's ghost was never questioned. Only John Thomas was too afraid to spread the tale for fear of embarrassment, since it seemed 'so incredible & unaccountable' that 'no man in his senses' could believe it.[152] If Quakers were circumspect in their public pronouncements on ghosts, the same was true of Baptist minister and schoolmaster John Ryland, even in spite of a strict Calvinist upbringing that led many before him to credit stories of avenging angels and ministering ghosts. Ryland's publications defended the orthodoxy of an immortal state and of future retribution for sinners, but he asserted these points by scriptural example, and through points of conscience, without recourse to ghost stories or other revelatory phenomena. In his restraint, Ryland stood apart from his close friend and Church of England clergyman Augustus Toplady, who endorsed such episodes as essential supports of the Christian faith.

The data gathered here in no way constitutes a comprehensive survey. Deists and Unitarians have received scant attention. More detailed research on those groups mentioned above will no doubt enrich the evidence gathered here. Nevertheless, what does emerge from this small labyrinth of evidence is the sense that public perceptions of ghost stories were more clearly determined by confessional rivalry and political crisis. Discourses of politeness and empiricism played an important part, as they were promoted by a shared and vibrant print culture which cut across confessional boundaries. At grass-roots level, however, personal convictions about the appearance and meanings of ghosts were sometimes related to, yet not exclusively dependent upon, confessional affiliation. Face-to-face encounters with ghosts were more closely tied to the mortuary culture of this period, with a host of idiosyncratic beliefs produced by local gossip, community traditions and individual imaginations blurring any clear-cut correlation between patterns of ghost belief and religious outlook.

Conclusion

If the likes of Joseph Priestley could have written the history of eighteenth-century religion then ideas about the perfectibility of man would have triumphed, along with general laws of providence that supported the idea of a self-regulating universe. God would have been the overseer of a well-oiled machine, and miraculous signs and wonders would no longer be needed to reinforce the Christian and moral duties of the faithful. The realities of Hanoverian England, however, bore little resemblance to this optimistic script, especially when the meanings of God, providence and scripture were hotly contested. Divine intervention in the material world was strictly limited, but not abandoned. Many grass-roots level ghost stories were able to traverse private and public worlds thanks to clergymen who teased out the fundamental spiritual and moral truths imputed by these episodes, and made them relevant to wider audiences. In this respect, the fortunes of ghost stories on the public stage were buoyed by daily evidence of immorality, vice and sin, which authorized occasional interventions from God. The relevance of ghost stories was also sustained by the explicit fashioning of these narratives as anti-consumerist tales, as they were pitched into the battle against luxury and immorality that was so often spearheaded by reformist Methodists, Presbyterians and clergymen of the established Church.

Nonetheless, ghosts did not escape unscathed from the changing intellectual climate of these years. Early opposition to Methodist evangelicalism compounded the difficulties of justifying providential signs and wonders as legitimate vehicles of religious instruction. These challenges led to a drive to curb the most incredible preternatural wonders. Yet with the aid of empirical discourse, a compromise was reached between the extremes of a reasonable and revelatory faith. Well-attested ghost stories that were couched within providential or civic humanist vocabularies could often be acceptable in promoting cautious engagement with the mystical elements of Christianity. Reports of departed souls appearing to the living were thus made to speak to general moral tenets, as well as to reinforce specific doctrinal positions that were under threat, notably the issue of the soul's immortality, bodily resurrection and the certitude of future rewards and punishments. These concerns were shared by a broad spectrum of Protestant apologists, and as such, responses to ghost stories highlight an important area of consensus in an age often characterized by confessional fragmentation. Prioritization of lay preferences also helps to explain the unexpected fluidity of religious allegiances that was sometimes apparent on the subject of ghosts.

Ghost stories were made acceptable for public consumption by overlaying accounts of their appearances with religious, civil and political orthodoxies, but this padding was often unnecessary in private. Personal attitudes could of course be influenced by philosophical fashion, but the idea that the soul persisted after death and retained some connection to those left behind, often commanded a powerful place within lay spirituality. Attitudes towards the preternatural world were also related to specific confessional identities. John Henderson's firm attachment to spirits and apparitions was, for example, ultimately shaped by his Methodist upbringing, and it remained undisturbed by his philosophical studies and correspondence with leading sceptics like Joseph Priestley.[153] That ghost beliefs were not the unique preserve of the vulgar sorts has again been demonstrated by the likes of William Legge, Earl of Dartmouth, whose Methodist sympathies sustained his conviction that departed souls retained agency to revisit the living. These associations, although powerful, did of course have exceptions. The notorious atheist Elizabeth Vassall Fox was terrified of ghosts throughout her life, and personal attitudes were fashioned by multiple forces, as the following chapter will make clear. Nevertheless, the confessional cultures of Enlightenment England must still be recognized as notable supports of publicly-professed ideas about ghosts, and privately-held notions of an invisible world.

6 LANDSCAPES OF BELIEF AND EVERYDAY LIFE IN LATE EIGHTEENTH-CENTURY ENGLAND

Individual perceptions of ghosts were shaped by forces beyond pen and pulpit. At grass-roots level, ghost stories and ghost beliefs were firmly embedded within the life-cycle structures, daily habits and physical landscapes of late eighteenth-century England. These localized and highly personal confrontations with ghost stories form the subject of this chapter. We have seen how abstract philosophical trends refashioned perceptions of ghosts, but what did it mean to experience ghosts within a spatially-bound community? Childhood recollections from the turn of the nineteenth century indicate that the idea of ghosts was one of the most formative experiences of social life, and one that made a long-lasting impression that continued into adulthood. Britain's colonial and commercial endeavours overseas created new spaces and motivations for the production and circulation of ghost stories. Ghost stories were also intimately linked with familiar geographical features of the natural environment. Evocative physical settings played a very significant role in determining the ways that people responded to these narratives. Local landscapes represented the primary sites in which most people *experienced* ghost stories, and as such they provide crucial contrasts to the appreciation of ghost stories through print. Reciprocal links between ghost stories, memory structures and physical landscapes further suggest that these narratives functioned as important expressions of personal and community identities. The cults of sensibility and romanticism will finally be examined for the ways in which they encouraged interest in wild, haunted landscapes. The impact of Gothic fictions and artworks upon the private leisure pursuits of the governing classes helps to create a more complete picture of how public and private perceptions of ghost beliefs were constantly interacting, and reshaping each other. By detailing how the idea of ghosts infiltrated everyday life, this chapter highlights reciprocal links between individual psychological structures and broader currents of social, religious and intellectual change.

Spectral Landscapes

The physical landscapes of societies past and present convey multiple meanings about the people who live, or who used to live, in them. Hills, mountains, lakes, fields, forests and the man-made constructions that accompany them are, at base, tangible features of the natural environment. Yet these persistent features of the landscape only acquire meaning through the ways in which people understand and interact with them. Physical landscapes therefore represent dynamic sites of interaction between natural environments and human societies. These apparently unchanging vistas are, in reality, multi-layered and constantly shifting repositories of memory, experience and belief. The meanings with which landscapes are invested are continually made and remade over time, and in their turn, they give form and structure to the cultural obsessions and preoccupations of their inhabitants. The infinite meanings of historical and contemporary landscapes have been skilfully illustrated by geographers, anthropologists, economists, literary scholars, art historians and sociologists, but historian Simon Schama stated their significance most eloquently when he commented that 'before it can ever be a repose for the senses, landscape is the work of the mind. Its scenery is built up as much from strata of memory as from layers of rock ... it is our shaping perception that makes the difference between raw matter and landscape.'[1]

Ghost beliefs, and the stories through which they were expressed, were products of this fertile conjunction between the physical and the imaginative. The rich cultural meanings attached to visions of the dead can therefore be significantly enhanced by recognizing the potent influence of *place* upon notions of the spectral. Haunted landscapes also provide important clues about the ways in which ghost beliefs were experienced, and the particular, familiar contexts in which they made sense. This discussion of spectral landscapes therefore provides an essential backdrop to the place of ghosts within the Gothic genre, and within the Romantic imagination, to which I shall shortly return.

The intimate and sometimes subconscious connections drawn between the idea of ghosts and eighteenth-century landscapes was manifest throughout the century, and it was especially pronounced in the vast array of topographical studies that were published by clergymen and antiquarians. John Aubrey's *Miscellanies* offered a particularly rich example. This work exhaustively catalogued the numerous tales of ghosts and spirits that Aubrey had encountered in his native Wiltshire at the close of the seventeenth century.[2] At about the same time, the Church of Scotland minister and printer Andrew Symson penned a *Large Description of Galloway*, partly in response to Sir Robert Sibbald's excited attempts to produce a Scottish atlas. Symson's *Description* recorded traditional farming methods alongside a variety of supernatural phenomena that were associated with his adopted home of Galloway. Although Symson's account was written around 1692, it was not until 1823 that it was edited and published for a wider audience.[3] In the mid-eighteenth century, Welsh independent minister Edmund Jones published a catalogue of ghosts, apparitions and fairies, and Jones's belief in these spirits was closely related to his old-style Puritanism. But Jones also interpreted these reports within the particular physical and imaginative frameworks supplied by the dramatic scenery of Wales. In *A Geographical, Historical, and Religious Account of the Parish of Aberystruth: In the County of Monmouth* (1779) and *A Relation of Apparition of Spirits, in the Principality of Wales* (1780), geography, spirituality and ghost stories went hand in hand. Jones made an irresistible correlation between divine creation, the mountains, valleys, forests and waterways of his homeland, and particular sites of memory where people had habitually reported encounters with the invisible world.

For Jones, the topography of Wales and the natural world in general bore witness to the complex, and often turbulent relationship between God and his children. Earthquakes were understood as divine curses sent to punish human sin, and the craggy mountains, treacherous pathways and dark valleys of Monmouthshire were interpreted as physical marks of God's displeasure. They were the scars and wounds that testified to original sin and human depravity. On a more comforting level, Jones believed that swallows, which slept in a 'death-like state' through the winter, were a mercy intended to remind people of the resurrection.[4] The same message of divine love and protection explained the existence of a medicinal well at Ffynnon y Rhiw Newith in the Church Valley. A small stone near the Church Valley at Abergavenney, which bore the imprint of a young lamb's foot, also seemed symbolic of heavenly comfort.[5] Jones clearly believed that the immediate landscape was deeply infused with spiritual meanings, and that its features were intended to chasten, edify and to comfort. Going further still, Jones also identified particular locations within this sacred topography where divine and demonic power was more directly experienced.

Local wisdom taught that forests and dry ground near trees and hedges were the favoured haunts of fairies, who were particularly attached to female oak trees.[6] By contrast, ghosts and apparitions roamed a little more freely. Lanhithel Mountain was much talked of by the parishioners of Lanhithel, largely because it was believed to be haunted by the ghost of an old woman, whose principal mischief was to lead weary travellers astray. Tradition held that this was the ghost of Juan White, who lived many years ago and had been suspected of witchcraft.[7] Juan's ghost had also troubled neighbouring areas, and she was said to haunt the Black Mountain in Breconshire on occasions.[8] The ghost of Thomas Cadogan was also notorious within the parish of Lanihangel Lantarnum. During his lifetime Cadogan owned a large estate, the boundaries of which he expanded at the expense of a poor widow without consent or remuneration. Cadogan's ghost was troubled by his scurrilous behaviour, and he appeared again to a local woman at a stile upon the land that he had encroached to confess his crime, and request that the widow reclaimed what was rightfully hers.[9] A gentleman of Pembrokeshire met with a spirit in a local field called the Cot-moor, which had a reputation as a haunted spot since it contained two stones which were known locally as 'the Devil's Nags'.[10] Similarly, it was no surprise that Henry Lewelin of Glamorganshire encountered a spirit near Clywd yr Helygen ale-house, which Edmund Jones recalled as a place where the Sabbath had been regularly profaned in times past. Lewelin's spirit therefore represented a sign of God's displeasure.[11] Edmund Jones was clearly not alone in superimposing sacred and profane meanings onto his immediate natural environment. The examples cited here are highly suggestive, since they show that, for most people, religious belief was not an abstract philosophy, but something that was rooted in time, space and personal experience. After all, particular scenes and landmarks only became sacred because of the memories and stories associated with them. They also illustrated the existence of a dynamic and mutually reinforcing relationship between ghost stories, landscapes and memory.

The meanings invested in natural environments were of course fluid, multi-layered and subject to change over time. So if Edmund Jones was quick to credit particular instances of preternatural activity, others were undoubtedly more circumspect. Yet even those who were wary of acknowledging the possibility of direct divine or demonic intervention were drawn to interpret their immediate physical environments within an overarching framework of Christian providentialism. As Robert Mayhew has suggested, the dominant strand of latitudinarian theology in eighteenth-century England favoured a particular view of the natural world. This view was one in which mountainous terrain, tempestuous waterways and dense forestry symbolized the unfathomable wonders of divine creation.[12] Gardens designed for the Denbie family, and for Alexander Pope, were pleasing to the eye. But these botanical delights were also inscribed with deeper spiritual meanings, and they deliberately evoked biblical parallels with the Garden of Eden.[13] The Lisbon earthquake of 1755 conjured up thoughts of the deluge and apocalypse, and the poetry of Thomas Gray deliberately evoked thoughts of human transience and mortality through the landscape of churchyards.[14] Close scrutiny of the natural world was then tantamount to an act of piety because it led the mind from the visible to the invisible and from secondary causes to the original cause. It was a cultural commonplace that God worked through nature, but the extent of his work was open to debate.

The final decades of the eighteenth century saw the rise to prominence of Romanticism, which was a pervasive social and cultural movement that Ian Whyte has credited with creating a unique 'mysticism of place'.[15] Novelists such as Ann Radcliffe, James Hogg, Sir Walter Scott and Charlotte and Emily Brontë in the early nineteenth century gave an ethereal, otherworldly quality to the rugged and imposing landscapes of the British Isles. In so doing, they reflected but also strengthened wider expectations that landscapes of great natural beauty or splendour were endowed with a particular sense of holiness that was missing from more mundane scenes. The history of ghost beliefs traced in this book suggests a strong connection between real-life expectations and artistic representations of haunted landscapes. The imposing mansions depicted in Matthew Lewis's play *Castle Spectre* had clear parallels with a female ghost that haunted Castle Russin on the Isle of Man, and with a spectre belonging to an 'antique mansion' in Berkshire.[16] According to antiquarian Henry Bourne, a decrepit mansion in the environs of Newcastle that was 'seated on some mellancholy Place, or built in some old Romantick Manner ... had a Mark set on it, and was afterwards esteemed the Habitation of a Ghost'.[17] Similarly, the ethereal mountain scenes of Radcliffe's *Mysteries of Udolpho* were analogous to the mountain spectres documented by Anne MacVicar Grant and the highland ghosts of Sir Walter Scott.[18] Novelists and poets also drew upon the passion for the sublime and picturesque, which stimulated polite fascination with the wild and untamed topography of the Peak District and Lake District, as seen in the art of Joseph Wright of Derby and John Robert Cozens.

The social and cultural milieu of the later eighteenth century therefore extended the possibilities for imaginative enchantments of place through drama, fiction, poetry and portraiture. The idea of ghosts was then partially internalized, or psychologized as an imaginative tool with which to refine emotional sensibilities and hone moral virtue. Nonetheless, the philosophical distinction between aesthetic appreciation of an invisible world and genuine belief had its limitations. In the 1790s Joseph Palmer encountered the story of an old woman's ghost whilst on a rambling tour of Westmoreland and Cumberland. Palmer gave no credit to the relation himself, but a fellow traveller was not so steadfast after reports of the ghost seemed 'instantly verified' by the appearance of a luminous white shadow.[19] Readers of Gothic fictions were also occasionally tempted to transgress the somewhat hazy boundary between fiction and reality upon encountering a ghost in the pages of a text. The essential point here is that romanticized perceptions of landscape provided an overarching interpretive framework that allowed both real and imagined ghost stories to coexist, and to circulate to wide audiences.

Within this general framework of landscape perceptions, particular sites of spectral activity stood out above others. In 1745, the gentleman Richard How, whom we met in the previous chapter, wrote to his friend William Tomlinson regarding a curious haunting in Northamptonshire. How had been engaged in amiable conversation with his friend Mr Bonell on the subject of apparitions, when the latter ventured the story of a marvellous well. This particular well was lately suspected of harbouring a ghost, which had been condemned to remain on earth because of sins committed during life. The well was located in the middle of a farmer's field, and it was clearly a source of local pride. Reports of the ghost attracted much local interest, especially following the disclosure that this erudite spirit could answer any question asked of it, whether in English, Latin or Greek. Many local inhabitants were convinced of the truth of the affair, and the local parson visited the well himself to question the ghost. He could, however, find no evidence of fraud. So it was left to Bonell to investigate, who was a man known to have 'no Faith in these kind of stories from the Impossibility of a Spirit's assuming a substantial form, & thinking God would never work a miracle to no purpose'.[20] Bonell's determination to explode the affair eventually paid off, and he discovered that it was in fact the farmer's university-educated son who had been posing as the ghost for his own amusement. This mischievous young scholar set out to pen a natural history of his home county after completing his studies, but the discovery of his father's well prompted him to hatch a diverting plan.[21] The manner in which this fraud was executed, and the reactions that it prompted, adhered to a well-established tradition of haunted wells in England. These prominent features of the landscape had long been associated with supernatural or divine power. The illuminating work of Alexandra Walsham has charted how these physical markers were renowned sites of holy pilgrimage in Catholic England. Far from being abandoned as popish outposts in Protestant England's war against idolatry, wells were instead incorporated within Protestant providential frameworks, and they were believed to convey curative powers, or to provide hiding places for the devil and his minions.[22] Many Protestants continued to believe that holy wells were places where the prayers of the laity might be more effectual. Many wells thus retained strong associations with holy and demonic powers long after they had been divested of popish associations.[23] If ghosts of the dead were to be expected anywhere, then a remote country well seemed a highly plausible location. Bonell's sceptical encounter with the Northamptonshire ghost does then highlight a degree of contestation about the meaning of particular landscapes. The wide variety of opinions on this subject was further evidenced by reports of a holy well that surfaced in Flintshire in 1797. St Winefred's well was formerly a site of Catholic pilgrimage, but its spiritual meanings had been reinterpreted rather than abandoned in post-Reformation England. The well continued to be revered by locals as a place of miraculous cures for physical ailments, notably smallpox, and for other 'curious and remarkable Things' that could not be explained by the ordinary laws of nature.[24]

Notions of an invisible world were nurtured within the individual imagination, yet they were also firmly rooted in the material environment. If vestiges of preternatural influence could sometimes be detected at holy wells, the churchyards of eighteenth-century England were also believed to witness frequent scenes of slippage between the visible and invisible worlds. The meanings attached to these spaces are particularly relevant, because churchyards represent a very specific kind of landscape, and one that was intimately associated with the fate of the dead. In 1725 the Newcastle clergyman and antiquary Henry Bourne noted with obvious disdain that the ignorant people of many English communities 'fear and tremble' to pass through churchyards at night.[25] The reason for this trepidation was given as the belief in 'frequent walking of Spirits at the *Dead-time* of Night' which Bourne traced to heathenish superstition.[26] Bourne himself confessed that churchyards were more solemn than most other places in the dark, but the idea that ghosts appeared more frequently here than elsewhere was 'intirely groundless, and without any Reason'.[27] Bourne's view was of course based on the theological commonplace that the age of miracles and wonders had ceased. This philosophy denied that any particular location was more or less sacred than any another and, as a result, the highly differentiated sacred landscape of pre-Reformation England was effectively democratized. Bourne's comments did of course function better in theory than in practice. A plethora of recent historical work has demonstrated how the complex sacred topography of Catholic England was replaced by an equally complex Protestant geography of holiness, in which the sanctity or otherworldly associations of particular sites was habitually disputed.[28] Discussions of sacred space in eighteenth-century England do, however, remain somewhat sketchy. Yet brief glimpses into the contested meanings of churchyards suggest that this issue was far from moribund. A case study from Hammersmith in London will help to elucidate some of these meanings.

In January 1804, excise officer Francis Smith was arrested for the murder of James Milwood, a local bricklayer who was shot in the head in his local churchyard one night. When Smith was questioned by the magistrate, he admitted discharging his gun at a shadowy white figure. But he claimed that his intended victim was not James Milwood, but the infamous ghost of Hammersmith. According to numerous reports within this community, a ghost had been terrifying the neighbourhood for the last two months. Here then was an extraordinary case of mistaken identity, and though Francis Smith delivered the fatal shot to Milwood's head, the unfortunate bricklayer was as much the victim of local superstition and gossip. The Hammersmith ghost was rumoured to be the unhappy spirit of a local man who had cut his own throat in 1802, and his disturbed spirit had been particularly active in the weeks leading up to Milwood's death. Local watchman William Girdle saw the apparition in the churchyard just a few days before Smith, and he recalled that it seemed to be covered 'with a [white] sheet or large tablecloth'. Others described this frightening vision 'all in white, with horns and glass eyes'.[29] However, it was the material injuries inflicted by the ghost that led Francis Smith with his gun into the churchyard on that fateful evening. The ghost had grabbed servant Thomas Groom by the throat as he passed through the haunted grounds one night, and another poor woman quite literally died of shock after seeing a tall white figure rising from the tombstones.[30] Parishioners could talk of little else, and few dared to venture out alone at night. Francis Smith was one of those who did and, being determined to put an end to the haunting, he lay in wait for the ghost to appear. When Milwood took a shortcut home through the churchyard dressed in his work clothes, top-to-toe in white (despite the advice of his mother-in-law, who had begged him to put on an overcoat to avoid being mistaken for the ghost), his fate was sealed. No doubt swayed by the copious amounts of alcohol he had drunk in the pub earlier that night, and desperate to avoid the unhappy fate of his neighbours, Francis Smith panicked and shot the ghost, or so he claimed, in self-defence. Despite Smith's protestations of innocence, he was tried at the Old Bailey for the murder of James Milwood, yet he seems to have received a sympathetic hearing. The jury initially refused to find him guilty of murder until instructed to do so by the judge, Lord Chief Baron. When Smith was eventually convicted, his initial sentence of death was commuted to just one year's imprisonment after he received a royal pardon.[31]

So why was Francis Smith treated with such leniency? On a personal level, the twelve witnesses that Smith called to vouch for his character affirmed that he was a gentle man, and well-liked by his neighbours.[32] Yet, beyond these neighbourly ties, could it be that the circumstances that led Smith to discharge his firearm were sufficiently plausible to convince a jury that he had been justified in confronting this spectral menace? Evidence to support this suggestion can be found in persistent associations between churchyards and preternatural visions of ghosts. In 1767 Walter Watkins of the parish of Landetty, who was noted as 'a man of virtue, sense and learning', reported a luminous vision that appeared to him next to the local chapel. Soon afterwards, a neighbour digging up the chapel field discovered the remains of a murdered man who had been secretly interred.[33] We have already met with the churchyard apparition at Harbury in 1755, and John Brand later publicized the commonplace notion that 'gross and Sensual souls' were thought to appear 'often, after their Separation, in *Church-Yards*' where their bodies had been buried.[34]

It is a mistake to assume that the kinds of beliefs and practices outlined here were remnants of pagan or Catholic superstitions, with physical objects and locations being frequently invested with supernatural agency.[35] A more convincing explanation emerges with a close, albeit brief, examination of eighteenth-century attitudes towards sacred and profane space. Churchyards in particular were very difficult to categorize as either sacred or profane, and no clear consensus existed about the nature of this space from clerical and lay commentaries. Churchyards had accommodated both religious and secular business for many centuries, both in England, Europe and further afield. David Dymond documented shifting usages of these spaces in medieval and early modern England. Churchyards provided a final resting place for the dead, but they also played host to regular commercial activities in the form of fairs and markets. This communal open space also provided an excellent venue for local sports and pastimes, which in the eighteenth century included 'handball, hammer-throwing, ninepins, bowls, bandy (a form of hockey), tennis and fives' as well as the drinking, dancing and general revelry that followed a funeral.[36] The status of churchyards as spiritual or secular spaces was constantly in flux in view of this varied job description. The arrival of Protestantism in mid-sixteenth century England did little to resolve these ambiguities. As Coster and Spicer point out, Puritan drives to relocate communal social events away from the churchyard may well have stemmed from a desire to impose a strict moral discipline upon wayward parishioners. Yet the result of these efforts was to effectively re-sacralize parts of the church fabric and its surroundings.[37]

The insistence on strict observance of the Sabbath was also commonplace amongst clergy and committed laymen and women from diverse confessional affiliations. If the outcry against Sabbath-breaking has been sufficiently documented for the seventeenth century, it mutated rather than disappeared in the eighteenth century. A sermon from 1733 entitled *A Dissuasive from Sabbath-Breaking* drew upon an earlier evangelical vocabulary to insist that churchyard activities like football and dancing were 'Profanations of God's Honour and Laws'.[38] Forceful as this sermon was, a clear shift of emphasis had occurred by the closing decades of the century. In 1800, James Stonhouse, the rector of Great and Little Cheveril in Wiltshire, published his *Admonitions against Swearing, Sabbath-Breaking and Drunkenness*.[39] Stonhouse was faithful to his clerical calling, and so was keen to warn his readers that cursing and profanation of the Sabbath were offences against God. Yet his tract also had a decidedly civic focus, with these kinds of transgressions described as 'a notorious Breach of Civility and good Manners'.[40] An anonymous clergyman claimed that keeping the Sabbath was not only advisable for the good of men's souls, but also for 'the *good* of the land'.[41] Jelinger Symons gave a similar justification in 1779 when he argued that sombre observance of the Sabbath indicated the correct exercise of 'reason and virtue'.[42] In the latter decades of the eighteenth century, clear links were drawn between Sabbath observance and notions of civility, politeness and good manners. The laws against Sabbath-breaking were also reiterated by the Society for the Reformation of Manners in the 1790s. Similarly, when advising young businessmen 'how they may attain the way to be rich and respectable', *The Remembrancer* insisted that reverence of the Lord's day was of 'admirable service to a state, considered merely as a civil institution', since it allowed for good conversation and good manners, and it also served as a useful means of health preservation to ensure that the state had a fit and profitable fleet of workers.[43] Sabbath observance was thus a religious requirement, but it also had a utilitarian purpose and was closely associated with the construction of gentlemanly respectability. It is therefore difficult to chart a progressive desacralization of church space in these years. Indeed, by strict regulation of the use and abuse of churchyards, civic and commercial interests may well have augmented the reverence with which these sites were associated.

The parish churchyard was a particularly logical place for ghosts to appear, since it was the central burial site for most communities. It was also close to the moist and slowly-decaying physical bodies that lay in the grave. Numerous reports of ghosts centred on churchyards, and they were similarly associated with the liminal period which immediately followed the physical death of a loved one. The liminal and ethereal qualities of burial grounds were again supported by contemporary poetry and drama. The action of Shakespeare's *Hamlet* established a firm link between the location of skeletal remains and contemplations of mortality, which was an essential accompaniment to the appearance of Hamlet's father's ghost.[44] The Graveyard poets whom we met in Chapter 4, similarly promoted burial grounds as logical spaces for spectral appearances.[45]

Identifying with Ghosts

Since ghost stories were intimately linked with particular places, buildings and landscapes, they played an important role in the formation of individual, community and regional identities. In fact late eighteenth-century England furnishes some of the richest evidence of these connections, which surfaced not only in folkloric collections, but also in a series of working-class autobiographies penned at the turn of the nineteenth century. The autobiography of Samuel Bamford, entitled *Early Days*, provides a case in point. Born in 1788 in Middleton, Lancashire, Bamford is most famous as a leading figure in working-class radical movements of the nineteenth century. His association with the Luddite rebellions and the Peterloo massacre of 1819 make him one of a handful of working men whose writing provides important insights into the manners, beliefs and quotidian preoccupations of ordinary men and women. Bamford's text was a very personal history, but one with a broader public purpose, and it was intended to further the social and moral improvement of an increasingly self-conscious working class. Just a few years later, William Lovett undertook a similar project. As part of the drive to improve the education and dignity of the common man, Lovett deliberately distanced himself from the taint of vulgar superstition by pouring scorn upon the ghostly tales that formed such a significant part of his childhood. Bamford was less bashful, and was inclined to catalogue, rather than condemn, the haunted stories that shaped his youth and fuelled his imagination.[46] Bamford recalled his childhood days in Middleton in the 1790s by writing a landscape history, or rather a spiritual topography, of this rural Lancashire parish. His remarkably vivid recollections of ghost stories and haunted spots formed an imaginative and physical blueprint that Bamford used to recall the contours and character of his childhood home. Few of the 'lonely, out-of-the-way places', he wrote, 'escaped the reputation of being haunted'. Experience taught that the school lane – a deep and narrow pathway with trees and bushes growing on either side, was to be avoided, since it was home to the apparition of a man killed during the civil wars.[47] Further east was Owler Bridge, said to be 'thronged by spirits', and leading on the other side to the 'haunted field'. The 'solitary footpath ... beneath the tall elms and sycamores, [and] past the lonely summer-house' was, according to Bamford, 'a favourite promenade to the beings of another world'. The footpath to the Black Bull public house was home to innumerable spirits and few that ventured through the churchyard after nightfall would leave without their hair standing on end.[48]

What Bamford's tract suggests is that ghost stories, and the physical markers with which they were associated, functioned as aids to memory, and they were powerful reference points which were internalized to spark personal and historical memories of home. Noted events and stories also gave individuality to local communities from which people derived a sense of their own identity.[49] In Bamford's case, this mnemonic function was especially significant since his chosen career meant that he had been displaced, both socially and geographically, from the community in which he had grown up and in which his earliest experiences and sense of belonging had been forged. David Vincent's work on working-class autobiography has reinforced this point, observing that self-improving men suffered from feelings of disorientation after they were separated from the inherited culture of their childhoods.[50]

Collier Timothy Mountjoy provided further evidence that self-improving men used ghost stories as a way of getting in touch with their roots. Writing in 1887 in recollection of his youth, Mountjoy described Grange House in the Forest of Dean, which had been haunted since time immemorial. He further observed that there was always a ghost to be seen 'at the crooked pear tree and one at the Temple'.[51] At the turn of the nineteenth century, a young William Lovett, though sceptical as an adult, feared the 'lonely roads' of his native Cornwall because 'popular credulity had peopled particular spots with ghosts and appearances of various kinds'.[52] William Borlase reinforced the strength of this tradition in Cornwall when he noted in his 1779 survey of Cornish antiquities that 'people in Cornwall will not be persuaded even at this day, but that there is something more than ordinary at such places; and their stories of apparitions gain greater credit, if the Spirit, Demon, or Hobgoblin, is said to have appeared where four Lanes meet; there they think apparitions are most frequent, and at such places it is common for these people travelling in the dark to be most afraid'.[53] John Harris also recalled the stock of ghost stories that added to the character of Camborne in late eighteenth-century Cornwall.[54] James Burn and Samuel Robinson wrote the haunted histories of late eighteenth-century Northumberland and the Scottish borders, and John Clare said of Helpston in Northamptonshire that it was impossible 'to travel more than half a mile in any direction without passing a spot where some apparition was said to be seen'.[55] Clare reflected these associations into his *Shepherd's Calendar* when he wrote of a dense wood that was 'dreaded as a haunted spot' on account of a gibbet which had once stood beside it.[56]

Penning a life history that was populated by ghost stories was then an important way of remembering. This kind of undertaking provided an opportunity to map the paths you had travelled, to acknowledge the influences that shaped you and to come to terms with a changed identity. Nostalgia for a lost home and uncertain identity is an oft-cited quality of John Clare's poetry, and his reminiscences contain a series of references to ghosts.[57] The sense of place implicit in tales of local haunting, and their intensely visual quality, became more important as patterns of migration intensified over the course of the eighteenth century. Recollection of these stories allowed people to remember the physical settings, customs and beliefs of home.

In addition to the mnemonic function of ghost stories, they also retained appeal as a source of community identity and pride. The legend of Catherine Ferrers, a notorious highwaywoman of the seventeenth century, persisted in her native Hertfordshire, where her ghost was said to assault local workmen, to disrupt village fêtes and to haunt her former home of Markyate Manor.[58] When a young woman was drowned by her lover at Miller's Pond in the New Forest, the site became the inspiration for a ghost story which immortalized this notorious murder. The tale was recalled in John Bullar's tour of Southampton, and its persistence was most likely connected to the local outcry that followed the lover's acquittal when brought to trial for the murder.[59] A similar tale from the 1780s secured the infamy of a lake in St James's Park. This body of water was reputedly haunted by the ghost of a headless woman whose husband had murdered her before throwing her body in the lake.[60] The apparition of a convict was seen running across Wimbledon Common in the late eighteenth century when the Common was fêted as a notorious haunt for footpads and highwaymen. In 1789 a procession of shadowy women carrying a coffin was seen in Greenwich Park. A local clergyman decided to investigate, only to discover that the site had once been used as a female burial ground in the fifth and sixth centuries.[61] It seems then that ghost stories, especially those that recalled bloody crimes or illustrious personages, represented an important source of local identity and subjectivity. Such narratives conferred a historical dimension and particularity to local communities, which reaffirmed a sense of place and belonging for residents.

Self-improving men experienced displacement from their homelands, but Britain's colonial endeavours also added to this tally. Overseas expansion ensured that thousands of soldiers and sailors were separated, at least temporarily, from the familiar sights and sounds of home. In this sense, the physical processes of imperial and commercial expansion gave extra impetus to the narration and circulation of ghost stories in the latter decades of the eighteenth century. Encounters with the wandering dead were commonplace on trawlers, gunboats and in military regiments, with soldiers and sailors deemed to be particularly credulous about the inhabitants of an invisible world. Many ghost stories from these years were set in and around coastal ports, with soldiers and sailors often taking starring roles. Jack Cremer observed that 'Sailors in generall have Noshern [notion] of fear of Aperishons', and a report in *The Times* from 1818 gave practical confirmation.[62] After a ghost was spotted near St Helena, British cruisers gave chase, prompting the journalist to wonder that 'Our seamen, who fear nothing human, are deadly cowards when opposed to spirits or apparitions'.[63] Sailors in the Georgian navy spent much of their time swapping stories and listening out for 'death-watches', which were visible signs and eerie noises that were thought to announce impending death.[64] Such notions were often perceived to be the result of a life spent at sea. Forced to live at the mercy of the elements, and faced by the constant threat of death, it seemed logical that military and commercial seamen placed their faith in providential omens and signs that were thought to provide guidance in an uncertain world.[65] Ship-owners in Rhode Island and Massachusetts made regular use of astrologers, fortune-tellers and horoscopes to predict 'what day, hour and minute was fortunate for vessels to sail'.[66] Marcus Rediker has also argued that the world-view of sailors was a mixture of 'religion and irreligion, magic and materialism, superstition and self-help'.[67] Nonetheless, evidence that sailors and soldiers were more superstitious than any other occupational group is highly problematic. Mortality rates associated with them are inconclusive and insufficient grounds upon which to base such an assumption.[68] Those deaths that did occur were more likely to have resulted from disease and poor living conditions than from direct combat or turbulent weather. Any analysis of the beliefs and attitudes of soldiers and sailors must also avoid buying into the romanticized, heroic depictions of military life which surfaced in hugely popular ballads and pamphlets. These texts were sensationalized to titillate the imagination of a hungry reading public. Links between identity, displacement and the telling of ghost stories do, however, offer a more convincing explanation of why soldiers and sailors appeared to be avid *narrators* of preternatural tales. Self-improvers like Samuel Bamford showed signs of both geographical and ideological dislocation, but soldiers and sailors usually suffered from prolonged physical separations from their homelands and from their families and loved ones. These separations were not always permanent, but they were significant enough to produce emotional stress, and a longing for what they had left behind.

Joseph Donaldson fought in Wellington's army in the Peninsular War of 1808–14 but his adventurous exploits began as a young boy when Donaldson joined the crew of a cargo ship bound for the West Indies. Every night instead of going below deck, the seamen gathered together to play games or tell stories. According to Donaldson, ghost stories were particular favourites and he noted that the legend of the Flying Dutchman and other naval apparitions 'were talked of and descanted on with much gravity' by the fascinated crew. British-owned vessels were staffed by sailors from Britain, Europe, North America, Africa and Asia and the tales of a Swedish sailor proved especially captivating. Donaldson thought that this man had as large a collection of tales 'as any person I ever knew: they were those of his country – mostly terrific – ghosts and men possessed of supernatural powers, were the heroes of his stories'. These chronicles clearly had an impact on the crew, and when a strange gleam of light was seen through the darkness one night, accompanied by a low murmuring sound, whispers began that something preternatural was afoot. The ship's mate was prompted to complain that 'there was a cursed deal too much of that ghost story-telling of late'.[69] As the example of the Swedish storyteller illustrates, naval ghost stories were not invented, but memorized from local traditions and legends that sailors brought with them from home. This conclusion has been further endorsed by David Hopkin, whose study of French military men showed that storytellers 'cut their coat from the material they had to hand'.[70] Clearly there was an element of pragmatism here, since storytelling was a cheap, easy and accessible form of sociability for men with limited resources and a lot of spare time on their hands. But the choice of narrative was no doubt conditioned by memories of familiar people and places from home. As Pamela Stewart and Andrew Strathern have argued, people travel 'with their own inner landscapes'. They recall scenes of personal significance, which give them 'a sense of "home"' when they are not "at home"'.[71]

Day-to-day activities on board ship also provided many practical opportunities for storytelling. Restricted living space made habits of sociability a routine part of daily life, which has led David Hopkin to observe that ships, as well as army barracks, artisan workshops and prisons, served as 'nurseries of narrative talent'.[72] The design and physical space available on ships thus played an important role in shaping narrative habits. The limited and uncomfortable arrangement of physical space below deck made the open space above deck a more appealing place to spend time. The close quarters at which these men lived no doubt created a sense of collegiality, which was forged by swapping experiences and stories from home. In these settings, narrators were assured of a broad and captive audience. The empty passages of time on long trading journeys or between battles also encouraged storytelling habits, which Hopkin describes as a crucial form of cultural capital which seamen exploited to ingratiate themselves with fellow crew members.[73]

Ghost stories provided on-board entertainment, but they also served a more serious purpose by providing emotional consolation for those at sea following the death of loved ones. On a trading journey to Jamaica at the turn of the nineteenth century, James Butler was told by locals that an apparition in the shape of 'a tall lusty man' had been spotted who appeared to have been slain in battle. Butler immediately thought of his brother ('a tall proper man of statture'), whom he had not heard from or seen in months. Sure enough, upon his return to England, Butler discovered that his brother had lately died in battle.[74] Towards the end of the eighteenth century, a mariner posted to the West Indies was visited by his mother's ghost after she expressed a desire to speak to him on her deathbed. Her spirit appeared late one night while her son was at the helm of his ship and, after speaking to him, the ghost 'descended the side regularly to the water, where she seemed to float for a while, and at last sunk and wholly disappeared'. The sailor suspected that this was some meaningful omen, and so he recorded the time, day, and the exact words of the ghost. On his return to dry land, he discovered that his mother had died at the precise moment that the ghost had appeared. This unfortunate sailor was drowned soon afterwards, which prompted fresh rumours that his mother's ghost had appeared to prophesy his own death.[75] The ballad of *Mary's Dream: or, Sandy's Ghost* (1790) also complemented these narratives. This ballad told the story of a sailor who was killed overseas, but his ghost appeared to his sweetheart to say a final farewell.[76]

A similar pattern was discernible amongst soldiers. Admiral Coates, commander of a squadron in the East Indies, 'saw the form of his wife standing at his bed-side', only to discover on his return home that she had died on the very day, and at the very time that her ghost had appeared.[77] A ghost also visited Sir John Sherbroke and General Wynyard when they were young officers in the army. Wynyard had received no word from his brother for some time, and he took the ghost to represent the spirit of his sibling. He soon discovered that his brother had indeed died 'on the day, and at the very hour on which the friends had seen his spirit pass so mysteriously through the apartment'.[78] It appears moreover that Wynyard's story was not unique. It may well have had wider resonance since the narrative was altered in subsequent retellings, and it ran through a number of versions, being alternately set in Gibraltar, England and America.[79] Visions of ghosts and the stories that accompanied them can be seen as important outlets for feelings of loss and bereavement. They functioned as emotional manifestations of anxiety and absence following enforced separation from well-loved friends and family, or following death. These episodes can therefore be closely related to the kind of lifestyle demanded by a career at sea or in military service. Increased contact with the wider world also opened up new channels for the exchange and circulation of ghost stories in an international context. Fresh and exotic tales were shipped in along commercial trade routes, notably from Holland, Russia, Germany, Rhode Island and South Carolina.[80] This traffic was a mutual process of exchange, with New England borrowing heavily from the wonder writings of London printers, and this was partly due to the comparable religious cultures between England and its American colonies.[81] A story from Boston in Massachusetts shows that ghosts were able to span the Atlantic divide, when the disturbed spirit of a murdered man claimed to have been murdered in a London brawl.[82] A brief comparison of publication lists from Britain and New England both before and after the War of Independence also highlights a marked degree of consensus about the uses to which ghost stories were put. They were not just used for entertainment, but also performed as religious and moral exemplars. *The Reprobate's Reward or a Looking Glass for Disobedient Children* was first published in London in 1788, and it told the story of a treacherous son who cut his own mother's throat as she rode to Chippenham market. The murderous deed was discovered by the mother's ghost, which brought her son to repent his sins before God. This cheap eight-page chapbook was penned by two Anglican ministers. Its final lines warned young readers against disobedience and immorality, and urged parents to raise their children in the fear of God.[83] Despite the local setting of this tale just outside of Bristol, its themes resonated widely and it was soon reprinted in Philadelphia in 1793, and again in 1798.[84] *The Babes in the Wood* was a similar tale of secret murder and immorality revealed by a ghost, and it was widely published: in London (1790), Edinburgh (1800) and Glasgow (1790), and in Philadelphia (1791), New York (1795), Albany (1799) and Poughkeepsie (1796).

Common themes also emerged from cheap printed literature aimed at the adult market. The account of *Thomas Ostrehan's Apparition*, published in Philadelphia in 1767, declared the certainty of life after death, warned against the errors of atheism and encouraged its readers to prepare for death. These concerns were traditional motifs of the ghost story in Britain, and they were echoed in *The Atheist's Reward*, published in London in 1788. Printers on both sides of the Atlantic reflected and sustained the lucrative market of ghost stories, with Anglican, Methodist and other dissenting ministers appropriating these tales for their own didactic ends. Britain's overseas endeavours thus opened up new physical and psychological spaces for the narration and circulation of ghost stories. They also secured new markets for the exchange and consumption of these tales.

The experience of childhood in late eighteenth-century England provides a final link between ghost beliefs and the construction of personal identities. George Boas was the first to identify a 'cult of childhood' in late eighteenth-century Europe, with Carolyn Steedman and Dror Wahrman adding further weight to the idea that these years witnessed a hitherto unknown focus upon children as the 'bud of potential' that would eventually mature into a thinking, feeling adult.[85] Contemporary educationalists and moral philosophers like David Fordyce drew heavily upon the educational ideas formulated by John Locke, in which each child was considered a tabula rasa. Children did not inherit habits, beliefs and sensibilities; they acquired them through experience and education.

The new obsession with the early years of life meant that the spotlight fell almost inevitably upon processes of child development. This was especially important in a nation that was concerned to produce a rational, well-educated and productive population. The activities of nursemaids and servants were put under the microscope since they played a crucial role in shaping the imaginations and experiences of the middling and upper-class infants in their charge. On a day-to-day basis, ghost stories served rather routine domestic functions. For female servants, and particularly nursemaids with young dependents to entertain, educate and discipline, ghost stories proved especially useful in capturing the imagination of children. John Brand complained in 1777 that when it came to stories of 'Spirit-walking ... the Nurse prevails over the Priest'.[86] In 1762, a fashionable magazine defined a ghost as a 'horrible representation, raised by terrible tales told in the nursery or kitchen'. Put very succinctly, this sort of tale served as 'a piece of domestic policy, contrived to make children go to bed early without crying'.[87] In 1770 the author of *The Compleat Wizzard* also claimed that 'Spectres and ghosts' were regularly described by 'old nurses to quiet their children with'.[88]

In Jonathan Swift's satirical *Directions to Servants*, the children's maid was suspected of telling her young charges 'Stories of Spirits, when they offer to cry'. Jane Eyre's early years in her aunt's house were similarly populated by 'tiny phantoms' that Bessie brought to life while she crimped Aunt Reed's nightcap borders at the nursery-hearth.[89] Jane also had the misfortune to be locked in the haunted red room in her aunt's house as punishment for striking her cousin John. It was here that Jane fancied she had seen the ghost of her dead uncle, who was disturbed in his grave by the evil treatment meted out to Jane at the hands of his widow.[90]

It is somewhat paradoxical that we are able to piece together glimpses of these narrative practices largely thanks to the growing number of complaints about them. The foundation for these criticisms was John Locke's attack on Cartesian philosophy in his *Essay Concerning Human Understanding*. Superstition was not innate, Locke claimed, rather it was instilled, 'the ideas of goblins and sprites have really no more to do with darkness than light: yet let but a foolish maid inculcate these often on the mind of a child and raise them there together, possibly he shall never be able to separate them again so long as he lives'.[91] In 1752, a posthumous edition of Daniel Defoe's *View of the Invisible World* added to the refrain. The anonymous author lamented the routine use of ghost stories by nursemaids 'to affright cross Children into Obedience', because this often left 'the most lasting Impressions of their Folly upon their unhappy Charge'.[92] In 1762, an anonymous author ascribed the persistence of ghost beliefs to 'ignorance and childish fear'. 'Children', he claimed, 'suck them in almost with their first milk; their nurses, no wiser than them, encourage the deceit; and so it is spread from one to another; till they have lost the grounds, from whence their foolish imaginations were derived; and never acquire strength enough of reason and judgement to examine their credibility, or to banish them afterward'.[93] Finally, in 1817 a letter to the editor of *The Times* complained that 'tales of *ghosts* and *hobgoblins* are often known to terrify and harrow up the infant mind, so as to render the most common, *twilight*, shadow, an ideal apparition of horror and dread'.[94]

Condemnation of these childcare practices formed part of broader anxieties among the middling and upper sorts about the 'nurturing but dangerous' status of the nurse in domestic households.[95] Educational theorists and physicians now claimed that children could inherit both physical *and* moral characteristics from their carers, and so their methods and practices were subject to close inspection. In 1743 Nicolas Andry de Bois-Regard's *Orthopaedia: or, The Art of Correcting and Preventing Deformities in Children* was published in London and in it he counselled parents to 'let none of your Servants, nor any other body, foolishly tell [children] any Stories' since 'they do a great deal of hurt to Children, and consequently to Mankind'. According to Andry, fear was a dangerous medical condition, which was prejudicial to the 'Bodies, Minds, and Manners' of children.[96] A wide range of instructional literature was published as the century wore on, and it contained advice for middle- and upper-class parents on how best to protect their children from the diseases of superstition, irrationality and vulgarity that ignorant servants threatened to transmit. In September 1748, the *Newcastle General Magazine* urged parents to pay special attention to the early years of their child's development since 'young minds are so soft and tender, that they take any Bent, and so empty, that they receive all Impressions ... Shall then the Youth, who is hereafter to command an Army, receive his first Principles from a Conversation with Servants'?[97] Contemporary medical theory allied with the cult of sensibility did little to allay these fears, because the nervous systems of infants were believed to be weak and easily excitable.[98] Although commentators primarily located ghost beliefs among impressionable children, their complaints may well have disguised deeper anxieties that lowly servants were sometimes capable of getting one over on their employers by manipulating fears of ghostly appearances. In May 1790 Lord Galway suffered this embarrassing fate when he was 'gull'd by his domestics into the perception of supernatural appearances' after he was persuaded that his rented estate was haunted by the ghost of the late incumbent. *The Times* newspaper reported Galway's folly as a salient warning to others.[99]

The association of ghost stories with the early years of development represents an important link in understanding how ghost beliefs were reproduced from generation to generation, and transmitted between different social levels. John Aubrey, Richard Baxter, John Wesley, Jonathan Swift, Samuel Romilly, William Wordsworth, Robert Burns and Samuel Taylor Coleridge all remembered hearing ghost stories as infants. The widespread condemnation of superstitious nursemaids in fashionable periodicals also indicates that these stories had powerful long-term effects upon the impressionable minds of those who heard them or read about them. Historians are used to making educated guesses about how stories, and particularly how oral narratives, were actually *received* by listeners in the past. But a number of autobiographies from the turn of the nineteenth century provide rare insights into the emotional reactions that ghost stories elicited. Samuel Bamford sat around the hearth as a child, while he allowed his aunt to excite his curiosity and wonder with 'strange and fearful tales of spirits, and apparitions'. He listened 'in silence and awe, and scarcely breathing, contemplated in imagination, the visions of an unseen world, which her narratives conjured up'.[100] In the early nineteenth-century, John Harris remembered listening to his mother's stories 'with wondering joy ... and as I listened my young heart beat, and imagination bore me away on her dazzling wings'.[101] The sense of wonder imparted by ghost stories was accompanied by fear in Alexander Somerville's childhood home at Berwick-on-Tweed. Here, children were taught by their elders 'that if they were afraid of such a thing as thunder, or a ghost ... the thunder or other thing of dread would come and kill them or take them away'.[102] Similarly, John Clare spoke of the 'fearful extacy' of listening to ghost stories in childhood:

The children – silent all the while –
And e'en repressed the laugh or smile –
Quake wi the ague chills of fear,
And tremble though they love to hear;
Starting, while they the tales recall,
At their own shadows on the wall[103]

William Lovett was born in Newlyn, Cornwall, at the turn of the century, and he first encountered ghosts from the numerous stories 'told to me in infancy, reiterated in boyhood, and authenticated and confirmed by one neighbour after another'. Lovett complained that these accounts instilled the reality of ghosts so firmly in his imagination that 'it was many years after I came to London before I became a sceptic in ghosts'.[104] The lawyer and politician Sir Samuel Romilly told a similar tale, lamenting that his early fascination with supernatural stories conjured up 'images of terror'. These memories remained 'very unwelcome intruders' upon Romilly's adult imagination.[105]

Lovett associated scepticism about ghosts with knowledge, literacy and ultimately with social progress, but David Hume was less optimistic about the power of print and education to overcome the effects of a good story. The question of how language and oral testimony convey authority has been pursued by socio-linguists in the twentieth century. But Hume anticipated this trend when he identified tale-telling as a major stumbling block to the cultivation of dispassionate reason. 'Eloquence' he complained, 'when at its highest pitch, leaves little room for reason or reflection; but addressing itself entirely to the fancy or the affections, captivates the willing hearers, and subdues their understanding'.[106] The ability to tell a good story was acknowledged as an important talent, and it was one that was encouraged by educationalists. An instructional guide for parents published in 1792 underlined the importance of narrative performance. Moral tales were to be told 'with warmth and interest, or they will have little effect; try to make them have the vivacity of plays, by assuming the voice and manner of the different persons who are mentioned; and, in the recital, do not forget the prints which represent them, for they will more deeply impress the truths they give life to on the children's minds, than mere words'.[107] Historians have all too often neglected the physical performance of storytelling, but this crucial aspect of communication must be reconstructed when attempting to understand how folk tales and oral narratives retained an unusually persuasive character.

Indeed, the second half of the eighteenth century saw a number of authors beginning to frame the rational rejection of ghosts within familiar narrative contexts to try to combat this pernicious tide of superstition. These years witnessed the emergence of a whole range of educational and entertaining texts produced specifically for children. This developing genre of literature was also an important arena for the contestation of preternatural ideas. It was against this backdrop that John Newbery first published *The History of Little Goody Two Shoes* in 1765.

Young readers, or rather their parents, were Newbery's target market, and the original book was bound in attractive flower and gilt patterned paper. By the third edition of 1766, however, Newbery expanded his potential audience as this small book became more affordable, priced at 6*d.* and including a series of lively woodcuts.[108] The story was set in a country village, and when the locals imagined that they had seen a ghost in the church one day, the heroine Margery intervened to quash the rumours. 'After this my dear Children', wrote the author, ' I hope you will not believe any foolish Stories that ignorant, weak, or designing People may tell you about Ghosts; for the Tales of Ghosts, Witches, and Fairies, are the Frolicks of a distempered Brain. No wise Man ever saw either of them.'[109] *Youth's Miscellany; or, A Father's Gift to his Children* taught 'Little Jack' not to believe in ghosts since his father 'had felt the pernicious effects of such inbred terrors himself'. Similarly, *The Children's Friend* recounted the tale of a young boy who thought he saw a ghost in the cellar, but which on closer inspection turned out to be a leg of mutton covered in a white tablecloth to keep the flies off.[110] Despite these efforts, however, the campaign to eradicate ghosts from children's literature only began in earnest in the later eighteenth century and it would be a number of years before the success of these efforts could be measured. In the meantime, it seems that children were still tempted to believe that ghosts were real, and this was confirmed in part by the publication history of *The Death-Watch* in 1796. Written by a country clergyman, this hefty tome took the form of a dialogue between four children, who pondered 'the important question relating to the real appearance of Departed Souls, and their power of making their second appearance in the world'.[111] The content was dreary, with no woodcuts or illustrations to liven up the dialogue. At 120 pages long and priced at 2*s.*, the readership of this text was restricted and it did not run into any further editions.[112] The young Joseph Donaldson preferred romances, fairy tales and Daniel Defoe's *Robinson Crusoe*, while Samuel Bamford's favourite books were *The Arminian Magazine*, *The Drummer of Tedworth*, *An Account of the Apparition of the Laird of Cool* and *An Account of the Disturbances at Glenluce*. In the market town of Penzance, William Lovett recalled only one bookseller's shop, in which, apart from 'Bibles and Prayer Books, spelling-books, and a few religious works, the only books in circulation for the masses were a few story-books and romances, filled with absurdities about ghosts, spirits, goblins, and supernatural horrors'.[113] Publication lists indicate that there was always money to be made from ghost stories. While the tensions between entertainment and instruction, fact and fiction are difficult to unravel, they were no doubt vital in preserving the dramatic potency and commercial appeal of these tales.

Childhood was, and still is, a crucial stage in the imaginative development of the individual. The fact that ghost stories were so firmly embedded in this fundamental life-cycle structure helps to explain why gentlemen and gentlewomen often remained convinced, or at least curious, about the existence of ghosts despite exposure to sceptical commentaries in later life. Moreover, William Lovett's example highlights the fact that currents of popular scepticism about the reality of ghosts co-existed with learned belief. Many educated men and women chose to preserve the idea that something otherworldly did exist. Tales of departed spirits reminded upper-class men and women of 'the Stories we have heard in our Child-hood', and that favoured 'those secret Terrours and Apprehensions to which the Mind of Man is naturally subject'.[114] As such, ghost beliefs cannot be so easily confined to the nursery since the spectral notions that were a marked feature of childhood often had a lingering effect upon adult imaginations. Publishers of cheap print also helped to sustain the presence of preternatural beings, since they specifically catered for schoolboys and adolescents with a fondness for blood and violence. The growing number of poltergeist narratives produced in post-Reformation England may well have satisfied these tastes, with young men also renowned for re-enacting these performances to frighten their friends and neighbours.[115] In 1765 William Gordon confirmed the fact that young boys revelled in the mysteries of the invisible world when he identified 'the common Notion of Spirits and Apparitions' among the readers of his *Young Man's Companion*. Gordon's instructional treatise chastised the credulity of his audience, lamenting that 'most Men are so prepared by Education to believe these Stories, that they will believe the Relation of them in these Cases, when they believe the Relators in nothing else'.[116]

Antiquarianism and Folklore

Fascination with ghost stories did of course extend beyond childhood. We have already seen how these narratives infiltrated colonial and military ventures. But the seductive effects of childhood ghost stories were supplemented or offset in later life by a vast repertoire of Gothic fictions, and by a body of antiquarian literature that foreshadowed the emergence of Victorian folklore. Before examining these genres in more detail, it is worth reiterating the point that ghosts were not simply to be encountered in fictional texts or romanticized surveys of English countryside lore. Rather these beliefs and narratives were part and parcel of the course of daily life, and they were firmly embedded in the life-cycle process. As such, the much touted notion that ghost beliefs were part of an alien folk culture that was 'rediscovered' by the educated classes through antiquarianism and romanticism is highly questionable. After all, a thing cannot be rediscovered if it never went away.

Nonetheless, the surveys of oral traditions and customs that accumulated towards the turn of the nineteenth century appeared to mark a new, more detached attitude towards ghost stories. The cataloguing and categorization of folk beliefs and practices was the hallmark of antiquarianism, and it drew on the language of empiricism. Antiquarianism had also become a highly respectable pursuit for the leisured classes following its early development in the hands of John Leland, William Camden, Edmund Gibson and John Aubrey. The ostensible motivation for compiling lists of superstitions was to preserve these rustic notions from extinction as the march of the printing press seemed to be undermining traditional oral culture. These stories were portrayed as static and unchanging parts of the English heritage. They were charming in their rusticity, but simultaneously appeared as hermetically sealed off from the enlightened, rational world of practising antiquarians.

This reading is of course far too neat. It accepts at face value the officially sanctioned notion that ghost stories were an embarrassment to the historical canon, and the stuff of frivolous fiction, rather than a subject worthy of serious contemplation. As Peter Marshall has pointed out, moreover, there was no such thing as pure oral folklore that was uncontaminated by print, and this was especially true of ghost stories. Catalogues of local superstitions were by no means stagnant or fixed, since they were influenced by both written and printed accounts of ghostly appearances, as well as by the physical landscapes in which they were set.[117] On occasion, the clinical and objective gaze of the antiquarian could also shade over into uncertainty or belief in the incidents they reported. In 1799 the budding antiquarian and man of letters Robert Southey confessed to a friend that he was 'not a disbeliever in these things'. The subject of ghosts and apparitions was, he claimed, 'a curious subject', that had 'never been fairly and reasonably examined'.[118] Despite folklorist William Hone's apparent distaste for ghost stories, his empirical approach led him to verify a 'spectral sight' which he had himself witnessed and which was included in his *Every-Day Book*.[119] Sir Walter Scott was also notoriously ambiguous about his own belief in ghosts. He conceded the possibility, but was reluctant to credit any particular episode unless it was corroborated by substantial witnesses and written accounts.[120] The individual and social impact of antiquarianism was rather unpredictable. Many antiquarians treated folk beliefs as an endangered species that was on the brink of extinction. Yet paradoxically, the effect of cataloguing and publicizing such tales was to open them up to fresh audiences who might otherwise have been ignorant of them. On a very basic level, folkloric collections of ghost stories functioned as important repositories of memory. Perhaps unwittingly, folklorists helped to preserve or even to revitalize interest in ghosts and other folk beliefs. This process may go some way towards explaining why nineteenth-century folklorists appeared circumspect about how much attention to devote to haunted spots and restless ghosts.[121]

Ghosts and the Gothic

Antiquarian texts were then just one of a number of ways in which people could engage with the idea of ghosts in late eighteenth-century England. An alternative path was provided by the burgeoning popularity of all things Gothic in art, poetry and literature that increasingly shaped the private pursuits of the moneyed, leisure-bound classes. The Gothic genre drew upon the emotional intensity of the sublime, which was first set out in Longinus's classical treatise *On the Sublime*. But it was Edmund Burke's more thorough treatment of this subject in his 1757 *Philosophical Enquiry into the Origin of Our Ideas of the Sublime and Beautiful* that established the relevance of this concept for eighteenth-century audiences. The guiding precept of the sublime was the confrontation of terror. Those authors who engaged with it stimulated the imaginations and emotions of readers with vivid depictions of violence, betrayal and death. Meanings of the eighteenth-century Gothic were fiercely contested, but historians and literary scholars generally agree that its emergence was motivated in part by a strong distaste for the enlightened proscription of marvellous, magical and seemingly irrational elements in artistic production, which was typified in many ways by the sentimental novels of Samuel Richardson. Authors of Gothic fictions believed that art should not be restricted to the domestic affairs of the natural world and, in order to excite the pleasures of the individual imagination, they set about reinserting suspense, fear and the supernatural into their work. This project was not only justified in the name of aesthetic pleasure, but also by moral tenets and by the dictates of sensibility which celebrated overt expressions of feeling and emotion among men and women of fashion.

The cultural discourse of sensibility and contemporary notions of the sublime thus provided a legitimating framework for the depiction of ghosts and other supernatural phenomena in literature and art. Ghostly figures were, after all, objects of fear and perennial reminders of human mortality. Anna Letitia Aikin (later Barbauld) affirmed the greediness with which stories of ghosts, goblins and other horrors were consumed by the reading public in her 1773 essay 'On the Pleasure Derived from Objects of Terror'. The intimate association of ghosts with tragedy was most famously captured by Shakespeare's *Hamlet*, and Aikin considered that the combination of suspense, curiosity and pain evoked by ghosts established their unrivalled power over the imagination. Musings on invisible beings allowed the human mind to embark upon explorations of new and exciting worlds, to indulge passionate and fanciful thoughts, and to escape from the insipid character of modern novels that Aikin herself considered 'tedious and disgusting'.[122]

A fine early example of how ghosts were employed to conjure fascination, fear and dread surfaced in Horace Walpole's 1764 *Castle of Otranto*, which has been widely identified as the foundation-stone of the English Gothic tradition. When

the young Conrad, heir to the house of Otranto, is improbably killed on his
wedding day, his father Manfred divorces his wife Hippolita to marry Conrad's
fiancée Isabella in the hope of producing a new heir. Manfred's ruthless ambition
is thwarted, however, by the realization of an ancient prophecy, which held that
the lordship of Otranto would pass to the true prince and heir whom Manfred
had usurped. The fulfilment of the prophecy involves many preternatural events,
including the seeming appearance of Conrad's ghost, the spectre of an old tutor
who drowned himself in the castle grounds and a skeletal ghost seeking to claim
the principality of Otranto for himself.[123] With the assistance of these ghosts,
Manfred's treachery is exposed and the true heir, Theodore, is installed as the
rightful Prince of Otranto.

Walpole's ghosts serve very familiar purposes, to uphold principles of social
and moral justice and to expose secrets and lies. Nevertheless, Walpole's engagement with these figures stemmed from his appreciation of their aesthetic value.
For Walpole, as for many of his readers, literary ghosts were a source of sublime
experience rather than a reflection of serious belief in the returning souls of the
dead. Walpole toured the dramatic landscapes of Europe with his poet-companion
Thomas Gray, and this grand tour confirmed his appreciation of scenes of terror.
But Walpole's sensual pleasures stopped short of true belief. Indeed Walpole had
made his views very clear on the subject of *real* ghosts when he scorned those who
had been duped by the infamous spectre of Cock Lane just a few years earlier.[124]
Walpole insisted that literary ghosts existed in an independent artistic sphere.
They retained the ability to stir the passions, but it was their fictional status that
made them both pleasurable and acceptable. So how do we explain Walpole's
initial reluctance to attach his name to *The Castle of Otranto* when it was first
published? Walpole's uncertainty about the reception of his work was partially
reflected in his decision to publish under the pseudonym of William Marshal.
He disguised his authorship still further by claiming that the tale was taken from
an Italian manuscript from the twelfth or thirteenth century, written by one
'Onuphrio Muralto, Canon of the Church of St. Nicholas at Otranto'.[125] Walpole
himself claimed to act merely as translator of the text, which he had lately discovered in the library of 'an ancient Catholic family in the north of *England*'.[126] This
elaborate pretence served an important purpose. By rooting the story within 'the
darkest days of Christianity', Walpole assigned real belief in ghosts to a bygone
age when the Catholic Church and its popish impostures reigned supreme. In so
doing, Walpole effectively dismissed the idea that enlightened and sophisticated
Englishmen could bear witness to real miracles, visions and ghosts. The point was,
however, that tales of avenging ghosts provided a spectacle for the mind or fuel to
enliven contemporary imaginations. It was only after Walpole's book had proved
popular enough to run through a series of editions that he confessed to its authorship. Yet if Walpole was correct to insist upon the fictional status of ghosts, why
resort to disguise and concealment? As Emma Clery has suggested, Walpole's

decision may have been shaped by civic humanist objections to extravagant forms of literature that indulged in frivolous irrationalities purely in the name of art. Yet his decision may have also been motivated by fears that he would be accused of encouraging vulgar superstition. The preceding chapters have made clear that Enlightenment England had refined, but not abandoned, the possibility of ghosts, and currents of religious belief lent public legitimacy to these notions. Indeed, an examination of critical reactions to the work of Clara Reeve further underlines the ambiguous epistemological status of ghosts in the final decades of the eighteenth century.

Reeve's *Champion of Virtue*, or *The Old English Baron* as it was reissued in 1778, adopted a broadly similar approach to Walpole, and Reeve herself declared her novel to be the 'literary offspring of the Castle of Otranto'.[127] *The Old English Baron* was then written with the express aim of blending the characteristics of ancient romances with modern novels, although Reeve intended to introduce a greater degree of verisimilitude and plausibility to the events she described. The tale centres on the young peasant Edmund, who is the true heir to the Lovel estate, which had been usurped by his kinsman Sir Walter Lovel many years before. Edmund's true identity is revealed by providential design, and through a series of supernatural revelations. The servants at the estate tell stories of how the former Lord and Lady Lovel haunt the east apartments, and Edmund has a vision, or perhaps a dream, in which he sees the ghosts of his parents. This vision is followed by a series of eerie sights and noises that ultimately lead Edmund to discover the body of his murdered father.[128] Reeve uses the marvellous to titillate and to tempt but, by suggesting that Edmund's vision may have been little more than a wishful reverie, she questions its reliability. Similarly, the reports of the servants remained unsubstantiated. Reeve was a specialist in romance rather than terror, and it is fair to say that she dipped her toes in preternatural fiction rather than immersing herself fully. Nonetheless, her ghost stories still function as essential plot devices that ensure the restoration of the Lovel estate to its rightful owner. The moral anatomy of Georgian England therefore gave respectability to Reeve's ghostly indulgence. Analogies between the preternatural and moral worlds were persistently articulated in the ghost stories of eighteenth-century England, and this association provided one of the most important contexts for sustaining the legitimacy of ghost stories in public life.

If Clara Reeve had hoped to improve upon Walpole's fanciful novel by integrating otherworldly mysteries within a more mundane, quotidian framework, her efforts provoked worried responses. In July 1778 the *Gentleman's Magazine* complained that 'some weak minds, perhaps, might be induced to think them true or possible, and thereby be led into superstition' if the epistemological ambiguity of ghost stories was not cleared up.[129] Anna Barbauld agreed that Reeve's novel introduced a potentially dangerous transgression of the boundaries between truth and fiction that might encourage credulity.[130] A degree of caution must be exercised before accepting such statements wholeheartedly, however, since many philosophers, moralists and literary critics were engaged in a campaign to stamp out excessive production and consumption of luxurious, trivial commodities. The seeming frivolity of Gothic novels made them a prominent target for attack. Nonetheless, the ability of ghost stories to excite curiosity about an invisible world was also borne out by private reflections on these narratives, to which I will shortly return.

The emotional effects produced by the Gothic-supernatural were therefore difficult to ascertain, and as a result the legitimacy of this nascent body of literature remained fiercely contested. This critical background no doubt proved an important influence upon the work of Ann Radcliffe, arguably the most influential author of Gothic romances in the 1780s and 1790s, when the English Gothic emerged as the most fashionable literary form of its day.[131] Like Walpole, Radcliffe used distancing techniques in her novels, which were often set in sublime landscapes – usually remote medieval castles in Catholic Europe or in the Scottish Highlands. But Radcliffe is most noted for perfecting the technique of what critics have termed the 'explained supernatural'. That is to say that Radcliffe introduces ghostly reports and rumour into her novels, and she depicts her characters in anxious states of fear and anticipation. These techniques are designed to evoke tension and suspense, but such fanciful notions are ultimately exploded by natural, commonsense explanations. *The Mysteries of Udolpho* provides an illustration of this technique in practice. The tale is based around the young heroine Emily, who was orphaned following the death of her father. As a result she is thrown into the clutches of her evil guardian Count Montoni who imprisons her in his medieval fortress in the Apennines. In her attempts to escape from her desperate situation, Emily fancies that she is visited by her father's ghost. Radcliffe, however, downplays these visions as 'thick-coming fancies' which obscure Emily's senses during her distress and grief.[132] Contrasted with Emily's usually incredulous rationality are the fears of her maidservant Annette, who is frequently terrified by ghosts, and she believes that she has seen an apparition on her way to her chamber. In addition, she spies a 'tall figure gliding along' in the dark gloomy corridor of Montoni's castle.[133] Annette's fears deepen further when her fellow servants insist that a room within the castle has been shut up on account of its being haunted by the late marchioness, who died in mysterious circumstances.[134] Radcliffe spins these mysteries out until the close of the novel when a natural explanation is finally produced to expose Annette's claims. Ludovico explains to Emily that pirates have been stashing their treasures in the vaults of Udolpho castle for many years. To avoid detection, they spread the rumour that a ghost haunted the fortress. The figures that Annette had seen in the rooms and corridors were none other than the pirates, who had discovered secret entrances to the castle's apartments.[135] Radcliffe's first novel, *The Castles of Athlin and Dunbayne*, published in 1789, also features a number of explained ghosts, but her final work,

Gaston de Blondeville, which was seemingly written for her own amusement and published posthumously in 1826, took a different approach. Curiously, it is the only one of Radcliffe's works in which an *unexplained* ghost appears, in this case to warn the king about Blondeville's despicable crimes. This ghost is central to the plot, and its revelations allow the working-class hero Woodreeve to triumph over his aristocratic oppressor.[136] It remains uncertain whether the ghost in *Gaston de Blondeville* reflects some discrepancy between Radcliffe's public and private opinions about the reality of ghosts. Nevertheless, her published work is characterized by an indulgent, yet ultimately incredulous, attitude towards preternatural phenomena. Radcliffe projected credulity onto uneducated servants, and she provided a logical explanation for their erroneous visions. In so doing, Radcliffe allowed her readers to be amused, fascinated and terrified by the idea of ghosts, whilst ultimately maintaining a sense of cultural superiority and distance from them. This technique also allowed Radcliffe to remain faithful to the sceptical principles of rational dissent in which she had been educated.

Radcliffe's exposition of the explained supernatural alongside Walpole and Reeve's veiled scepticism might also be collectively termed the 'polite supernatural'. Their treatment of ghost stories revealed a seemingly paradoxical fascination with these tales, whilst simultaneously ridiculing them in the name of taste and politeness. But three writers do not a genre make, and an important counter-current within the English Gothic aggressively asserted itself in the work of Anne Fuller and, perhaps most notably, in that of Matthew Lewis. In the 1780s Fuller depicted a real ghost in *Alan Fitz-Osborne*. The novel claims to be 'An Historical Tale' and it recounts the appearance of Matilda's ghost, who has been brutally murdered by Walter. As Walter retires to his bedchamber one night, Matilda's 'pale, ghastly, and bloody' form appears before him, still bearing the dagger in her breast where she had been slain.[137] Walter tries to convince himself that the vision was an 'illusion of the senses', but his efforts are in vain. He finally admits that 'the object that I saw, the accents which I heard owed their being to reality, not fancy'.[138]

Fuller was not alone in producing a more fearful, realistic description of avenging ghosts. Born in 1775, Matthew Lewis was just nineteen years old when his best-selling novel *The Monk* was first published. *The Monk* proved shocking to critics, and it sensationalized the reading public, who eagerly devoured its violent descriptions of rape, murder and betrayal. What made these deeds all the more outrageous was the fact that they were carried out by a once devout Capuchin monk named Ambrosio who had been the toast of Catholic Madrid. Ambrosio is tortured by the affections of the beautiful Matilda who declares her love for him. This temptation renders him unable to honour his monastic vows, and he finally succumbs to his sexual fantasies by raping the innocent Antonia, and then murdering her to conceal his guilt. In stark contrast to Radcliffe, Lewis's novel revels in unexplained supernatural phenomena. Numerous spectres appear to characters of high and low birth, and the author drew on familiar themes of social justice in his description of the bleeding nun's apparition. This ghost could find no rest in death because she had been a murderer during life until she was violently killed herself, with her remains left unburied.[139] At a time when literature was perceived not merely as entertainment, but also as a tool for education and refinement, condemnations of *The Monk* as depraved and immoral were highly significant. Yet, in many ways, Lewis's ghosts represent the voices, or figures of conscience in the novel, exhibiting a concern to expose and avenge sinful deeds. As such, there are important elements of continuity between the meanings and functions of real-life hauntings in Georgian England and the ghosts that were created for the simple pleasure of readers. The ghosts of Lewis, Fuller and Radcliffe were therefore proponents of a strongly articulated moral world-view that would have undoubtedly met with the approval of readers and critics concerned about the potentially subversive messages of contemporary fiction. Likewise, in spite of the anti-consumerist rhetoric levelled at such texts, ghostly figures championed principles of social justice and morality, restoring inheritances to their rightful owners and condemning sinners. In 1796 for example, Regina Maria Roche weaved traditional themes of ghost-lore into her novel, *The Children of the Abbey*. Here, ghosts were positioned as protectors of the central protagonists, the orphaned children, against the evil designs of their aunt and cousin who try to steal their inheritance.[140] Ghost stories then, whether or not they were perceived as factual, were used to reinforce moral tenets that permeated Georgian England. Whilst ghosts were certainly appreciated for their aesthetic value, they simultaneously inhabited a semi-autonomous sphere of artistic production that looked to social life, expectations and understandings for its inspiration. Moreover, despite Walpole's parodies and Radcliffe's naturalistic explanations, there remained sufficient disagreement within the varied Gothic genre about how best to represent ghosts. This in itself indicates that both authors and readers were unsure about how these figures should be represented.

It is similarly misleading to posit that aesthetic appreciation of ghosts was only skin-deep. Samuel Taylor Coleridge's example suggests that it was possible for artists to combine aesthetic appreciation with real curiosity about the invisible world. Coleridge confessed to having witnessed numerous unexplained visions during his lifetime and, when asked if he believed in ghosts and apparitions, he said, with a large dose of irony, 'No, Madam! I have seen far too many myself.'[141] Echoes of a real-life seventeenth-century ghost story may also be detected in Coleridge's most famous work, *The Rime of the Ancient Mariner*.[142] Similarly, the work of watercolour painter John Varley was strongly influenced by his avowed belief in ghosts and visions. Varley's faith in the preternatural realm also provided an important foundation for his friendship with William Blake, who was himself convinced that the world swarmed with ghosts and apparitions, and who was reportedly visited by the ghost of his dead brother Robert.[143] Southey, Varley and

Blake demonstrate that the idea of ghosts troubled but also inspired some of the greatest minds of the age. These figures were in many ways complementary to the Romantic impulse for imagination, emotion and feeling, and consequently ghosts became fashionable subjects for artistic representation.

The first major work by painter Charles Robert Leslie was a sombre 1814 depiction of *The Witch of Endor Raising the Ghost of Samuel before Saul*. Benjamin West contributed his own contemplative representation of this scriptural episode, which was reproduced by a number of engravers at the turn of the nineteenth century.[144] Iconographic representations of ghosts from this period oscillated between the contemplative and the satirical, again reflecting the ambiguity of their status and the diverse responses that they evoked. Images of credulous servants and naive country-folk were common, and Portbury's engraving *The Exorcism of a Ghost* features a fainting woman. The anonymous etching *Two Figures Terrified by a Ghost at their Table* also depicts two poor cottagers exclaiming in fright as they perceive a ghost in the candlelight. More overtly satirical depictions appear in several renditions of the Cock Lane episode, including the 1762 *English Credulity, or The Invisible Ghost*. Here a frantic scene includes several well-dressed gentlemen searching a bedchamber in vain for a ghost. On the opposite side of the bed, credulous female servants pray for deliverance. The sketches of George Woodward present a series of comical or mock-ghosts. His *Gravedigger* drawing, created some time between 1780 and 1799, features a white creature which resembles an animal, with blazing yellow eyes, emerging from a coffin. His *Ghost of St Stephen's* is merely a political squib. On the other hand, a more serious, contemplative image is presented in an engraving of the Hammersmith Ghost of 1804. This portrait evokes awe and trepidation from the viewer, with the ghost dressed from head to toe in a luminous white winding sheet. The ghost stands with arms raised to heaven, surveying the empty moonlit landscape which he dominates. An image of Mary Robinson's *The Haunted Beach*, first penned in 1800, similarly focused on the otherworldly glory of the three ghosts it depicted (see Figure 4). But in an interesting shift from the fleshy, familiar bodies of traditional ghostly figures, these ghosts were airy and transparent. This iconographical shift was important since the flimsy indeterminacy of these images mirrored weakening certainties about the nature and probability of ghosts that surfaced in contemporary commentaries. Significantly, Robinson was inspired to write her poem following a real-life episode that she witnessed from her window one evening. On the beach outside she perceived two fishermen bringing a lifeless body to the shore. Attempts to revive the man failed, and his corpse was abandoned on the beach, where it laid unburied for several days. It was only after Robinson intervened that the unfortunate stranger was buried on a nearby cliff under a pile of stones, without ceremony or prayer. The poem clearly expresses Robinson's horror, and her concern for the fate of this stranger's soul given the indecency of his death.[145]

H Corbould *delin.*   C Knight *sculp.* 1814

The Haunted Beach.

Figure 4. 'The Haunted Beach', in J. Taylor, *Apparitions; or, The Mystery of Ghosts, Hobgoblins, and Haunted Houses Developed*, 2nd edn (London: Lackington, Allen & Co., 1815). Reproduced with the kind permission of the Wellcome Trust Library, London.

What all of these texts and images suggest is that the link between ghost stories and ghost beliefs had yet to be completely severed. As a result, ghostly figures occupied a highly ambiguous cultural space in the latter decades of the eighteenth century. If we adhere to scholarly assessments of the Gothic as a mirror of human fears and forbidden desires, then we have to recognize that the status of the invisible world and its inhabitants had yet to be conclusively resolved. Jerrold Hogle voiced a now standard view that 'the longevity and power of Gothic fiction unquestionably stem from the way it helps us address and disguise some of the most important desires, quandaries, and sources of anxiety, from the most internal and mental to the widely social and cultural'.[146] The nature of these longings and anxieties remains at issue, but they are specific to time and place. Ghosts and apparitions have generally been cast as empty vehicles or functions of plot without any meaning in themselves. They existed to articulate bourgeois fears about the transference of property, and voiced concerns about gender distinctions. Yet it is not inconceivable to suggest that the figure of the ghost itself numbered among those cultural problems and contradictions that the Gothic tried to address. The prominence of ghostly figures within Gothic texts, Romantic poems and portraits strongly suggests that ghosts formed an important source of anxiety and confusion. Attempts to work through these confusions may well be reflected in the vacillation between realism and parody that we see in narrative and portraiture. When these artistic productions are placed within their correct historical context, it is clear that ghost stories, whether real or not, retained very important meanings above and beyond an empty aesthetic value.

Nonetheless, despite the existence of texts and imagery supporting the possibility of returning ghosts, the connection needs to be made between this artistic production and individual belief. The role of Gothic texts in shaping the imagination and fuelling the anxieties of readers is suggested by complaints that habits of late-night reading gave rise to irrational fears and even to insomnia. This was especially true for fashionable young women who, according to prevalent medical discourse, suffered from weak nerves and impressionable imaginations. George Cheyne and Samuel Tissot represented a cluster of physicians who associated disorders of the nervous system with women, but also with educated people of lively imaginations and delicate feeling.[147] Portraits such as Robert Buss's *The Ghost Story* supported these notions. This image depicts a gentlewoman who is terrified out of her wits after reading an evocative novel with spectral overtones. The middling and upper sorts, who were keen to immerse themselves within the cult of sensibility, deliberately cultivated such expressions of human emotion. Ghost stories and all things Gothic formed an important part of this cultural preoccupation. The emergence of private and comfortable reading practices also allowed ghost stories to find another point of access into the private lives of the wealthy and fashionable. But these narratives were not just confined to works of fiction. A ghost story dating back to the turn of the nineteenth century also illustrates that these narratives formed a staple part of correspondence and gossip networks. A letter from Catherine Marlay to Georgiana, Lady Chatterton and later wife of Edward Dering, tells of the ghost of a 'very dark-eyed young man' that appeared many years earlier to Lady Paulet and some female friends at Baddesley Clinton, Warwickshire.[148] It is said that Lady Paulet had been sceptical of such instances until this encounter. Her fellow percipients seemed equally affected by the vision – one of them fainted and the other 'fell into hysterics'. The servants meanwhile calmly searched the haunted room for signs of a prankster. The event was clearly noteworthy. It was spread far and wide amongst Lady Paulet's correspondents and is said to have 'made a great sensation at the time'.[149]

Conclusion

William Lovett's autobiography was first published in 1876, and in it the author referred to ghostly superstitions as 'the curse of my boyhood'.[150] Lovett lived through a period of rapid social change, and after moving to London in 1821 he became an important figure in campaigns to improve the social and political condition of the working classes. Along with a number of his contemporaries, Lovett recognized that a sound education held the key to long-term social change. Throughout his life he worked for the reform of infant, primary and secondary education as well as for the establishment of circulating libraries and the employment of educational missionaries, and he also wrote a number of school textbooks. There was no place for ghost beliefs or ghost stories within Lovett's project, since the category of superstition into which he had packed them had by now taken on highly negative social and political connotations. Described by Adam Smith in 1776 as a social poison and cited as evidence for the inferiority of the vulgar sorts, it is little wonder that Lovett was so keen to exorcize spirits from the minds of his peers.[151] Nonetheless, Lovett's avowed scepticism was out of step with the views of his native townsfolk, and he was forced to acknowledge that the belief they entertained about ghosts was borne out of conviction rather than ignorance. Lovett was reminded of the reverence with which ghosts were regarded when he revisited his home town of Newlyn in Cornwall as an adult. The local baker reprimanded him for laughing at reports of a headless ghost that were circulating in the neighbourhood. He also told Lovett that if he did not believe in ghosts then he certainly 'could not believe the Bible', going on to cite the story of the Witch of Endor as scriptural justification. By the 1870s Lovett was forced to admit that 'notwithstanding the progress of knowledge among our people, by means of the press, the school, and the rail, the belief in ghosts is still widely entertained'.[152] If Lovett was unable to account for the stubborn persistence of spectral notions, this chapter has offered some possible answers to this conundrum.

Imperial expansion and the printing press were conceived as agents of modernization, but they also threw up a series of contradictions. First, they created new spaces for the burgeoning narrative talents of soldiers and sailors for whom ghost stories formed a staple part of the imaginative diet. Second, they spread preternatural tales to national and international audiences on an unprecedented scale. The importation of ghost stories from overseas was an important development of these years, and the commercial ethos of many publishers ensured that spectral sightings were exchanged across Europe, America and the West Indies. Ghost stories also helped to stave off feelings of isolation and homesickness among those who, for one reason or another, were absent from their homelands. Ghost stories conjured up an inner landscape of home. As such, these stories were an important source of emotional support and psychological comfort.

Closer to home, ghost stories were intimately associated with the activities and experiences of everyday life. They were sustained by local memories and traditions, and they were embedded within working patterns and life-cycle structures. The inculcation of ghost beliefs in childhood was particularly effective in allowing fascination about the invisible world to pass from one generation to the next, and across social divides. The curiosity with which people approached the subject of ghosts was excited further still by the surfeit of Gothic fictions that were produced in these years. The ambiguous legacy of the Gothic genre did at the very least establish that ghost stories were useful vehicles with which to affirm tenets of civic and moral virtue within polite society, whatever individual readers were inclined to believe on this matter. Ghost stories were not simply intended to stimulate sensual passions, since they were consistently overlaid with instructive moral discourses.

Finally, the vibrant connections between landscape, memory and ghost stories secured powerful attachments to notions of the spectral which formed an integral part of personal, regional and social identities. Conceptions of landscape were by no means uniform in these years, but the class-specific explanation suggested by polite interest in antiquarianism is overly simplistic. Preternatural legends attached to specific locations ensured that the idea of ghosts influenced people with diverse class, gender and religious affiliations. To quote a perceptive phrase from Belden Lane, what is most striking about the individual experience of place is its 'messiness, ambiguity and mystery'.[153] This certainly applied to the period under study here, in which ghost stories spoke to both materialist and symbolist understandings of landscape. The natural world was widely recognized as a canvas that bore distinct marks of divine craftsmanship. Ghost stories therefore help us to understand how people saw themselves, not just socially, but also in relation to their environment. If Simon Schama is right to say that landscapes were inscribed with cultural obsessions, then the ghostly narrative has to be recognized as a flexible and meaningful cultural resource in late eighteenth-century England.[154]

CONCLUSION

Multiple discussions of an idea suggest its topicality. Whilst this study is by no means exhaustive, enough evidence has emerged to state with some confidence that the idea of ghosts shaped some of the most pivotal debates and discussions that preoccupied the people of late seventeenth- and eighteenth-century England. The precise meanings of ghost stories were energetically contested, and interpretations reflected a circularity of influences in which the ideas of natural philosophers, politicians and clergymen overlapped with, and drew upon, those of ordinary men and women. Whether ghosts were conceived as tangible entities or as symbolic representations of spiritual or moral truths, the idea of the preternatural realm was sufficiently elastic to allow ghost beliefs and stories to adapt to the contours of a rapidly changing cultural environment. The boundaries between the natural and preternatural worlds were certainly redrawn in these years, and in some respects they became more stringent, yet the souls of the dead continued to haunt the physical and imaginative landscapes of English society.

One vital reason that ghost stories were able to maintain their relevance against the often corrosive critique of scientists and satirists was due to the flexible literary conventions of these tales. The fact that ghosts drifted through so many different print media highlights the fact that a settled genre of ghost stories had yet to emerge. Ghost stories maintained a powerful reputation for exposing immorality and sin, but the nature of such transgression was not confined to a particular time and place. As a result, ghost stories could be easily updated to reflect the specific problems of eighteenth-century life. The changing form and content of these narratives therefore tells the historian a great deal about the cultural preoccupations that shaped Augustan and Georgian England.

Ghost stories were cast as moral censors of an increasingly commercially-focused society. This assumed particular importance in a climate where fragile personal reputations were made and broken by strict codes of personal and civic morality. Persuasive connections between ghost stories, physical landscapes and memory also suggest that these narratives performed as coping mechanisms for the dislocations brought about by commercial and imperial expansion, and by social stratification. Support for ghost stories also came from a more traditional source. Clergymen from Anglican and dissenting backgrounds used reports of ghostly activity to respond to the particular challenges of religious life both on the public stage and at grass-roots level. The fit between Protestant theologies and ghost beliefs was by no means perfect, but their occasional intrusion into the human world could be justified in particular contexts. The shaky empirical foundations of ghostly reports were sometimes overlooked if these episodes could be moulded to encourage loyalty to the Holy Trinity, to the doctrine of immortality, and to promote the devotional habits of the laity. As Samuel Gray put it in 1797, 'If then the great causes of morality and religion may be thus benefited by it, let us not hastily erase from the mind an opinion which, at the worst, is perfectly harmless. Let us not, in our admiration of personal courage, contemn that disposition to dread which is one of the first principles of society'.[1] Public support for these reports was increasingly limited to moments of religious and political crisis. Yet the acceptability of ghost beliefs at parish level was more consistently expressed. Community-level hauntings were interpreted as visible sermons to a sinful people, and they gave clergymen important opportunities to influence the behaviour of errant parishioners. Some of these adoptions were cynically manufactured, but clergymen were often no strangers to genuine belief in preternatural activity. Attitudes towards ghosts were after all shaped by a complex network of forces including religious belief, intellectual trends, life-cycle structures, local memory and tradition, and the relationship of individuals to the physical landscape.

Due to the limitations of evidence, historians know much more about the perceptions and world-views of the educated elite who left a deeper impression upon the historical record. Yet by focusing upon the meanings ascribed to ghosts in printed matter, the intention here has been to show how ghost beliefs and ghost stories interacted with the daily lives of men, women and children from a wide spectrum of social backgrounds. The preceding chapters have shown how these narratives were firmly rooted within life-cycle structures, including childhood, courtship, marriage and death. These were experiences shared by all members of society. The ghost stories included here also provide access to the voices of domestic servants, women, working men and children, who used them to make sense of their own lives and experiences. Ghost stories provided a way for socially and economically marginalized groups to influence their social superiors, to enforce certain codes of conduct, and to sculpt the contours of the society in which they lived. When set in their original contexts, ghost stories were both affective and effective narratives, manifestations of emotional attachments to the dead and to a sense of personal immortality, but they were also rational strategies used to achieve very practical objectives.

This analysis adds depth to histories of the marginalized and dispossessed, but the interest excited by ghost stories in this period has highlighted a circularity of influences between the governing classes and the governed, between local and national communities, and between the spoken word and printed texts. Eighteenth-century ghost stories commanded the attention of natural phi-losophers, clergymen, ladies and gentlemen of fashion, royalty and less wealthy spectators. As a result, they encouraged a vibrant exchange of ideas about the meanings of such occurrences. When framed in an appropriate manner, ghost stories were able to traverse social boundaries, and to move between public and private worlds with relative ease. This traffic was facilitated by authors, print-ers and publishers whose products appealed to diverse audiences. Texts also emphasized points of overlap in form and content between expensive canonical publications and the ephemeral products of the cheap print market. The value of studying changing perceptions of ghosts partly lies therefore in illustrating a non-linear and multifaceted process of cultural change. The complex web of factors that shaped public and private attitudes towards ghosts complicates neat models of social and economic polarization favoured by some historians of this period.[2] Despite clear disparities of wealth and lifestyle, there were issues upon which rich, poor and all those in between could share an opinion. Likewise, this study adds another layer to the growing corps of work currently revising Max Weber's propo-sition that the eighteenth century saw a progressive disenchantment of the world. To accurately describe the public fortunes of ghost stories, it is better to think of them as an underlying cultural resource which could be called upon at moments of social, political or religious tension. These moments did not of course corre-spond to a linear timescale, which makes it very difficult, if not impossible, to specify a particular date by which ghost stories had ceased to be relevant to the intellectual and social lives of English people.

Language was of course crucial in constructing systems of meaning and belief, and so some brief reflections upon the changing language of ghosts will help to sum up shifting attitudes towards the preternatural realm by the turn of the nineteenth century.[3] In 1818, the new edition of Samuel Johnson's *Dictionary* defined the term 'Ghost' as 'a spirit appearing after death'. The meaning of this term remained largely unchanged throughout the eighteenth century, but by 1818 it had been joined by 'Ghostlike', which described something or somebody 'withered; having hollow, sad, or sunk-in eyes'.[4] 'Ghostlike' was not the only new spectral descriptor that had emerged by the turn of the nineteenth century. In 1815 Joseph Taylor referred to 'ghost-mongers' to describe mischievous individu-als who faked the appearance of ghosts, or who spread tales of their exploits with alacrity. Just such a ghost-monger featured that same year in Holborn, London. Sixteen-year old James Cainess terrified his neighbours by dressing as a ghost in a white jacket, trousers and cotton cap. It was in this guise that he skipped among the tombstones of the local churchyard, bellowing 'sepulchral groans' for added effect. When summoned before the magistrate for this disruptive behaviour, Cainess claimed that his intention had been to 'undeceive' rather than to impose upon the credulous multitude who gathered each night to view the spectacle.[5]

The linguistic shifts documented by Johnson and typified by Taylor reflected the increasingly problematic belief that ghosts were a tangible, physical presence within the human world. The scorn directed towards James Cainess can also be linked to ongoing efforts to dissolve supposedly preternatural events into natural explanations.[6] In 1815 Taylor advertised his own folly when he described how he had mistaken a snow-white dressing gown for a ghost – all in an effort to warn his readers to guard against fraud and imposture.[7] In a similar vein Stephen Fovargue advanced 'a little Dissertation upon Optics' to explain how visions of ghosts could trick the eye.[8] The excitement raised in Taunton by the so-called Sampford Ghost was similarly dampened down by a report in the *Times* in October 1810. The local clergyman Reverend Colton could find no human agency responsible for the knockings and noises in Sampford. Yet the reporter for the *Times* averred that preternatural activity was unlikely given the questionable reliability of human senses and diseases of the nerves, which were apt to create false illusions.[9] According to this author, the supposed ghost was more likely to reflect a disturbed state of mind than an 'actual occurrence'.[10]

Other terms that reflect important changes in conceptions of ghosts included the notion of a 'Bugbear'. This was positively dismissed by Samuel Johnson as 'A frightful object; a walking spectre' that was only 'imagined to be seen' and that was 'generally now used for a false terrour to frighten babes'.[11] Nonetheless, the relegation of this term to the nursery was countered by Johnson's definition of 'Spectre', which was an altogether more ambiguous term that was judged to denote 'an image, or figure, seen either truly, or but in conceit'. Johnson's notes also emphasized the increasingly familiar poetical use of this term, which did not undermine the reality of spectres but was instead used to 'imply an exact resemblance to some real being it represents'.[12] Daniel Defoe's work further suggested that ladies and gentlemen of fashion increasingly favoured the term 'Apparition' instead of 'Ghost' to describe a shadowy preternatural appearance. Whereas the latter was more indicative of vulgar usage, the former encapsulated a more pleasing degree of indistinctness. 'Apparition' also had the flexibility to describe a more general appearance or 'visible object', as well as 'a spectre' or 'walking spirit'.[13] For fashionable sceptics, Johnson's 'Apparition' allowed for the appearance of something 'only apparent, not real', but the term was also given authority by its association with optical theories and astronomical research.[14] 'Apparition' thus acknowledged a wider variety of interpretative viewpoints, catering for a cautious, yet more sophisticated engagement with ill-defined preternatural events, as well as for doubt and outright rejection. Linguistic shifts thus highlight a deep sense of uncertainty about the epistemological status of ghosts. They also suggest that a hierarchy of spectral visions now existed, with ghost stories of superior rank and quality holding more sway in polite society.

The degree to which this formal terminology reflected widespread shifts in attitudes remains uncertain. Johnson's lexicon probably catered for more educated outlooks, it was after all a commercially focused product, published by the highly successful bookseller William Strahan and issued in four hefty leather-bound volumes.[15] Nonetheless, the uncertainties suggested by Johnson's classifications connect up to a broader range of activities and publications from the late eighteenth and early nineteenth centuries. On 12 April 1790, Capel Court in Bartholomew Lane, London, hosted a series of debates regarding the nature of 'GHOSTS, Apparitions, Fortune-Telling, and Dreams'.[16] The event was advertised in the classified section of the *The Times*. The main speaker, Dr Ranger, professor of astral science, was to demonstrate the practice of 'foretelling future Events by the Position of the Stars', and his presentation was to be followed the next Monday by discussion of 'the strange Apparition of the Woman murdered at Pancras'.[17] Similarly, in 1791, Coachmakers Hall Society in Cheapside debated whether it was 'consistent with the Character of a Christian and a Man of Sense, to believe that the Death of a Friend may be known by a supernatural Token, or that a departed Spirit ever appeared and conversed with any mortal'. Promising to reflect on the 'eminent' views of Lord Clarendon, Charles Drelincourt, Samuel Johnson and John Wesley, the discussion was promoted as 'one of the most important that ever engaged the Attention of intelligent Beings'.[18] The precise essence and meaning of ghosts remained highly controversial, which allowed them to be cast as intriguing subjects for empirical investigation and imaginative speculation.[19]

We have seen that the flexible discourse of empiricism could be fashioned in support of ghost stories as well as in opposition to them. The configuration of ghost stories as legitimate subjects of scientific enquiry also gave important succour to experimental pursuits, and it opened up new avenues of investigation. Indeed, as Alex Owen has argued, the spiritualist movement of nineteenth-century England was the product of an uneasy, but workable marriage between scientific naturalism and a commitment to a vibrant world of spirits. Many believers strove for scientific proof of the survival of the spirit after death. They exhibited a desire similar to that of eighteenth-century Romantics, who were anxious to balance the 'gross materialism' of the age with contemplation of a higher spiritual order.[20] Between the close of the eighteenth century and the heyday of spiritualist séances in the 1860s and 1870s, the balance of power between the living and the dead had shifted firmly in favour of the former. The ghost stories of eighteenth-century England were often conceived within a religious and sometimes providential framework, yet the meaning of the term 'providence' usually denoted 'divine superintendence'. It had also acquired both secular and commercial meanings by the early nineteenth century.[21] Nonetheless, as the evangelical texts of John Wesley attested, the impenetrable mysteries of God occasionally allowed the dead to appear of their own volition in the service of the divine. However, the late nineteenth-century séance stripped the dead of independent agency. Contact with the spirit world was now subject to strict rules of conduct, with spirits at the beck and call of mediums who invoked and orchestrated their appearances. The years under study here in many ways laid the foundations for these later changes. Enlightened philosophers who tried to satisfy a constant thirst for knowledge toiled hard to achieve mastery of the preternatural world, but ghosts remained irritatingly resistant to intellectual domination and categorization.

The iconography of ghosts provides further testament to the haziness which often characterized perceptions of ghosts, spectres and apparitions. The familiar ghost, recognizable by its facial contours or by its clothing, persisted throughout this period. But it was also joined by a more indistinct and anonymous substance that was impossible to identify as the returning soul of a particular person. This kind of ghost featured strongly in fictional representations and especially in poems, where the precise identity of the ghost was less important than the broader meanings it embodied. The now familiar image of a ghost as a floating figure in white began to creep into more common usage towards the close of the eighteenth century. No doubt this was connected to the more traditional image of the ghost in winding sheet that was prominent throughout the medieval and early modern period. But this trend may also bear connections to increasingly familiar accounts of fraudulent ghost-mongers who dressed up in white sheets to play pranks. When a ghost was pursued through St Paul's churchyard in 1804, it was unveiled as a fraudster 'attired in a muslin robe'.[22] Although the connections remain oblique, the shifting imagery of eighteenth-century ghosts again suggests important links to optical and astronomical technologies. The visual vocabulary of the age was considerably expanded by refractions and reflections of light, alongside the identification of new celestial phenomena. Medical probing under the human skin and into the unconscious mind laid similar emphasis upon transparency, and on the ability to see through and within material substance. Visual representations of ghosts were in a state of flux between two different worlds. They were destabilized by increased knowledge of the human body, but also by new explorations of astronomical objects, which expanded the category of apparitions and brought them closer to the knowable human world.

What emerges from this maze of words and images is a dualistic conception of ghosts that allowed for physical and psychological interpretations to coexist and overlap. This coexistence was of course nothing new in the eighteenth century, but the tools and the vocabulary now existed to define these categories more carefully. If ghosts became less viable as a physical presence in Georgian society, the stories associated with them became more rather than less meaningful in psychological settings. Ghost stories expressed curiosity about the nature of life after death, and they reflected desires to confirm the post-mortem fate of the individual. These years witnessed a significant burgeoning in the material culture of death, and ghost stories deserve a place alongside the elaborate tombs, eulogies and funereal ephemera that were dedicated to sanctifying the memory of the dead.[23] This commemorative urge formed an important expression of historical subjectivity, and allowed people to maintain crucial links with the past. Ghost stories must then be situated within a history of memory since they were expressions of individual and communal identity, and they preserved the histories of particular families, communities and localities. Caroline Bynum has shown that proof of individual souls persisting beyond the grave was, and continues to be, one of the most fundamental obsessions of human societies across the world.[24] Furthermore, Fernando Vidal has demonstrated that the seat of individuality or selfhood was by no means settled in the eighteenth century. Materialistic conceptions of the soul were supported by both theological argument and chemical experimentation, before the 'self' was gradually disembodied and became coterminous with the brain.[25] For people contemplating their own mortality, or that of loved ones, comfort was taken in the possibility that ghosts *might* exist, even if specific instances of them appearing on earth could rarely be verified. Following the death of his wife, Samuel Johnson comforted himself with the hope that his beloved might communicate with him 'whether exercised by appearance, impulses, dreams, or in any other manner'.[26] The living had then discovered new ways to interact with the dead, perhaps most notably through the medium of dreams. Alongside concrete, physical reports of ghostly activity, this somatic trend exemplified a growing tendency for ghostly encounters to take place as part of an interior psychological world. Yet whether conceived as physical or psychological embodiments of immortality, ghost stories articulated the same deep-seated emotional attachments to the dead, and to the concept of future spiritual reward.

Also prominent in these years were attempts to drive a wedge between factual and fictional ghost stories, though considerable seepage has been witnessed from both sides. The result of this separation was the greater extension of ghost stories into fictional spaces where emphasis on the aesthetic value of ghosts as an imaginative resource invested these tales with an important role in developing notions of the sublime, Romanticism and interiority. Romantic novels, ethereal poetry and Gothic fictions provided fresh vehicles for contemplating ghostly figures. They simultaneously incited and assuaged the terrors and uncertainties of death, but from a safe distance that did not offend the prevailing canons of taste and politeness. Contemplation of ghosts could then be the mark of a cultivated mind that was able to extend its imaginative faculties beyond the mundane and domestic. This was particularly important in an age fixated upon the mind as the seat of human reason and emotion. If philosophical trends insisted upon a strict separation between ghost beliefs and ghost stories, fictional representations of ghosts were highly ambiguous. The ability to appreciate the aesthetics of ghost stories, without at least conceding the possibility that returning souls of the dead might revisit the living, required a careful balancing act, and one that was not always successfully achieved. The experiences of childhood may well have coloured opinions on this subject, since Walter Scott observed that affections for marvellous and supernatural wonders occupied 'a hidden corner in almost every ones bosom'.[27] Notwithstanding the vehement and genuine disavowal of some commentators that the ghosts of the dead could appear amongst the living, it was often a matter of taste rather than conviction that dictated public indictments of ghost stories. Nevertheless, irrespective of their epistemological status, ghost stories were good for thinking with. At the very least they had the potential to dramatize real events and emotions, and to frame important questions about social life, spirituality and morality.

Brief glimpses of private reflections certainly suggest that genuine belief in ghosts retreated from public spaces into private, domestic worlds over the course of this period. Personal experience and memory also played a crucial formative role in determining individual attitudes towards ghost stories, either alongside or instead of the dictates of philosophy, fashion and confessional strife. There were, however, important exceptions to this trend and more extensive quarrying of private papers, diaries and journals must add depth and complexity to this observation. The discussion of local landscapes in the preceding chapter also suggests that a detailed regional analysis of ghost beliefs will add important new layers to the research presented here. Historians of ghost beliefs and supernatural phenomena must build upon the work of folklorists who have, for example, identified important divergences in regional conceptions of fairies in the British Isles, which seem to relate at least in part to different physical landscapes and forms of social organization.[28] It is beyond the scope of this study to assess the distinctive features of ghost beliefs in urban and industrial settings, but the work of Owen Davies suggests that important lessons can be learned about the ways in which ghosts and other supernatural phenomena adapted to particular physical and social environments.[29] Similarly, there has been room for just a few anecdotal comparisons between English ghost stories and those originating in other parts of the British Isles and the wider world. Sustained comparison of British ghost beliefs will serve to mark out both similarities and peculiarities between different native traditions. Studies of ghost beliefs in different locations may also highlight an alternative pattern of cultural change than that identified here.

The fortunes of other supernatural phenomena remain relatively obscure in this period, with the notable exception of witches. I look forward to hearing how fairies and angels fared in these years, and to revising my own thoughts on the significance of supernatural belief in Georgian society.[30] Detailed studies will help to distinguish important points of overlap and difference between the assorted phenomena included under the heading of superstition. This term is tainted by its polemical associations and, although sceptics chose not to untangle its diverse meanings, it is increasingly clear that many contemporaries understood the inhabitants of the invisible world to correspond to an organized hierarchy of spirits. On occasion the ghosts of the dead became associated with cases of possession, or they were spied in the company of fairies, yet the attributes associated with different types of spirit were for the most part clearly demarcated. The souls of the dead did not have the power of enchantment or healing enjoyed by fairies, nor could they perform magical acts in the manner of witches. Angels were shining examples of chastity and humility and were perceived to hold superior knowledge of the occult world than other types of spirit. In contrast, the powers commonly associated with ghosts were more closely tied to the human world, which made sense since this was the sphere that they had formerly inhabited. The less fantastical, rather modest capabilities of ghosts may then provide one explanation for why their ministrations appear to have remained more acceptable. A strictly ordered hierarchy of the supernatural had thus emerged by the close of the eighteenth century.

Finally, the extent to which a common print culture homogenized views of the preternatural world is a topic that certainly deserves more sustained attention. The relationship between historical change and literary genres has been foundational to this study. Without reducing the literary to the historical, or the historical to the literary, I have tried to acknowledge intimate links between the two. It should be clear by now that the increasingly diverse ways in which ghost stories were interpreted paralleled their differentiation in form and content within assorted print media. There is no doubt that the absorption of ghosts within new forms of literature, including periodicals and novels, had an immense impact upon the ways in which people thought about them. As the work of Michael MacDonald, Terence Murphy and Daniel Woolf illustrates, the epistemological assumptions of print, and especially the periodical press, could have a corrosive, de-contextualizing effect upon local reports of suicides, or in this case of ghosts. Ultimately, they argue, print undermined oral tradition because it distanced these kinds of reports from their original legitimating contexts. What I have tried to suggest here is that this de-contextualizing effect varied in degree across different categories of print. There was moreover considerable overlap between the techniques used to tell ghost stories verbally and in print. The deliberate inclusion of dialogue, imagery and credible circumstantial detail in textual performances was designed to persuade readers and to compensate for the sanitizing tendencies of print. Many printed ghost stories were also designed to flow back into speech, allowing them to be re-animated with physical gestures and persuasive linguistic techniques. Just as some print forms discouraged speculation about the existence of ghosts, it was equally possible for other genres to stir curiosity. Ghost stories were, after all, collective expressions of the beliefs and practices of the people of Georgian England. As such, these narratives reveal scepticism, but also intense curiosity about the souls of the dead. They also tell us a great deal about the evolving climate of English society, and about the intricate, complicated nature of cultural change.

NOTES

Introduction

1. S. Johnson in J. Boswell, *Everybody's Boswell, Being the Life of Samuel Johnson Abridged from James Boswell's Complete Text and from the "Tour to the Hebrides"*, illustrated by E. H. Shepard (Ware: Wordsworth Editions, 1989), p.290.
2. Printer and magazine proprietor Edward Cave confessed to Johnson that he had seen a ghost, as did Rev. Goldsmith, brother of Oliver Goldsmith, ibid., p. 154.
3. J. Boswell, *The Life of Samuel Johnson, LLD, Comprehending an Account of his Studies and Numerous Works*, 4 vols (London, 1799), vol. 3, p. 318.
4. M. R. James, 'Twelve Medieval Ghost-Stories', *English Historical Review*, 37:147 (1922), pp. 413–22; K. Thomas, *Religion and the Decline of Magic, Studies in Popular Beliefs in Sixteenth- and Seventeenth-Century England* (London: Penguin, 1991), pp. 701–4; J.-C. Schmitt, *Ghosts in the Middle Ages: The Living and the Dead in Medieval Society*, trans. T. L. Fagan (Chicago, IL, and London: University of Chicago Press, 1998).
5. P. Marshall, *Beliefs and the Dead in Reformation England* (Oxford: Oxford University Press, 2002), pp. 12–18.
6. For a comprehensive discussion of theological debates surrounding purgatory see ibid., pp. 47–73.
7. E. Sandys, *Sermons*, ed. J. Ayre (Cambridge: Parker Society, 1841), p. 60.
8. Marshall, *Beliefs and the Dead*, pp. 245–64.
9. Affiliations between science, magic and the occult have been documented in M. Hunter, *The Occult Laboratory: Magic, Science and Second Sight in Late Seventeenth-Century Scotland* (Woodbridge: Boydell Press, 2001); J. Barry, 'Public Infidelity and Private Belief? The Discourse of Spirits in Enlightenment Bristol', in O. Davies and W. de Blécourt (eds), *Beyond the Witch Trials, Witchcraft and Magic in Enlightenment Europe* (Manchester: Manchester University Press, 2004); S. Clark, *Thinking with Demons: The Idea of Witchcraft in Early Modern Europe* (Oxford: Oxford University Press, 1997); J. Shaw, *Miracles in Enlightenment England* (New Haven, CT, and London: Yale University Press, 2006).
10. E. Birkhead, *The Tale of Terror: A Study of Gothic Romance* (London: Constable & Co., 1921); J. Briggs, *Night Visitors: The Rise and Fall of the English Ghost Story* (London:

Faber and Faber, 1977); G. Cavaliero, *The Supernatural and English Fiction* (Oxford: Oxford University Press, 1995); E. J. Clery, *The Rise of Supernatural Fiction, 1762–1800* (Cambridge: Cambridge University Press, 1995); R. Geary, *The Supernatural in Gothic Fiction: Horror, Belief, and Literary Change* (New York: Lampeter, 1992).

11. Thomas, *Religion and the Decline of Magic*, p. 724.

12. R. C. Finucane, *Appearances of the Dead: A Cultural History of Ghosts* (Buffalo, NY: Prometheus Books, 1984).

13. L. Daston and K. Park, *Wonders and the Order of Nature, 1150–1750* (New York: Zone Books, 1998), pp. 14, 20, 331.

14. D. Spadafora, *The Idea of Progress in Eighteenth-Century Britain* (New Haven, CT, and London: Yale University Press, 1990).

15. Barry, 'Public Infidelity and Private Belief?'; Clark, *Thinking with Demons*; M. Gibson, *Possession, Puritanism and Print: Darrell, Harsnett, Shakespeare and the Elizabethan Exorcism Controversy* (London: Pickering & Chatto, 2006); P. Lake with M. Questier, *The Antichrist's Lewd Hat, Protestants, Papists and Players in Post-Reformation England* (New Haven, CT, and London: Yale University Press, 2002); Shaw, *Miracles in Enlightenment England*; A. Walsham, *Providence in Early Modern England* (Oxford: Oxford University Press, 1999).

16. O. Davies, *Witchcraft, Magic and Culture, 1736–1951* (Manchester: Manchester University Press, 1999); R. Hutton, 'The English Reformation and the Evidence of Folklore', *Past and Present*, 148: 1 (1995) pp. 89–116.

17. Schmitt, *Ghosts in the Middle Ages*; N. Caciola, 'Wraiths, Revenants and Ritual in Medieval Culture', *Past and Present*, 152:1 (1996), pp. 3–45; Marshall, *Beliefs and the Dead*, pp. 232–64.

18. L. Roper, *Oedipus and the Devil: Witchcraft, Sexuality and Religion in Early Modern Europe* (London: Routledge, 1994).

19. I. Bostridge, *Witchcraft and its Transformations c. 1650–c. 1750* (Oxford and New York: Clarendon Press, 1997), pp. 180–202.

20. Davies, *Witchcraft, Magic and Culture*.

21. P. Burke, *Popular Culture in Early Modern Europe* (London: Temple Smith, 1978).

22. 'Ghost', in S. Johnson, *A Dictionary of the English Language*, 2 vols (London, 1755).

23. 'Apparition' and 'Spectre', in ibid.

24. J. Boswell, *The Life of Dr Johnson, LLD*, abridged by F. Thomas (London, 1792), p. 73.

25. See for example 'The Hammersmith Ghost', *The Times*, 6 January 1804, p. 3.

26. B. Capp, *Astrology and the Popular Press, English Almanacs 1500–1800* (London and Boston, MA: Faber and Faber, 1979); M. Spufford, *Small Books and Pleasant Histories: Popular Fiction and its Readership in Seventeenth-Century England* (Cambridge: Cambridge University Press, 1985); T. Watt, *Cheap Print and Popular Piety, 1550–1640* (Cambridge: Cambridge University Press, 1996).

27. Jonathan Barry has called for 'a social analysis in which gender, age and position in the life-cycle are integrated with notions of class derived from birth, occupation or wealth', J. Barry and C. Brooks (eds), *The Middling Sort of People, Culture, Society and Politics in England, 1550–1800* (Basingstoke: Macmillan, 1994), pp. 2–3.

28. P. Bourdieu, *The Field of Cultural Production: Essays on Art and Literature*, ed. R. Johnson (Cambridge: Polity Press, 1993), p. 37.

29. K. Sharpe and S. N. Zwicker (eds), *Reading, Society and Politics in Early Modern England* (Cambridge and New York: Cambridge University Press, 2003), p. 23.

30. T. Eagleton, *Literary Theory: An Introduction* (Oxford: Blackwell, 1988), p. 11.

31. L. J. Davis, *Factual Fictions: The Origins of the English Novel* (New York and Guildford: Columbia University Press, 1983), pp. 1–10.

32. W. J. Ong, 'Writing is a Technology that Restructures Thought', in G. Baumann (ed.), *The Written Word: Literacy in Transition* (Oxford: Clarendon Press, 1986), pp. 23–50, on p. 38. Similar points have been made by M. MacDonald and T. R. Murphy, *Sleepless Souls: Suicide in Early Modern England* (Oxford: Clarendon Press, 1990), pp. 301–2; see also D. Woolf, 'The "Common Voice": History, Folklore and Oral Tradition in Early Modern England', *Past and Present*, 120:1 (1988), pp. 26–52, on p. 52.

33. E. Duffy, 'The Godly and the Multitude in Stuart England', *Seventeenth Century*, 1 (1986), pp. 31–55; I. Green, *Print and Protestantism in Early Modern England* (Oxford and New York: Oxford University Press, 2003); P. Lake, 'Popular Form, Puritan Content? Two Puritan Appropriations of the Murder Pamphlet from Mid-Seventeenth-Century London', in A. Fletcher and P. Roberts (eds), *Religion, Culture and Society in Early Modern Britain* (Cambridge: Cambridge University Press, 1994), pp. 313–34; Walsham, *Providence in Early Modern England*; Watt, *Cheap Print and Popular Piety*.

34. R. Chartier (ed.), *The Culture of Print, Power and the Uses of Print in Early Modern Europe* (Cambridge: Polity Press, 1989), p. 6.

35. A. Fox, *Oral and Literate Culture in England, 1500–1700* (Oxford: Clarendon Press, 2000).

36. Watt, *Cheap Print and Popular Piety*, pp. 14–30; Spufford, *Small Books and Pleasant Histories*, pp. 5–6; Capp, *Astrology and the Popular Press*, p. 287.

37. For full description see J. Brewer, *The Pleasures of the Imagination, English Culture in the Eighteenth Century* (Chicago, IL: University of Chicago Press, 1997), pp. 167–97.

38. Ibid., p. 179.

39. W. J. Ong, *Orality and Literacy: The Technologising of the Word* (London: Methuen, 1982), p. 8.

40. J. Locke, *An Essay Concerning Human Understanding*, 9th edn, 2 vols (London, 1726), vol. 1, p. 368.

41. R. Houlbrooke, *Death, Religion, and the Family in England, 1480–1750* (Oxford: Clarendon Press, 1998), pp. 40, 291.

42. C. Gittings, *Death, Burial and the Individual in Early Modern England* (London: Croom Helm, 1984), p. 111.

43. P. Ariès, *The Hour of our Death*, trans. Helen Weaver (London: Allen Lane, 1981), pp. 337–48. John McManners advanced a similar argument for Enlightenment France, suggesting that emphasis on hope and consolation in death outweighed concepts of fear and judgement, J. McManners, *Death and the Enlightenment: Changing Attitudes to Death among Christians and Unbelievers in Eighteenth-Century France* (Oxford: Oxford University Press, 1981), pp. 202–3.

44. R. Richardson, *Death, Dissection and the Destitute* (London: Routledge & Kegan Paul, 2001), pp .7, 13.

45. 'Ghost' and 'Ghostliness', in Johnson, *A Dictionary* (1755).
46. A. Armstrong, *The Church of England, the Methodists and Society 1700–1850* (London: University of London Press, 1973); W. Gibson, *The Church of England 1688–1832, Unity and Accord* (London: Routledge, 2001); J. Gregory, *Restoration, Reformation and Reform, 1660–1828* (Oxford and New York: Oxford University Press, 2000); D. A. Spaeth, *The Church in An Age of Danger: Parsons and Parishioners, 1660–1740* (Cambridge: Cambridge University Press, 2000); J. Spurr, *The Restoration Church of England* (New Haven, CT, and London: Yale University Press, 1991).
47. M. Gaskill, 'Reporting Murder: Fiction in the Archives in Early Modern England', *Social History*, 23:3 (1998), pp. 1–30.
48. M. Berg, *The Age of Manufactures, 1700–1820* (London: Fontana, 1985), pp. 46, 94, 124, 127, 203.
49. B. Capp, *When Gossips Meet: Women, Family and Neighbourhood in Early Modern England* (Oxford: Oxford University Press, 2003), pp. 67–126; L. Gowing, 'The Haunting of Susan Lay: Servants and Mistresses in Seventeenth-Century England', *Gender and History*, 14:2 (2002), pp. 183–201.
50. Eagleton, *Literary Theory*, p. 2.
51. R. Williams, *Keywords: A Vocabulary of Culture and Society* (London: Fontana Press, 1988), p. 135.
52. R. Williams, *Culture* (London: Fontana, 1981); R. Williams, *Culture and Society, 1780–1950* (New York: Columbia University Press, 1958).
53. Davis, *Factual Fictions*, p. 86.
54. Samuel Taylor Coleridge, cited in M. H. Abrams, *A Glossary of Literary Terms*, 7th edn (New York and London: Harcourt and Brace, 1999), p. 96.
55. Chartier, *The Culture of Print*, p. 2.
56. Hutton, 'The English Reformation', pp. 93–6.
57. L. Colley, *Britons, Forging the Nation 1707–1837* (London: Vintage, 1996).
58. See for example E. Jones, *A Relation of Apparitions of Spirits in the Principality of Wales* (Trevecca, 1780), p. v.

1 Restoration Hauntings

1. *Athenian Mercury*, 7:28 (1692), p. 2.
2. Individual editorial responses were anonymous but, as a practising clergyman, questions relating to religion were most likely to have been answered by Samuel Wesley.
3. C. Hill, *The World Turned Upside Down: Radical Ideas During the English Revolution* (London: Penguin, 1991), p. 182; C. Hill, 'Irreligion in the "Puritan" Revolution', in J. F. McGregor and B. Reay (eds), *Radical Religion in the English Revolution* (Oxford: Oxford University Press, 1986), pp. 191–211.
4. Hill, *The World Turned Upside Down*, pp. 151–83. B. Reay, *The Quakers and the English Revolution* (London: Temple Smith, 1985), p. 15.
5. R. Overton, *Mans Mortallitie* (London, 1643).
6. Lawrence Clarkson in Hill, *The World Turned Upside Down*, p. 339.
7. G. Fox, *The Journal of George Fox*, ed. N. Penney, 2 vols (Cambridge: Cambridge University Press, 1911), vol. 1, p. 228.

8. R. Moore, 'Late Seventeenth-Century Quakerism and the Miraculous: A New Look at George Fox's "Book of Miracles"', in K. Cooper and J. Gregory (eds), *Signs, Wonders, Miracles: Representations of Divine Power in the Life of the Church*, Studies in Church History, vol. 41 (Woodbridge: Boydell Press, 2005), pp. 335–44, on p. 338.

9. Jones, *A Relation of Apparitions*, pp. 1–2.

10. J. Glanvill, *A Blow at Modern Sadducism in Some Philosophical Considerations about Witchcraft* (London, 1668), pp. 115–17.

11. W. Turner, *A Compleat History of the Most Remarkable Providences* (London, 1697), p. v.

12. Ibid., p. 2.

13. R. Cudworth, *The True Intellectual System of the Universe* (London, 1678), p. 642.

14. B. Camfield, *A Theological Discourse of Angels and their Ministries* (London, 1678), p. 172.

15. Distaste for religious pluralism was expressed in a series of measures against nonconformity. See P. C. Almond, *Heaven and Hell in Enlightenment England* (Cambridge: Cambridge University Press, 1994), pp. 40–3; J. Spurr, 'Religion in Restoration England', in L. K. J. Glassey (ed.), *The Reigns of Charles II and James VII & II* (Basingstoke: Macmillan, 1997), pp. 90–124, on pp. 92–4.

16. S. Clarke, *A Demonstration of the Being and Attributes of God* (London, 1705), preface.

17. Burnet, cited in M. Hunter, *Science and Society in Restoration England* (Cambridge: Cambridge University Press, 1981), p. 173; Wilkins, cited in R. S. Westfall, *Science and Religion in Seventeenth-Century England*, (New Haven, CT, and London: Yale University Press, 1958), p. 34.

18. A. A. Cooper, 'A Letter Concerning Enthusiasm, to My Lord *****' (1708), in *Characteristics of Men, Manners, Opinions, Times*, ed. L. E. Klein (Cambridge and New York: Cambridge University Press, 1999), pp. 4–28.

19. T. Hobbes, *Leviathan*, ed. R. E. Flathman (London: W. W. Norton & Co., 1997), p. 247.

20. Westfall, *Science and Religion*, pp. 146–61.

21. James and Margaret Jacob, cited in R. Kroll, R. Ashcraft and P. Zagorin (eds), *Philosophy, Science, and Religion in England 1640–1700* (Cambridge and New York: Cambridge University Press, 1994), p. 2.

22. P. Elmer, 'Valentine Greatrakes, the Body Politic and the Politics of the Body in Restoration England' (unpublished paper prepared for 'Medicine and Religion in Enlightenment Europe' conference, Cambridge University, 20–1 September 2004), p. 86.

23. Cooper, 'A Letter Concerning Enthusiasm', p. 5.

24. E. Fowler, *Reflections upon a Letter Concerning Enthusiasm to my Lord *****(London, 1709), p. 63.

25. S. Hutton, 'More, Henry (1614–1687)', *Oxford Dictionary of National Biography* (Oxford: Oxford University Press, 2004), hereafter *ODNB*, http://www.oxforddnb.com/view/article/19181 (accessed 21 February 2005).

26. H. More, *Antidote of Atheism, or An Appeal to the Natural Faculties of the Minde of Man, whether there be not a God* (London, 1653), p. 164.

27. Hunter, *Science and Society*, p. 181.
28. M. Hope Nicolson (ed.), *The Conway Letters: The Correspondence of Anne, Viscountess Conway, Henry More, and their Friends 1642–1684* (Oxford: Clarendon Press, 1992), p. xv.
29. Taylor was most famous for his devotional writings, especially *The Rule and Exercise of Holy Living* (London, 1650) and *The Rule and Exercise of Holy Dying* (London, 1651).
30. Nicolson, *The Conway Letters*, p. 175.
31. More, *Antidote of Atheism*, p. 147.
32. J. Glanvill, *Saducismus Triumphatus, or, Full and Plain Evidence Concerning Witches and Apparitions*, ed. H. More (London, 1681), p. 286.
33. Henry More, cited in R. Baxter, *Of the Immortality of Mans Soul, and the Nature of it and other Spirits* (London, 1682), p. 4.
34. More, *Antidote of Atheism*, p. 145.
35. Term coined by R. M. Burns, *The Great Debate on Miracles, from Joseph Glanvill to David Hume* (Lewisburg: Bucknell University Press, 1981), p. 12.
36. Glanvill, *Saducismus Triumphatus*, p. 7.
37. Almond, *Heaven and Hell*, p. 35.
38. Glanvill, *A Blow at Modern Sadducism*, pp. 115–17.
39. Glanvill, *Saducismus Triumphatus*, p. 269.
40. Ibid., p. 54.
41. William Bayly took Goddard's deposition and he was further examined by Lypyatt Major, town clerk Rolf Bayly and by Joshuah Sacheverell, rector of St Peters in Marlborough, ibid., pp. 210–19.
42. Ibid., pp. 238–42.
43. Burns, *The Great Debate on Miracles*, p. 31.
44. Hunter, *Science and Society*, p. 180.
45. J. Glanvill, *Some Philosophical Considerations touching the Being of Witches and Witchcraft Written in a Letter to the Much Honour'd Robert Hunt, Esq.* (London, 1667), p. 60.
46. Glanvill, *Saducismus Triumphatus*, p. 277.
47. This tale is also recounted in the ballad *The Disturbed Ghost* (London, 1675).
48. The two accounts use strikingly similar language to describe the Tedworth spirit. The providential interpretation given by Glanvill to the drumming also matches the ballad, A. Miles, 'A Wonder of Wonders', in H. E. Rollins (ed.), *The Pack of Autolycus: or, Strange and Terrible News of Ghosts, Apparitions, Monstrous Births, Showers of Wheat, Judgments of God, and Other Prodigious and Fearful Happenings as Told in Broadside Ballads* (Cambridge, MA: Harvard University Press, 1969), pp. 118–19; Glanvill, *Saducismus Triumphatus*, pp. 90–118. According to Hay and Craven, linguistic affinities suggest important patterns of borrowing and exchange, which can be applied to the language of ghost stories, D. Hay and P. Craven (eds), *Masters, Servants, and Magistrates in Britain and the Empire, 1562–1955* (Chapel Hill, NC: University of North Carolina Press, 2004), pp. 15–21.
49. Turner, *A Compleat History*, preface.
50. Elmer, 'Valentine Greatrakes', p. 92.
51. Almond, *Heaven and Hell*, p. 34.

52. T. Bromhall, *A Treatise of Specters, or, An History of Apparitions, Oracles, Prophecies, and Predictions* (London, 1658), p. 343. Thomas Browne reaffirmed the centrality of believing in ghosts since those that denied them were, he argued, 'a sort, not of Infidels, but Atheists', Almond, *Heaven and Hell*, p. 41.

53. W. K. Lowther Clarke, *A History of the SPCK* (London: Society for Promoting Christian Knowledge, 1959), p. 2.

54. Elmer, 'Valentine Greatrakes', p. 75.

55. N. H. Keeble, *The Restoration: England in the 1660s* (Oxford: Blackwell, 2002), pp. 116–20. Spurr, 'Religion in Restoration England', p. 106.

56. Lowther Clarke counted thirty-nine societies in London and Westminster alone, *A History of the SPCK*, p. 3.

57. N. H. Keeble and G. F. Nuttall (eds), *Calendar of the Correspondence of Richard Baxter* (Oxford: Clarendon Press, 1991).

58. Keeble, *The Restoration*, p. 126.

59. Duffy, 'The Godly and the Multitude in Stuart England'.

60. R. Baxter, *The Certainty of the World of Spirits Fully Evinced* (London, 1691), pp. 3–4.

61. Ibid.

62. Ibid., p. 23.

63. Ibid., p. 25.

64. Ibid., p. 60

65. Ibid.

66. *The History of the Athenian Society*, 1 (1691), p. 10.

67. G. D. McEwen, *The Oracle of the Coffee House, John Dunton's Athenian Mercury* (San Marino, CA: Huntingdon Library, 1972), p. 18. See also H. Berry, *Gender, Society and Print Culture, The Cultural World of the Athenian Mercury* (Aldershot: Ashgate, 2003).

68. Anon., 'Epistle Dedicator, to the Gentleman of the Athenian Society', *Athenian Mercury*, 1 (1691), p. 1.

69. With the exception of the *London Gazette*, the *Athenian Mercury* enjoyed the longest publication run of any periodical of its generation.

70. *Athenian Mercury*, 1:29 (1691), p. 1; 1:28 (1691), p. 1; 2:7 (1691), p. 2; 4:28 (1691), p. 2.

71. *Athenian Mercury*, 4:10 (31 October 1691), p. 1.

72. Ibid.

73. Marshall, *Beliefs and the Dead*, pp. 245–64. F. Valletta, *Witchcraft, Magic and Superstition in England 1640–70* (Aldershot: Ashgate, 2000), pp. 80–1.

74. *Athenian Oracle*, 4 (1710), p. 288.

75. More, in Glanvill, *Saducismus Triumphatus*, pp. 229–30.

76. *Athenian Mercury*, 2:7 (1691), p. 1; 1:25 (1691), p. 2; 1:20 (1691), p. 1.

77. Philip Almond noted increasing desires for spousal reunion in heaven in the later seventeenth century, which he ascribed to the growth of companionate marriage. Almond, *Heaven and Hell*, p. 104.

78. Ibid., p. 25.

79. Ibid., pp. 25, 44.

80. Ibid., p. 156; D. P. Walker, *The Decline of Hell: Seventeenth-Century Discussions of Eternal Torment* (Chicago, IL: University of Chicago Press, 1964), pp. 9, 108.

81. Barrow, cited in Almond, *Heaven and Hell*, p. 148.

82. *Athenian Mercury*, 4:10 (1691), p. 1.

83. Ibid.

84. Turner, *A Compleat History*, title-page.

85. Baxter, *The Certainty of the World of Spirits*, p. 88.

86. Ibid., p. 147.

87. Anon., *An Exact Narrative of Many Surprizing Matters of Fact Uncontestably Wrought by an Evil Spirit or Spirits, in the House of Master Jan Smagge* (London, 1709), pp. 25–8.

88. Anon., *The Wonderful and Strange Apparition and Ghost of Edward Ashley* (London, 1712), title-page.

89. Spurr, 'Religion in Restoration England', p. 113.

90. Ibid., p. 112. For ghost stories in Cambridge see C. Jackson (ed.), *The Diary of Abraham De La Pryme, The Yorkshire Antiquary*, Surtees Society, vol. 54 (Durham, 1870), pp. 39–42.

91. R. Wodrow, *Analecta, or, Materials for a History of Remarkable Providences, mostly relating to Scotch Ministers and Christians*, ed. M. Leishman, Maitland Club, 60, 4 vols ([Edinburgh], 1842–3), vol. 1, pp. 201–2, 215; vol. 4, pp. 88–90.

92. Anon., *A True Relation of the Dreadful Ghost Appearing to one John Dyer* (London, 1691).

93. Samuel Harsnett described ghost stories as the work of 'craftie priests and leacherous friers', S. Harsnett, *A Declaration of Egregious Popish Impostures*, reprinted in F. W. Brownlow, *Shakespeare, Harsnett, and the Devils of Denham* (London and Cranbury, NJ: Associated University Presses, 1993), pp. 191–335, on p. 309. W. Perkins, *A Discourse of the Damned Art of Witchcraft* (Cambridge, 1610), pp. 115–16.

94. A. Marshall, 'Stephen Dugdale', *ODNB*, http://www.oxforddnb.com/view/article/19181 (accessed 26 February 2006).

95. 'The Duchess of York's Ghost' (1691), in G. de F. Lord (ed.), *Poems on Affairs of State: August Satirical Verse, 1660–1714*, 7 vols (New Haven, CT, and London: Yale University Press, 1971), vol. 5, p. 299.

96. Duffy, 'The Godly and the Multitude in Stuart England', pp. 47–8.

97. F. Perrault, *The Divell of Masçon: or, A True Relation of the Chiefe Things which an Uncleane Spirit did, and said at Masçon in Burgundy* (London, 1669).

98. Ibid., preface.

99. 'Du Moulin's letter to Robert Boyle', in ibid., preface.

2 Printing the Preternatural in the Late Seventeenth Century

1. Anon., *Tears of the Press* (London, 1681), p. 7.

2. A. McShane Jones, '"Rime and Reason": The Political World of the English Broadside Ballad, 1640–1689' (PhD thesis, University of Warwick, 2004), p. 10; Mark Knights calculates that five to ten million pamphlets were in circulation from 1678–1681,

M. Knights, *Politics and Opinion in Crisis, 1678–1681* (Cambridge: Cambridge University Press, 1994), p. 168.

3. Watt, *Cheap Print and Popular Piety*; Lake, 'Popular Form, Puritan Content?'; Walsham, *Providence in Early Modern England*.

4. This does not include reprints, which were common throughout this period, nor is it an exhaustive analysis of ballad collections, being largely based on the Pepys and Douce collections, 'The Douce Ballads', http://www.bodley.ox.ac.uk/ballads/ (accessed 5 September 2006); W. G. Day (ed.), *Catalogue of the Pepys Library. The Pepys Ballads*, 5 vols (Cambridge: D. S. Brewer, 1987).

5. McShane Jones, '"Rime and Reason"', p. 33.

6. Watt, *Cheap Print and Popular Piety*, pp. 76–7, 11, 42, 275.

7. D. Cressy, *Literacy and the Social Order: Reading and Writing in Tudor and Stuart England* (Cambridge: Cambridge University Press, 1980).

8. Fox, *Oral and Literate Culture*, p. 19.

9. Fox argues that reading was prioritized in Protestant England because salvation became intrinsically linked with the ability to read scripture for oneself, ibid., pp. 16–17.

10. Spufford, *Small Books and Pleasant Histories*, p. 20; Fox, *Oral and Literate Culture*, p. 13.

11. The concept of 'societal bilingualism' is drawn from D. Leith, *A Social History of English* (London: Routledge, 1997), p. 12.

12. Walter Ong argues that 'the written text, for all its permanence means nothing, is not even a text, except in relationship to the spoken word', Ong, 'Writing is a Technology that Restructures Thought', p. 31.

13. For more detail see McShane Jones, '"Rime and Reason"', p. 11.

14. Anon., *The Two Unfortunate Lovers, or, A True Relation of the Lamentable End of John True and Susan Mease* (London, 1670), p. 1.

15. Anon., *A Godly Warning to all Maidens* (London, 1670), p. 1. This tale had a long shelf life both before and after this period, see Walsham, *Providence in Early Modern England*, pp. 111–12.

16. J. A. Sharpe, '"Last Dying Speeches": Religion, Ideology and Public Execution in Seventeenth-Century England', *Past and Present*, 107 (1985), pp. 144–67. Bateman's tragedy was the best-selling ballad of this genre, enjoying several reprints in the eighteenth century. It was also turned into a play, *The Vow Breaker*, by William Samson. See MacDonald and Murphy, *Sleepless Souls*, p. 47.

17. Spufford, *Small Books and Pleasant Histories*, p. 157.

18. Anon., *The Suffolk Miracle, or, A Relation of a Young Man who a Month After his Death Appeared to his Sweetheart* (London, 1670), p. 1.

19. Anon., *The Leicestershire Tragedy: or, The Fatal Overthrow of two Unfortunate Lovers, caus'd by Susanna's Breach of Promise* (London, 1685), p. 1.

20. McShane Jones, '"Rime and Reason"', p. 6.

21. Davis, *Factual Fictions*, p. 28.

22. Ibid., p. 74.

23. Walter Ong's contention that print was a technology of decontextualization has recently been challenged in the field of psycho-linguistics, D. R. Olson, *The World on*

Paper: The Conceptual and Cognitive Implications of Writing and Reading (Cambridge: Cambridge University Press, 1994), p. 38.

24. Cited in Knights, *Politics and Opinion in Crisis*, p. 170.

25. Anon., *Great News from Middle-Row in Holbourn or A True Relation of a Dreadful Ghost which Appeared in the Shape of one Mrs. Adkins* (London, 1680), pp. 1–4.

26. Ibid., p. 4.

27. Lake, 'Popular Form, Puritan Content?'. McShane Jones illustrated how elites used ballads to influence popular opinion, '"Rime and Reason"', p. 6.

28. Anon., *A Strange, but True Relation, of the Discovery of a Most Horrid and Bloody Murder* (London, 1678), p. 2.

29. Ibid., p. 4.

30. Anon., *Strange and Wonderful News from Lincolnshire* (London, 1679).

31. Anon., *A True and Perfect Relation from the Faulcon at the Banke-side* (London, 1661), p. 1. This devotional strategy had clear affinities to traditional ways of conjuring ghosts and it was repeated in a number of other ballads, including Anon., *Strange and Wonderful News from Northampton-shire, or, The Discontented Spirit* (London, 1674).

32. Ibid., p. 1.

33. Bernard Capp, in B. Reay (ed.), *Popular Culture in Seventeenth-Century England* (London: Croom Helm, 1985), p. 220.

34. McShane Jones, '"Rime and Reason"', p. 19.

35. Anon., *Mr. Ashton's Ghost to his Late Companion in the Tower* (London, 1691), p. 1; Anon., *Murder Will Out: Being a Relation of the Late Earl of Essex's Ghost* (London, 1683), p. 1.

36. Anon., *Bradshaw's Ghost: Being a Dialogue between the said Ghost, and an Apparition of the Late King Charles* (London, 1659), pp. 1–12; Anon., *Lilburn's Ghost* (London, 1659) served a very similar purpose.

37. Anon., *Sir Edmundbury Godfreys Ghost* (London, 1682); J. Oldham, *Garnets Ghost Addressing to the Jesuits, Met in Private Caball, just after the Murther of Sir Edmund-Bury Godfrey* (London, 1679). See also Anon., *A New Apparition of S. Edmund-Bery Godfrey's Ghost to the Earl of Danby in the Tower* (London, 1681); A. Roper, 'Absalom's Issue: Parallel Poems in the Restoration', *Studies in Philology*, 99:3 (2002), pp. 276–8.

38. For parallel argument see A. E. Bakos, 'Images of Hell in the Pamphlets of the Fronde', *Historical Reflections*, 26:2 (2000), pp. 339–52.

39. Anon., *The Midwives Ghost* (London, 1680); Anon., *A New Ballad of The Midwives Ghost*, (London, 1680), p. 1.

40. Ibid.

41. Ibid.

42. Anon., *Strange and Wonderful News from Lincolnshire*, p. 1.

43. Ibid., p. 2.

44. Ibid., p. 3.

45. Ibid., p. 4.

46. Ibid., title-page.

47. Gaskill, 'Reporting Murder'. See also M. Gaskill, *Crime and Mentalities in Early Modern England* (Cambridge: Cambridge University Press, 2000), p. 233; Gowing, 'The Haunting of Susan Lay', p. 198.

48. The unceremonious interment of this man meant that his corpse was denied the customary rituals of cleansing and of decent burial. For details of these customs see D. Cressy, *Birth, Marriage and Death: Ritual, Religion and the Life-Cycle in Tudor and Stuart England* (Oxford: Oxford University Press, 1997), pp. 421–55.

49. Anon., *The Wonder of this Age: or, God's Miraculous Revenge against Murder* (London, 1677), pp. 1–5.

50. Ibid.

51. Anon., *The Duke's Daughter's Cruelty: or, The Wonderful Apparition of Two Infants whom she Murther'd and Buried in a Forrest, for to Hide her Shame* (London, 1692), p. 1.

52. Ibid.

53. For descriptions of the ballad partners see Spufford, *Small Books and Pleasant Histories*, pp. 84 ff.

54. In 1674 Philip Brooksby published the ballad of *The Disturbed Ghost* that featured in Chapter 1.

55. J. Aubrey, *Remains of Gentilisme and Judaisme*, 1686–7, ed. J. Britten (London, 1881), p. 104.

56. Jackson (ed.), *The Diary of Abraham De La Pryme*, p. 5.

57. D. Defoe, *An Essay on the History and Reality of Apparitions* (London, 1727), p. 280.

58. Anon., *The Rich Man's Warning-Piece; or, The Oppressed Infants in Glory* (London, 1683 and 1770), p. 1.

59. O. Hufton, *The Prospect Before Her: A History of Women in Western Europe* (London: HarperCollins, 1995).

60. Gowing, 'The Haunting of Susan Lay', p. 196.

61. Anon., *An Account of a Most Horrid and Barborous Murther and Robbery, Committed on the Body of Captain Brown, near Shrewsbury in Shropshire* (London, 1694).

62. Royal Commission, *Fifth Report of the Royal Commission on Historical Manuscripts*, 1:4 (London, 1876), p. 384.

63. Defoe, *An Essay on the History and Reality of Apparitions*, pp. 376–9.

64. For a fuller description of the spread of regional printing after 1695 see T. Jones, *Street Literature in Birmingham: A History of Broadside and Chapbook* (Oxford: Polytechnic, 1970).

65. Anon., *The Wonder of this Age*, title-page.

66. Anon., *A Strange, but True Relation*, p. 1.

67. Anon., *A Warning Piece for the World, or, A Watch-Word to England* (London, 1655), pp. 1–8.

68. Anon., *The Examination of Isabel Binnington of Great-Driffield* (York, 1662); Anon., *A Strange and Wonderfull Discovery of a Horrid and Cruel Murther Committed Fourteen Years Since, upon the Person of Robert Eliot of London, at Great Driffield in the East-Riding of the County of York* (London, 1662).

69. This detail supported a verdict of murder since it was a well-documented belief that driving a stake through a corpse would prevent its ghost from returning to identify the killer. See Caciola, 'Wraiths, Revenants and Ritual', pp. 29–30.

70. Anon., *The Rest-less Ghost: or, Wonderful News from Northamptonshire and Southwark* (London, [1675]), title-page.

71. Ibid.

72. Anon., 'Strange News and Wonderful News from Northampton-shire, or, The Discontented Spirit', in Rollins (ed.), *The Pack of Autolycus*, pp. 179–84.

73. Ibid., p. 179.

74. Anon., *A True Relation of the Dreadful Ghost*, pp. 1–8.

75. Ibid.

76. Ong, 'Writing is a Technology that Restructures Thought', p. 31.

77. David Olson for example notes that variations of intonation in speech give rise 'to radically different interpretations' among listeners, *The World on Paper*, p. 8.

78. Leith, *A Social History of English*, p. 89.

79. K. Thomas, 'The Meaning of Literacy', in Baumann (ed.), *The Written Word*, pp. 97–131, on p. 99.

80. Cressy, *Literacy and the Social Order*, p. 14.

81. A number of 'ghosts' were employed in this polemical battle, usually being used to claim authority from the words of the dead. C. Ness, *The Lord Stafford's Ghost: or, A Warning to Traitors* (London, 1680).

82. McShane Jones, '"Rime and Reason"', p. 28.

83. N. Llewellyn, *The Art of Death: Visual Culture in the English Death Ritual c.1500–1800* (London: Reaktion Books, 1997), pp. 16–34.

84. All three painters contributed work related to the context of death: Robert Walker painted a famous oil canvas of John Evelyn in 1648, John Souch produced the portrait entitled *Sir Thomas Aston at the Deathbed of his Wife* in 1636 and Thomas Stothard's 1792 watercolour *Burying the Dead* evoked similar contemplations of mortality. See Llewellyn, *The Art of Death*, pp. 6, 48, 82.

85. This sketch appeared in a 1605 edition of Pierre Le Loyer's *A Treatise of Specters or Straunge Sights, Visions and Apparitions Appearing Sensibly unto Men* (London, 1605). This text was reprinted in English in 1658 and 1659.

3 A New Canterbury Tale

1. *The Loyal Post: With Foreign and Inland Intelligence*, 14 (21–4 December 1705), reproduced in M. Schonhorn (ed.), *Accounts of the Apparition of Mrs. Veal by Daniel Defoe and Others*, Augustan Reprint Society, 115 (Los Angeles, CA: William Andrews Clark Memorial Library, University of California, 1965), pp. 1–3

2. 'Letter from E. B. at Canterbury to an Unknown Lady', 13 September 1705. This letter survives in manuscript form in the correspondence of John Flamsteed, but was probably addressed to his wife. It is reproduced in full in ibid., p. 1.

3. 'Letter from Lucy Lukyn at Canterbury to her Aunt', 9 October 1705, in ibid., p. 1.

4. 'Letter from Stephen Gray at Canterbury to John Flamsteed at the Royal Observatory at Greenwich', 15 November 1705, Papers of John Flamsteed, Royal Greenwich

Observatory, MS London, 37, f. 16, in Schonhorn (ed.), *Accounts of the Apparition of Mrs. Veal*, p. 3.

5. C. Drelincourt, *The Christian's Defence Against the Fears of Death: With Directions how to Dye Well, with an Account of Mrs. Veal's Apparition to Mrs. Bargrave* (London, 1720), p. xiii.

6. [D. Defoe], *A True Relation of the Apparition of one Mrs. Veal, the Next Day After her Death, to one Mrs. Bargrave, at Canterbury, the 8th of September, 1705* (London, 1706), p. vii. George Starr has cast doubt on Defoe's authorship due to his religious sensibilities. Starr's comments are however inconclusive, not least because Defoe's true opinions are characteristically difficult to ascertain. G. Starr, 'Why Defoe Probably Did Not Write the Apparition of Mrs Veal', *Eighteenth Century Fiction*, 15:3–4 (2003), pp. 421–50. Rodney Baine supplies evidence contrary to Starr's claim in R. M. Baine, *Daniel Defoe and the Supernatural* (Athens, GA: University of Georgia Press, 1968), pp. 91–108.

7. Rev. Payne, *An Account of Mrs Veal's Appearance to Mrs Bargrave at Canterbury* (London, 1722), in Schonhorn (ed.), *Accounts of the Apparition of Mrs. Veal*, p. xiv.

8. See Baine, *Daniel Defoe and the Supernatural*, pp. 80–1.

9. 'Letter from E. B.', in Schonhorn (ed.) *Accounts of the Apparition of Mrs. Veal*, p. 1.

10. The same excitement can be detected in the 'Letter from Lucy Lukyn', in ibid., pp. 1–2.

11. For in-depth discussion of parish boundaries see D. Gardiner, 'What Canterbury knew of Mrs. Veal and her Friends', *Review of English Studies*, 7:26 (1931), pp. 188–97, on p. 191.

12. 'Letter from E. B', in Schonhorn (ed.), *Accounts of the Apparition of Mrs. Veal*, p. 2.

13. Ibid.

14. Ibid., p. 3.

15. Ibid.

16. 'Letter from Lucy Lukyn', in ibid., p. 2.

17. Ibid., p. 1.

18. Anthony Oughton, an apothecary, was landlord of Mrs Bargrave's house. In 1687 he became a freeman of Canterbury and later served as common councillor (1690), sheriff (1697), alderman (1700), chamberlain (1706) and mayor (1702 and 1730), Gardiner, 'What Canterbury knew', pp. 188, 195, 196.

19. The letter is also reproduced in D. H. Clark and S. P. H. Clark, *Newton's Tyranny: The Suppressed Scientific Discoveries of Stephen Gray and John Flamsteed* (New York: W. H. Freeman & Co., 2001), p. 123.

20. John Flamsteed was also known for his disagreements with Sir Isaac Newton, president of the Royal Society. This culminated in a battle to prevent the forced publication of Flamsteed's Star Catalogue by Newton in 1712. With royal backing Newton prevailed, see ibid., pp. 48–9, 102.

21. M. Hunter, 'Science and Astrology in Seventeenth-Century England: An Unpublished Polemic by John Flamsteed', in P. Curry (ed.) *Astrology and Society, Historical Essays* (Woodbridge, Boydell, 1987), pp. 261–300, on p. 267.

22. Clark and Clark, *Newton's Tyranny*, p. 123.

23. John Arbuthnot held the title of physician extraordinary from 1705 to 1709 and of physician in ordinary from 1709 to 1714.

24. R. C. Steensma, *Dr John Arbuthnot* (Boston, MA: Twayne Publishers, 1979), p. 19.

25. 'Peter Wentworth to Lord Raby, 25 August 1710', Wentworth Papers, reproduced in E. Gregg, *Queen Anne* (London: Routledge & Kegan Paul, 1980), p. 234.

26. Ibid., p. 246.

27. Further proof of the favour Arbuthnot enjoyed is underlined by his attendance during Queen Anne's final illness in 1714.

28. Queen Anne is identified as the 'very great person' by Clark and Clark in *Newton's Tyranny*, and this is further reinforced by Arbuthnot's reference to the Queen as 'the great person' in a letter to Jonathan Swift, see G. A. Aitken, *The Life and Works of John Arbuthnot* (Oxford: Clarendon Press, 1892), pp. 74–5.

29. Stephen Gray is best remembered for his electrical experiments, detailed by Clark and Clark, *Newton's Tyranny*, p. 159.

30. Canterbury became a major silk centre in the later seventeenth century after the Edict of Nantes was revoked by Louis XIV in 1685. This led to a large influx of French Protestants skilled in this trade, ibid., p. 17.

31. S. Shapin and S. Schaffer, *Leviathan and the Air-Pump: Hobbes, Boyle, and the Experimental Life* (Princeton, NJ: Princeton University Press, 1989), p. 59.

32. 'Letter from Stephen Gray', in Schonhorn (ed.), *Accounts of the Apparition of Mrs. Veal*, p. 1.

33. Reverend John Lodowick was embroiled in a contentious pew dispute between parishioners, local magistrates and councilmen after the latter tried to override customary pew distribution by altering the layout of the seating. Lodowick led the parish opposition, threatening to libel jurats in the Consistory Court at Canterbury for removing the communion table. Rev. J. Lyon, *The History of the Town and Port of Dover, and of Dover Castle; with a Short Account of the Cinque Ports*, 2 vols (London, 1813), vol. 1, pp. 98–115.

34. Shapin and Schaffer, *Leviathan and the Air-Pump*, p. 65.

35. 'Letter from Stephen Gray', in Schonhorn (ed.), *Accounts of the Apparition of Mrs. Veal*, p. 6.

36. Ibid.

37. 'Letter from E. B.', in ibid., p. 3.

38. Capp, *When Gossips Meet*, p. 377.

39. Ibid., p. 85.

40. 'Letter from Stephen Gray', in Schonhorn (ed.), *Accounts of the Apparition of Mrs. Veal*, p. 3.

41. 'An Account of the Journeys I have Taken & Where I have Been since March 1695', the travel journal of Cassandra Willoughby, cited in E. Hagglund, 'Tourists and Travellers: Women's Non-Fictional Writing about Scotland, 1770–1830' (PhD thesis, University of Birmingham, 2000).

42. 'Letter from Stephen Gray', in Schonhorn (ed.), *Accounts of the Apparition of Mrs. Veal*, p. 2.

43. Payne, *An Account of Mrs Veal's Appearance*, in Schonhorn (ed.), *Accounts of the Apparition of Mrs. Veal*, p. x.

44. Shapin and Schaffer, *Leviathan and the Air-Pump*, pp. 44–63.

45. M. McKeon, *The Origins of the English Novel, 1600–1740* (Baltimore, MD: Johns Hopkins University Press, 1988), p. 47.

46. 'Letter from Stephen Gray', in Schonhorn (ed.), *Accounts of the Apparition of Mrs. Veal*, p. 3.
47. Ibid., p. 5.
48. Ibid., p. 6.
49. S. Shapin, '"A Scholar and a Gentleman": The Problematic Identity of the Scientific Practitioner in Early Modern England', *History of Science*, 29 (1991), pp. 279–327, on pp. 303–4.
50. D. S. Lux and H. J. Cook, 'Closed Circles or Open Networks?: Communicating at a Distance During the Scientific Revolution', *History of Science*, 36 (1998), pp. 179–211, on p. 180.
51. *Loyal Post*, in Schonhorn (ed.), *Accounts of the Apparition of Mrs. Veal*, pp. 1–3.
52. Ibid., p. 1.
53. Davis, *Factual Fictions*, pp. 42–70.
54. *Loyal Post*, in Schonhorn (ed.), *Accounts of the Apparition of Mrs. Veal*, p. 1.
55. Ibid., p. 3.
56. Ibid., p. 1.
57. [Defoe], *A True Relation*, in Schonhorn (ed.), *Accounts of the Apparition of Mrs. Veal*, pp. 1–12. See note 6 above for doubts regarding the authorship of this text.
58. S. Schaffer, 'Defoe's Natural Philosophy and the Worlds of Credit', in J. Christie and S. Shuttleworth (eds), *Nature Transfigured: Science and Literature 1700–1900* (Manchester: Manchester University Press, 1989), pp. 13–44, on p. 22, for an exploration of Defoe's 'creditable reportage' see p. 14. Defoe's use of natural philosophical methods is described in McKeon, *The Origins of the English Novel*, p. 85.
59. Christie and Shuttleworth provide a fuller description of how Defoe fused science with novelistic realism, *Nature Transfigured*, p. 6.
60. J. Aubrey, *Miscellanies upon the Following Subjects* (London, 1696).
61. Baine, *Daniel Defoe and the Supernatural*, pp. 80–1.
62. [Defoe], *A True Relation*, in Schonhorn (ed.), *Accounts of the Apparition of Mrs. Veal*, p. 3.
63. Ibid.
64. Ibid., pp. 3–4.
65. Ibid., p. 3.
66. Defoe, *An Essay on the History and Reality of Apparitions*, p. 2.
67. Ibid., preface.
68. Drelincourt, *The Christian's Defence*, preface.
69. *The Universal Spectator*, 209 (7 October 1732), p. 1; *The Universal Spectator*, 320 (23 November 1734), reproduced in Baine, *Daniel Defoe and the Supernatural*, p. 93.
70. *The Penny London Post*, 171 (3 May 1726), p. 4.
71. A. M. Toplady, *Works*, 6 vols (London, 1825), vol. 4, p. 234, reproduced in Baine, *Daniel Defoe and the Supernatural*, p. 94.
72. 'Letter from Stephen Gray', in Schonhorn (ed.), *Accounts of the Apparition of Mrs. Veal*, p. 1.
73. McKeon, *The Origins of the English Novel*, p. 3.
74. Davis, *Factual Fictions*, p. 87.
75. D. Defoe, *The Farther Adventures of Robinson Crusoe*, 2nd edn (London, 1719), p. 3.

76. T. Luckman, in Payne, *An Account of Mrs Veal's Appearance*, in Schonhorn (ed.), *Accounts of the Apparition of Mrs. Veal*, preface.

77. Ibid.

78. The author of these comments remains anonymous, but they appeared in manuscript notes in Latin in the fourth edition of *A True Relation*. The recorded date of the interview with Mrs Bargrave was 21 May 1714, Baine, *Daniel Defoe and the Supernatural*, p. 107.

79. Payne, *An Account of Mrs Veal's Appearance*, in Schonhorn (ed.), *Accounts of the Apparition of Mrs. Veal*, p. ix.

80. J. Nichols, *Literary Anecdotes of the Eighteenth Century; comprising Biographical Memoirs of William Bowyer, Printer, F.S.A. and Many of his Learned Friends*, 9 vols (London, 1812), vol. 4, pp. 150–9.

81. Payne, *An Account of Mrs Veal's Appearance*, in Schonhorn (ed.), *Accounts of the Apparition of Mrs. Veal*, p. xv.

82. Drelincourt, *The Christian's Defence*, p. 16.

83. Ibid., p. 95.

84. Ibid., preface.

85. Ibid.

86. Bostridge, *Witchcraft and its Transformations*, pp. 92–4; W. E. Burns, *An Age of Wonder: Prodigies, Politics and Providence in England 1657–1727* (Manchester and New York: Manchester University Press, 2002), pp. 185–7.

87. Defoe, *An Essay on the History and Reality of Apparitions*, p. 44.

88. Ibid., p. 50.

89. Starr, 'Why Defoe Probably Did Not Write the Apparition of Mrs Veal', p. 422.

90. See for example H. Welby, *Signs Before Death, and Authenticated Apparitions* (London, 1825), pp. 254–64, 297–301.

91. Defoe, *An Essay on the History and Reality of Apparitions*, pp. 94–5.

92. Ibid., p. 103.

93. Ibid., pp. 132–50.

94. Ibid., p. 150.

95. Schaffer, 'Defoe's Natural Philosophy', pp. 17–18.

96. Defoe, *An Essay on the History and Reality of Apparitions*, p. 118.

97. Ibid., p. 337.

98. Ibid., pp. 99–100.

99. Ibid., p. 100.

100. Barry, 'Public Infidelity and Private Belief?', p. 127.

101. For further details of Arbuthnot's collection see P. Koster (intro.), *Arbuthnotiana: The Story of the St Alb-ns Ghost* (1712), Augustan Reprint Society, 154 (Los Angeles, CA: William Andrews Clark Memorial Library, University of California, 1972), pp. i–iv.

102. J. Arbuthnot, *An Essay Concerning the Effects of Air on Human Bodies* (London, 1702).

103. [J. Arbuthnot], *The Story of the St. Albans Ghost, or the Apparition of Mother Haggy* (London, 1712). The authorship of this tract is somewhat contested but has been attributed to Arbuthnot by Patricia Koster in *Arbuthnotiana*, pp. i–iv.

104. McKeon, *The Origins of the English Novel*, p. 20.

4 Ghost Stories in the Periodical Press

1. MacDonald and Murphy, *Sleepless Souls*, p. 302.
2. The association of 'enlightenment' and the 'anti-marvellous' has for example featured in the work of Daston and Park, *Wonders and the Order of Nature*, pp. 329 ff.
3. J. P. Carson, 'Enlightenment, Popular Culture, and Gothic Fiction', in J. Richetti (ed.), *The Cambridge Companion to the Eighteenth-Century Novel* (Cambridge: Cambridge University Press, 2002), pp. 255–76, on p. 268.
4. See, for example, J. Dunton, *The Night-Walker, or, Evening Rambles in Search after Lewd Women* (London, 1696).
5. J. Winship, *Inside Women's Magazines* (London: Pandora Press, 1987), pp. 66–7.
6. See, for example, T. Burnet, *The Theory of the Earth containing an Account of the Original of the Earth* (London, 1684); Almond, *Heaven and Hell*, pp. 119–23; Houlbrooke, *Death, Religion, and the Family*, pp. 50–1. See also John Locke's assertion that personal identity lay in individual consciousness, not in the physical body, *An Essay Concerning Human Understanding*, vol. 1, p. 287.
7. J. Asgill, *An Argument Proving, that According to the Covenant of Eternal Life Revealed in the Scriptures, Man may be Translated from Hence into that Eternal Life, Without Passing Through Death* (London, 1715), p. 46.
8. T. Milles, *The Natural Immortality of the Soul Asserted, and Proved from the Scriptures, and First Fathers: In Answer to Mr Dodwell's Epistolary Discourse* (Oxford, 1707); S. Clarke, *A Defense of an Argument made use of in a Letter to Mr Dodwel, to Prove the Immateriality and Natural Immortality of the Soul* (London, 1707); J. Norris, *A Philosophical Discourse Concerning the Natural Immortality of the Soul* (London, 1708).
9. L. Smith, *The Evidence of Things Not Seen: or, The Immortality of the Human Soul* (London, 1701, reprinted 1703, 1706); C. Trotter, *A Defence of the Essay of Human Understanding, Written by Mr. Lock* (London, 1702); J. Taylor, *A Golden Chain to Link the Penitent Sinner unto God. Whereunto is added, A Treatise of the Immortality of the Soul* (London, 1704); W. Reeves, *A Sermon Concerning the Natural Immortality of the Soul* (London, 1704); Joseph Addison, cited in R. Porter, *Flesh in the Age of Reason* (London: Allen Lane, 2003), p. 127.
10. John Locke believed that the 'self' resided in the conscious mind, whilst Shaftesbury insisted that identity was psychological and moral, not physical, R. Voitle, *The Third Earl of Shaftesbury, 1671–1713* (Baton Rouge, LA, and London: Louisiana State University Press, 1984), pp. 118–20.
11. Anon., *The Possibility of Apparitions. Being an Answer to this Question, Whether can Departed Souls (Souls Separated from their Bodies) so Appear, as to be Visibly Seen and Conversed With here upon Earth?* (London, 1706), p. 11.
12. Ibid., p. 17, 19.
13. Ibid., pp. 18–19.
14. The Thomist tradition held that the resurrected body would be as material as its terrestrial form. St Paul defended the bodily resurrection of Christ to the Corinthians as the foundation of the Christian faith and, in spite of discoveries that substances were transmutable, Robert Boyle used chemical principles to demonstrate that the material body could be resurrected following decomposition. For a fuller explanation

see F. Vidal, 'Brains, Bodies, Selves, and Science: Anthropologies of Identity and the Resurrection of the Body', *Critical Inquiry*, 28:4 (2002), pp. 930–74, on pp. 940, 946, 949. See also C. Bynum, 'Why all the Fuss about the Body? A Medievalist's Perspective', *Critical Inquiry*, 22:1 (1995), pp. 1–33, on pp. 9, 12, 32.

15. *The British Apollo, or, Curious Amusements for the Ingenious*, 96 (7–12 January 1709), p. 1.

16. *British Apollo*, 26 (7–12 May 1708), p. 1.

17. 'A Supplement to the Advice from the Scandalous Club', *Review*, 3 (November 1704), p. 5.

18. Ibid., p. 6.

19. Ibid.

20. Ibid.

21. J. Donovan, *A Sketch of Opticks: Displaying the Wonders of Sight and Manner of Vision* (Cork, 1795).

22. R. Smith, *A Compleat System of Opticks* (Cambridge, 1738).

23. B. M. Stafford, *Body Criticism: Imaging the Unseen in Enlightenment Art and Medicine* (Cambridge, MA, and London: MIT Press, 1994), p. 11.

24. Donovan, *A Sketch of Opticks*, p. 8.

25. Smith, *A Compleat System of Opticks*, p. 96.

26. Stafford, *Body Criticism*, pp. 5, 11.

27. J. Shuttleworth, *A Treatise of Opticks Direct* (London, 1709); E. Wells, *The Young Gentleman's Opticks* (London, 1713).

28. Anon., *Observations on the Use of Spectacles* (London, 1753).

29. Cited in Stafford, *Body Criticism*, p. 348.

30. Brewer, *The Pleasures of the Imagination*, p. 135; W. Graham, *The Beginnings of English Literary Periodicals: A Study of Periodical Literature 1665–1715* (New York: Octagon, 1972), p. 69; P. Smithers, *The Life of Joseph Addison* (Oxford: Clarendon Press, 1968), p. 250.

31. Cited in ibid., p. 463.

32. Spurr, *The Restoration Church of England*, p. 392.

33. Smithers, *The Life of Joseph Addison*, p. 212.

34. J. Addison, *The Spectator*, ed. D. F. Bond, 4 vols (Oxford: Clarendon Press, 1965), vol. 1, no. 7 (8 March 1711), p. 34. All subsequent references are to this edition.

35. Stafford, *Body Criticism*, pp. 404–5.

36. Ibid., p. 432.

37. Ibid., pp. 431–2.

38. I. Newton, *Opticks: or, A Treatise of the Reflexions, Refractions, Inflexions and Colours of Light* (London, 1704), pp.10–11.

39. Anon., *Observations on the Use of Spectacles*, p. 8.

40. *Spectator*, vol. 1, no. 110 (6 July 1711), pp. 453–6.

41. Ibid., vol. 3, no. 419 (1 July 1712), p. 571, and vol. 1, no. 110 (6 July 1712), p. 455.

42. Carolyn Steedman surveyed classical and godly education in the pedagogy of West Riding schools for the late eighteenth century, C. K.Steedman, *Master and Servant: Love and Labour in the English Industrial Age*, Cambridge Cultural History Series, 10 (Cambridge: Cambridge University Press, 2007), pp. 110–30, 152–75.

43. *Spectator*, vol. 1, no. 90 (13 June 1711), p. 381.

44. R. Steele (ed.), *The Tatler*, 2 vols (London, 1777), vol. 1, no. 152 (30 March 1710), pp. 193–4. All subsequent references are to this edition.
45. *Spectator*, vol. 2, no. 110 (6 July 1711), p. 456.
46. Ibid.
47. C. Fox, *Locke and the Scriblerians: Identity and Consciousness in Early Eighteenth-Century Britain* (Berkeley, CA, and London: University of California Press, 1988), p. 81.
48. H. Curzon, *The Universal Library: or, Compleat Summary of Science*, 2 vols (London, 1722), vol. 2, p. 360.
49. The *Tatler* was published thrice weekly from 12 April 1709 to 2 January 1711 and cost 1*d*.
50. *Tatler*, vol. 1, no. 152 (30 March 1710), p. 193.
51. As Henry Fielding noted in his *History of Tom Jones*, John Dryden defended the use of ghosts in heroic poetry in the preface to *The Conquest of Granada* (London, 1672). See J. Dryden, *Three Plays*, ed. G. Saintsbury (New York: Hill and Wang, 1957).
52. *Tatler*, vol. 1, no. 152 (30 March 1710), p. 192.
53. *Spectator*, vol. 3, no. 419 (1 July 1712), p. 571.
54. E. J. Clery and R. Miles, *Gothic Documents: A Sourcebook, 1700–1820* (Manchester: Manchester University Press, 2000), p. 113.
55. E. Burke, *A Philosophical Enquiry into the Origins of our Ideas of the Sublime and Beautiful* (London, 1757), p. 53.
56. *Spectator*, vol. 3, no. 419 (1 July 1712), pp. 572, 570.
57. Ibid., p. 572.
58. Ibid., p. 570.
59. Ibid., p. 573.
60. T. Parnell, *Poems on Several Occasions* (London, 1747), p. 148.
61. Ibid., p. 149.
62. Ibid.
63. J. Hervey, *Meditations Among the Tombs* (London, 1756), preface.
64. Ibid., p. 63.
65. N. L. Beaty, *The Craft of Dying: A Study in the Literary Tradition of the Ars Moriendi in England* (New Haven, CT, and London: Yale University Press, 1970).
66. I. Barrow, *Practical Discourses upon the Consideration of Our Latter End* (1694; 2nd edn, London, 1712); J. Woodward, *Fair Warnings to a Careless World* (London, 1707).
67. R. Blair, *The Grave. A Poem* (London, 1743), p. 4.
68. Ibid., p. 26.
69. L. Dacome, 'Resurrecting by Numbers in Eighteenth-Century England', *Past and Present*, 193:1 (2006), pp. 73–110, on pp. 84–7.
70. Gittings, *Death, Burial and the Individual*, p. 59.
71. J. Kristeva, *Powers of Horror: An Essay on Abjection*, trans. Leon S. Roudiez (New York and Oxford: Columbia University Press, 1982).
72. Arbuthnot, *An Essay Concerning the Effects of Air*; R. Boyle, 'New Pneumatical Experiments about Respiration', *Philosophical Transactions of the Royal Society*, 5 (1665–78), pp. 2011–31.
73. McManners, *Death and the Enlightenment*, pp. 308–19.

74. Ariès, *The Hour of our Death*, p. 351.

75. Richardson, *Death, Dissection and the Destitute*, pp. 75–99.

76. J. C. Riley, *The Eighteenth-Century Campaign to Avoid Disease* (Basingstoke: Macmillan, 1987), p. 109.

77. Brewer, *The Pleasures of the Imagination*, p. 172.

78. Davis, *Factual Fictions*, p. 155; I. P. Watt, *The Rise of the Novel: Studies in Defoe, Richardson and Fielding* (London: Hogarth, 1957).

79. Gabriel Odingsells's *The Capricious Lovers* (London, 1726), first performed at Lincoln's Inn Fields, featured the ghost of a lawyer who came to confess that he had forged wills for his clients.

80. *Spectator*, vol. 1, no. 44 (20 April 1711), p. 186.

81. D. E. Heddon, 'Bellamy, George Anne', *ODNB*, http://www.oxforddnb.com/view/article/19181 (accessed 25 February 2007).

82. *Spectator*, vol. 1, no. 44 (20 April 1711), p. 186.

83. *Spectator*, vol. 4, no. 502 (6 October 1712), p. 282.

84. *Spectator*, vol. 1, no. 44 (20 April 1711), p. 187.

85. Ibid., p. 186.

86. H. Fielding, *The Tragedy of Tragedies, or The Life and Death of Tom Thumb the Great* (London, 1731), p. 40.

87. Ibid., III.ii, p. 39.

88. H. Fielding, *The History of Tom Jones, a Foundling* (1749), The Wesleyan Edition of the Works of Henry Fielding, ed. Fredson Bowers, 2 vols (Oxford: Clarendon Press, 1974), vol. 1, p. 387.

89. Ibid., vol. 1, p. 388.

90. Emma Clery credits Radcliffe with introducing 'the device of the "explained supernatural" in order to reconcile Protestant incredulity and the taste for ghostly terror', E. J. Clery, 'The Genesis of "Gothic" Fiction', in J. E. Hogle (ed.), *The Cambridge Companion to Gothic Fiction* (Cambridge: Cambridge University Press, 2002), pp. 21–39, on pp. 26–7. A. Radcliffe, *The Mysteries of Udolpho*, ed. B. Dobree, intro. and notes T. Castle (Oxford: Oxford University Press, 1998).

91. Fielding, *The History of Tom Jones*, vol. 1, p. 406.

92. Ibid., vol. 1, p. 399.

93. Ibid.

94. *Spectator*, vol. 3, no. 419 (1 July 1712), p. 571.

95. *Gentleman's Magazine, or, Monthly Intelligencer*, 2:10 (1732), title-page; Graham, *The Beginnings of English Literary Periodicals*, p. 55.

96. *Gentleman's Magazine*, 1:1 (1731), p. 31.

97. Ibid.

98. Ibid.

99. *Gentleman's Magazine*, 1:2 (1731), p. 32.

100. *Gentleman's Magazine*, 2:10 (1732), p. 1001.

101. Ibid., p. 1002. The ghost of George Villiers was a popular ghost narrative published in a number of formats, notably by Clarendon, Aubrey and Defoe, and in a separate pamphlet account entitled *A Full, True and Particular Account of the Ghost or Apparition of the Late Duke of Buckingham's Father* (London, 1700).

102. *Gentleman's Magazine*, 17:11 (1747), p. 524.

103. Ibid.

104. *Gentleman's Magazine*, 17:12 (1747), pp. 611–12.

105. Ibid.

106. Curzon, *The Universal Library*, vol. 2, pp. 367–8.

107. *Gentleman's Magazine*, 17:12 (1747), pp. 611–12.

108. Curzon, *The Universal Library*, vol. 2, pp. 369–70.

109. Anon., *A Warning Piece Against the Crime of Murder* (London and Sherborne, 1752), p. 88.

110. John Fletcher, the vicar of Madeley in Shropshire, was seen many times in dreams. His wife Mary Fletcher had a well-known dream in which he appeared in the late eighteenth century, 'Letter from Miles Martindale in Leeds to Mary Fletcher', Methodist Church Archive, MS Manchester, Fletcher-Tooth Collection, MAM FL 5/1/9. In a letter from Clifton in 1800 George Fothy claimed to have seen the ghost of his neighbour Joseph Bradley in a dream, 'Letter from George Fothy to Mary Fletcher', Fletcher-Tooth Collection, MAM FL 6/7/19.

111. J. Norris, cited in L. L. Whyte, *The Unconscious Before Freud* (London: Freidmann, 1978), p. 96.

112. Locke, *An Essay Concerning Human Understanding*, vol. 1, p. 185.

113. Stafford, *Body Criticism*, p. 437.

114. J. Trenchard, *Natural History of Superstition* (London, 1709), pp. 10–12.

115. Donovan, *A Sketch of Opticks*; Stafford, *Body Criticism*, pp. 366, 371–3.

116. Anon., *Gale's Cabinet of Knowledge; or, Miscellaneous Recreations* (London, 1796), p. 201.

117. G. Smith, *The Laboratory; or, School of Arts* (London, 1799), p. 167.

118. Terry Castle, cited in Carson, 'Enlightenment, Popular Culture, and Gothic Fiction', p. 269.

119. D. Simpson, *Discourse on Dreams and Night Visions* (London, 1791), pp. 36, 102, 104.

120. G. C. Lichtenberg, cited in Whyte, *The Unconscious Before Freud*, p. 114.

121. Ibid., p.69.

122. J. Addison, *The Drummer; or, The Haunted-House, a Comedy, as it is Acted at the Theatre-Royal in Drury Lane, by His Majesty's Servants* (London, 1715), p. 12.

123. K. Wilson, *The Sense of the People: Politics, Culture and Imperialism in England, 1715–1785* (Cambridge: Cambridge University Press, 1998), p. 305.

124. H. Crossgrove, *The Accurate Intelligencer, Containing Answers to a Number of Curious Letters Never Yet Publish'd in the Norwich Gazette* (Norwich, 1708), title-page.

125. Ibid., pp. 23–4.

126. J. Dunton, *An Essay Proving we Shall Know our Friends in Heaven* (London, 1698); Curzon, *The Universal Library*, vol. 2, p. 367.

127. Anon., 'The Fruits of Enthusiasm', *Norwich Mercury* (15–22 February 1752), p. 3.

128. Ibid.

129. Wilson, *The Sense of the People*, p. 405.

130. Soon after this letter was published, the *Norwich Mercury* printed a weekly letter addressed to Mr Wheatley, complaining of the latest excesses of Methodist converts, Anon., 'Letter to Mr Wheatley', *Norwich Mercury* (4–11 April 1752), p. 3.

131. *Norwich Mercury* (16–23 May 1752), p. 3; *Norwich Mercury* (23–30 May 1752), p. 4; *Norwich Mercury* (6–13 June 1752), p. 3.
132. Anon., *A Warning Piece Against the Crime of Murder*, preface.
133. Those found guilty were now to be fed with only bread and water, they would be hanged within forty-eight hours of sentencing and their bodies dissected as a final mark of infamy.
134. Anon., *The Rich Man's Warning-Piece*, p. 229.
135. Ibid., p. 231.
136. Ibid., p. 279.
137. Apart from the initial advertisement, the book was recommended by the *Norwich Mercury* in issues on 23 May, 6 June, 8 and 15 August 1752.
138. *Newcastle General Magazine* (June 1747), pp. 153–4; (September 1747), pp. 237, 241–5.
139. *Newcastle General Magazine* (February 1748), p. 102.
140. Anon., *Lovat's Ghost: or The Courtier's Warning Piece* (London, 1747) was a satire on the debauched life of Lord Lovat, who was executed in 1747. *Anon., Scelus's Ghost: or, The Lawyer's Warning Piece* (London, 1748) was another satirical polemic, this time attacking the morality of treacherous and greedy lawyers.
141. Brewer, *The Pleasures of the Imagination*, pp. 184–5.
142. J. Derrida, *Specters of Marx, The State of the Debt, The Work of Mourning, and The New International*, trans. P. Kamuf (New York and London, Routledge, 1994), pp. 125–76.

5 Confessional Cultures and Ghost Beliefs

1. D. Grant, *The Cock Lane Ghost* (New York: St Martin's Press, 1965), p. 110.
2. Reports of the Cock Lane ghost appeared in Jackson's *Oxford Journal, Lloyd's Evening Post, London Chronicle, Public Ledger, Public Advertiser, St. James's Chronicle, The Annual Register, The Beauties of All the Magazines, The Gentleman's Magazine, The London Magazine, The Monthly Chronicle* and *The Universal Magazine*. See Grant, *The Cock Lane Ghost*, preface.
3. J. M. Beattie suggests that, although the pillory was still used, it was much more likely to be restricted to one session rather than three, *Policing and Punishment in London 1660–1720: Urban Crime and the Limits of Terror* (Oxford: Oxford University Press, 2001), pp. 307–8.
4. O. Goldsmith, *The Mystery Revealed; Containing a Series of Transactions and Authentic Testimonials, Respecting the Supposed Cock-Lane Ghost* (London, 1762), p. 15.
5. Relations between Kent and the Lynes family soured further when he inherited £150 after the death of Fanny's brother Thomas and a further £94 12s. 7d. from property sale. When part of this sum had to be repaid due to a mistake in the original sale, Kent refused to contribute and John Lynes began proceedings in Chancery against him, Grant, *The Cock Lane Ghost*, pp. 7, 18–19.
6. As Douglas Grant notes, Kent's reputation was key to his success in business and in marriage negotiations with the family of his third wife. Indeed, plans for Kent to

go into partnership with her brother were shelved after the affair became common knowledge, ibid., p. 38.

7. Ibid., p. 27.

8. H. D. Rack, *Reasonable Enthusiast: John Wesley and the Rise of Methodism* (London: Epworth, 1989), p. 281. Even Joseph Priestley commended Wesley for spreading the gospel among the poor. Although he disapproved of Wesley's promotion of the supernatural, he conceded that these accounts were 'exceeding lively and entertaining', *Original Letters by the Rev. John Wesley, and his Friends, Illustrative of his Early History, with other Curious Papers, Communicated by the late Rev. S. Badcock, to which is prefixed, An Address to the Methodists by Joseph Priestley* (Birmingham, 1791), p. xi.

9. Richard Parsons and a local publican also claimed to have seen the dead woman 'with hands, all luminous and shining', Goldsmith, *The Mystery Revealed*, p. 18.

10. Grant, *The Cock Lane Ghost*, p. 52.

11. Walpole, cited in Clery, *The Rise of Supernatural Fiction*, p. 24.

12. H. Walpole, *The Yale Edition of Horace Walpole's Correspondence*, ed. W. S. Lewis , 48 vols (New Haven, CT, and London: Yale University Press, 1983), vol. 10, pp. 5–7.

13. Grant, *The Cock Lane Ghost*, p. 38.

14. Ibid., p. 45. See also Anon., *Genuine and Impartial Memoirs of Elizabeth Canning* (London, 1754); H. Fielding, *A Clear State of the Case of Elizabeth Canning* (London, 1753).

15. Grant, *The Cock Lane Ghost*, p. 12. Despite the outcome of the Cock Lane case, Johnson insisted some years later that 'it is undecided whether or not there has ever been an instance of the spirit of any person appearing after death', in Boswell, *Everybody's Boswell*, p. 290.

16. Grant, *The Cock Lane Ghost*, pp. 71–2.

17. *Gentleman's Magazine*, 32:1 (1762), pp. 43–4, 81–4.

18. Archer went to the vault to produce illustrations for Charles Mackay's *Memoirs of Extraordinary Popular Delusions* (London, 1841). His suspicions were raised by the fact that Fanny's remains were 'perfectly preserved' – a tell-tale sign of poisoning, Grant, *The Cock Lane Ghost*, p. 2.

19. Thomas, *Religion and the Decline of Magic*, p. 712.

20. Clery, *The Rise of Supernatural Fiction*, p. 17.

21. Even after Aldrich's committee had concluded their investigation, the Cock Lane episode had a vibrant afterlife. Poor Elizabeth Parsons was taken to a house near Covent Garden where she was forced to sleep 'in a kind of hammock with her hands and feet fastened with fillets' to see if the scratching continued, Grant, *The Cock Lane Ghost*, p. 75; Drelincourt, *The Christian's Defence*; D. Defoe, *The Secrets of the Invisible World Laid Open: or, An Universal History of Apparitions, Sacred and Prophane* (London, 1770).

22. Jane Shaw has identified this literary preference in sceptical rebuttals of miracle claims in the early eighteenth century in *Miracles in Enlightenment England*, p. 176.

23. D. Hume, *Of Miracles* (1748), ed. A. Flew (LaSalle, III: Open Court, 1985), p. 39.

24. C. Coote, *The History of England*, 9 vols (London, 1791–8), vol. 9, pp. 242–3.

25. J. Adams, *Elegant Anecdotes, and Bon-Mots of the Greatest Princes, Politicians, Philosophers, Orators, and Wits of Modern Times* (London, 1790), p. 147.

26. Following the murder of thirteen-year-old Anne Naylor in 1758, the locals of Farringdon came into regular contact with her ghost. A headless spectre haunting St James's Park was thought to be the ghost of a woman who was brutally murdered by her husband in the 1780s. Admiralty House in Whitehall was haunted by the ghost of Martha Ray, mistress of the Earl of Sandwich, first lord of the Admiralty, see R. Jones, *Walking Haunted London* (London: New Holland Publishers, 1999), pp. 36, 66, 103.

27. Anon., *Anti-Canidia: or, Superstition Detected and Exposed* (London, 1762), p. 3.

28. Ibid., pp. 5, 3.

29. More details can be found in Burns, *An Age of Wonder*, pp. 149–74.

30. P. Annet, *Supernaturals Examined* (London, 1747).

31. W. Sturch, *Apeleutherus, or, An Effort to Attain Intellectual Freedom* (London, 1799), p. 72.

32. J. Wesley, 3 June 1756, *The Journal of the Reverend John Wesley*, ed. N. Curnock, 8 vols (London: Robert Culley, 1909–16), vol. 2, pp. 165–6.

33. *Arminian Magazine*, 12 (1789), p. 436.

34. Wesley, 25 May 1768, *The Journal*, vol. 5, pp. 266–75.

35. Johnson's interest in this affair resulted in his first meeting with John Wesley. Although Johnson admired Wesley's 'pious zeal', he declared that 'His statement of the evidence as to the ghost did not satisfy me', Wesley, 25 May 1768, *The Journal*, vol. 5, p. 275.

36. Wesley quoted wholesale from Baxter's *The Certainty of the World of Spirits* in the *Arminian Magazine*, 6 (1783), pp. 212 ff.

37. J. Wesley, 'Serious Address to the Preachers of the Gospel of Christ', *Arminian Magazine*, 20 (1797), pp. 123–4.

38. J. Wesley, 'Guardian Angels', *Bicentennial Edition of the Works of John Wesley*, ed. F. Baker and R. Heitzenrater, 23 vols (Oxford: Clarendon Press, 1980–2003), vol. 4, pp. 225–35.

39. G. M. Ditchfield, *The Evangelical Revival* (London: University College London Press, 1998), pp. 46–50.

40. G. Lavington, *The Enthusiasm of Methodists and Papists Compared* (London, 1749), preface.

41. N. Rogers, *Whigs and Cities: Popular Politics in the Age of Walpole and Pitt* (Oxford: Clarendon Press, 1989), p. 379.

42. C. Haydon, *Anti-Catholicism in Eighteenth-Century England, c.1714–80* (Manchester: Manchester University Press, 1993), p. 10. The slur of 'Papist' was a traditional rhetorical device, used by King James I, who compared puritan and Jesuit enthusiasm in his *Daemonologie, in Forme of a Dialogue* (London, 1603), pp. 52–4.

43. Lavington, *The Enthusiasm of Methodists and Papists Compared*, pp. 48–9.

44. Ibid., p. 76.

45. Ibid., p. 25.

46. Anon., *Anti-Canidia*, p. 23.

47. Wesley, 28 March 1736, *The Journal*, vol. 1, p. 187.

48. A. Cockburn, *A Philosophical Essay Concerning the Intermediate State of Blessed Souls* (London, 1722), pp. 39–41.

49. Ibid., p. 70.

50. Anon., *An Account of the Apparition of the Late Lord Kilmarnock to the Reverend Mr. Foster* (London, 1747), p. 7.
51. Ibid., pp. 2–3, 7.
52. Ibid., pp. 27–8.
53. Anon., *The Ghost, or A Minute Account of the Appearance of the Ghost of John Croxford Executed at Northampton, August the 4ᵗʰ 1764* ([[London?]], 1764), reprinted in Anon., *A True and Circumstantial Relation of a Cruel and Barbarous Murder* (Northampton, 1848), p. 12.
54. Ibid., p. 14.
55. Ibid.
56. Ibid., pp. 18, 19.
57. Ibid., p. 3.
58. Ibid., p. 5.
59. Ibid., p. 33.
60. Colley, *Britons*, p. 26.
61. *Arminian Magazine*, 7 (1784), p. 488.
62. Anon., *Admiral Vernon's Ghost* (London, 1758), pp. 6–7.
63. Rogers, *Whigs and Cities*, p. 375.
64. Anon., *A Full and Particular Account of a Most Dreadful and Surprising Apparition* (London, 1757).
65. P. Langford, *A Polite and Commercial People: England, 1727–1783* (Oxford: Oxford University Press, 1989), p. 202. Colin Haydon suggests that anti-Catholicism was 'the chief ideological commitment of the nation, a set of generally held attitudes, not the obsession of 'ultra-Protestants', *Anti-Catholicism*, p. 18.
66. The anti-Catholic dimension of the Gordon Riots is described by N. Rogers, *Crowds, Culture, and Politics in Georgian Britain* (Oxford: Clarendon Press, 1998), pp. 152–75.
67. *Arminian Magazine*, 8 (1785), p. 378.
68. For discussion of John Wesley's interest in 'angelology' see R. Webster, 'Those Distracting Terrors of the Enemy: Demonic Possession and Exorcism in the Thought of John Wesley', *Bulletin of the John Rylands University Library of Manchester*, 85:2/3 (2003), pp. 373–85.
69. Gibson, *The Church of England*, pp. 11, 126.
70. A. Webster, *Supernatural Religion the Only Sure Hope of Sinners* (London, 1741).
71. J. Leland, *The Advantage and Necessity of the Christian Revelation, Shewn from the State of Religion in the Antient Heathen World* (London, 1764).
72. See Chapter 1, pp. 41–4, for full details.
73. In 1698 Samuel Wesley preached at the Society for the Reformation of Manners at Westminster. He later began a religious society of his own following correspondence with the Society for the Promotion of Christian Knowledge, Rack, *Reasonable Enthusiast*, p. 53.
74. Armstrong, *The Church of England*, p. 20.
75. Ditchfield, *The Evangelical Revival*, p. 36. See also J. Reed, *A Rope's End for Hempen Monopolists; or, A Dialogue between a Broker, a Rope Maker, and the Ghost of Jonas Hanway* (London, 1786). This tract criticized companies and entrepreneurs trying

to monopolize the hemp market. *Admiral Vernon's Ghost* similarly complained about 'vice', 'corrupters' and 'gamesters' that had made England a 'steril isle', pp. 5, 8.

76. Armstrong, *The Church of England*, p. 19.

77. Gibson, *The Church of England*, p. 1.

78. Thomas Hayter saw the defeat of the rebels as 'a recent instance of such divine providence vouchsafed to our gracious sovereign in the suppression of an attempt to rob him of his Kingdom', cited in ibid., p. 39.

79. At the battle of Dettingen in 1743 the ghost of General Jasper Clayton was rumoured to have appeared before an enemy soldier, warning him to renounce his Jacobite sympathies or face certain destruction, Anon., *The Most Strange, Wonderful and Surprising Apparition of the Ghost of General Clayton, which Appeared to the Man, who Wore the Yellow Sash at the Battle of Dettingen* (London, 1743). Sir John Temple's *The Irish Rebellion* was also reprinted in 1746. His account included a number of apparitions of murdered Protestants who returned to expose their Catholic killers, J. Temple, *The Irish Rebellion* (London, 1746), pp. 100, 121–2; J. Hogg, *The Long Pack, or The Mysterious Pedlar* (Leeds, 1870), p. 27.

80. Gibson, *The Church of England*, p. 153.

81. F. Blackburne, *No Proof in the Scriptures of an Intermediate State of Happiness or Misery between Death and the Resurrection* (London, 1755) and *A Short Historical View of the Controversy Concerning an Intermediate State and the Separate Existence of the Soul between Death and the General Resurrection* (London, 1765).

82. G. Killingworth, *On the Immortality of the Soul, the Resurrection of the Body, the Glorius Millennium, the Most Glorious Kingdom of God, and the Prophet Daniel's Numbers* (London, 1761), p. 11.

83. R. Dean, *On the Future Life of Brutes, Introduced with Observations upon Evil, its Nature and Origin* (London, 1767), pp. 81, 91–9.

84. D. Allan, 'Richard Dean', *ODNB*, http://www.oxforddnb.com/view/article/7383 (accessed 12 April 2007).

85. Proposals for the professorship survive among the Wodehouse family papers from 1767. Norris's will of 1770 established an annuity of £120 for the position, Papers of the Wodehouse Family of Kimberley, Norfolk Record Office, MS Norfolk, KIM 16/4, 1767.

86. B. Caulfield, *An Essay on the Immateriality and Immortality of the Soul* (London, 1778), pp. 12, 6.

87. See for example Philanthropus, *An Essay on the Existence of God, and the Immortality of the Soul* (London, 1750), title-page.

88. John Tillotson's writings pioneered this work in the Restoration period, Rack, *Reasonable Enthusiast*, p. 29.

89. Armstrong, *The Church of England*, p. 76.

90. Ibid., p. 79.

91. See, for example, the anonymous *Ghost of Edward Ashley* and *Life After Death; or The History of Apparitions, Ghosts, Spirits or Spectres* (London, 1758).

92. R. Jago, *The Causes of Impenitence Consider'd: As Well in the Case of Extraordinary Warnings, as Under the General Laws of Providence, and Grace* (Oxford, 1755), title-page.

93. Ibid., p. 4.

94. Ibid., p. 24.
95. Ibid., p. 18.
96. J. Williams, *Extracts from the Diary, Meditations and Letters of Mr Joseph Williams of Kidderminster* (Shrewsbury, 1779), pp. 50–1.
97. Jago was also a successful poet and part of 'the Warwickshire Coterie', a local literary circle. The group was centred on Henrietta, Lady Luxborough, and included William Shenstone, William Somerville and Richard Graves. Members of the coterie were highly educated and in tune with new philosophical trends.
98. Jago, *The Causes of Impenitence*, p. 21.
99. Lawford Hall was pulled down in 1790 when the Boughtons sold the property to the Caldecote family, who declared it 'a thing accursed', M. E. Atkins, *Haunted Warwickshire: A Gazetteer of Ghosts and Legends* (London: Hale, 1981), pp. 52–5, 57, 122.
100. Jago, *The Causes of Impenitence*, preface.
101. E. Kimber, *The Life and Adventures of James Ramble*, 2 vols (London, 1755), vol. 1, p. 24.
102. Ibid., vol. 1, p. 29.
103. R. Polwhele, *Traditions and Recollections*, 2 vols (London, 1826), vol. 2, p. 605.
104. J. C. Atkinson, *Countryman on the Moors*, ed. J. G. O'Leary, Fitzroy edn (London: MacGibbon & Kee, 1967), p. 25.
105. 'Report given to Robert Withers, Vicar of Gateley, of the Appearance of a Ghost 1706', Parish Records of Gateley, Norfolk Record Office, MS Norfolk, MS PD 9/1.
106. Brewer, *The Pleasures of the Imagination*, pp. 170–2. Reasons for the popularity of eighteenth-century sermons are also set out in J. Downey, *The Eighteenth Century Pulpit: A Study of the Sermons of Butler, Berkeley, Secker, Sterne, Whitefield and Wesley* (Oxford: Clarendon Press, 1969), pp. 1–29.
107. A. Russell, *The Clerical Profession* (London: Society for Promoting Christian Knowledge, 1980), p. 87.
108. J. Tillotson, *A Discourse Against Transubstantiation* (London, 1797).
109. Russell, *The Clerical Profession*, pp. 87, 89.
110. William Gibson cites civic humanism as one of the key values of eighteenth-century Anglicanism. It was a means by which the Church could participate in the cultural life of the nation, Gibson, *The Church of England*, p. 2.
111. Jago, *The Causes of Impenitence*, preface.
112. A. M. Toplady, 'The Existence and the Creed of Devils Considered: With a Word Concerning Apparitions. A Discourse Preached in the Parish Church of St. Olave, Jewry, 29 October 1775', in *Sermons and Essays* (London, 1793), p. 282.
113. Ibid.
114. Toplady, *Sermons and Essays*, p. 282.
115. J. Priestley, *An History of the Corruptions of Christianity*, 2 vols (Birmingham, 1782), vol. 1, p. 345.
116. Ibid., vol. 1, p. 425.
117. 'Letters Concerning some Supernatural Disturbances at the House of the Reverend Mr Samuel Wesley, in Epworth, Lincolnshire', Notebook of Charles Wesley (1716–17), Methodist Church Archives, MS Manchester, DDCW 8/15, 8.
118. Ibid.

119. Joseph Hoole was a learned man, educated at Sydney College, Cambridge, and was vicar of Haxey in Lincolnshire from 1712 to 1736, ibid.

120. A. Clarke, *The Miscellaneous Works of Adam Clarke, Memoirs of the Wesley Family*, 2nd edn, 13 vols (London, 1836), vol. 1, pp. 285–91.

121. Priestley, in Wesley, *Original Letters*, p. ix.

122. Ibid., p. iv.

123. H. T. Dickinson (ed.), *Britain and the French Revolution, 1789–1815* (Basingstoke: Macmillan, 1994), p. 8.

124. An influx of Irish artisans into Britain exacerbated anti-Catholic sentiments, see Colley, *Britons*, pp. 87–9; Haydon, *Anti-Catholicism*, p. 247.

125. Dickinson, *Britain and the French Revolution*, p. 17.

126. J. C. D. Clark, *English Society 1688–1832* (Cambridge: Cambridge University Press, 1985), p. 220.

127. On 14 July 1791 Priestley's house, library and laboratory in Birmingham were destroyed. He finally fled Britain in April 1794. Priestley's views also contrasted markedly with the outbreak of millenarian thought in these years, J. F. C. Harrison, *The Second Coming: Popular Millenarianism 1780–1850* (London: Routledge & Kegan Paul, 1979), p. 30.

128. B. Hilton, *The Age of Atonement: The Influence of Evangelicalism on Social and Economic Thought, 1795–1865* (Oxford: Clarendon Press, 1988), p. 13.

129. J. Whitaker, *The Real Origin of Government, deriving the State from Revelation, not Natural Religion* (London, 1795).

130. Anon., *The Atheist's Reward: or, A Call from Heaven, To which is Annexed an Account of the Apparition of the Ghost of Major George Sydenham* (London, 1788), p. 8.

131. Ibid., title-page.

132. Hilton, *The Age of Atonement*, p. 7.

133. Anon., *A Full and Particular Account, of the Wonderful Apparition of Mary Nicholson* (Durham, 1799), p. 1.

134. Anon., *An Account of a Most Horrid, Bloody, and Terrible Apparition, which Lately Appeared in the Parish of Shotts* (London, 1793), p. 1.

135. B. Krysmanski, 'We See a Ghost: Hogarth's Satire on Methodists and Connoiseurs', *Art Bulletin*, 80:2 (1998), pp. 292–310, on p. 292.

136. A. Butler, *The Moveable, Feasts, Fasts, and Other Annual Observances of the Catholic Church* (London, 1774), p. 158.

137. J. Berington, 'On Ghosts' (c. 1820), Birmingham Archdiocesan Archives, MS Birmingham, C2365, p. 1.

138. Ibid.

139. Ibid.

140. Letter from Richard How II to William Tomlinson, 21 July 1745, Bedfordshire and Luton Archives, MS Bedford, Letters & Papers of the How Family, HW/87/118, p. 4.

141. Ibid.

142. Moore, 'Late Seventeenth-Century Quakerism and the Miraculous'.

143. Shaw notes the case of Sarah Wiltshire, a former Quaker who became involved with the French Prophets in London in the first decade of the eighteenth century.

Wiltshire claimed to perform miracle cures through the power of the Holy Spirit, Shaw, *Miracles in Enlightenment England*, p. 154.

144. A vision which Samuel Spavold had when he was in London, 1754, 'A Collection of Letters, Dreams and Visions and other Remarkable Occurrences of the People called Quakers' (1788), Friends House Library, MS London, S78, pp. 123–5.

145. J. Churchman, *An Account of the Gospel Labours and Christian Experiences of a Faithful Minister of Christ, John Churchman* (London, 1780), pp. 185–6.

146. See Chapter 1, p. 27.

147. Lydia Fear's account, given to John Clark, Somerset Record Office, MS Somerset, 'Papers relating to the Sidcot Ghost' (*c.* 1780), DD/SC/G/1393/57.

148. John Benwell's account, given to John Clark *c.* 1814, in ibid.

149. Letter to Mr John Clarke, 19 Februrary 1846, in ibid.

150. Ibid.

151. Ibid.

152. Thomas Tanner's account, given to John Clark, 1828, in ibid..

153. J. Sambrook, 'John Henderson (1757–1788)', *ODNB*, http://www.oxforddnb.com/view/article/12911?docPos=3 (accessed 14 April 2007).

6 Landscapes of Belief and Everyday Life

1. S. Schama, *Landscape and Memory* (London: Fontana Press, 1996), pp. 6–7, 10.

2. Aubrey, *Miscellanies*, pp. 59–82.

3. A. Symson, *A Large Description of Galloway*, ed. T. Maitland (Edinburgh, 1823).

4. E. Jones, *A Geographical, Historical, and Religious Account of the Parish of Aberystruth: In the County of Monmouthshire* (Trevecca, 1779), p. 63.

5. Ibid., pp. 18–19, 62.

6. Ibid., pp. 76–8.

7. Jones, *A Relation of Apparitions*, p. 25.

8. Ibid.

9. Ibid., p. 43.

10. Ibid., pp. 76–7.

11. Ibid., pp. 29–30.

12. R. J. Mayhew, *Landscape, Literature and English Religious Culture, 1660–1800* (Basingstoke: Palgrave Macmillan, 2004), pp. 70–126.

13. Ibid., p. 42.

14. Ibid., p. 44; T. Gray, *Elegy Written in a Country Church-Yard* (London, 1751).

15. Ian D. Whyte, *Landscape and History Since 1500* (London: Reaktion Books, 2002), p. 120.

16. Francis Grose reported the ghost of Castle Russin, which was said to be the spirit of a woman who had been executed for the murder of her child. The ghost was credited by many locals and soldiers of a local garrison, but Grose took his account from a learned gentleman of 'good understanding' and 'veracity', F. Grose, *The Antiquities of England and Wales* (London, 1773), p. 210. Reports of the Berkshire ghost appeared in the private diary of Captain Allen, cited in J. P. Andrews, *Anecdotes, &c. Antient and Modern. With Observations* (London, 1790), p. 441.

17. Bourne went on to say that 'Stories of this Kind are infinite, and there are few Villages, which have not either had such an House in it, or near it', H. Bourne, *Antiquitates Vulgares; or, The Antiquities of the Common People* (Newcastle, 1725), p. 87.

18. R. M. Dorson, *The British Folklorists: A History*, 2 vols (London: Routledge, 2001), vol. 1, pp. 113–16, 155.

19. J. Palmer, *A Fortnights' Ramble to the Lakes in Westmoreland, Lancashire and Cumberland* (London, 1795), p. 284.

20. Letter from Richard How II to William Tomlinson, 21 July 1745, MS HW/87/118, p. 4.

21. Ibid., pp. 3–4.

22. A. Walsham, 'Reforming the Waters: Holy Wells and Healing Springs in Protestant England', in D. Wood (ed.), *Life and Thought in the Northern Church c.1100–c.1700: Essays in Honour of Claire Cross* (Woodbridge: Boydell Press, 1999), pp. 227, 234, 245. On curative powers see also J. Brand, *Observations on Popular Antiquities: Including the Whole of Mr Bourne's Antiquitates Vulgares, with Addenda to Every Chapter of That Work* (Newcastle upon Tyne, 1777), pp. 85–6.

23. R. Gillespie, *Devoted People: Belief and Religion in Early Modern Ireland* (Manchester: Manchester University Press, 1997), p. 94.

24. Anon., *A Description of St. Winefred's Well, at Holy-Well, in Flintshire, North Wales* (Liverpool, 1797), p. 1.

25. Brand, *Observations on Popular Antiquities*, p. 76.

26. Ibid., pp. 76–7.

27. Ibid., p. 77.

28. W. Coster and A. Spicer (eds), *Sacred Space in Early Modern Europe* (Cambridge: Cambridge University Press, 2005), pp. 1–16.

29. 'Francis Smith, Killing: Murder, 11th January 1804', in *The Proceedings of the Old Bailey Online*, http://www.oldbaileyonline.org/html_units/1800s/t18040111-79.html (accessed 15 April 2007). See also National Archives Home Office, Criminal Registers, Middlesex, 1791–1849, National Archives, Kew.

30. 'Francis Smith: Condemned to Death on 13th of January 1804, for the Murder of the supposed Hammersmith ghost, but pardoned soon afterwards', *The Newgate Calendar*, 1804, http://www.exclassics.com/newgate/ng470.htm (accessed 15 April 2007).

31. Ibid.. The case was also followed in *The Times*, 6 January 1804, p. 3.

32. 'Francis Smith, Killing'.

33. Jones, *A Relation of Apparitions*, pp. 55–6.

34. Brand, *Observations on Popular Antiquities*, p. 78.

35. Bourne, cited in ibid., p. 83; Hutton, 'The English Reformation', pp. 91–3.

36. D. Dymond, 'God's Disputed Acre', *Journal of Ecclesiastical History*, 50:3 (1999), pp. 464–97, on p. 491.

37. Coster and Spicer (eds), *Sacred Space*, p. 7.

38. Anon., *A Dissuasive from Sabbath-Breaking; Deliver'd in a Sermon on April the 22d, 1733* (Cambridge: 1735), p. 4.

39. J. Stonhouse, *Admonitions against Swearing, Sabbath-Breaking and Drunkenness* (London, 1800).

40. Ibid., pp. 3–4.

41. Clergyman, *Sabbath-Keeping the Support of our Religion and Nation* (London, 1767), p. 9.
42. J. Symons, *An Enquiry into the Design of the Christian Sabbath* (London, 1779), p. 12.
43. Committee of Special Constables, and the Society for the Reformation of Manners, *Abstract of the Laws Against Sabbath-Breaking, Swearing, and Drunkenness* (Stockport, 1797); *The Remembrancer: Addressed to Young Men in Business. Shewing How they May Attain the Way to be Rich and Respectable* (London, 1794), pp. 55–6.
44. W. Shakespeare, *Hamlet, a Tragedy*, I.i.; V.i.
45. See Chapter 4, pp. 120–2.
46. David Vincent observed that many working-class autobiographers 'retained a deep respect for the education and stimulus to their imagination that they had received from the story-tellers of their youth', *Bread, Knowledge and Freedom: A Study of Nineteenth-Century Working Class Autobiography* (London: Methuen, 1982), p. 21.
47. S. Bamford, *The Autobiography of Samuel Bamford*, ed. W. H. Chaloner, 2 vols (London: Frank Cass & Co., 1967), vol. 1, p. 29.
48. Ibid., vol. 1, pp. 27–8.
49. A similar point has been made by B. C. Lane, *Landscapes of the Sacred: Geography and Narrative in American Spirituality* (Baltimore, MD, and London: Johns Hopkins University Press, 2002), pp. 6, 8, 24.
50. D. Vincent, *Literacy and Popular Culture: England 1750–1914* (Cambridge: Cambridge University Press, 1989), pp. 270–80.
51. T. Mountjoy, *Hard Times in the Forest, Extracts from "62 Years in the life of a Forest of Dean Collier" by Timothy Mountjoy and The Forest in my Younger Days; by Fred Boughton* (Coleford, Forest of Dean Newspapers, 1971), p. 15.
52. W. Lovett, *Life and Struggles of William Lovett, in his Pursuit of Bread, Knowledge and Freedom, with Some Short Account of the Different Associations he Belonged to and of the Opinions he Entertained*, preface R. H. Tawney (London: MacGibbon & Kee, 1967), p. 8.
53. W. Borlase, *Antiquities, Historical and Monumental, of the County of Cornwall* (London, 1769), p. 122.
54. J. Harris, *My Autobiography* (London, 1882), p. 39.
55. Vincent, *Bread, Knowledge and Freedom*, p. 168; J. Clare, *Sketches in the Life of John Clare, Written by Himself*, intro. E. Blunden (London: Cobden-Sanderson, 1931), p. 56.
56. J. Clare, *The Shepherd's Calendar* (1827), intro. J. Wordsworth (Oxford and New York: Woodstock Books, 1991), p. 10.
57. Clare's work contained a number of references to ghosts, spirits and haunted spots, see ibid., pp. 10, 33–4, 73, 89.
58. B. White, 'Catherine Ferrers', *ODNB*, http://www.oxforddnb.com/view/article/73927 (accessed 21 April 2007).
59. J. Bullar, *A Companion in a Tour Round Southampton, comprehending Various Particulars, Ancient and Modern, of the New Forest* (Southampton, 1799), p. 176.
60. Jones, *Walking Haunted London*, p. 66.
61. Ibid., pp. 90, 134.

62. J. Cremer, *Ramblin' Jack. The Journal of Captain John Cremer, 1700–1774* (London, 1936), p. 90 cited in M. Rediker, *Between the Devil and the Deep Blue Sea: Merchant Seamen, Pirates and the Anglo-American Maritime World, 1700–1750* (Cambridge: Cambridge University Press, 1989), p. 183.

63. 'Editorials/Leaders', *The Times*, 11 November 1818, p. 2

64. H. Teonge, *The Diary of Henry Teonge*, ed. G. E. Manwaring (London: G. Routledge, 1927), p. 169. When the crew of the *William Galley* saw an apparition in 1705, they concluded that it came to warn of the death of Mr Nesbitt, who died the night following, F. Rogers, *The Journal of Francis Rogers* (London, 1936), pp. 223–4.

65. See C. Thomson, *The Autobiography of an Artisan* (London, 1847), p. 148.

66. R. Godbeer, *The Devil's Dominion: Magic and Religion in Early New England* (Cambridge and New York: Cambridge University Press, 1992), p. 232.

67. Rediker, *Between the Devil and the Deep Blue Sea*, p. 185.

68. Ibid., pp. 2–3, 40, 92–3, 186, 293.

69. J. Donaldson, *Recollections of an Eventful Life Chiefly Passed in the Army* (Glasgow, 1825), pp. 38–43.

70. D. M. Hopkin, 'Storytelling, Fairytales and Autobiography: Some Observations on Eighteenth- and Nineteenth-Century French Soldiers' and Sailors' Memoirs', *Social History*, 29:2 (2004), pp. 188–98, on p. 196.

71. P. J. Stewart and A. Strathern, *Landscape, Memory and History: Anthropological Perspectives* (London: Pluto Press, 2003), pp. 4–5.

72. Rediker, *Between the Devil and the Deep Blue Sea*, p. 190; Hopkin, 'Storytelling, Fairytales and Autobiography', p. 187.

73. Ibid., p. 187.

74. Recounted in W. H. D. Longstaffe (ed.), *Memoirs of the Life of Mr. Ambrose Barnes, Late Merchant and Sometime Alderman of Newcastle Upon Tyne*, Publications of the Surtees Society, vol. 50 (Durham, 1867), pp. 59–60.

75. J. Tregortha, *News from the Invisible World* (Burslem, 1808), p. 345.

76. Anon., *Mary's Dream: or, Sandy's Ghost* (London, 1790).

77. *Scientific Magazine, and Freemasons' Repository*, 1 (1797), p. 331.

78. Welby, *Signs Before Death*, p. 80.

79. Ibid., p. 81.

80. G. Sinclair, *Satan's Invisible World Discovered* (Edinburgh, 1789), pp. 20–1, 87; Anon., *The Compleat Wizzard: Being a Collection of Authentic and Entertaining Narratives of the Real Existence and Appearance of Ghosts, Demons, and Spectres* (London, 1770), p. 270; Tregortha, *News from the Invisible World*, p. 345; 'Camden (South Carolina), Aug. 11', *The Times*, 2 December 1803, p. 3; J. Andrews, *A Review of the Characters of the Principal Nations in Europe*, 2 vols (London, 1770), vol. 2, pp. 105–6.

81. D. D. Hall, *Worlds of Wonder, Days of Judgment: Popular Religious Belief in Early New England* (New York: Knopf, 1989), pp. 46–9.

82. Tregortha, *News from the Invisible World*, p. 49.

83. Anon., *The Reprobate's Reward or a Looking Glass for Disobedient Children* (London, 1788), p. 8

84. The 1798 version was set in Cork not Bristol, but the main characters and plot remained the same.

85. G. Boas, *The Cult of Childhood*, Studies of the Warburg Institute, vol. 29 (London: Warburg Institute, 1966); C. K. Steedman, *Strange Dislocations: Childhood and the Idea of Human Interiority* (Cambridge, MA: Harvard University Press, 1995), pp. 1–20; D. Wahrman, *The Making of the Modern Self: Identity and Culture in Eighteenth-Century England* (New Haven, CT, and London: Yale University Press, 2004), p. 282.

86. Brand, *Observations on Popular Antiquities*, p. 71.

87. *Beauties of all the Magazines Selected*, 1 (1762), p. 12.

88. Anon., *The Compleat Wizzard*, preface.

89. Anon., 'Of Ghosts, Daemons, and Spectres', *Gentleman's Magazine*, 2:10 (1732); C. H. Flynn, *The Body in Swift and Defoe* (Cambridge: Cambridge University Press, 1990), p. 103; C. Brontë, *Jane Eyre* (London: Penguin, 1994), pp. 42–6.

90. Ibid., pp. 48–9.

91. Locke, *An Essay Concerning Human Understanding*, vol. 1, p. 368.

92. D. Defoe, *A View of the Invisible World: or, General History of Apparitions* (London, 1752), pp. iii–iv.

93. Anon., *Anti-Canidia*, p. 20.

94. 'To the Editor of the Times', *The Times*, 26 November 1817, p. 3.

95. Flynn, *The Body in Swift and Defoe*, pp. 101 ff.

96. N. Andry de Bois-Regard, *Orthopaedia: or, The Art of Correcting and Preventing Deformities in Children*, 2 vols (London, 1743), vol. 2, pp. 210–11.

97. 'Essay on the Education of Children', *Newcastle General Magazine* (September 1748).

98. A. Hamilton, *A Treatise on the Management of Female Complaints, and of Children in Early Infancy* (Edinburgh, 1792), p. 395.

99. Anon., 'Lord Galway and the Ghost', *The Times*, 5 May 1790, p. 2.

100. Bamford, *Autobiography*, vol. 1, p. 162.

101. Harris's mother probably had a good stock of ghost stories up her sleeve because the town of Camborne reportedly had a 'white-sheeted spectre' for 'every large rock and abandoned mine-pit', Harris, *Autobiography*, pp. 14, 39.

102. A. Sommerville, *The Autobiography of a Working Man, by one who has Whistled at the Plough* (London, 1848), p. 59.

103. Clare, *The Shepherd's Calendar*, p. 14.

104. Lovett, *Life and Struggles*, p. 8.

105. S. Romilly, *Memoirs of the Life of Sir Samuel Romilly*, 3 vols (London, 1840), vol. 1, p. 11.

106. Hume, *Of Miracles*, p. 36. In the 1970s, socio-linguists studied the use of oral testimonies in capturing audiences and creating authority for the narrator. See W. Labov, *Language in the Inner City: Studies in the Black English Vernacular* (Oxford: Blackwell, 1977).

107. Anon., *Elements of Morality for the Use of Children; with an Introductory Address to Parents*, 2 vols (London, 1792), vol. 1, p. xvii.

108. Anon., *The History of Little Goody Two Shoes; Otherwise Called, Mrs Margery Two-Shoes* (London, 1766).

109. Ibid., p. 56.

110. Anon., *Youth's Miscellany; or, A Father's Gift to his Children* (London, 1798), pp. 54–6; M. Berquin, *The Children's Friend; Consisting of Apt Tales, Short Dialogues, and Moral Dramas*, 24 vols (London, 1786), vol. 15, pp. 27–30.

111. Country Clergyman, *The Death-Watch. Dialogues upon Spirits; or, A Curious, Interesting, and Entertaining Disquisition on the Important Question relating to the Real Appearance of Departed Souls, and their Power of Making their Second Appearance in the World* (London, 1796), title-page.

112. From the evidence that does survive detailing the reading habits of youngsters in the late eighteenth and early nineteenth centuries, *The Death Watch* made a poor showing. Although *The History of Little Goody Two Shoes* ran through ten English editions by 1830, it enjoyed greater popularity in the second half of the nineteenth century, being reprinted seventeen times between 1855 and 1901.

113. Donaldson, *Recollections of an Eventful Life*, pp. 1–3; Bamford, *Autobiography*, p. 110; Lovett, *Life and Struggles*, p. 17.

114. *Spectator*, 3:419 (1 July 1712), p. 570.

115. Spufford, *Small Books and Pleasant Histories*, p. 72; J. Bath, '"In the Divell's Likenesse": Interpretation and Confusion in Popular Ghost Belief', in J. Newton (ed.), *Early Modern Ghosts: Proceedings of the Early Modern Ghosts Conference held at St John's College, Durham University, 24 March 2001* (Durham: Centre for Seventeenth Century Studies, Durham University, 2002).

116. W. Gordon, *Every Young Man's Companion* (London, 1765), p. 427.

117. P. Marshall, *Mother Leakey and the Bishop: A Ghost Story* (Oxford: Oxford University Press, 2007), p. 256.

118. 'Letter from Robert Southey to C. W. Williams, Bristol, January 15, 1799', in, R. Southey, *Letters of Robert Southey*, ed. J. Wood Warter, 4 vols (London, 1856), vol. 1, p. 64. Also cited in Dorson, *The British Folklorists*, vol. 1, pp. 92–3.

119. Cited in ibid., vol. 1, p. 42.

120. Marshall, *Mother Leakey and the Bishop*, p. 253.

121. MacDonald and Murphy, *Sleepless Souls*, pp. 351–3.

122. J. Aikin and A. L. Aikin, *Miscellaneous Pieces, in Prose* (London, 1773), p. 124.

123. H. Walpole, *The Castle of Otranto: A Gothic Story* (London, 1766), pp. 36, 53.

124. See Chapter 5, pp. 144–5.

125. Clery, *The Rise of Supernatural Fiction*, p. 53.

126. Walpole, *The Castle of Otranto*, preface.

127. C. Reeve, *The Old English Baron: A Gothic Story* (London, 1778), preface.

128. Ibid., pp. 42–4.

129. *Gentleman's Magazine*, 48:7 (1778), pp. 325–6.

130. A. Barbauld, 'Critical Preface', in *The Old English Baron: A Gothic Story, by Clara Reeve, and The Castle of Otranto, by Horace Walpole*, The British Novelists, vol. 22 (London, 1810), p. ii. Also cited in Clery, *The Rise of Supernatural Fiction*, p. 89.

131. Robert Miles estimates that Gothic texts had a market share of about thirty per cent of novel production between 1788 and 1807, rising to thirty-eight per cent in 1795, R. Miles, 'The 1790s: The Effulgence of Gothic' in Hogle (ed.), *Companion to Gothic Fiction*, pp. 41–62, on p. 42.

132. Radcliffe, *The Mysteries of Udolpho*, pp. 102–3.

133. Ibid., pp. 300–1.

134. Ibid., p. 300.
135. Ibid., p. 633.
136. A. Radcliffe, *Gaston de Blondeville and St. Albans Abbey* (London, 1826), pp. 114–24.
137. A. Fuller, *Alan Fitz-Osborne, an Historical Tale*, 2 vols (London, 1787), vol. 1, title-page, pp. 82–3.
138. Ibid., vol. 1, p. 86.
139. M. Lewis, *Ambrosio, or The Monk: A Romance*, 2 vols (London, 1798), vol. 2, pp. 21–5, 85.
140. R. M. Roche, *The Children of the Abbey* (London, 1796).
141. S. T. Coleridge, *The Oxford Authors: Samuel Taylor Coleridge*, ed. H. J. Jackson (Oxford: Oxford University Press, 1985) p. 632.
142. Marshall, *Mother Leakey and the Bishop*, pp. 255–6.
143. C. M. Kauffmann, *John Varley, 1778–1842* (London: Victoria and Albert Museum, 1984), p. 39. On Blake's ghost see notes by J. T. Smith (1828) in G. E. Bentley, *Blake Records* (Oxford: Clarendon Press, 1969), p. 460.
144. See for example R. I. Martin's engraving, *The Witch of Endor Conjures up the Ghost of Samuel at the Request of Saul, who Lies Petrified on the Ground* (1811).
145. M. Robinson, 'The Haunted Beach', in *Romanticism: An Anthology*, ed. D. Wu (Oxford: Blackwell, 2006).
146. Hogle (ed.), *The Cambridge Companion to Gothic Fiction*, p.4.
147. G. Cheyne, *The English Malady* (London, 1733); S. Tissot, *Essay on the Disorders of People of Fashion* (London, 1771).
148. 'Letters and Papers of Georgiana, Lady Chatterton', Shakespeare Birthplace Trust, MS Warwickshire, DR 495/101, p. 4.
149. Ibid., p. 5.
150. Lovett, *Life and Struggles*, p. 11.
151. A. Smith, *An Inquiry into the Nature and Causes of the Wealth of Nations*, 2 vols (London, 1778), vol. 2, p. 386.
152. Lovett, *Life and Struggles*, p. 11.
153. Lane, *Landscapes of the Sacred*, p. 6.
154. Schama, *Landscape and Memory*, p. 12.

Conclusion

1. S. F. Gray, *Phantasmatophaneia; or Anecdotes of Ghosts and Apparitions* (London, 1797), p. 4.
2. Thomas, *Religion and the Decline of Magic*; Burke, *Popular Culture in Early Modern Europe*; K. Wrightson, *English Society 1580–1680* (London: Routledge, 1982). A similar point has been made by MacDonald and Murphy in their survey of changing attitudes towards suicide in this chronology, *Sleepless Souls*, p. 343.
3. Clark, *Thinking with Demons*, pp. 3–11.
4. S. Johnson, *A Dictionary of the English Language*, 4 vols (London, 1818).
5. Anon., 'The Ghost of St. Andrews', *The Times*, 26 August 1815, p. 3, col. G.

6.   J. Taylor, *Apparitions; or, The Mystery of Ghosts, Hobgoblins, and Haunted Houses Developed*, 2nd edn (London: Lackington, Allen & Co., 1815), p. viii.
7.   Ibid., p. vii.
8.   S. Fovargue, *A New Catalogue of Vulgar Errors* (Cambridge, 1767), p. 60.
9.   Anon., 'On the Sampford Ghost, And on Human Testimony to Supernatural Occurrences', *The Times*, 22 October 1810, p. 3, col. C.
10. Ibid.
11. Johnson, *A Dictionary* (1818).
12. Ibid.
13. Defoe, *An Essay on the History and Reality of Apparitions*, pp. 25–43.
14. Johnson, *A Dictionary* (1818).
15. For a study of Strahan's career in printing see J. A. Cochrane, *Dr. Johnson's Printer: The Life of William Strahan* (London: Routledge & Kegan Paul, 1964).
16. Advertisements, *The Times*, 12 April 1790, p. 4.
17. Ibid.
18. Advertisements, *The Times*, 14 April 1791, p. 3.
19. In 1821 *The Times* advertised 'Ghostiana, with a New Theory of Apparitions', underlining the topicality of this subject, Advertisements, *The Times*, 26 February 1821, p. 3.
20. A. Owen, *The Darkened Room: Women, Power and Spiritualism in Late Victorian England* (London: Virago, 1989), Introduction. See also J. Oppenheim, *The Other World: Spiritualism and Psychical Research in England, 1850–1914* (Cambridge: Cambridge University Press, 1985).
21. Johnson, *A Dictionary* (1818).
22. News, *The Times*, 28 April 1804, p. 2.
23. For a fuller description see Llewellyn, *The Art of Death*.
24. Bynum, 'Why all the Fuss about the Body?', pp. 32–3.
25. Vidal, 'Brains, Bodies, Selves, and Science', pp. 958, 965, 969, 973.
26. *Boswell's Life of Johnson*, ed. G. B. Hill and L. F. Powell, 4 vols (Oxford: Clarendon Press, 1934–50), vol. 3, pp. 298, 235, cited in Thomas, *Religion and the Decline of Magic*, p. 703.
27. Walter Scott, cited in H. Walpole, *The Castle of Otranto*, ed. and intro. M. Gamer (London: Penguin, 2001), p. 135.
28. See for example L. Henderson and E. J. Cowan, *Scottish Fairy Belief* (East Linton: Tuckwell Press, 2001), pp. 18, 39, 44.
29. O. Davies, 'Urbanization and the Decline of Witchcraft: An Examination of London', *Journal of Social History*, 30:3 (1997), pp. 597–617.
30. In the case of angels, important first steps have already been taken to measure their significance in early modern European culture. See P. Marshall and A. Walsham (eds), *Angels in the Early Modern World* (Cambridge: Cambridge University Press, 2006).

WORKS CITED

Manuscript Sources

Bedfordshire and Luton Archives, MS Bedford, Letters & Papers of the How Family, Letter from Richard How II to William Tomlinson, 21 July 1745, HW/87/118.

Birmingham Archdiocesan Archives, MS Birmingham, J. Berington, 'On Ghosts' (*c.* 1820), C2365.

Friends House Library, MS London, 'A Collection of Letters, Dreams and Visions and other Remarkable Occurrences of the People called Quakers' (1788), S78.

Methodist Church Archives, MS Manchester:

'Letters Concerning some Supernatural Disturbances at the House of the Reverend Mr Samuel Wesley, in Epworth, Lincolnshire', Notebook of Charles Wesley (1716–17), DDCW 8/15.

Fletcher-Tooth Collection, Letter from George Fothy to Mary Fletcher, 1800, MAM FL 6/7/19

Fletcher-Tooth Collection, Letter from Miles Martindale in Leeds to Mary Fletcher, 14 January 1811, MAM FL 5/1/9.

National Archives, Kew, National Archives Home Office, Criminal Registers, Middlesex, 1791–1849.

Norfolk Record Office, MS Norfolk:

'Report given to Robert Withers, Vicar of Gateley, of the Appearance of a Ghost 1706', Parish Records of Gateley, MS PD 9/1.

Papers of the Wodehouse Family of Kimberley, KIM 16/4, 1767.

Royal Greenwich Observatory, MS London, Papers of John Flamsteed, 37, f. 16.

Somerset Record Office, MS Somerset, 'Papers relating to the Sidcot Ghost' (*c.* 1780), DD/SC/G/1393/57.

Shakespeare Birthplace Trust, MS Warwickshire, 'Letters and Papers of Georgiana, Lady Chatterton', DR 495/101.

Journals and Magazines

Arminian Magazine, 20 vols (London, 1783–97).

Athenian Mercury, The (London, 1691–7).

Beauties of all the Magazines Selected, The, 3 vols (London, 1762).

British Apollo; or Curious Amusements for the Ingenious, The, 3 vols (London, 1708-1710).

Gentleman's Magazine, or, Monthly Intelligencer, 103 vols (London, 1731–1833).

Loyal Post: with Foreign and Inland Intelligence, The, 14 (1705).

Newcastle General Magazine, The, 14 vols (Newcastle, 1747-60).

Norwich Mercury, The (1752).

Penny London Post, The, vol. 171, 3 May 1726.

Remembrancer: Addressed to Young Men in Business. Shewing How they May Attain the Way to be Rich and Respectable, The (London, 1794).

Scientific Magazine, and Freemasons' Repository, The, 2 vols (London, 1797).

Universal Spectator, The (London, 1732).

Primary Printed Sources

Adams, J., *Elegant Anecdotes, and Bon-Mots of the Greatest Princes, Politicians, Philosophers, Orators, and Wits of Modern Times* (London, 1790).

Addison, J., *The Drummer; or, The Haunted-House, a Comedy, as it is Acted at the Theatre-Royal in Drury Lane, by His Majesty's Servants* (London, 1715).

—, *The Spectator*, ed. D. F. Bond, 4 vols (Oxford: Clarendon Press, 1965).

Aikin, J., and A. L. Aikin, *Miscellaneous Pieces, in Prose* (London, 1773).

Aitken, G. A., *The Life and Works of John Arbuthnot* (Oxford: Clarendon Press, 1892).

Andrews, J., *A Review of the Characters of the Principal Nations in Europe*, 2 vols (London, 1770).

Andrews, J. P., *Anecdotes, &c. Antient and Modern. With Observations* (London, 1790).

Andry de Bois-Regard, N., *Orthopaedia: or, The Art of Correcting and Preventing Deformities in Children*, 2 vols (London, 1743).

Annet, P., *Supernaturals Examined* (London, 1747).

Anon., *An Account of a Most Horrid and Barborous Murther and Robbery, Committed on the Body of Captain Brown, near Shrewsbury in Shropshire* (London, 1694).

—, *An Account of a Most Horrid, Bloody, and Terrible Apparition, which Lately Appeared in the Parish of Shotts* (London, 1793).

—, *An Account of the Apparition of the Late Lord Kilmarnock to the Reverend Mr. Foster* (London, 1747).

—, *Admiral Vernon's Ghost* (London, 1758).

—, *Anti-Canidia: or, Superstition Detected and Exposed* (London, 1762).

—, *The Atheist's Reward: or, A Call from Heaven, To which is Annexed an Account of the Apparition of the Ghost of Major George Sydenham* (London, 1788).

—, *Bradshaw's Ghost: Being a Dialogue between the said Ghost, and an Apparition of the Late King Charles* (London, 1659).

—, *The Compleat Wizzard: Being a Collection of Authentic and Entertaining Narratives of the Real Existence and Appearance of Ghosts, Demons, and Spectres* (London, 1770).

—, *A Description of St. Winefred's Well, at Holy-Well, in Flintshire, North Wales* (Liverpool, 1797).

—, *A Dissuasive from Sabbath-Breaking; Deliver'd in a Sermon on April the 22d, 1733* (Cambridge, 1735).

—, *The Disturbed Ghost* (London, 1675).

—, *The Duke's Daughter's Cruelty: or, The Wonderful Apparition of Two Infants whom she Murther'd and Buried in a Forrest, for to Hide her Shame* (London, 1692).

—, *Elements of Morality for the Use of Children; with an Introductory Address to Parents*, 2 vols (London, 1792).

—, Epistle Dedicator, to the Gentleman of the Athenian Society', *Athenian Mercury*, 1 (1691), p. 1.

—, 'Essay on the Education of Children', *Newcastle General Magazine* (September 1748).

—, *An Exact Narrative of Many Surprizing Matters of Fact Uncontestably Wrought by an Evil Spirit or Spirits, in the House of Master Jan Smagge* (London, 1709).

—, *The Examination of Isabel Binnington of Great-Driffield* (York, 1662).

—, 'The Fruits of Enthusiasm', *Norwich Mercury*, 15–22 February 1752, p. 3.

—, *A Full and Particular Account of a Most Dreadful and Surprising Apparition* (London, 1757).

—, *A Full and Particular Account of the Wonderful Apparition of Mary Nicholson* (Durham, 1799).

—, *A Full, True and Particular Account of the Ghost or Apparition of the Late Duke of Buckingham's Father* (London, 1700).

—, *Gale's Cabinet of Knowledge; or, Miscellaneous Recreations* (London, 1796).

—, *Genuine and Impartial Memoirs of Elizabeth Canning* (London, 1754).

—, 'The Ghost of St. Andrews', *The Times*, 26 August 1815, p. 3, col. G.

—, *The Ghost, or, A Minute Account of the Appearance of the Ghost of John Croxford Executed at Northampton, August the 4th 1764* ([London?], 1764).

—, *A Godly Warning to all Maidens* (London, 1670).

—, *Great News from Middle-Row in Holbourn or A True Relation of a Dreadful Ghost which Appeared in the Shape of one Mrs. Adkins* (London, 1680).

—, *The History of Little Goody Two Shoes; Otherwise Called, Mrs Margery Two-Shoes* (London, 1766).

—, *The Leicestershire Tragedy: or, The Fatal Overthrow of two Unfortunate Lovers, Caus'd by Susanna's Breach of Promise* (London, 1685).

—, 'Letter to Mr Wheatley', *Norwich Mercury*, 4 April 1752, p. 3.

—, *Life After Death; or The History of Apparitions, Ghosts, Spirits or Spectres* (London, 1758).

—, *Lilburn's Ghost* (London, 1659).

—, 'Lord Galway and the Ghost', *The Times*, 5 May 1790, p. 2.

—, *Lovat's Ghost: or The Courtier's Warning Piece* (London, 1747).

—, *Mary's Dream: or, Sandy's Ghost* (London, 1790).

—, *The Midwives Ghost* (London, 1680).

—, *The Most Strange, Wonderful and Surprising Apparition of the Ghost of General Clayton, which Appeared to the Man, who Wore the Yellow Sash at the Battle of Dettingen* (London, 1743).

—, *Mr. Ashton's Ghost to his Late Companion in the Tower* (London, 1691).

—, *Murder Will Out: Being a Relation of the Late Earl of Essex's Ghost* (London, 1683).

—, *A New Apparition of S. Edmund-Bery Godfrey's Ghost to the Earl of Danby in the Tower* (London, 1681).

—, *A New Ballad of the Midwives Ghost* (London, 1680).

—, *Observations on the Use of Spectacles* (London, 1753).

—, 'Of Ghosts, Daemons, and Spectres', *Gentleman's Magazine*, 2:10 (1732).

—, 'On the Sampford Ghost, And on Human Testimony to Supernatural Occurrences', *The Times*, 22 October 1810, p. 3, col. C.

—, *The Possibility of Apparitions. Being an Answer to this Question, Whether can Departed Souls (Souls Separated from their Bodies) so Appear, as to be Visibly Seen and Conversed With here upon Earth?* (London, 1706).

—, *The Reprobate's Reward or a Looking Glass for Disobedient Children* (London, 1788).

—, *The Rest-less Ghost: or, Wonderful News from Northamptonshire and Southwark* (London, [1675]).

—, *The Rich Man's Warning-Piece; or, The Oppressed Infants in Glory* (London, 1683 and 1770).

—, *Scelus's Ghost: or, The Lawyer's Warning Piece* (London, 1748).

—, *Sir Edmundbury Godfreys Ghost* (London, 1682).

—, *A Strange and Wonderfull Discovery of a Horrid and Cruel Murther Committed Fourteen Years Since, upon the Person of Robert Eliot of London, at Great Driffield in the East-Riding of the County of York* (London, 1662).

—, *Strange and Wonderful News from Lincolnshire* (London, 1679).

—, *Strange and Wonderful News from Northampton-shire, or, The Discontented Spirit* (London, 1674).

—, *A Strange, but True Relation, of the Discovery of a Most Horrid and Bloody Murder* (London, 1678).

—, *The Suffolk Miracle, or, A Relation of a Young Man who a Month After his Death Appeared to his Sweetheart* (London, 1670).

—, 'A Supplement to the Advice from the Scandalous Club', *Review*, 3 (London, 1704).

—, *Tears of the Press* (London, 1681).

—, *A True and Circumstantial Relation of a Cruel and Barbarous Murder* (Northampton, 1848).

—, *A True and Perfect Relation from the Faulcon at the Banke-side* (London, 1661).

—, *A True Relation of the Dreadful Ghost Appearing to one John Dyer* (London, 1691).

—, *The Two Unfortunate Lovers, or, A True Relation of the Lamentable End of John True and Susan Mease* (London, 1670).

—, *A Warning Piece Against the Crime of Murder* (London and Sherborne, 1752).

—, *A Warning Piece for the World, or, A Watch-Word to England* (London, 1655).

—, *The Wonder of this Age: or, God's Miraculous Revenge against Murder* (London, 1677).

—, *The Wonderful and Strange Apparition and Ghost of Edward Ashley* (London, 1712).

—, *Youth's Miscellany; or, A Father's Gift to his Children* (London, 1798).

Arbuthnot, J., *An Essay Concerning the Effects of Air on Human Bodies* (London, 1702).

[Arbuthnot, J.], *The Story of the St. Albans Ghost, or the Apparition of Mother Haggy* (London, 1712).

Asgill, J., *An Argument Proving, that According to the Covenant of Eternal Life Revealed in the Scriptures, Man may be Translated from Hence into that Eternal Life, Without Passing Through Death* (London, 1715).

Atkinson, J. C., *Countryman on the Moors*, ed. J. G. O'Leary, Fitzroy edn (London: MacGibbon & Kee, 1967).

Aubrey, J., *Remains of Gentilisme and Judaisme* (1686–7), ed. J. Britten (London, 1881).

—, *Miscellanies upon the Following Subjects* (London, 1696).

Bamford, S., *The Autobiography of Samuel Bamford*, ed. W. H. Chaloner, 2 vols (London: Frank Cass & Co., 1967).

Barbauld, A., 'Critical Preface', in *The Old English Baron: A Gothic Story, by Clara Reeve, and The Castle of Otranto, by Horace Walpole*, The British Novelists, vol. 22 (London, 1810).

Barrow, I., *Practical Discourses upon the Consideration of Our Latter End* (1694; 2nd edn, London, 1712).

Baxter, R., *Of the Immortality of Mans Soul, and the Nature of it and other Spirits* (London, 1682).

—, *The Certainty of the World of Spirits Fully Evinced* (London, 1691).

Berquin, M., *The Children's Friend; Consisting of Apt Tales, Short Dialogues, and Moral Dramas*, 24 vols (London, 1786).

Blackburne, F., *No Proof in the Scriptures of an Intermediate State of Happiness or Misery between Death and the Resurrection* (London, 1755).

—, *A Short Historical View of the Controversy Concerning an Intermediate State and the Separate Existence of the Soul between Death and the General Resurrection* (London, 1765).

Blair, R., *The Grave. A Poem* (London, 1743).

Borlase, W., *Antiquities, Historical and Monumental, of the County of Cornwall* (London, 1769).

Boswell, J., *Everybody's Boswell, Being the Life of Samuel Johnson Abridged from James Boswell's Complete Text and from the "Tour to the Hebrides"*, illustrated by E. H. Shepard (Ware: Wordsworth Editions, 1989).

—, *The Life of Dr Johnson, LLD*, abridged by F. Thomas (London, 1792).

—, *The Life of Samuel Johnson, LLD, Comprehending an Account of his Studies and Numerous Works*, 4 vols (London, 1799).

Bourne, H., *Antiquitates Vulgares; or, The Antiquities of the Common People* (Newcastle, 1725).

Boyle, R., 'New Pneumatical Experiments about Respiration', *Philosophical Transactions of the Royal Society*, 5 (1665–78), pp. 2011–31.

Brand, J., *Observations on Popular Antiquities: Including the Whole of Mr Bourne's Antiquitates Vulgares, with Addenda to Every Chapter of That Work* (Newcastle upon Tyne, 1777).

Bromhall, T., *A Treatise of Specters, or, An History of Apparitions, Oracles, Prophecies, and Predictions* (London, 1658).

Brontë, C., *Jane Eyre* (London: Penguin, 1994).

Bullar, J., *A Companion in a Tour Round Southampton, comprehending Various Particulars, Ancient and Modern, of the New Forest* (Southampton, 1799).

Burke, E., *A Philosophical Enquiry into the Origins of our Ideas of the Sublime and Beautiful* (London, 1757).

Burnet, T., *The Theory of the Earth containing an Account of the Original of the Earth* (London, 1684).

Butler, A., *The Moveable, Feasts, Fasts, and Other Annual Observances of the Catholic Church* (London, 1774).

Camfield, B., *A Theological Discourse of Angels and their Ministries* (London, 1678).

Caulfield, B., *An Essay on the Immateriality and Immortality of the Soul* (London, 1778).

Cheyne, G., *The English Malady* (London, 1733).

Churchman, J., *An Account of the Gospel Labours and Christian Experiences of a Faithful Minister of Christ, John Churchman* (London, 1780).

Clare, J., *The Shepherd's Calendar* (1827), intro. J. Wordsworth (Oxford and New York: Woodstock Books, 1991).

—, *Sketches in the Life of John Clare, Written by Himself*, intro. E. Blunden (London: Cobden-Sanderson, 1931).

Clarke, A., *The Miscellaneous Works of Adam Clarke, Memoirs of the Wesley Family*, 2nd edn, 13 vols (London, 1836).

Clarke, S., *A Demonstration of the Being and Attributes of God* (London, 1705).

—, *A Defense of an Argument made use of in a Letter to Mr Dodwel, to Prove the Immateriality and Natural Immortality of the Soul* (London, 1707).

Clergyman, *Sabbath-Keeping the Support of our Religion and Nation* (London, 1767).

Cockburn, A., *A Philosophical Essay Concerning the Intermediate State of Blessed Souls* (London, 1722).

Coleridge, S. T., *The Oxford Authors: Samuel Taylor Coleridge*, ed. H. J. Jackson (Oxford: Oxford University Press, 1985).

Committee of Special Constables, and the Society for the Reformation of Manners, *Abstract of the Laws Against Sabbath-Breaking, Swearing, and Drunkenness* (Stockport, 1797).

Cooper, A. A., 'A Letter Concerning Enthusiasm to My Lord *****' (1708), in Lawrence E. Klein, ed., *Characteristics of Men, Manners, Opinions, Times* (Cambridge and New York, Cambridge University Press, 1999), pp. 4–28.

Coote, C., *The History of England*, 9 vols (London, 1791–8).

Country Clergyman, *The Death-Watch: Dialogues upon Spirits; or, A Curious, Interesting, and Entertaining Disquisition on the Important Question relating to the Real Appearance of Departed Souls, and their Power of Making their Second Appearance in the World* (London 1796).

Crossgrove, H., *The Accurate Intelligencer, Containing Answers to a Number of Curious Letters Never Yet Publish'd in the Norwich Gazette* (Norwich, 1708).

Cudworth, R., *The True Intellectual System of the Universe* (London, 1678).

Curzon, H., *The Universal Library: or, Compleat Summary of Science*, 2 vols (London, 1722).

Day, W. G. (ed.), *Catalogue of the Pepys Library. The Pepys Ballads*, 5 vols (Cambridge: D. S. Brewer, 1987).

Dean, R., *On the Future Life of Brutes, Introduced with Observations upon Evil, its Nature and Origin* (London, 1767).

Defoe, D., *The Farther Adventures of Robinson Crusoe*, 2nd edn (London, 1719).

—, *An Essay on the History and Reality of Apparitions* (London, 1727).

—, *A View of the Invisible World: or, General History of Apparitions* (London, 1752).

—, *The Secrets of the Invisible World Laid Open: or, An Universal History of Apparitions, Sacred and Prophane* (London, 1770).

[Defoe, D.], *A True Relation of the Apparition of one Mrs. Veal, the Next Day After her Death, to one Mrs. Bargrave, at Canterbury, the 8th of September, 1705* (London, 1706).

Donaldson, J., *Recollections of an Eventful Life Chiefly Passed in the Army* (Glasgow, 1825).

Donovan, J., *A Sketch of Opticks: Displaying the Wonders of Sight and Manner of Vision* (Cork, 1795).

Drelincourt, C., *The Christian's Defence Against the Fears of Death: With Directions how to Dye Well, with an Account of Mrs. Veal's Apparition to Mrs. Bargrave* (London, 1720).

Dryden, J., *Three Plays*, ed. G. Saintsbury (New York: Hill and Wang, 1957).

Dunton, J., *The Night-Walker, or, Evening Rambles in Search after Lewd Women* (London, 1696).

—, *An Essay Proving we Shall Know our Friends in Heaven* (London, 1698).

Fielding, H., *The Tragedy of Tragedies, or The Life and Death of Tom Thumb the Great* (London, 1731).

—, *The History of Tom Jones, a Foundling* (1749), The Wesleyan Edition of the Works of Henry Fielding, 2 vols, ed. Fredson Bowers (Oxford: Clarendon Press, 1974).

—, *A Clear State of the Case of Elizabeth Canning* (London, 1753).

Fovargue, S., *A New Catalogue of Vulgar Errors* (Cambridge, 1767).

Fowler, E., *Reflections upon a Letter Concerning Enthusiasm to my Lord* ***** (London, 1709).

Fox, G., *The Journal of George Fox*, ed. N. Penney, 2 vols (Cambridge: Cambridge University Press, 1911).

Fuller, A., *Alan Fitz-Osborne, an Historical Tale*, 2 vols (London, 1787).

Glanvill, J., *Some Philosophical Considerations touching the Being of Witches and Witchcraft Written in a Letter to the Much Honour'd Robert Hunt, Esq.* (London, 1667).

—, *A Blow at Modern Sadducism in Some Philosophical Considerations about Witchcraft* (London, 1668).

—, *Saducismus Triumphatus, or, Full and Plain Evidence Concerning Witches and Apparitions*, ed. H. More (London, 1681).

Goldsmith, O., *The Mystery Revealed; Containing a Series of Transactions and Authentic Testimonials, Respecting the Supposed Cock-Lane Ghost* (London, 1762).

Gordon, W., *Every Young Man's Companion* (London, 1765).

Gray, S. F. *Phantasmatophaneia; or Anecdotes of Ghosts and Apparitions* (London, 1797).

Gray, T., *Elegy Written in a Country Church-Yard* (London, 1751).

Grose, F., *The Antiquities of England and Wales* (London, 1773).

Hamilton, A., *A Treatise on the Management of Female Complaints, and of Children in Early Infancy* (Edinburgh, 1792).

Harris, J., *My Autobiography* (London, 1882).

Harsnett, S., *A Declaration of Egregious Popish Impostures*, reprinted in F. W. Brownlow, *Shakespeare, Harsnett, and the Devils of Denham* (London and Cranbury, NJ: Associated University Presses, 1993), pp. 191–335.

Hervey, J., *Meditations Among the Tombs* (London, 1756).

Hobbes, T., *Leviathan*, ed. R. E. Flathman (London: W. W. Norton & Co., 1997).

Hogg, J., *The Long Pack, or The Mysterious Pedlar* (Leeds, 1870).

Hume, D., *Of Miracles* (1748), ed. A. Flew (LaSalle, III: Open Court, 1985).

Jackson, C. (ed.), *The Diary of Abraham De La Pryme, The Yorkshire Antiquary*, Surtees Society, vol. 54 (Durham, 1870).

Jago, R., *The Causes of Impenitence Consider'd: As Well in the Case of Extraordinary Warnings, as Under the General Laws of Providence, and Grace* (Oxford, 1755).

James, M. R., 'Twelve Medieval Ghost-Stories', *English Historical Review*, 37:147 (1922), pp. 413–22.

James I, King, *Daemonologie, in Forme of a Dialogue* (London, 1603).

Johnson, S., *A Dictionary of the English Language*, 2 vols (London, 1755).

—, *A Dictionary of the English Language*, 4 vols (London, 1818).

Jones, E., *A Geographical, Historical, and Religious Account of the Parish of Aberystruth: In the County of Monmouth* (Trevecca, 1779).

—, *A Relation of Apparitions of Spirits in the Principality of Wales* (Trevecca, 1780).

Keeble, N. H., *The Restoration: England in the 1660s* (Oxford: Blackwell, 2002).

Keeble, N. H., and G. F. Nuttall (eds), *Calendar of the Correspondence of Richard Baxter* (Oxford: Clarendon Press, 1991).

Killingworth, G., *On the Immortality of the Soul, the Resurrection of the Body, the Glorious Millennium, the Most Glorious Kingdom of God, and the Prophet Daniel's Numbers* (London, 1761).

Kimber, E., *The Life and Adventures of James Ramble*, 2 vols (London, 1755).

Lavington, G., *The Enthusiasm of Methodists and Papists Compared* (London, 1749).

Leland, J., *The Advantage and Necessity of the Christian Revelation, Shewn from the State of Religion in the Antient Heathen World* (London, 1764).

Le Loyer, Pierre, *A Treatise of Specters or Straunge Sights, Visions and Apparitions Appearing Sensibly unto Men* (London, 1605).

Lewis, M., *Ambrosio, or The Monk: A Romance*, 2 vols (London, 1798).

Locke, J., *An Essay Concerning Human Understanding*, 9th edn, 2 vols (London, 1726).

Longstaffe, W. H. D. (ed.), *Memoirs of the Life of Mr. Ambrose Barnes, Late Merchant and Sometime Alderman of Newcastle Upon Tyne*, Publications of the Surtees Society, vol. 50 (Durham, 1867).

Lord, G. de F. (ed.), *Poems on Affairs of State: August Satirical Verse, 1660–1714*, 7 vols (New Haven, CT, and London: Yale University Press, 1971).

Lovett, W., *Life and Struggles of William Lovett, in his Pursuit of Bread, Knowledge and Freedom, with Some Short Account of the Different Associations he Belonged to and of the Opinions he Entertained*, preface R. H. Tawney (London: MacGibbon & Kee, 1967).

Lyon, J., *The History of the Town and Port of Dover, and of Dover Castle; with a Short Account of the Cinque Ports*, 2 vols (London, 1813).

Mackay, C., *Memoirs of Extraordinary Popular Delusions* (London, 1841).

Milles, T., *The Natural Immortality of the Soul Asserted, and Proved from the Scriptures, and First Fathers: In Answer to Mr Dodwell's Epistolary Discourse* (Oxford, 1707).

More, H., *Antidote of Atheism, or An Appeal to the Natural Faculties of the Minde of Man, whether there be not a God* (London, 1653).

Mountjoy, T., *Hard Times in the Forest: Extracts from "62 Years in the Life of a Forest of Dean Collier" by Timothy Mountjoy and The Forest in my Younger Days; by Fred Boughton* (Coleford: Forest of Dean Newspapers, 1971).

Ness, C., *The Lord Stafford's Ghost: or, A Warning to Traitors* (London, 1680).

Newton, I., *Opticks: or, A Treatise of the Reflexions, Refractions, Inflexions and Colours of Light* (London, 1704).

Nichols, J., *Literary Anecdotes of the Eighteenth Century; comprising Biographical Memoirs of William Bowyer, Printer, F.S.A. and Many of his Learned Friends*, 9 vols (London, 1812).

Nicolson, M. H. (ed.), *The Conway Letters: The Correspondence of Anne, Viscountess Conway, Henry More, and their Friends 1642–1684* (Oxford: Clarendon Press, 1992).

Norris, J., *A Philosophical Discourse Concerning the Natural Immortality of the Soul* (London, 1708).

Odingsells, G., *The Capricious Lovers* (London, 1726).

Oldham, J., *Garnets Ghost Addressing to the Jesuits, Met in Private Caball, just after the Murther of Sir Edmund-Bury Godfrey* (London, 1679).

Overton, R., *Mans Mortallitie* (London, 1643).

Palmer, J., *A Fortnights' Ramble to the Lakes in Westmoreland, Lancashire and Cumberland* (London, 1795).

Parnell, T., *Poems on Several Occasions* (London, 1747).

Payne, Rev., *An Account of Mrs Veal's Appearance to Mrs Bargrave at Canterbury* (London, 1722).

Perkins, W., *A Discourse of the Damned Art of Witchcraft* (Cambridge, 1610).

Perrault, F., *The Divell of Masçon: or, A True Relation of the Chiefe Things which an Uncleane Spirit did, and said at Masçon in Burgundy* (London, 1669).

Philanthropus, *An Essay on the Existence of God, and the Immortality of the Soul* (London, 1750).

Polwhele, R., *Traditions and Recollections*, 2 vols (London, 1826).

Priestley, J., *An History of the Corruptions of Christianity*, 2 vols (Birmingham, 1782).

Radcliffe, A., *The Mysteries of Udolpho* (1794), ed. B. Dobree, intro. and notes T. Castle (Oxford: Oxford University Press, 1998).

—, *Gaston de Blondeville and St. Albans Abbey* (London, 1826).

Reed, J., *A Rope's End for Hempen Monopolists, or, A Dialogue between a Broker, a Rope Maker, and the Ghost of Jonas Hanway* (London, 1786).

Reeve, C., *The Old English Baron: A Gothic Story* (London, 1778).

Reeves, W., *A Sermon Concerning the Natural Immortality of the Soul* (London, 1704).

Roche, R. M., *The Children of the Abbey* (London, 1796).

Rogers, F., *The Journal of Francis Rogers* (London, 1936).

Romilly, S., *Memoirs of the Life of Sir Samuel Romilly*, 3 vols (London, 1840).

Royal Commission, *Fifth Report of the Royal Commission on Historical Manuscripts*, 1:4 (London, 1876).

Sandys, E., *Sermons*, ed. J. Ayre (Cambridge: Parker Society, 1841).

Schonhorn, Manuel (ed.) *Accounts of the Apparition of Mrs. Veal by Daniel Defoe and Others*, Augustan Reprint Society, 115 (Los Angeles, CA: William Andrews Clark Memorial Library, University of California, 1965).

Shuttleworth, J., *A Treatise of Opticks Direct* (London, 1709).

Simpson, D., *Discourse on Dreams and Night Visions* (London, 1791).

Sinclair, G., *Satan's Invisible World Discovered* (Edinburgh, 1789).

Smith, A., *An Inquiry into the Nature and Causes of the Wealth of Nations*, 2 vols (London, 1778).

Smith, G., *The Laboratory; or, School of Arts* (London, 1799).

Smith, L., *The Evidence of Things Not Seen: or, The Immortality of the Human Soul* (London, 1701).

Smith, R., *A Compleat System of Opticks* (Cambridge, 1738).

Sommerville, A., *The Autobiography of a Working Man, by one who has Whistled at the Plough* (London, 1848).

Southey, R., *Letters of Robert Southey*, ed. J. Wood Warter, 4 vols (London, 1856).

Steele, R. (ed.), *The Tatler*, 2 vols (London, 1777).

Stonhouse, J., *Admonitions against Swearing, Sabbath-Breaking and Drunkenness* (London, 1800).

Sturch, W., *Apeleutherus, or, An Effort to Attain Intellectual Freedom* (London, 1799).

Symons, J., *An Enquiry into the Design of the Christian Sabbath* (London, 1779).

Symson, A., *A Large Description of Galloway*, ed. T. Maitland (Edinburgh, 1823).

Taylor, J., *The Rule and Exercise of Holy Living* (London, 1650).

—, *The Rule and Exercise of Holy Dying* (London, 1651).

Taylor, J., *A Golden Chain to Link the Penitent Sinner unto God. Whereunto is added, A Treatise of the Immortality of the Soul* (London, 1704).

Taylor, J., *Apparitions; or, The Mystery of Ghosts, Hobgoblins, and Haunted Houses Developed*, 2nd edn (London: Lackington, Allen & Co., 1815).

Temple, J., *The Irish Rebellion* (London, 1746).

Teonge, H., *The Diary of Henry Teonge*, ed. G. E. Manwaring (London: G. Routledge, 1927).

Thomson, C., *The Autobiography of an Artisan* (London, 1847).

Tillotson, J., *A Discourse Against Transubstantiation* (London, 1797).

Tissot, S., *Essay on the Disorders of People of Fashion* (London, 1771).

Toplady, A. M., *Sermons and Essays* (London, 1793).

—, *Works*, 6 vols (London, 1825).

Tregortha, J., *News from the Invisible World* (Burslem, 1808).

Trenchard, J., *Natural History of Superstition* (London, 1709).

Trotter, C., *A Defence of the Essay of Human Understanding, Written by Mr. Lock* (London, 1702).

Turner, W., *A Compleat History of the Most Remarkable Providences* (London, 1697).

Walpole, H., *The Castle of Otranto: A Gothic Story* (London, 1766).

—, *The Castle of Otranto*, ed. and intro. M. Gamer (London: Penguin, 2001).

—, *The Yale Edition of Horace Walpole's Correspondence*, ed. W.S. Lewis, 48 vols (New Haven, CT, and London: Yale University Press, 1983).

Webster, A., *Supernatural Religion the Only Sure Hope of Sinners* (London, 1741).

Welby, H., *Signs Before Death, and Authenticated Apparitions* (London, 1825).

Wells, E., *The Young Gentleman's Opticks* (London, 1713).

Wesley, J., *Original Letters by the Rev. John Wesley, and his Friends, Illustrative of his Early History, with other Curious Papers, Communicated by the Late Rev. S. Badcock, to which is prefixed, An Address to the Methodists by Joseph Priestley* (Birmingham, 1791).

—, 'Serious Address to the Preachers of the Gospel of Christ', *Arminian Magazine*, 20 (1797), pp. 123–4.

—, *The Journal of the Reverend John Wesley*, ed. N. Curnock, 8 vols (London: Robert Culley, 1909–16).

—, 'Guardian Angels', *Bicentennial Edition of the Works of John Wesley*, ed. F. Baker and R. Heitzenrater, 23 vols (Oxford: Clarendon Press, 1980–2003).

Whitaker, J., *The Real Origin of Government, deriving the State from Revelation, not Natural Religion* (London, 1795).

Williams, J., *Extracts from the Diary, Meditations and Letters of Mr Joseph Williams of Kidderminster* (Shrewsbury, 1779).

Wodrow, R., *Analecta, or, Materials for a History of Remarkable Providences, mostly relating to Scotch Ministers and Christians*, ed. M. Leishman, Maitland Club, 60, 4 vols ([Edinburgh], 1842–3).

Woodward, J., *Fair Warnings to a Careless World* (London, 1707).

Secondary Sources

Abrams, M. H., *A Glossary of Literary Terms*, 7th edn (New York and London: Harcourt Brace, 1999).

Almond, P. C., *Heaven and Hell in Enlightenment England* (Cambridge: Cambridge University Press, 1994).

Anon., 'Strange and Wonderful News from Northampton-shire, or, The Discontented Spirit', in H. E. Rollins (ed.), *The Pack of Autolycus: or, Strange and Terrible News of Ghosts, Apparitions, Monstrous Births, Showers of Wheat, Judgments of God, and Other Prodigious and Fearful Happenings as Told in Broadside Ballads* (Cambridge, MA: Harvard University Press, 1969), pp. 179–84.

Ariès, P., *The Hour of our Death*, trans. H. Weaver (London: Allen Lane, 1981).

Armstrong, A., *The Church of England, the Methodists and Society 1700–1850* (London: University of London Press, 1973).

Atkins, M. E., *Haunted Warwickshire: A Gazetteer of Ghosts and Legends* (London: Hale, 1981).

Baine, R. M., *Daniel Defoe and the Supernatural* (Athens, GA: University of Georgia Press, 1968).

Bakos, A. E., 'Images of Hell in the Pamphlets of the Fronde', *Historical Reflections*, 26:2 (2000), pp. 339–52.

Barry, J., 'Public Infidelity and Private Belief? The Discourse of Spirits in Enlightenment Bristol', in O. Davies and W. de Blécourt (eds), *Beyond the Witch Trials, Witchcraft and Magic in Enlightenment Europe* (Manchester: Manchester University Press, 2004).

Barry, J., and C. Brooks (eds), *The Middling Sort of People: Culture, Society and Politics in England, 1550–1800* (Basingstoke: Macmillan, 1994).

Bath, J., '"In the Divell's Likenesse": Interpretation and Confusion in Popular Ghost Belief', in J. Newton (ed.), *Early Modern Ghosts: Proceedings of the Early Modern Ghosts*

Conference held at St. John's College, Durham University, 24 March 2001 (Durham: Centre for Seventeenth Century Studies, Durham University, 2002).

Beattie, J. M., *Policing and Punishment in London 1660–1720: Urban Crime and the Limits of Terror* (Oxford: Oxford University Press, 2001).

Beaty, N. L., *The Craft of Dying: A Study in the Literary Tradition of the Ars Moriendi in England* (New Haven, CT, and London: Yale University Press, 1970).

Bentley, G. E., *Blake Records* (Oxford: Clarendon Press, 1969).

Berg, M., *The Age of Manufactures, 1700–1820* (London: Fontana, 1985).

Berry, H., *Gender, Society and Print Culture, The Cultural World of the Athenian Mercury* (Aldershot: Ashgate, 2003).

Birkhead, E., *The Tale of Terror: A Study of Gothic Romance* (London: Constable & Co., 1921).

Boas, G., *The Cult of Childhood*, Studies of the Warburg Institute, vol. 29 (London: Warburg Institute, 1966).

Bostridge, I., *Witchcraft and its Transformations c. 1650–c. 1750* (Oxford and New York: Clarendon Press, 1997).

Bourdieu, P., *The Field of Cultural Production: Essays on Art and Literature*, ed. R. Johnson (Cambridge: Polity Press, 1993).

Brewer, J., *The Pleasures of the Imagination, English Culture in the Eighteenth Century* (Chicago, IL: University of Chicago Press, 1997).

Briggs, J., *Night Visitors: The Rise and Fall of the English Ghost Story* (London: Faber and Faber, 1977).

Burke, P., *Popular Culture in Early Modern Europe* (London: Temple Smith, 1978).

Burns, R. M., *The Great Debate on Miracles, from Joseph Glanvill to David Hume* (Lewisburg: Bucknell University Press, 1981).

Burns, W. E., *An Age of Wonder: Prodigies, Politics and Providence in England 1657–1727* (Manchester and New York: Manchester University Press, 2002).

Bynum, C., 'Why all the Fuss about the Body? A Medievalist's Perspective', *Critical Inquiry*, 22:1 (1995), pp. 1–33.

Caciola, N., 'Wraiths, Revenants and Ritual in Medieval Culture', *Past and Present*, 152:1 (1996), pp. 3–45.

Capp, B., *Astrology and the Popular Press, English Almanacs 1500–1800* (London and Boston, MA: Faber and Faber, 1979).

—, *When Gossips Meet: Women, Family and Neighbourhood in Early Modern England* (Oxford: Oxford University Press, 2003).

Carson, J. P., 'Enlightenment, Popular Culture, and Gothic Fiction', in J. Richetti (ed.), *The Cambridge Companion to the Eighteenth-Century Novel* (Cambridge: Cambridge University Press, 2002), pp. 255–76.

Cavaliero, G., *The Supernatural and English Fiction* (Oxford: Oxford University Press, 1995).

Chartier, R. (ed.), *The Culture of Print, Power and the Uses of Print in Early Modern Europe* (Cambridge: Polity Press, 1989).

Christie, J., and S. Shuttleworth (eds), *Nature Transfigured: Science and Literature 1700–1900* (Manchester: Manchester University Press, 1989).

Clark, D. H., and S. P. H. Clark, *Newton's Tyranny: The Suppressed Scientific Discoveries of Stephen Gray and John Flamsteed* (New York: W. H. Freeman & Co., 2001).

Clark, J. C. D., *English Society 1688–1832* (Cambridge: Cambridge University Press, 1985).

Clark, S., *Thinking with Demons: The Idea of Witchcraft in Early Modern Europe* (Oxford: Oxford University Press, 1997).

Clery, E. J., *The Rise of Supernatural Fiction, 1762–1800* (Cambridge: Cambridge University Press, 1995).

—, 'The Genesis of "Gothic" Fiction', in J. E. Hogle (ed.), *The Cambridge Companion to Gothic Fiction* (Cambridge: Cambridge University Press, 2002), pp. 21–39.

Clery, E. J., and R. Miles, *Gothic Documents: A Sourcebook, 1700–1820* (Manchester: Manchester University Press, 2000).

Cochrane, J. A., *Dr. Johnson's Printer: The Life of William Strahan* (London: Routledge & Kegan Paul, 1964).

Colley, L., *Britons, Forging the Nation 1707–1837* (London: Vintage, 1996).

Coster, W., and A. Spicer (eds), *Sacred Space in Early Modern Europe* (Cambridge: Cambridge University Press, 2005).

Cressy, D., *Literacy and the Social Order: Reading and Writing in Tudor and Stuart England* (Cambridge: Cambridge University Press, 1980).

—, *Birth, Marriage and Death: Ritual, Religion and the Life-Cycle in Tudor and Stuart England* (Oxford: Oxford University Press, 1997).

Dacome, L., 'Resurrecting by Numbers in Eighteenth-Century England', *Past and Present*, 193:1 (2006), pp. 73–110.

Daston, L., and K. Park, *Wonders and the Order of Nature, 1150–1750* (New York: Zone Books, 1998).

Davies, O., 'Urbanization and the Decline of Witchcraft: An Examination of London', *Journal of Social History*, 30:3 (1997), pp. 597–617.

—, *Witchcraft, Magic and Culture, 1736–1951* (Manchester: Manchester University Press, 1999).

Davis, L. J., *Factual Fictions: The Origins of the English Novel* (New York and Guildford: Columbia University Press, 1983).

Derrida, J., *Specters of Marx, The State of the Debt, The Work of Mourning, and The New International*, trans. P. Kamuf (New York and London: Routledge, 1994).

Dickinson, H. T. (ed.), *Britain and the French Revolution, 1789–1815* (Basingstoke: Macmillan, 1994).

Ditchfield, G. M., *The Evangelical Revival* (London: University College London Press, 1998).

Dorson, R. M., *The British Folklorists: A History*, 2 vols (London: Routledge, 2001).

Downey, J., *The Eighteenth Century Pulpit: A Study of the Sermons of Butler, Berkeley, Secker, Sterne, Whitefield and Wesley* (Oxford: Clarendon Press, 1969).

Duffy, E., 'The Godly and the Multitude in Stuart England', *Seventeenth Century*, 1 (1986), pp. 31–55.

Dymond, D., 'God's Disputed Acre', *Journal of Ecclesiastical History*, 50:3 (1999), pp. 464–97.

Eagleton, T., *Literary Theory: An Introduction* (Oxford: Blackwell, 1988).

Elmer, P., 'Valentine Greatrakes, the Body Politic and the Politics of the Body in Restoration England' (unpublished paper prepared for 'Medicine and Religion in Enlightenment Europe' conference, Cambridge University, 20–1 September 2004).

Finucane, R., C., *Appearances of the Dead: A Cultural History of Ghosts* (Buffalo, NY: Prometheus Books, 1984).

Flynn, C. H., *The Body in Swift and Defoe* (Cambridge: Cambridge University Press, 1990).

Fox, A., *Oral and Literate Culture in England, 1500–1700* (Oxford: Clarendon Press, 2000).

Fox, C., *Locke and the Scriblerians: Identity and Consciousness in Early Eighteenth-Century Britain* (Berkeley, CA, and London: University of California Press, 1988).

Gardiner, D., 'What Canterbury knew of Mrs. Veal and her Friends', *Review of English Studies*, 7:26 (1931), pp. 188–97.

Gaskill, M., 'Reporting Murder: Fiction in the Archives in Early Modern England', *Social History*, 23:3 (1998), pp. 1–30.

—, *Crime and Mentalities in Early Modern England* (Cambridge: Cambridge University Press, 2000).

Geary, R., *The Supernatural in Gothic Fiction: Horror, Belief, and Literary Change* (New York: Lampeter, 1992).

Gibson, M., *Possession, Puritanism and Print: Darrell, Harsnett, Shakespeare and the Elizabethan Exorcism Controversy* (London: Pickering & Chatto, 2006).

Gibson, W., *The Church of England 1688–1832, Unity and Accord* (London: Routledge, 2001).

Gillespie, R., *Devoted People: Belief and Religion in Early Modern Ireland* (Manchester: Manchester University Press, 1997).

Gittings, C., *Death, Burial and the Individual in Early Modern England* (London: Croom Helm, 1984).

Godbeer, R., *The Devil's Dominion: Magic and Religion in Early New England* (Cambridge and New York: Cambridge University Press, 1992).

Gowing, L., 'The Haunting of Susan Lay: Servants and Mistresses in Seventeenth-Century England', *Gender and History*, 14:2 (2002), pp. 183–201.

Graham, W., *The Beginnings of English Literary Periodicals: A Study of Periodical Literature 1665–1715* (New York: Octagon, 1972).

Grant, D., *The Cock Lane Ghost* (New York: St Martin's Press, 1965).

Green, I., *Print and Protestantism in Early Modern England* (Oxford and New York: Oxford University Press, 2003).

Gregg, E., *Queen Anne* (London: Routledge & Kegan Paul, 1980).

Gregory, J., *Restoration, Reformation and Reform, 1660–1828* (Oxford and New York: Oxford University Press, 2000).

Hagglund, E., 'Tourists and Travellers: Women's Non-Fictional Writing about Scotland, 1770–1830' (PhD thesis, University of Birmingham, 2000).

Hall, D. D., *Worlds of Wonder, Days of Judgment: Popular Religious Belief in Early New England* (New York: Knopf, 1989).

Harrison, J. F. C., *The Second Coming: Popular Millenarianism 1780–1850* (London: Routledge & Kegan Paul, 1979).

Hay, D., and P. Craven (eds), *Masters, Servants, and Magistrates in Britain and the Empire, 1562–1955* (Chapel Hill, NC: University of North Carolina Press, 2004).

Haydon, C., *Anti-Catholicism in Eighteenth-Century England, c.1714–80* (Manchester: Manchester University Press, 1993).

Henderson, L., and E. J. Cowan, *Scottish Fairy Belief* (East Linton: Tuckwell Press, 2001).

Hill, C., 'Irreligion in the "Puritan" Revolution', in J. F. McGregor and B. Reay (eds), *Radical Religion in the English Revolution* (Oxford: Oxford University Press, 1986), pp. 191–211.

—, *The World Turned Upside Down: Radical Ideas During the English Revolution* (London: Penguin, 1991).

Hilton, B., *The Age of Atonement: The Influence of Evangelicalism on Social and Economic Thought, 1795–1865* (Oxford: Clarendon Press, 1988).

Hogle, Jerrold E. (ed.), *The Cambridge Companion to Gothic Fiction* (Cambridge: Cambridge University Press, 2002).

Hopkin, D. M., 'Storytelling, Fairytales and Autobiography: Some Observations on Eighteenth- and Nineteenth-Century French Soldiers' and Sailors' Memoirs', *Social History*, 29:2 (2004), pp. 188–98.

Houlbrooke, R., *Death, Religion, and the Family in England, 1480–1750* (Oxford: Clarendon Press, 1998).

Hufton, O., *The Prospect Before Her: A History of Women in Western Europe* (London: HarperCollins, 1995).

Hunter, M., *Science and Society in Restoration England* (Cambridge: Cambridge University Press, 1981).

—, 'Science and Astrology in Seventeenth-Century England: An Unpublished Polemic by John Flamsteed', in P. Curry (ed.) *Astrology and Society, Historical Essays* (Woodbridge: Boydell, 1987), pp. 261–300.

—, *The Occult Laboratory: Magic, Science and Second Sight in Late Seventeenth-Century Scotland* (Woodbridge: Boydell Press, 2001).

Hutton, R., 'The English Reformation and the Evidence of Folklore', *Past and Present*, 148:1 (1995), pp. 89–116.

Jones, R., *Walking Haunted London* (London: New Holland Publishers, 1999).

Jones, T., *Street Literature in Birmingham: A History of Broadside and Chapbook* (Oxford: Polytechnic, 1970).

Kauffmann, C. M., *John Varley, 1778–1842* (London: Victoria and Albert Museum, 1984).

Knights, M., *Politics and Opinion in Crisis, 1678–1681* (Cambridge: Cambridge University Press, 1994).

Koster, P. (intro.), *Arbuthnotiana: The Story of the St Alb-ns Ghost* (1712), Augustan Reprint Society, 154 (Los Angeles, CA: William Andrews Clark Memorial Library, University of California, 1972).

Kristeva, J., *Powers of Horror: An Essay on Abjection*, trans. Leon S. Roudiez (New York and Oxford: Columbia University Press, 1982).

Kroll, R., R. Ashcraft and P. Zagorin (eds), *Philosophy, Science, and Religion in England 1640–1700* (Cambridge and New York: Cambridge University Press, 1994).

Krysmanski, B., 'We See a Ghost: Hogarth's Satire on Methodists and Connoiseurs', *Art Bulletin*, 80:2 (1998), pp. 292–310.

Labov, W., *Language in the Inner City: Studies in the Black English Vernacular* (Oxford: Blackwell, 1977).

Lake, P., 'Popular Form, Puritan Content? Two Puritan Appropriations of the Murder Pamphlet from Mid-Seventeenth-Century London', in A. Fletcher and P. Roberts (eds), *Religion, Culture and Society in Early Modern Britain* (Cambridge: Cambridge University Press, 1994), pp. 313–34.

Lake, P., with M. Questier, *The Antichrist's Lewd Hat, Protestants, Papists and Players in Post-Reformation England* (New Haven, CT, and London: Yale University Press, 2002).

Lane, B. C., *Landscapes of the Sacred: Geography and Narrative in American Spirituality* (Baltimore, MD, and London: Johns Hopkins University Press, 2002).

Langford, P., *A Polite and Commercial People: England, 1727–1783* (Oxford: Oxford University Press, 1989).

Leith, D., *A Social History of English* (London: Routledge, 1997).

Llewellyn, N., *The Art of Death: Visual Culture in the English Death Ritual c.1500–1800* (London: Reaktion Books, 1997).

Lowther Clarke, W. K., *A History of the SPCK* (London: Society for Promoting Christian Knowledge, 1959).

Lux, D. S., and H. J. Cook, 'Closed Circles or Open Networks?: Communicating at a Distance During the Scientific Revolution', *History of Science*, 36 (1998), pp. 179–211.

MacDonald, M., and T. R. Murphy, *Sleepless Souls: Suicide in Early Modern England* (Oxford: Clarendon Press, 1990).

McEwen, G. D., *The Oracle of the Coffee House, John Dunton's Athenian Mercury* (San Marino, CA: Huntingdon Library, 1972).

McKeon, M., *The Origins of the English Novel, 1600–1740* (Baltimore, MD: Johns Hopkins University Press, 1988).

McManners, J., *Death and the Enlightenment: Changing Attitudes to Death among Christians and Unbelievers in Eighteenth-Century France* (Oxford: Oxford University Press, 1981).

McShane Jones, A., '"Rime and Reason": The Political World of the English Broadside Ballad, 1640–1689' (PhD thesis, University of Warwick, 2004).

Marshall, P., *Beliefs and the Dead in Reformation England* (Oxford: Oxford University Press, 2002).

—, *Mother Leakey and the Bishop: A Ghost Story* (Oxford: Oxford University Press, 2007).

Marshall, P., and A. Walsham (eds), *Angels in the Early Modern World* (Cambridge: Cambridge University Press, 2006).

Mayhew, R. J., *Landscape, Literature and English Religious Culture, 1660–1800* (Basingstoke: Palgrave Macmillan, 2004).

Miles, A., 'A Wonder of Wonders', in H. E. Rollins (ed.), *The Pack of Autolycus: or, Strange and Terrible News of Ghosts, Apparitions, Monstrous Births, Showers of Wheat, Judgments of God, and Other Prodigious and Fearful Happenings as Told in Broadside Ballads* (Cambridge, MA: Harvard University Press, 1969), pp. 118–19.

Miles, R., 'The 1790s: The Effulgence of Gothic', in J. E. Hogle (ed.), *The Cambridge Companion to Gothic Fiction* (Cambridge: Cambridge University Press, 2002), pp. 41–62.

Moore, R., 'Late Seventeenth-Century Quakerism and the Miraculous: A New Look at George Fox's "Book of Miracles"', in K. Cooper and J. Gregory (eds), *Signs, Wonders, Miracles: Representations of Divine Power in the Life of the Church*, Studies in Church History, vol. 41 (Woodbridge: Boydell Press, 2005), pp. 335–44.

Olson, D. R., *The World on Paper: The Conceptual and Cognitive Implications of Writing and Reading* (Cambridge: Cambridge University Press, 1994).

Ong, Walter J., *Orality and Literacy: The Technologising of the Word* (London: Methuen, 1982).

—, 'Writing is a Technology that Restructures Thought', in G. Baumann (ed.), *The Written Word: Literacy in Transition* (Oxford: Clarendon Press, 1986), pp. 23–50.

Oppenheim, J., *The Other World: Spiritualism and Psychical Research in England, 1850–1914* (Cambridge: Cambridge University Press, 1985).

Owen, A., *The Darkened Room: Women, Power and Spiritualism in Late Victorian England* (London: Virago, 1989).

Porter, R., *Flesh in the Age of Reason* (London: Allen Lane, 2003).

Rack, H. D., *Reasonable Enthusiast: John Wesley and the Rise of Methodism* (London: Epworth, 1989).

Reay, B. (ed.), *Popular Culture in Seventeenth-Century England* (London: Croom Helm, 1985).

—, *The Quakers and the English Revolution* (London: Temple Smith, 1985).

Rediker, M., *Between the Devil and the Deep Blue Sea: Merchant Seamen, Pirates and the Anglo-American Maritime World, 1700–1750* (Cambridge: Cambridge University Press, 1989).

Richardson, R., *Death, Dissection and the Destitute* (London: Routledge & Kegan Paul, 2001).

Riley, J. C., *The Eighteenth-Century Campaign to Avoid Disease* (Basingstoke: Macmillan, 1987).

Rogers, N., *Whigs and Cities: Popular Politics in the Age of Walpole and Pitt* (Oxford: Clarendon Press, 1989).

—, *Crowds, Culture, and Politics in Georgian Britain* (Oxford: Clarendon Press, 1998).

Roper, A., 'Absalom's Issue: Parallel Poems in the Restoration', *Studies in Philology*, 99:3 (2002), pp. 268–94.

Roper, L., *Oedipus and the Devil: Witchcraft, Sexuality and Religion in Early Modern Europe* (London: Routledge, 1994).

Russell, A., *The Clerical Profession* (London: Society for Promoting Christian Knowledge, 1980).

Schaffer, S., 'Defoe's Natural Philosophy and the Worlds of Credit', in J. Christie and S. Shuttleworth (eds), *Nature Transfigured: Science and Literature 1700–1900* (Manchester: Manchester University Press, 1989), pp. 13–44.

Schama, S., *Landscape and Memory* (London: Fontana Press, 1996).

Schmitt, J.-C., *Ghosts in the Middle Ages: The Living and the Dead in Medieval Society*, trans. T. L. Fagan (Chicago, IL, and London: University of Chicago Press, 1998).

Shapin, S., '"A Scholar and a Gentleman": The Problematic Identity of the Scientific Practitioner in Early Modern England', *History of Science*, 29 (1991), pp. 279–327.

Shapin, S., and S. Schaffer, *Leviathan and the Air-Pump: Hobbes, Boyle, and the Experimental Life* (Princeton, NJ: Princeton University Press, 1989).

Sharpe, J. A., '"Last Dying Speeches": Religion, Ideology and Public Execution in Seventeenth-Century England', *Past and Present*, 107 (1985), pp. 144–67.

Sharpe, K., and S. N. Zwicker (eds), *Reading, Society and Politics in Early Modern England* (Cambridge and New York: Cambridge University Press, 2003).

Shaw, J., *Miracles in Enlightenment England* (New Haven, CT, and London: Yale University Press, 2006).

Smithers, P., *The Life of Joseph Addison* (Oxford: Clarendon Press, 1968).

Spadafora, D., *The Idea of Progress in Eighteenth-Century Britain* (New Haven, CT, and London: Yale University Press, 1990).

Spaeth, D. A., *The Church in An Age of Danger: Parsons and Parishioners, 1660–1740* (Cambridge: Cambridge University Press, 2000).

Spufford, M., *Small Books and Pleasant Histories: Popular Fiction and its Readership in Seventeenth-Century England* (Cambridge: Cambridge University Press, 1985).

Spurr, J., *The Restoration Church of England, 1646–1689* (New Haven, CT, and London: Yale University Press, 1991).

—, 'Religion in Restoration England', in L. K. J. Glassey (ed.), *The Reigns of Charles II and James VII & II* (Basingstoke: Macmillan, 1997), pp. 90–124.

Stafford, B. M., *Body Criticism: Imaging the Unseen in Enlightenment Art and Medicine* (Cambridge, MA, and London: MIT Press, 1994).

Starr, G., 'Why Defoe Probably Did Not Write the Apparition of Mrs Veal', *Eighteenth Century Fiction*, 15:3-4 (2003), pp. 421–50.

Steedman, C. K., *Strange Dislocations: Childhood and the Idea of Human Interiority* (Cambridge. MA: Harvard University Press, 1995).

—, *Master and Servant: Love and Labour in the English Industrial Age*, Cambridge Cultural History Series, 10 (Cambridge: Cambridge University Press, 2007).

Steensma, R. C., *Dr John Arbuthnot* (Boston, MA: Twayne Publishers, 1979).

Stewart, P. J., and A. Strathern, *Landscape, Memory and History: Anthropological Perspectives* (London: Pluto Press, 2003).

Thomas, K., 'The Meaning of Literacy', in G. Baumann (ed.), *The Written Word: Literacy in Transition* (Oxford: Clarendon Press, 1986), pp. 97–131.

—, *Religion and the Decline of Magic, Studies in Popular Beliefs in Sixteenth- and Seventeenth-Century England* (London: Penguin, 1991).

Valletta, F., *Witchcraft, Magic and Superstition in England 1640–70* (Aldershot: Ashgate, 2000).

Vidal, F., 'Brains, Bodies, Selves, and Science: Anthropologies of Identity and the Resurrection of the Body', *Critical Inquiry*, 28:4 (2002), pp. 930–74.

Vincent, D., *Bread, Knowledge and Freedom: A Study of Nineteenth-Century Working Class Autobiography* (London: Methuen, 1982).

—, *Literacy and Popular Culture: England 1750–1914* (Cambridge: Cambridge University Press, 1989).

Voitle, R., *The Third Earl of Shaftesbury, 1671–1713* (Baton Rouge, LA, and London: Louisiana State University Press, 1984).

Wahrman, D., *The Making of the Modern Self: Identity and Culture in Eighteenth-Century England* (New Haven, CT, and London: Yale University Press, 2004).

Walker, D. P., *The Decline of Hell: Seventeenth-Century Discussions of Eternal Torment* (Chicago, IL: University of Chicago Press, 1964).

Walsham, A., *Providence in Early Modern England* (Oxford: Oxford University Press, 1999).

—, 'Reforming the Waters: Holy Wells and Healing Springs in Protestant England', in D. Wood (ed.), *Life and Thought in the Northern Church c.1100–c.1700: Essays in Honour of Claire Cross* (Woodbridge: Boydell Press, 1999).

Watt, I. P., *The Rise of the Novel: Studies in Defoe, Richardson and Fielding* (London: Hogarth, 1957).

Watt, T., *Cheap Print and Popular Piety, 1550–1640* (Cambridge: Cambridge University Press, 1996).

Webster, R., 'Those Distracting Terrors of the Enemy: Demonic Possession and Exorcism in the Thought of John Wesley', *Bulletin of the John Rylands University Library of Manchester*, 85:2/3 (2003), pp. 373–85.

Westfall, R. S., *Science and Religion in Seventeenth-Century England* (New Haven, CT, and London: Yale University Press, 1958).

Whyte, I. D., *Landscape and History since 1500* (London: Reaktion Books, 2002).

Whyte, L. L., *The Unconscious Before Freud* (London: Freidmann, 1978).

Williams, R., *Culture and Society, 1780–1950* (New York: Columbia University Press, 1958).

—, *Culture* (London: Fontana, 1981).

—, *Keywords: A Vocabulary of Culture and Society* (London: Fontana Press, 1988).

Wilson, K., *The Sense of the People: Politics, Culture and Imperialism in England, 1715–1785* (Cambridge: Cambridge University Press, 1998).

Winship, J., *Inside Women's Magazines* (London: Pandora Press, 1987).

Woolf, D., 'The "Common Voice": History, Folklore and Oral Tradition in Early Modern England', *Past and Present*, 120:1 (1988), pp. 26–52.

Wrightson, K., *English Society 1580–1680* (London: Routledge, 1982).

Wu, Duncan (ed.), *Romanticism: An Anthology* (Oxford: Blackwell, 2006).

Websites

'The Douce Ballads', http://www.bodley.ox.ac.uk/ballads/ (accessed 5 September 2006).

'Francis Smith: Condemned to Death on 13th of January 1804, for the Murder of the supposed Hammersmith ghost, but pardoned soon afterwards', *The Newgate Calendar*, 1804, http://www.exclassics.com/newgate/ng470.htm (accessed 17 April 2007).

'Francis Smith, Killing: Murder, 11th January 1804', in *The Proceedings of the Old Bailey Online*, http://www.oldbaileyonline.org/html_units/1800s/t18040111-79.html (accessed 15 April 2007).

Oxford Dictionary of National Biography, online edition, http://www.oxforddnb.com.

The Times, Digital Archive, http://infotrac.galegroup.com/itw/infomark/0/1/1/purl=rc6_TTDA?sw_aep=jrycal5 (accessed 28 April 2007).

INDEX